Hana-Kimi

For You in Full Blossom

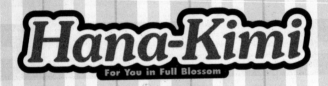

20

story and art by
HISAYA NAKAJO

HANA-KIMI
For You in Full Blossom
VOLUME 20

STORY & ART BY HISAYA NAKAJO

Translation & English Adaptation/David Ury
Touch-Up Art & Lettering/Primary Graphix
Design/Izumi Evers
Editor/Jason Thompson

Editor in Chief, Books/Alvin Lu
Editor in Chief, Magazines/Marc Weidenbaum
VP of Publishing Licensing/Rika Inouye
VP of Sales/Gonzalo Ferreyra
Sr. VP of Marketing/Liza Coppola
Publisher/Hyoe Narita

Published by VIZ Media, LLC, P.O. Box 77010, San Francisco, CA 94107

Shôjo Edition
10 9 8 7 6 5 4 3 2 1

First printing, October 2007

T 251558

www.viz.com
store.viz.com

PARENTAL ADVISORY
HANA-KIMI is rated T+ for Older Teen and is
recommended for ages 16 and up. Contains strong
language, sexual themes and alcohol and tobacco usage.

RATED
T+
FOR OLDER
TEEN

ratings.viz.com

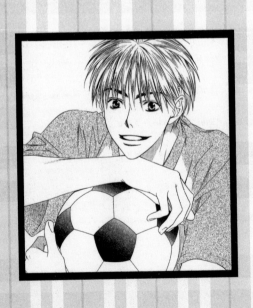

CONTENTS

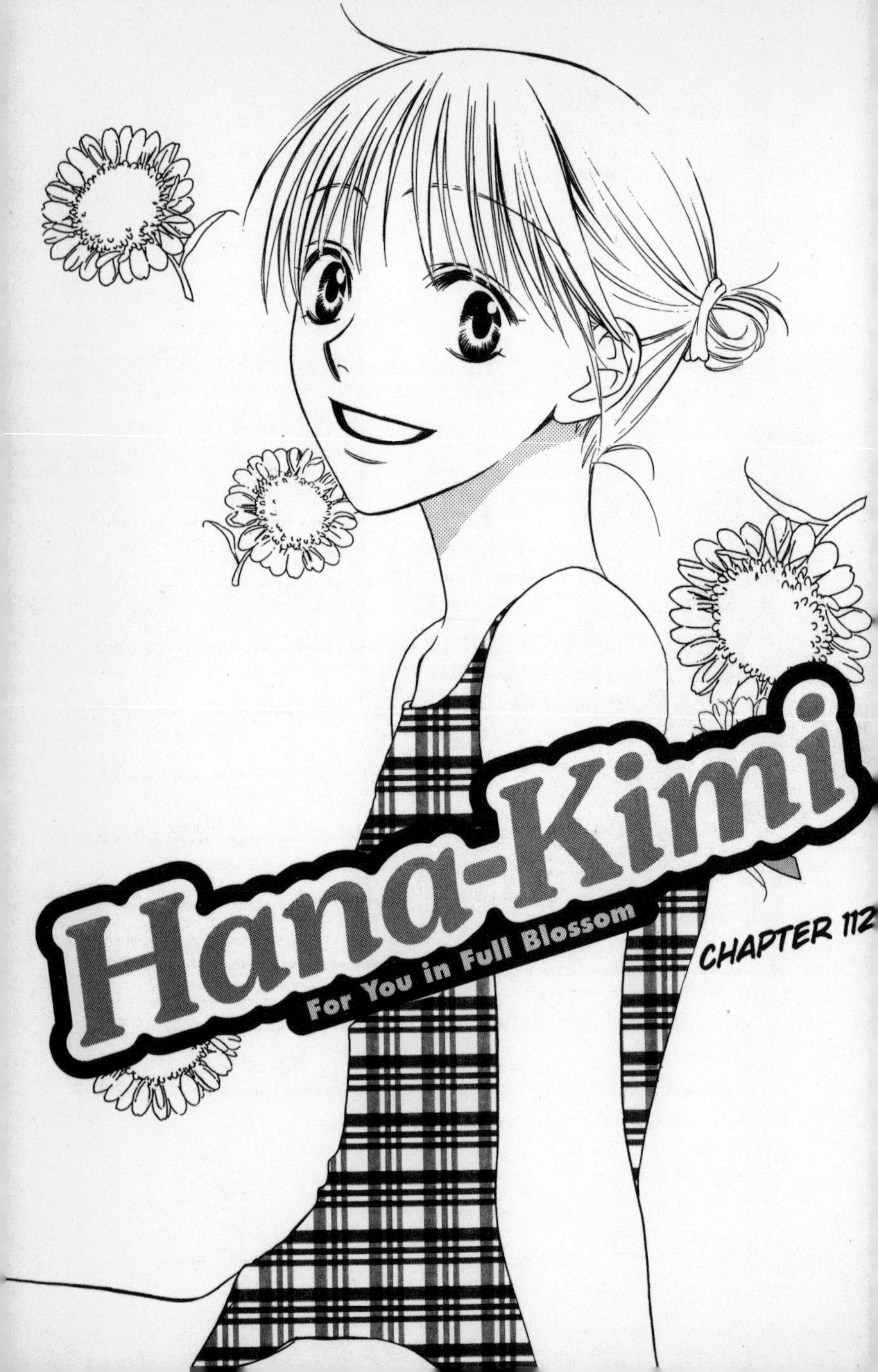
Hana-Kimi
For You in Full Blossom
CHAPTER 112

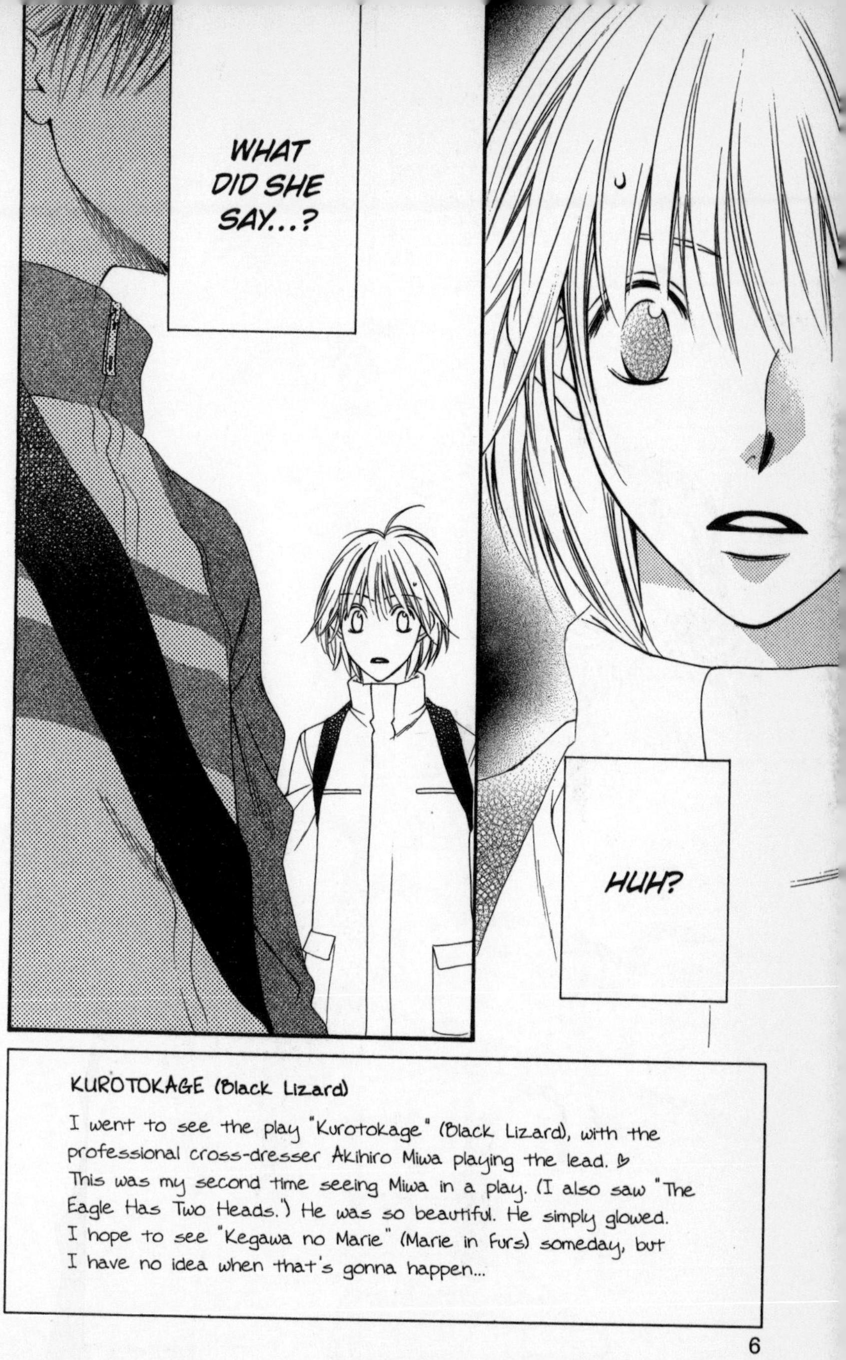
HUH?
WHAT DID SHE SAY...?

KUROTOKAGE (Black Lizard)

I went to see the play "Kurotokage" (Black Lizard), with the professional cross-dresser Akihiro Miwa playing the lead. ♥
This was my second time seeing Miwa in a play. (I also saw "The Eagle Has Two Heads.") He was so beautiful. He simply glowed.
I hope to see "Kegawa no Marie" (Marie in Furs) someday, but I have no idea when that's gonna happen...

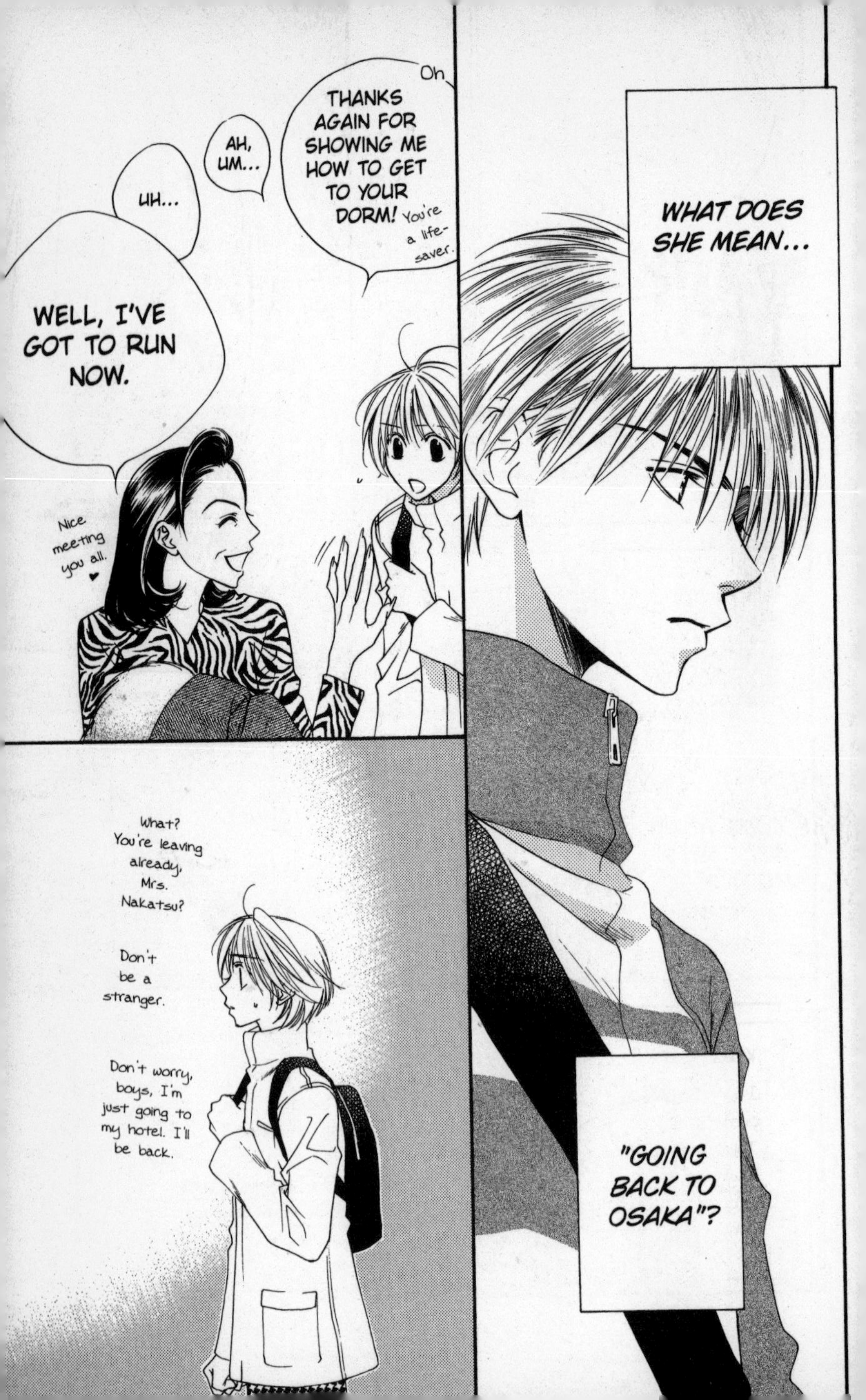
WHAT DOES SHE MEAN...
"GOING BACK TO OSAKA"?
Oh
THANKS AGAIN FOR SHOWING ME HOW TO GET TO YOUR DORM!
You're a life-saver.
AH, UM...
UH...
WELL, I'VE GOT TO RUN NOW.
Nice meeting you all. ♥
What? You're leaving already, Mrs. Nakatsu?
Don't be a stranger.
Don't worry, boys, I'm just going to my hotel. I'll be back.

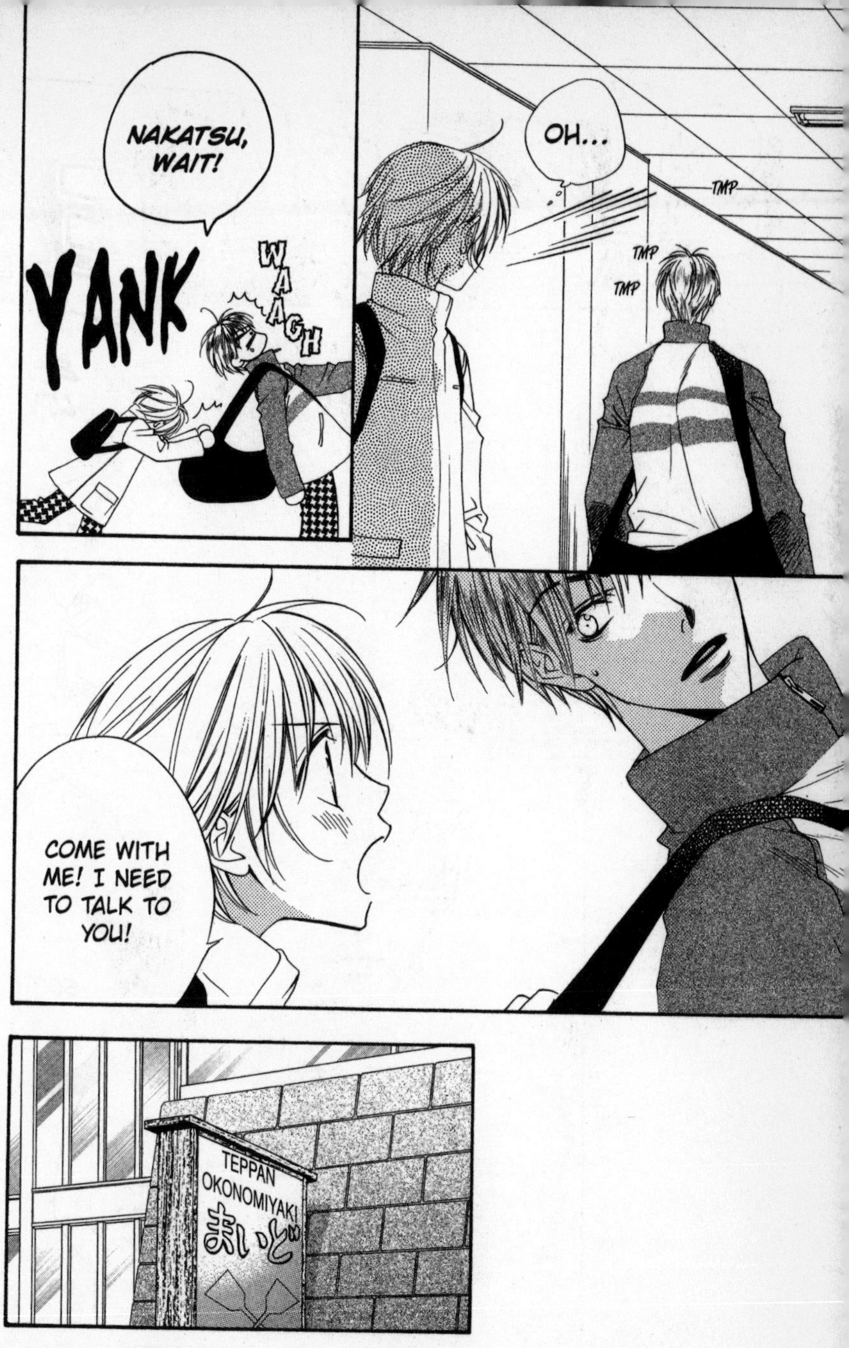
OH...
TMP
TMP
TMP
NAKATSU, WAIT!
YANK
WAAGH
COME WITH ME! I NEED TO TALK TO YOU!
TEPPAN OKONOMIYAKI
まいど

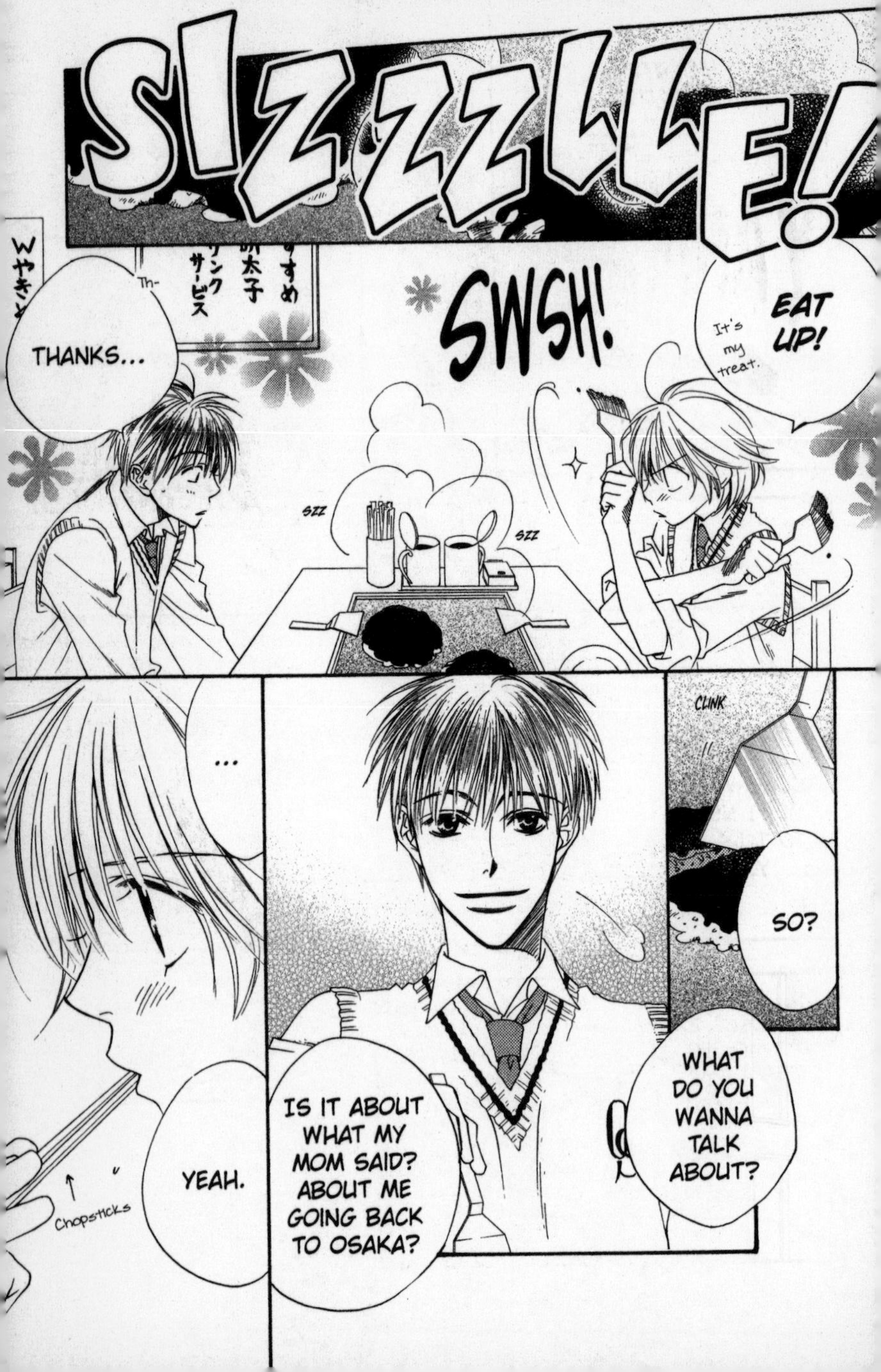
SIZZLLE!
EAT UP!
It's my treat.
SWSH!
SZZ
SZZ
Th-
THANKS...
CLINK
SO?
WHAT DO YOU WANNA TALK ABOUT?
IS IT ABOUT WHAT MY MOM SAID? ABOUT ME GOING BACK TO OSAKA?
...
YEAH.
Chopsticks

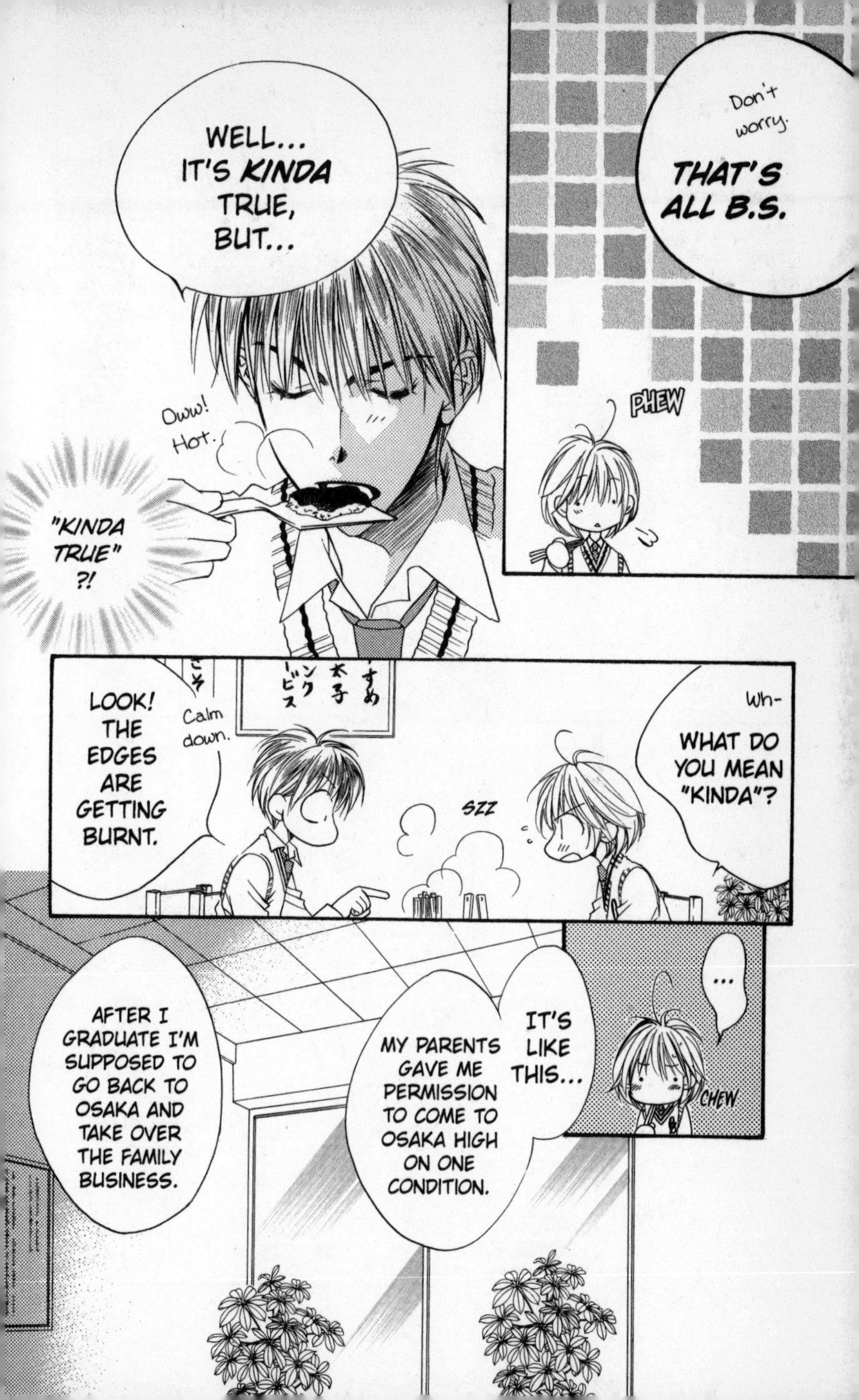
Don't worry.
THAT'S ALL B.S.
PHEW
WELL... IT'S KINDA TRUE, BUT...
Oww! Hot.
"KINDA TRUE"?!
Wh-
WHAT DO YOU MEAN "KINDA"?
SZZ
Calm down.
LOOK! THE EDGES ARE GETTING BURNT.
...
CHEW
IT'S LIKE THIS...
MY PARENTS GAVE ME PERMISSION TO COME TO OSAKA HIGH ON ONE CONDITION.
AFTER I GRADUATE I'M SUPPOSED TO GO BACK TO OSAKA AND TAKE OVER THE FAMILY BUSINESS.

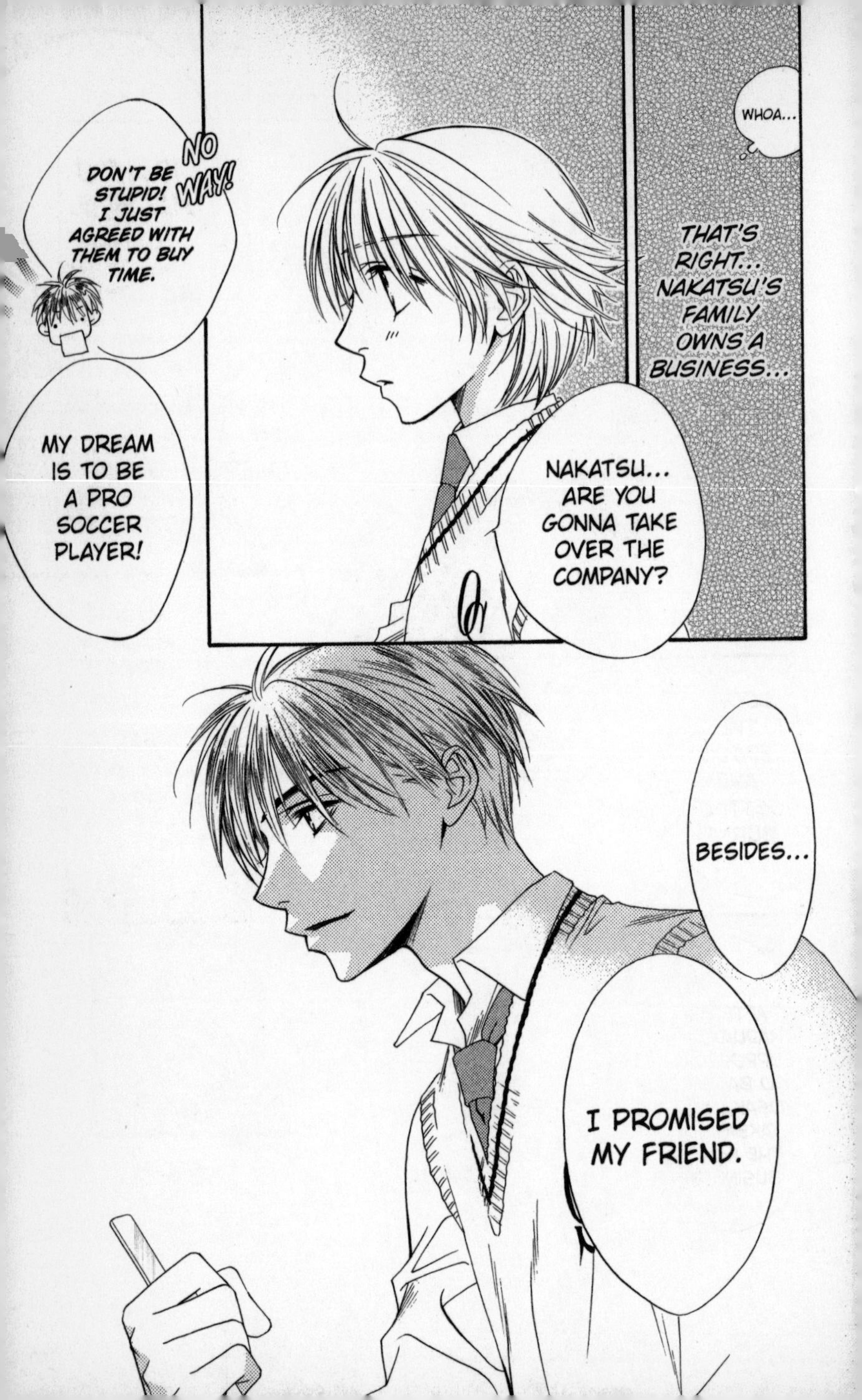
WHOA...
THAT'S RIGHT... NAKATSU'S FAMILY OWNS A BUSINESS...
NAKATSU... ARE YOU GONNA TAKE OVER THE COMPANY?
NO WAY!
DON'T BE STUPID! I JUST AGREED WITH THEM TO BUY TIME.
MY DREAM IS TO BE A PRO SOCCER PLAYER!
BESIDES...
I PROMISED MY FRIEND.

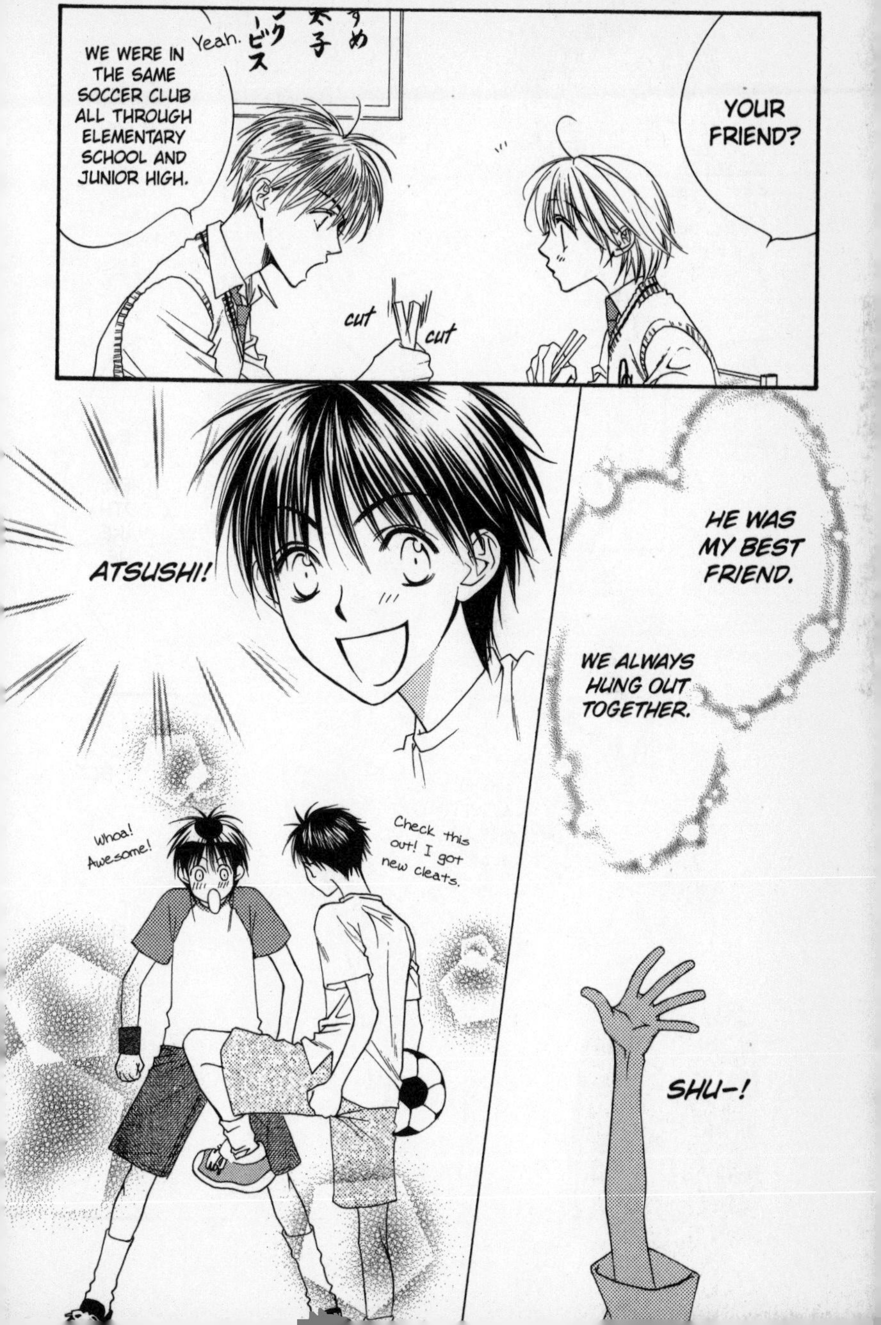
YOUR FRIEND?
Yeah.
WE WERE IN THE SAME SOCCER CLUB ALL THROUGH ELEMENTARY SCHOOL AND JUNIOR HIGH.
cut cut
HE WAS MY BEST FRIEND.
WE ALWAYS HUNG OUT TOGETHER.
SHU-!
ATSUSHI!
Check this out! I got new cleats.
Whoa! Awesome!

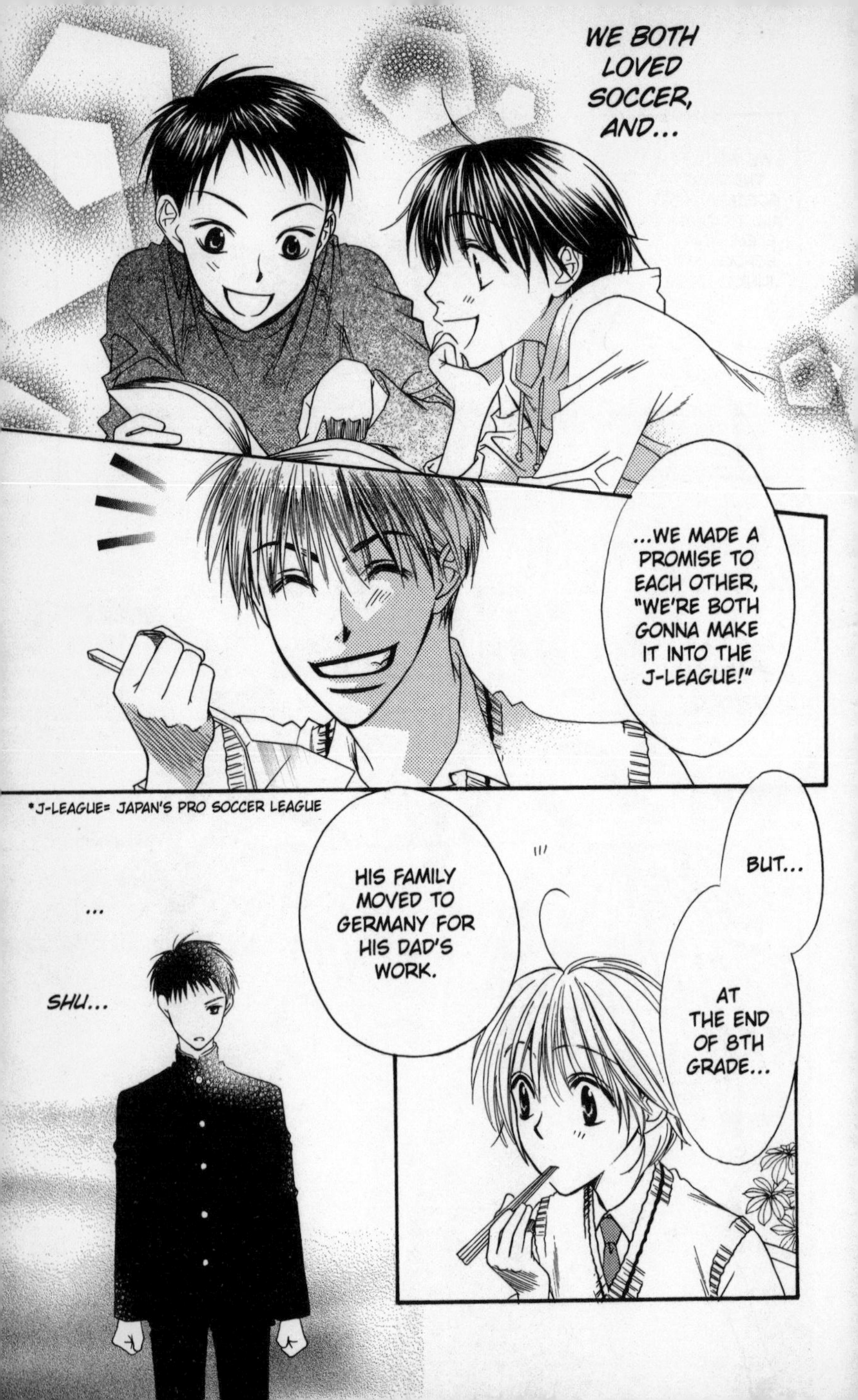
WE BOTH LOVED SOCCER, AND...
...WE MADE A PROMISE TO EACH OTHER, "WE'RE BOTH GONNA MAKE IT INTO THE J-LEAGUE!"
BUT...
AT THE END OF 8TH GRADE...
HIS FAMILY MOVED TO GERMANY FOR HIS DAD'S WORK.
...
SHU...
*J-LEAGUE= JAPAN'S PRO SOCCER LEAGUE

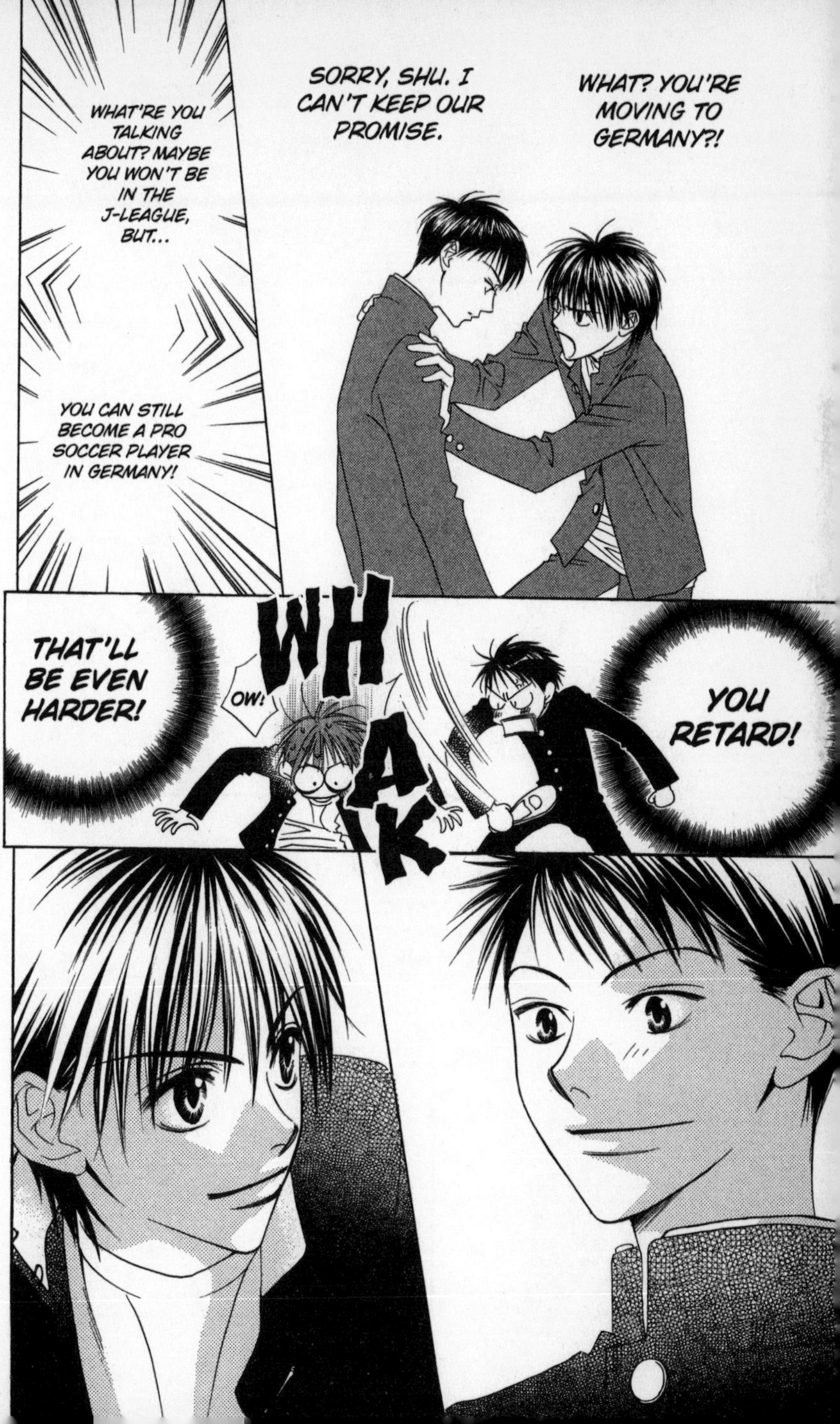
WHAT? YOU'RE MOVING TO GERMANY?!
SORRY, SHU. I CAN'T KEEP OUR PROMISE.
WHAT'RE YOU TALKING ABOUT? MAYBE YOU WON'T BE IN THE J-LEAGUE, BUT...
YOU CAN STILL BECOME A PRO SOCCER PLAYER IN GERMANY!
YOU RETARD!
WHAK!
OW!
THAT'LL BE EVEN HARDER!

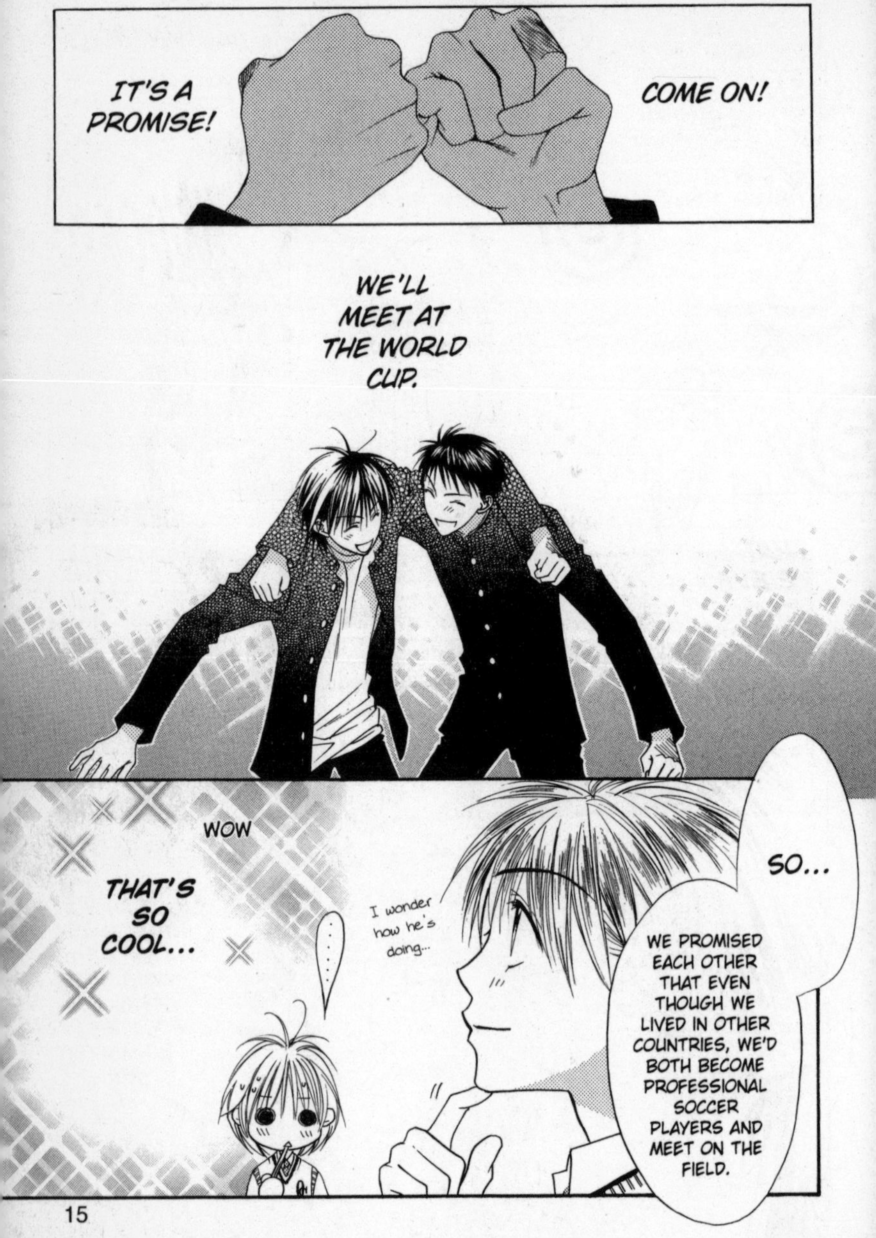
COME ON!
IT'S A PROMISE!
WE'LL MEET AT THE WORLD CUP.
SO...
WE PROMISED EACH OTHER THAT EVEN THOUGH WE LIVED IN OTHER COUNTRIES, WE'D BOTH BECOME PROFESSIONAL SOCCER PLAYERS AND MEET ON THE FIELD.
I wonder how he's doing...
......
WOW
THAT'S SO COOL...

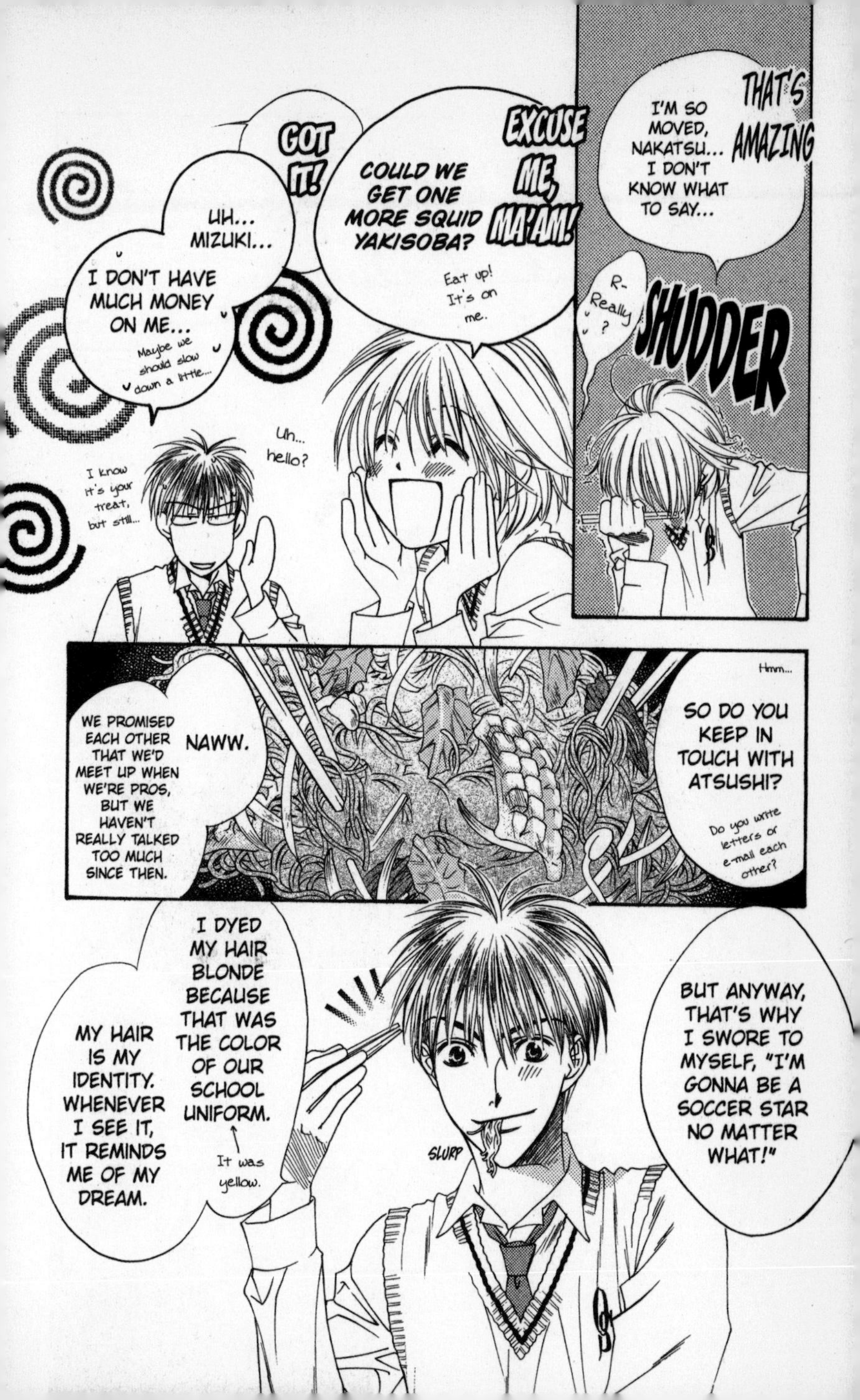
THAT'S AMAZING
I'M SO MOVED, NAKATSU... I DON'T KNOW WHAT TO SAY...
R-Really?
SHUDDER
EXCUSE ME, MA'AM!
COULD WE GET ONE MORE SQUID YAKISOBA?
GOT IT!
Eat up! It's on me.
UH... MIZUKI...
I DON'T HAVE MUCH MONEY ON ME...
Maybe we should slow down a little...
Uh... hello?
I know it's your treat, but still...
Hmm...
SO DO YOU KEEP IN TOUCH WITH ATSUSHI?
Do you write letters or e-mail each other?
NAWW.
WE PROMISED EACH OTHER THAT WE'D MEET UP WHEN WE'RE PROS, BUT WE HAVEN'T REALLY TALKED TOO MUCH SINCE THEN.
BUT ANYWAY, THAT'S WHY I SWORE TO MYSELF, "I'M GONNA BE A SOCCER STAR NO MATTER WHAT!"
SLURP
I DYED MY HAIR BLONDE BECAUSE THAT WAS THE COLOR OF OUR SCHOOL UNIFORM.
It was yellow.
MY HAIR IS MY IDENTITY. WHENEVER I SEE IT, IT REMINDS ME OF MY DREAM.

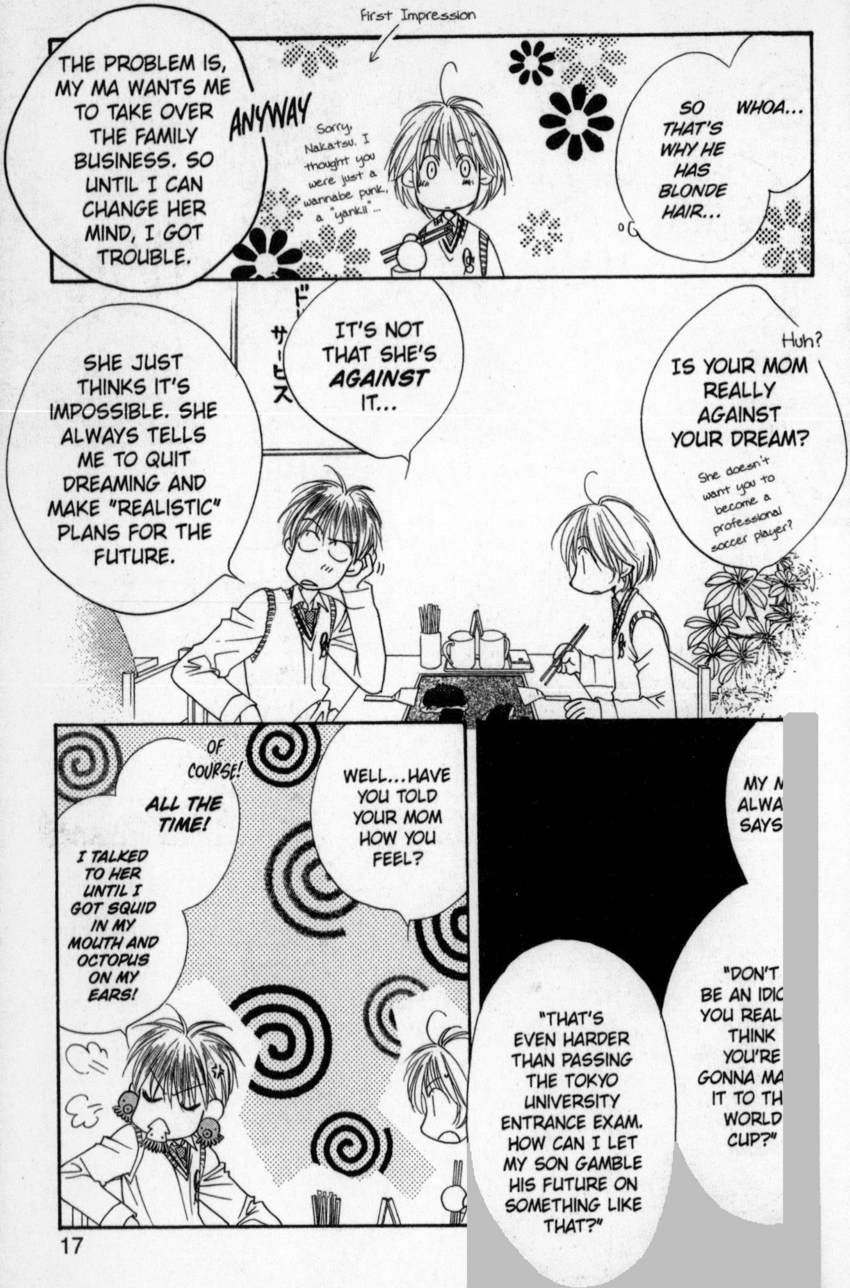
WHOA...
SO THAT'S WHY HE HAS BLONDE HAIR...
First Impression
Sorry, Nakatsu. I thought you were just a wannabe punk, a "yankii"...
ANYWAY
THE PROBLEM IS, MY MA WANTS ME TO TAKE OVER THE FAMILY BUSINESS. SO UNTIL I CAN CHANGE HER MIND, I GOT TROUBLE.
Huh?
IS YOUR MOM REALLY AGAINST YOUR DREAM?
She doesn't want you to become a professional soccer player?
IT'S NOT THAT SHE'S AGAINST IT...
SHE JUST THINKS IT'S IMPOSSIBLE. SHE ALWAYS TELLS ME TO QUIT DREAMING AND MAKE "REALISTIC" PLANS FOR THE FUTURE.
MY M ALWA SAYS
"DON'T BE AN IDIC YOU REAL THINK YOU'RE GONNA MA IT TO TH WORLD CUP?"
"THAT'S EVEN HARDER THAN PASSING THE TOKYO UNIVERSITY ENTRANCE EXAM. HOW CAN I LET MY SON GAMBLE HIS FUTURE ON SOMETHING LIKE THAT?"
WELL...HAVE YOU TOLD YOUR MOM HOW YOU FEEL?
OF COURSE!
ALL THE TIME!
I TALKED TO HER UNTIL I GOT SQUID IN MY MOUTH AND OCTOPUS ON MY EARS!

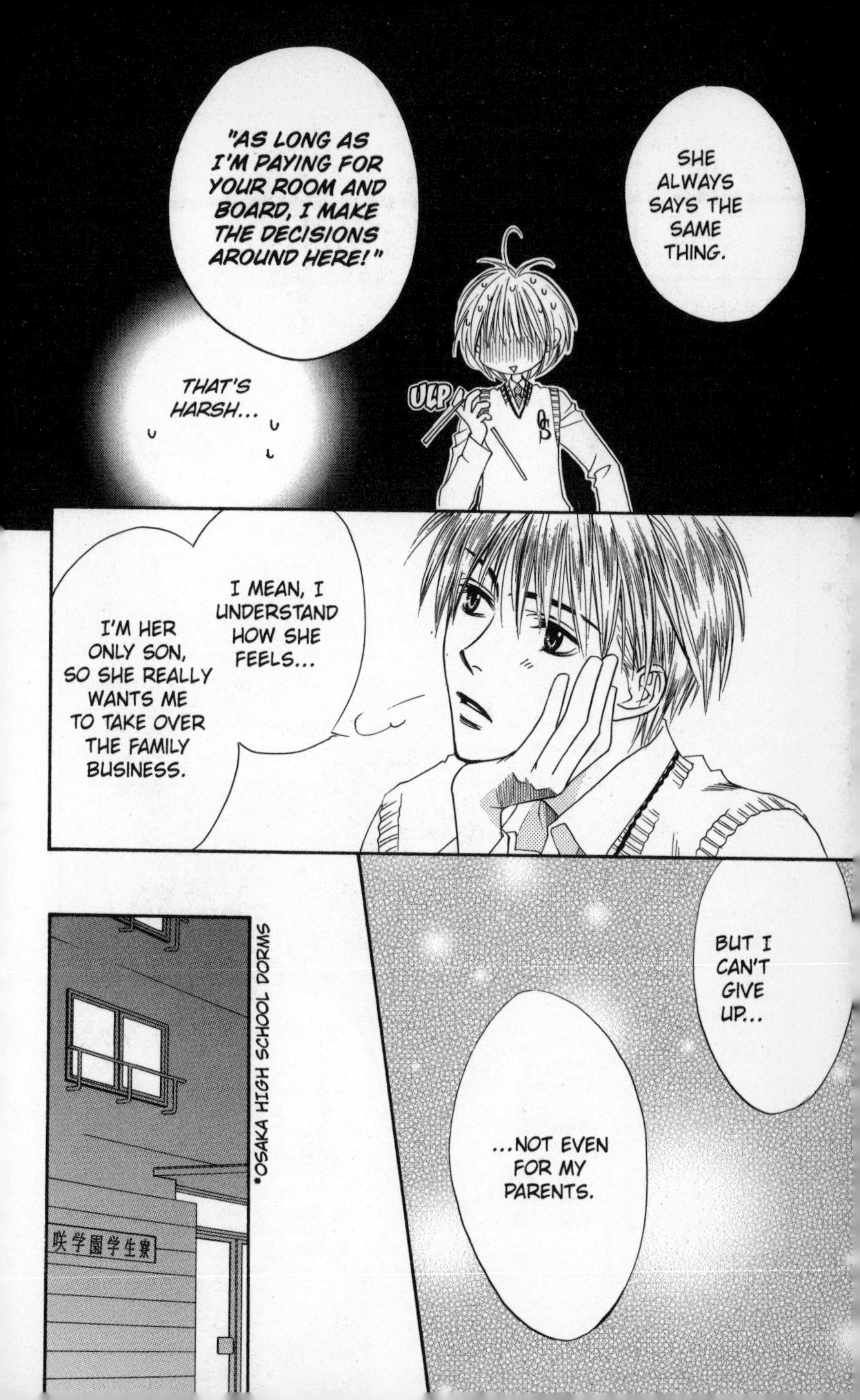
SHE ALWAYS SAYS THE SAME THING.
"AS LONG AS I'M PAYING FOR YOUR ROOM AND BOARD, I MAKE THE DECISIONS AROUND HERE!"
ULP
THAT'S HARSH...
I MEAN, I UNDERSTAND HOW SHE FEELS...
I'M HER ONLY SON, SO SHE REALLY WANTS ME TO TAKE OVER THE FAMILY BUSINESS.
BUT I CAN'T GIVE UP...
...NOT EVEN FOR MY PARENTS.
*OSAKA HIGH SCHOOL DORMS
咲学園学生寮

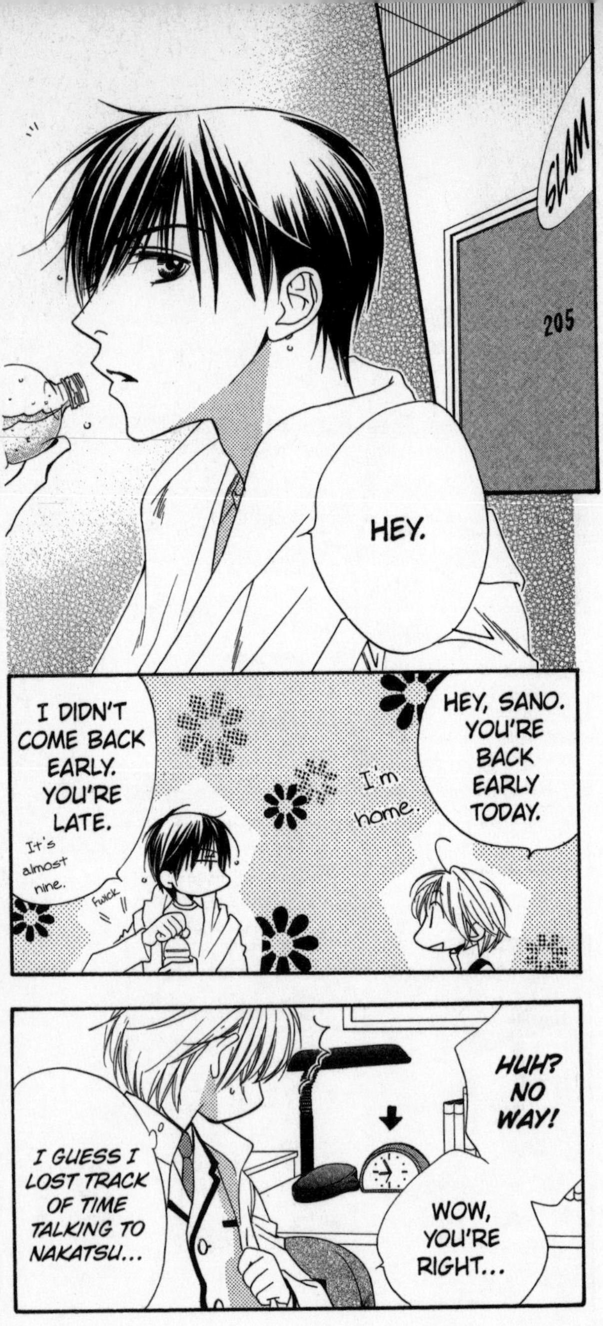
SLAM
205
HEY.
HEY, SANO. YOU'RE BACK EARLY TODAY.
I'm home.
I DIDN'T COME BACK EARLY. YOU'RE LATE.
It's almost nine.
Fwick
HUH? NO WAY!
WOW, YOU'RE RIGHT...
I GUESS I LOST TRACK OF TIME TALKING TO NAKATSU...

20

It's Hana-Kimi Book 20. Wow... This is the first time I've ever made it to book 20, so I'm pretty surprised. Sure, I was surprised when I wrote episode 100, but book 20... Oh my god!

Duh...

Seriously, that's my reaction.

But, even though I can hardly believe it, this really is book 20. Pull yourself together, Nakajo!

Okay... I'm fine... really.... Anyway, I hope you all enjoy book 20!

20

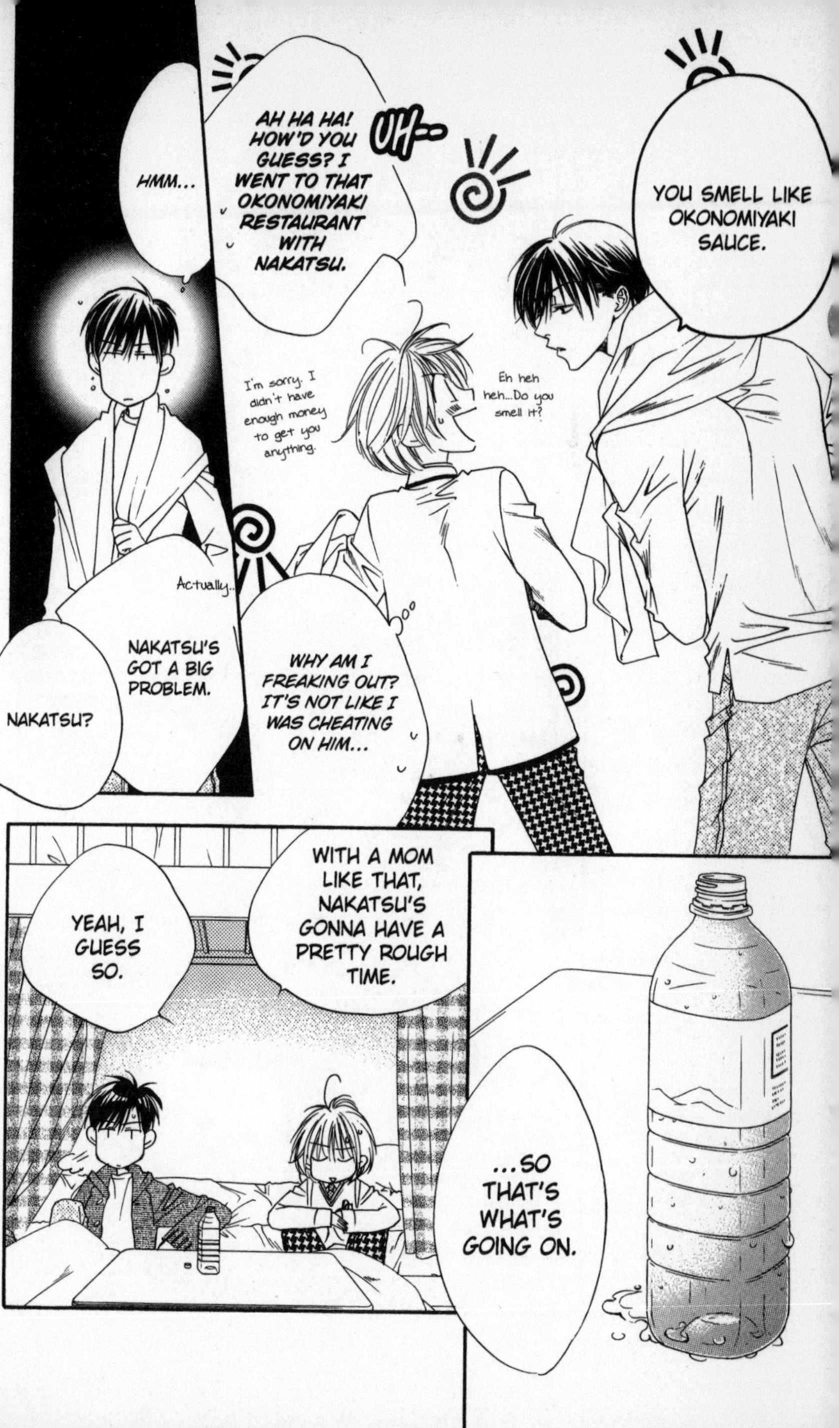
YOU SMELL LIKE OKONOMIYAKI SAUCE.
Eh heh heh...Do you smell it?
UH--
AH HA HA! HOW'D YOU GUESS? I WENT TO THAT OKONOMIYAKI RESTAURANT WITH NAKATSU.
I'm sorry. I didn't have enough money to get you anything.
WHY AM I FREAKING OUT? IT'S NOT LIKE I WAS CHEATING ON HIM...
HMM...
Actually...
NAKATSU'S GOT A BIG PROBLEM.
NAKATSU?
...SO THAT'S WHAT'S GOING ON.
WITH A MOM LIKE THAT, NAKATSU'S GONNA HAVE A PRETTY ROUGH TIME.
YEAH, I GUESS SO.

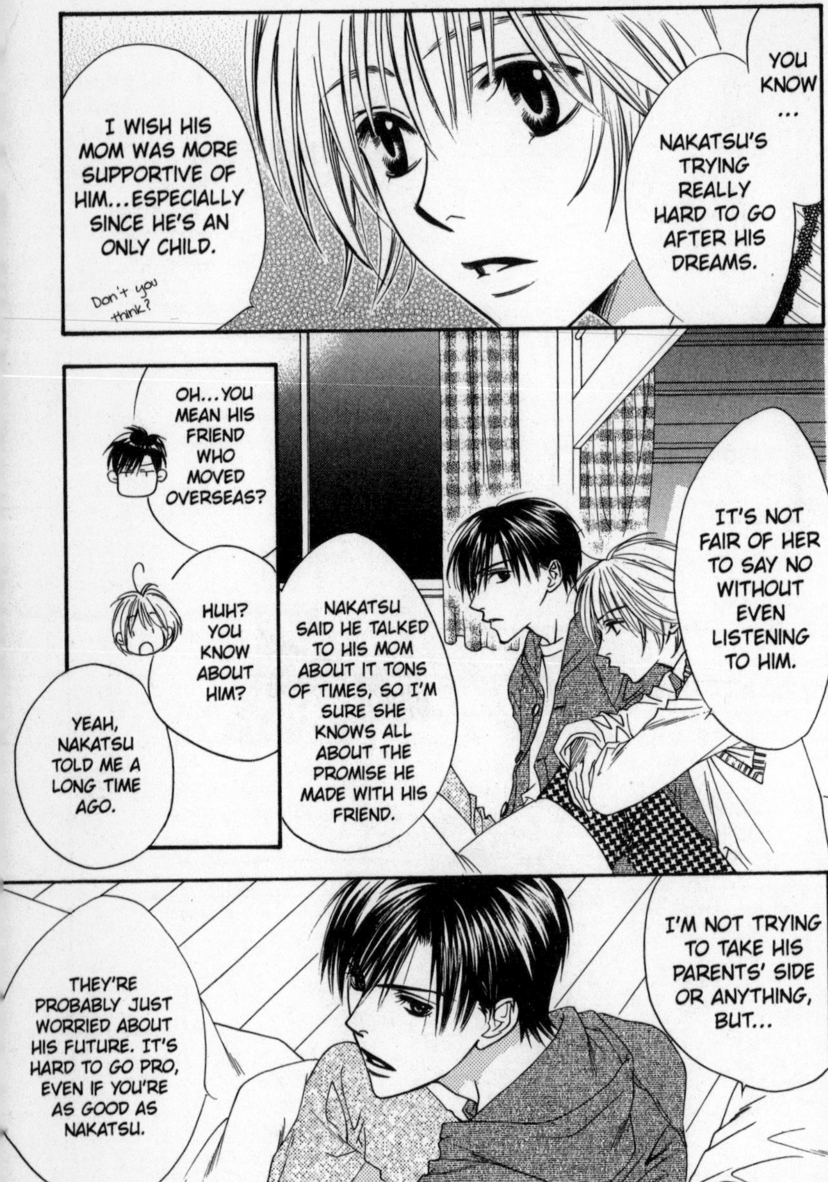
YOU KNOW ...
NAKATSU'S TRYING REALLY HARD TO GO AFTER HIS DREAMS.
I WISH HIS MOM WAS MORE SUPPORTIVE OF HIM...ESPECIALLY SINCE HE'S AN ONLY CHILD.
Don't you think?
IT'S NOT FAIR OF HER TO SAY NO WITHOUT EVEN LISTENING TO HIM.
NAKATSU SAID HE TALKED TO HIS MOM ABOUT IT TONS OF TIMES, SO I'M SURE SHE KNOWS ALL ABOUT THE PROMISE HE MADE WITH HIS FRIEND.
OH...YOU MEAN HIS FRIEND WHO MOVED OVERSEAS?
HUH? YOU KNOW ABOUT HIM?
YEAH, NAKATSU TOLD ME A LONG TIME AGO.
I'M NOT TRYING TO TAKE HIS PARENTS' SIDE OR ANYTHING, BUT...
THEY'RE PROBABLY JUST WORRIED ABOUT HIS FUTURE. IT'S HARD TO GO PRO, EVEN IF YOU'RE AS GOOD AS NAKATSU.

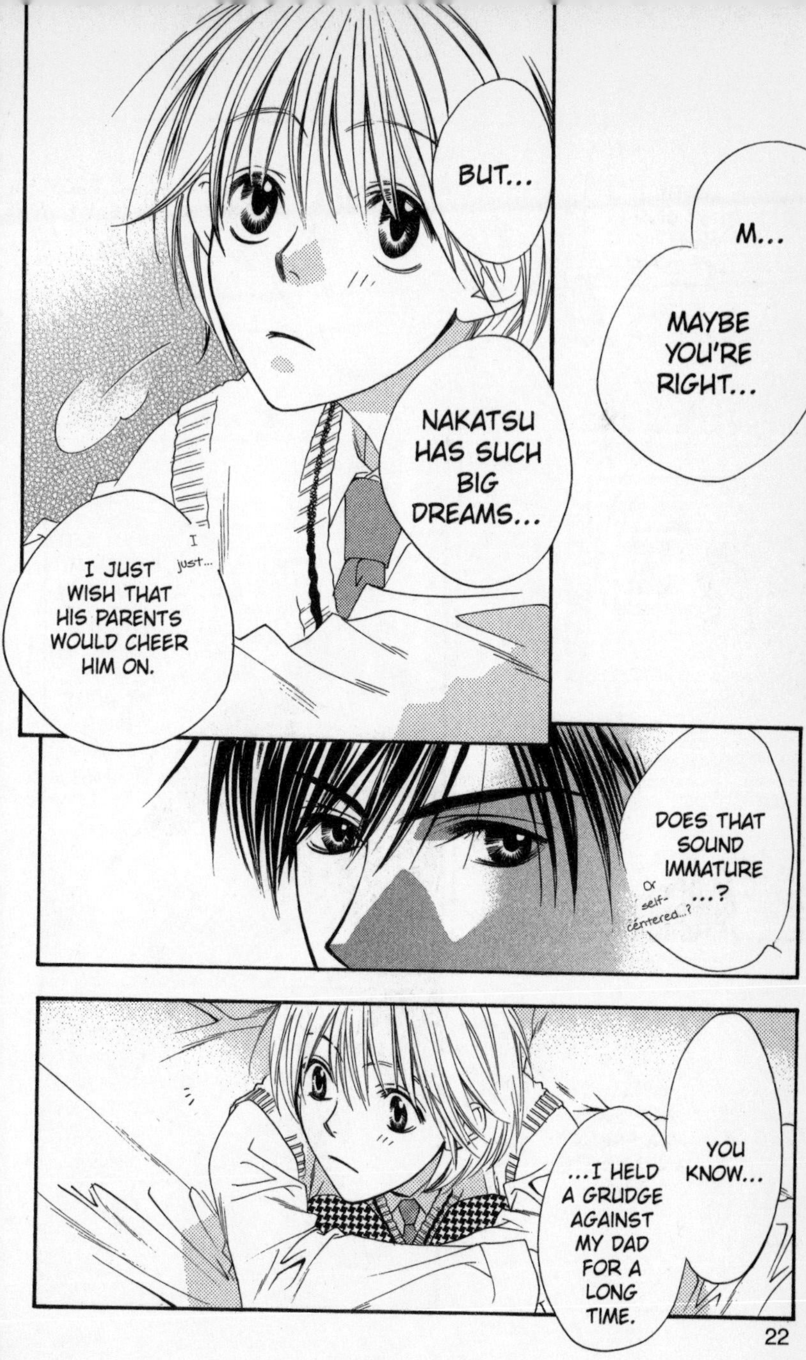
M...
MAYBE YOU'RE RIGHT...
BUT...
NAKATSU HAS SUCH BIG DREAMS...
I just...
I JUST WISH THAT HIS PARENTS WOULD CHEER HIM ON.
DOES THAT SOUND IMMATURE ...?
Or self-centered...?
YOU KNOW...
...I HELD A GRUDGE AGAINST MY DAD FOR A LONG TIME.

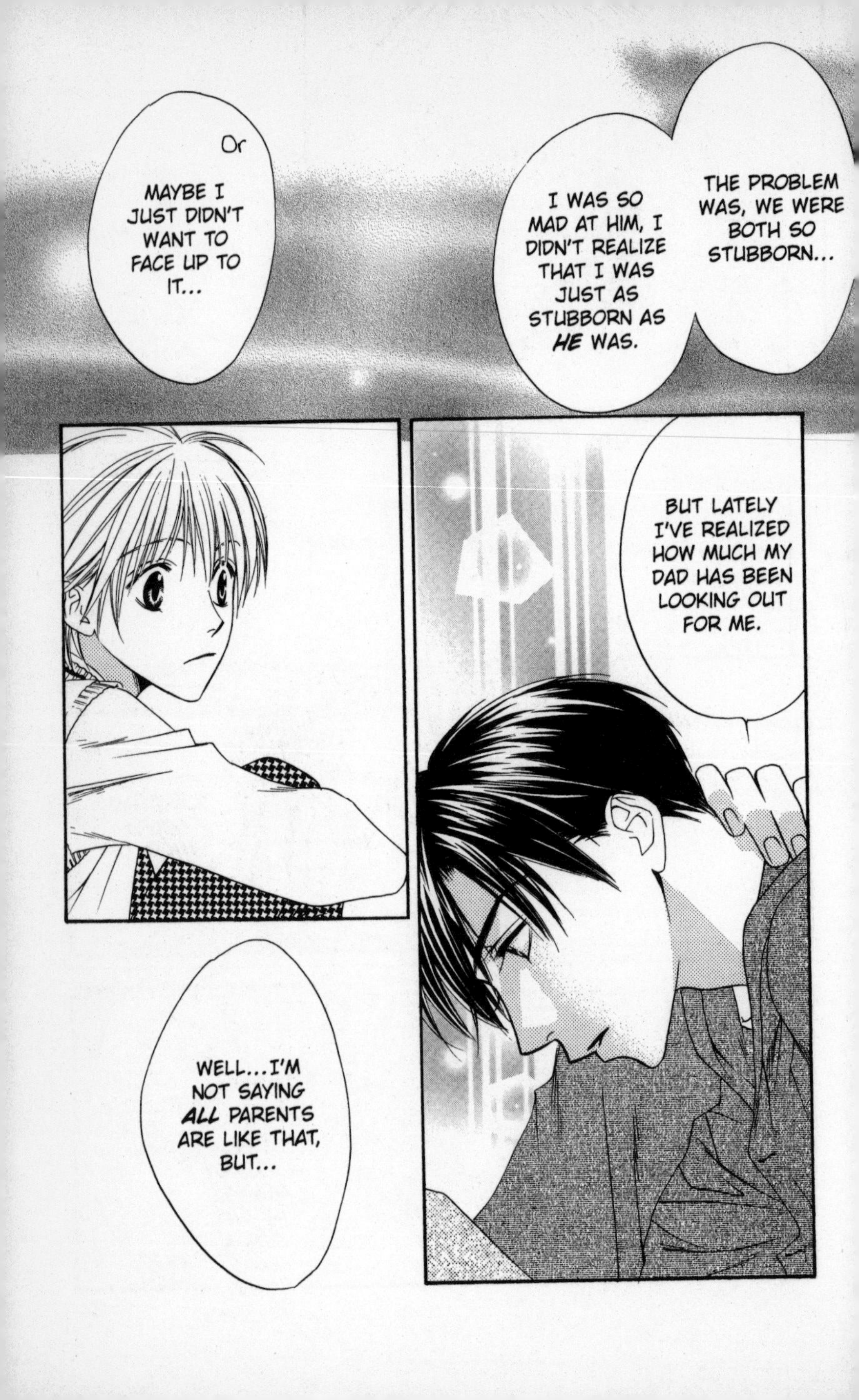
THE PROBLEM WAS, WE WERE BOTH SO STUBBORN...
I WAS SO MAD AT HIM, I DIDN'T REALIZE THAT I WAS JUST AS STUBBORN AS *HE* WAS.
Or
MAYBE I JUST DIDN'T WANT TO FACE UP TO IT...
BUT LATELY I'VE REALIZED HOW MUCH MY DAD HAS BEEN LOOKING OUT FOR ME.
WELL...I'M NOT SAYING *ALL* PARENTS ARE LIKE THAT, BUT...

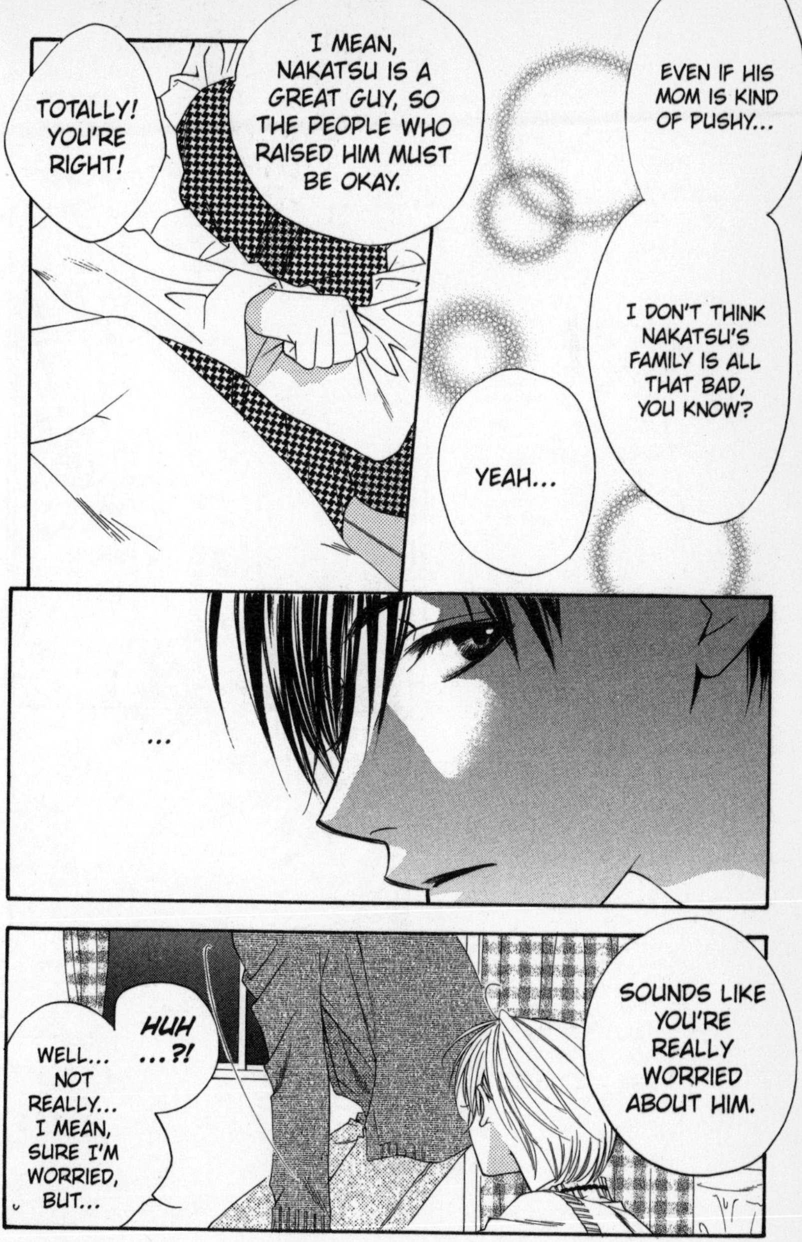
EVEN IF HIS MOM IS KIND OF PUSHY...
I DON'T THINK NAKATSU'S FAMILY IS ALL THAT BAD, YOU KNOW?
YEAH...
I MEAN, NAKATSU IS A GREAT GUY, SO THE PEOPLE WHO RAISED HIM MUST BE OKAY.
TOTALLY! YOU'RE RIGHT!
...
SOUNDS LIKE YOU'RE REALLY WORRIED ABOUT HIM.
HUH ...?!
WELL... NOT REALLY... I MEAN, SURE I'M WORRIED, BUT...

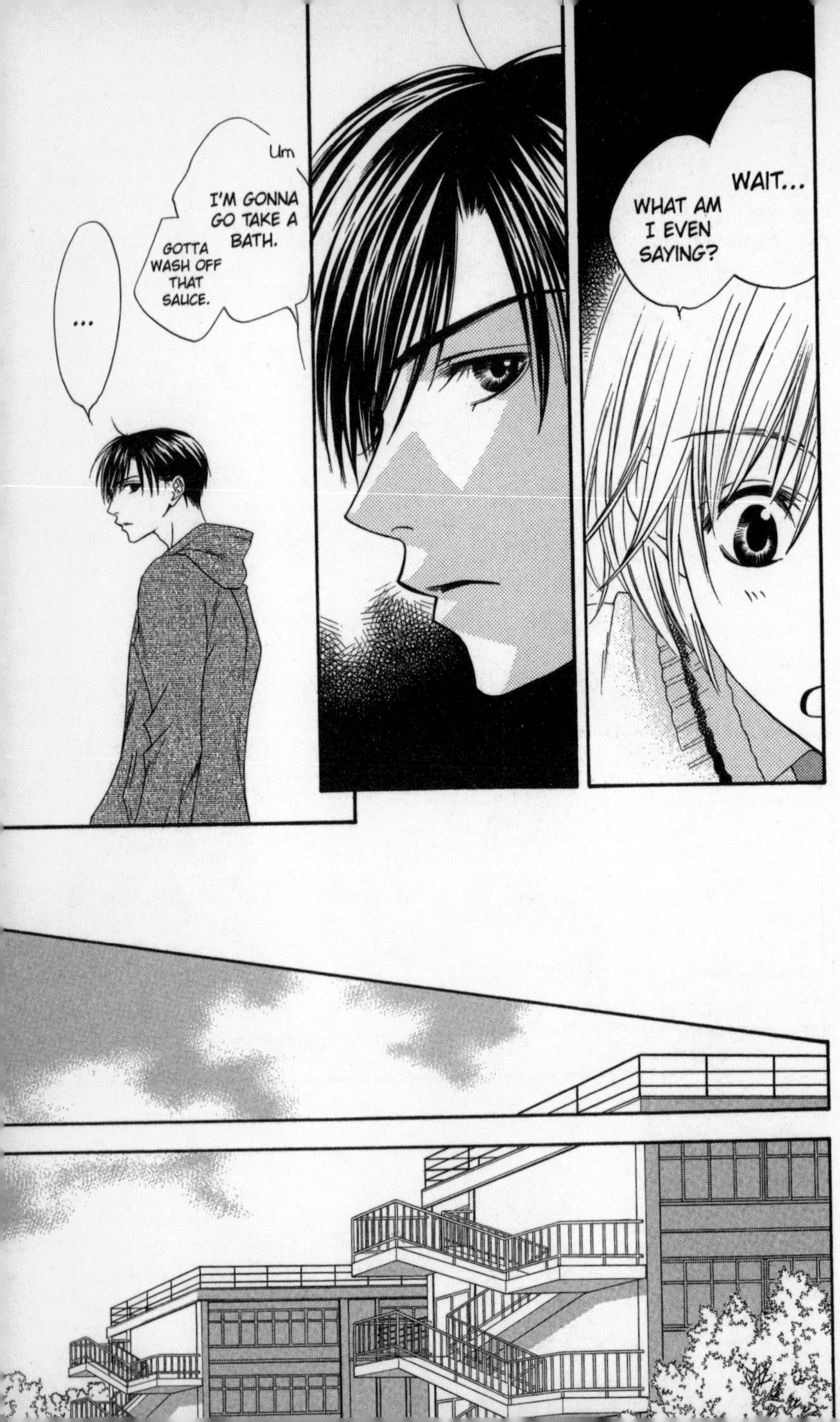
WAIT... WHAT AM I EVEN SAYING?
Um
I'M GONNA GO TAKE A BATH. GOTTA WASH OFF THAT SAUCE.
...

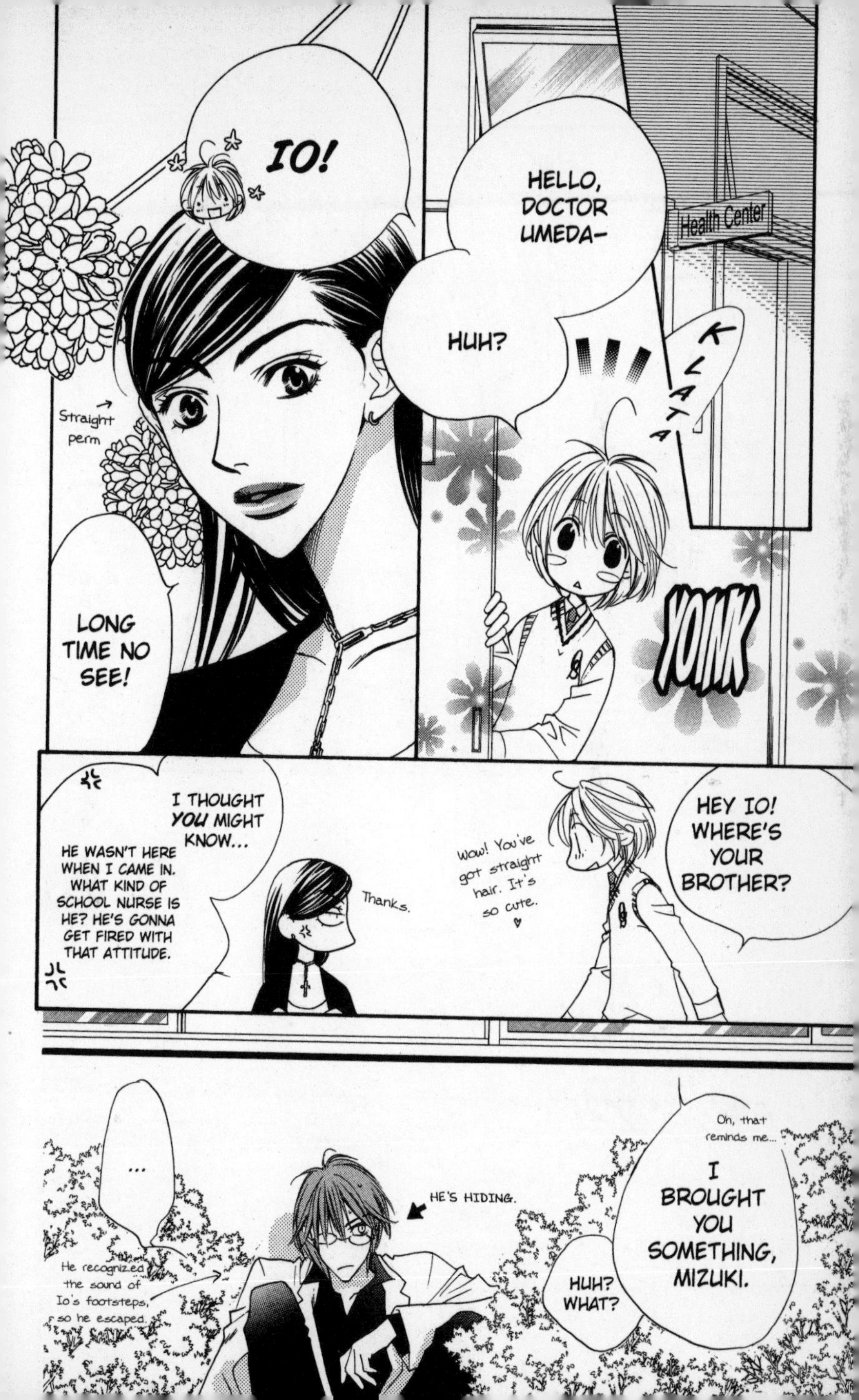
Health Center
HELLO, DOCTOR UMEDA-
KLATA
HUH?
YOINK
IO!
Straight perm
LONG TIME NO SEE!
HEY IO! WHERE'S YOUR BROTHER?
Wow! You've got straight hair. It's so cute.
Thanks.
I THOUGHT YOU MIGHT KNOW...
HE WASN'T HERE WHEN I CAME IN. WHAT KIND OF SCHOOL NURSE IS HE? HE'S GONNA GET FIRED WITH THAT ATTITUDE.
Oh, that reminds me...
I BROUGHT YOU SOMETHING, MIZUKI.
HUH? WHAT?
HE'S HIDING.
...
He recognized the sound of Io's footsteps, so he escaped.

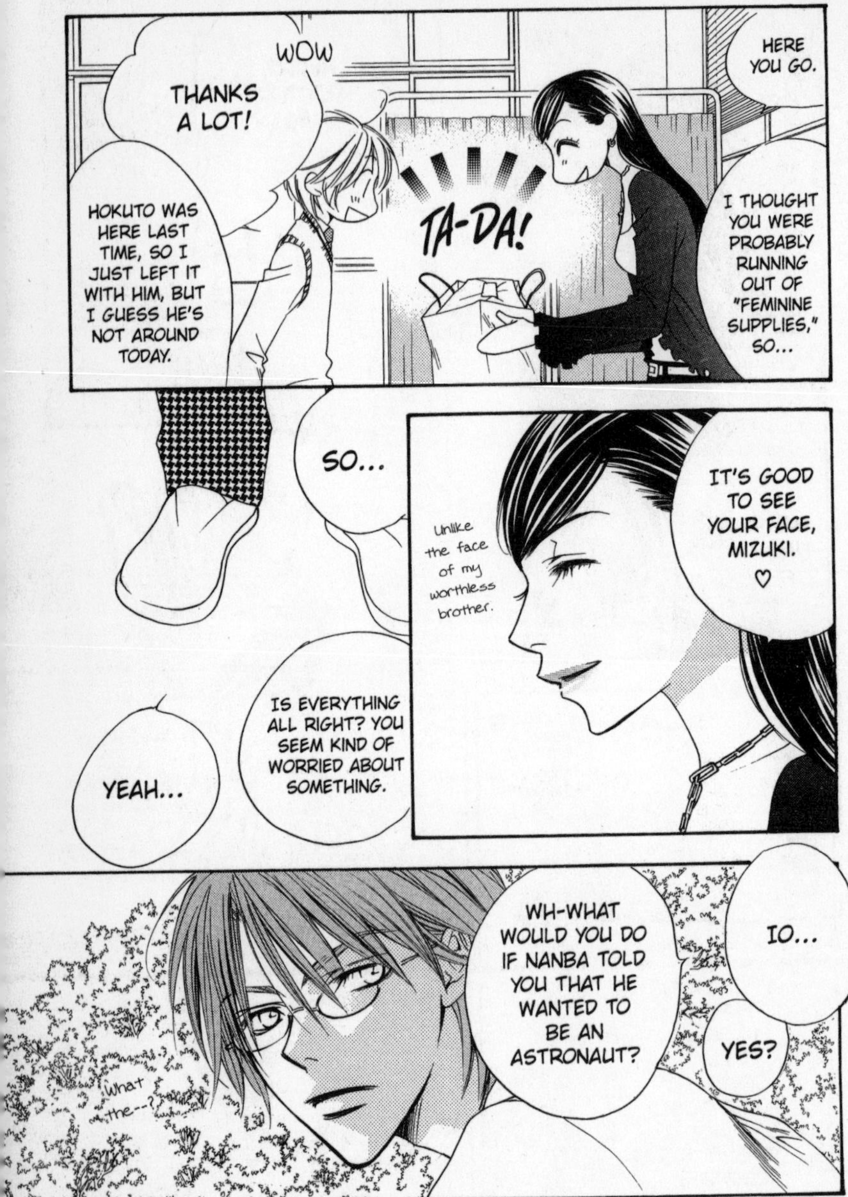
HERE YOU GO.
I THOUGHT YOU WERE PROBABLY RUNNING OUT OF "FEMININE SUPPLIES," SO...
TA-DA!
WOW
THANKS A LOT!
HOKUTO WAS HERE LAST TIME, SO I JUST LEFT IT WITH HIM, BUT I GUESS HE'S NOT AROUND TODAY.
IT'S GOOD TO SEE YOUR FACE, MIZUKI. ♡
Unlike the face of my worthless brother.
SO...
IS EVERYTHING ALL RIGHT? YOU SEEM KIND OF WORRIED ABOUT SOMETHING.
YEAH...
IO...
YES?
WH-WHAT WOULD YOU DO IF NANBA TOLD YOU THAT HE WANTED TO BE AN ASTRONAUT?
What the--?

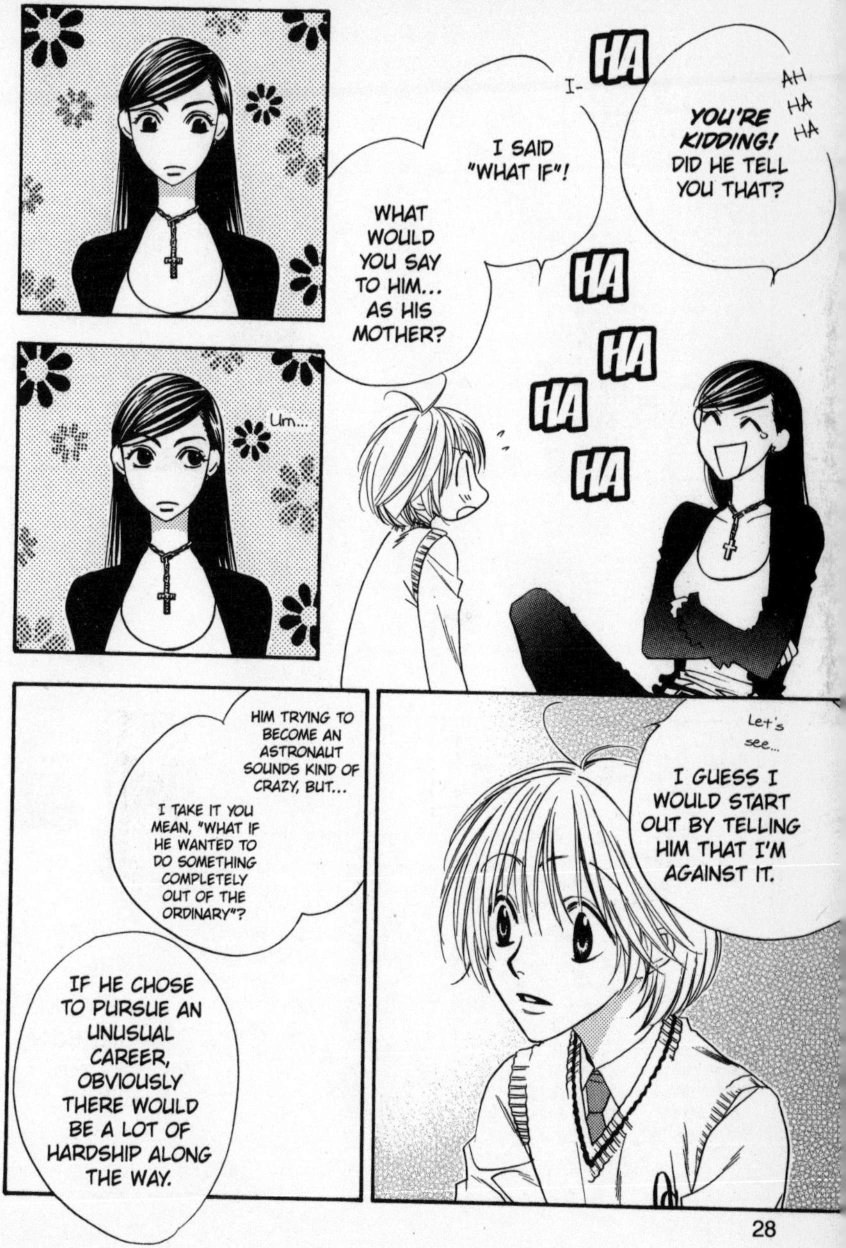
HA
AH HA HA
YOU'RE KIDDING! DID HE TELL YOU THAT?
I-
I SAID "WHAT IF"!
WHAT WOULD YOU SAY TO HIM... AS HIS MOTHER?
HA
HA
HA
HA
Um...
Let's see...
I GUESS I WOULD START OUT BY TELLING HIM THAT I'M AGAINST IT.
HIM TRYING TO BECOME AN ASTRONAUT SOUNDS KIND OF CRAZY, BUT...
I TAKE IT YOU MEAN, "WHAT IF HE WANTED TO DO SOMETHING COMPLETELY OUT OF THE ORDINARY"?
IF HE CHOSE TO PURSUE AN UNUSUAL CAREER, OBVIOUSLY THERE WOULD BE A LOT OF HARDSHIP ALONG THE WAY.

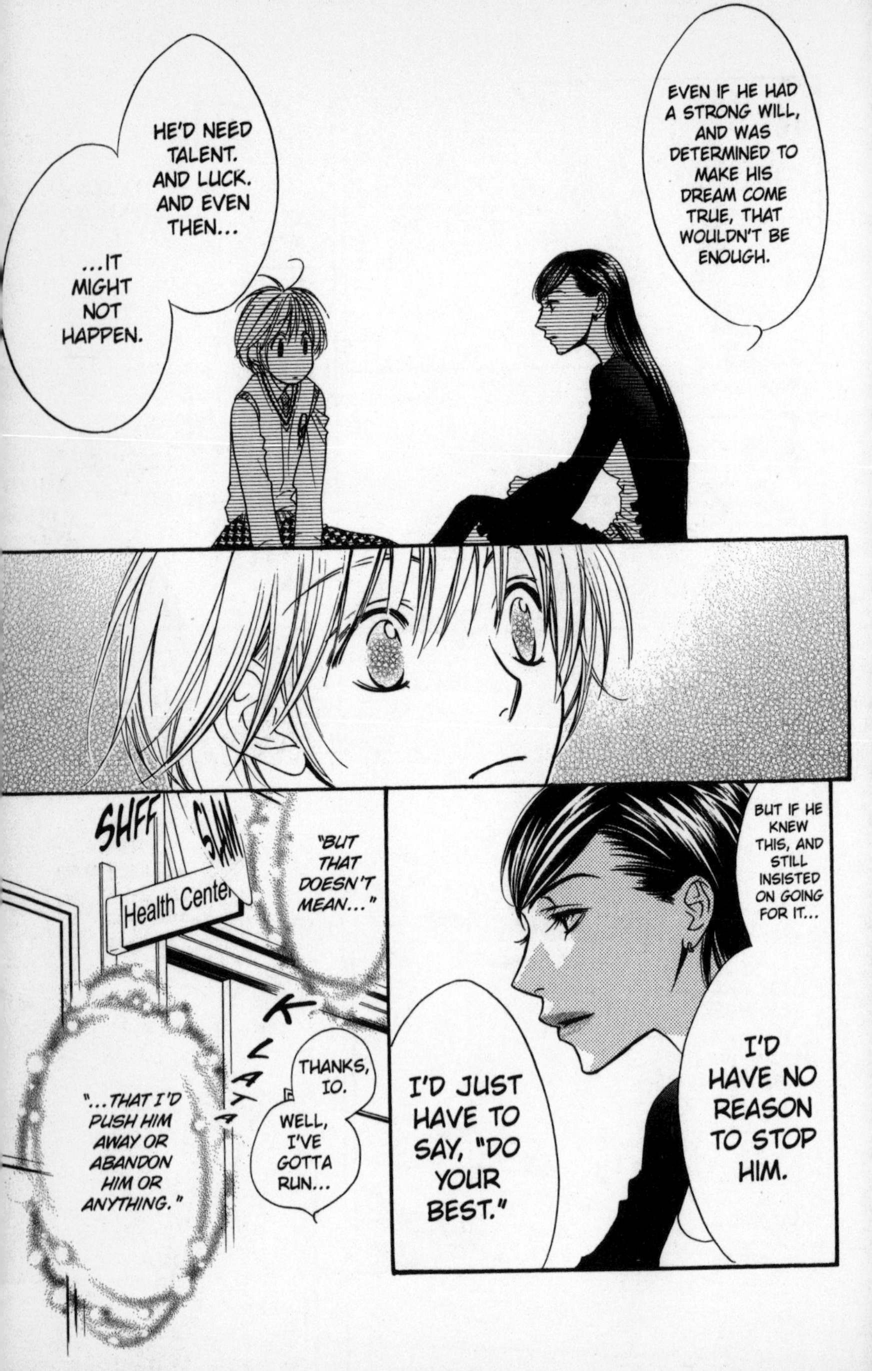
EVEN IF HE HAD A STRONG WILL, AND WAS DETERMINED TO MAKE HIS DREAM COME TRUE, THAT WOULDN'T BE ENOUGH.
HE'D NEED TALENT. AND LUCK. AND EVEN THEN...
...IT MIGHT NOT HAPPEN.
BUT IF HE KNEW THIS, AND STILL INSISTED ON GOING FOR IT...
I'D HAVE NO REASON TO STOP HIM.
I'D JUST HAVE TO SAY, "DO YOUR BEST."
"BUT THAT DOESN'T MEAN..."
SLAM
SHFF
Health Center
KLATA
THANKS, IO.
WELL, I'VE GOTTA RUN...
"...THAT I'D PUSH HIM AWAY OR ABANDON HIM OR ANYTHING."

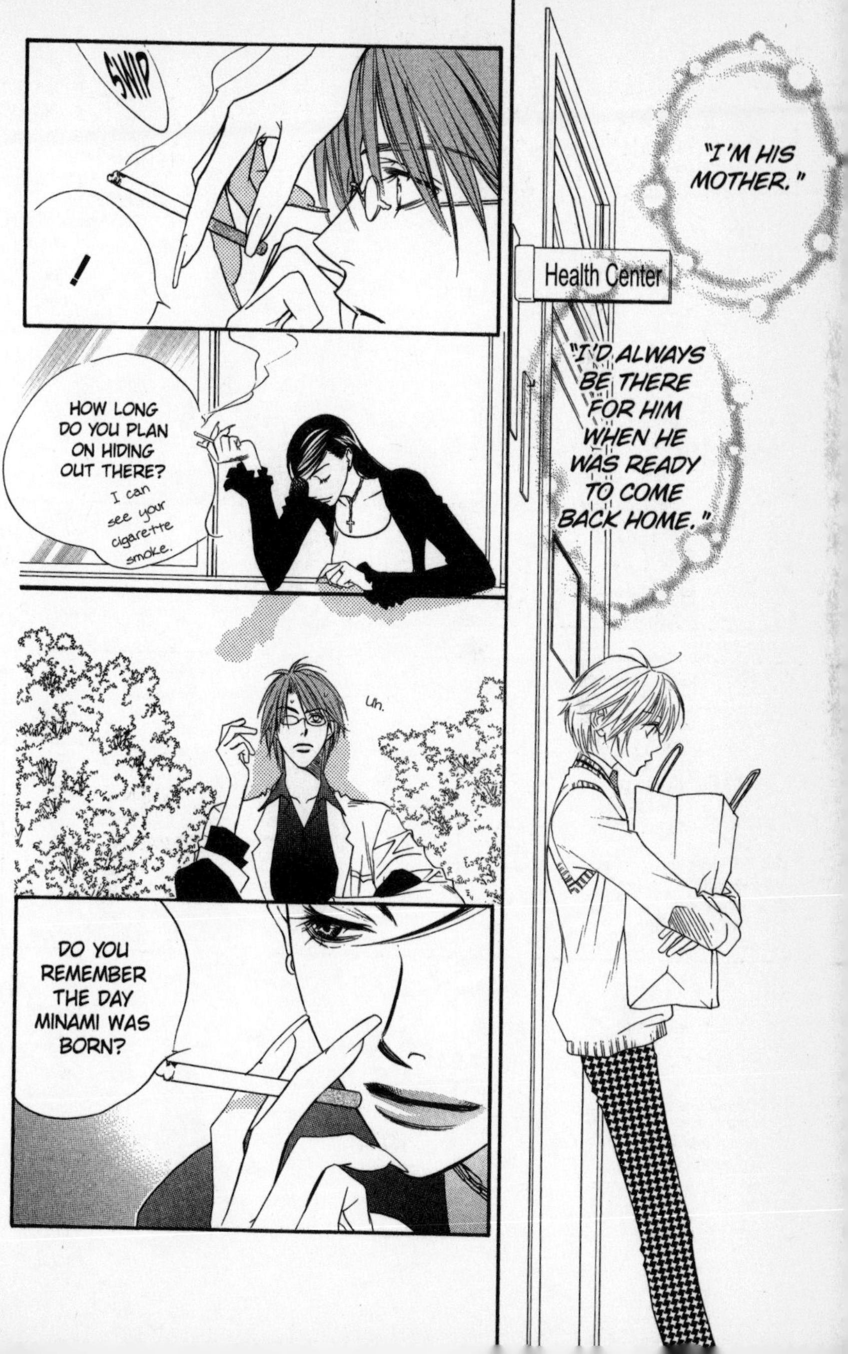
"I'M HIS MOTHER."
Health Center
"I'D ALWAYS BE THERE FOR HIM WHEN HE WAS READY TO COME BACK HOME."
SWIP
!
HOW LONG DO YOU PLAN ON HIDING OUT THERE?
I can see your cigarette smoke.
Uh.
DO YOU REMEMBER THE DAY MINAMI WAS BORN?

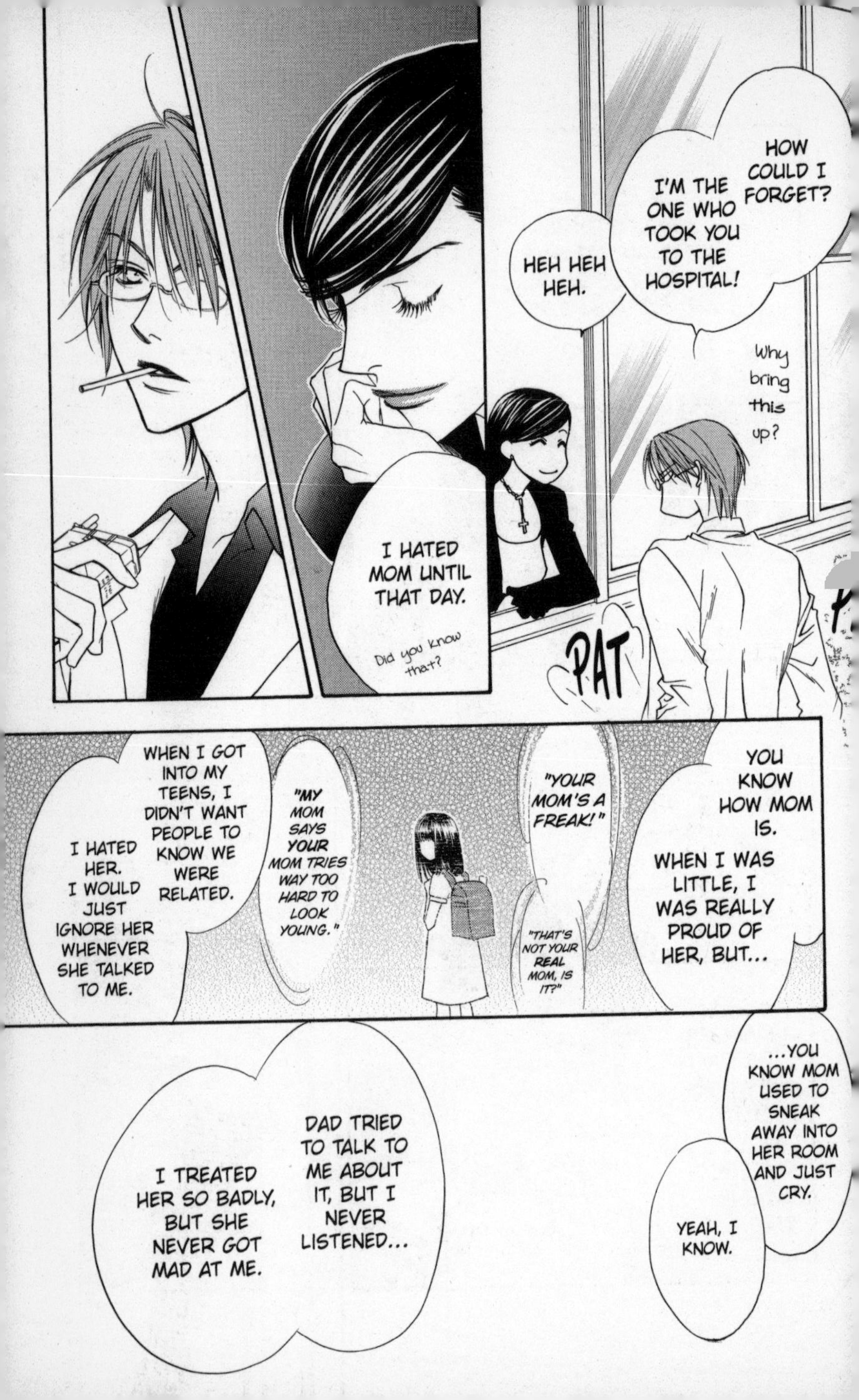
HOW COULD I FORGET?
I'M THE ONE WHO TOOK YOU TO THE HOSPITAL!
HEH HEH HEH.
Why bring this up?
PAT
I HATED MOM UNTIL THAT DAY.
Did you know that?
YOU KNOW HOW MOM IS.
WHEN I WAS LITTLE, I WAS REALLY PROUD OF HER, BUT...
"YOUR MOM'S A FREAK!"
"THAT'S NOT YOUR REAL MOM, IS IT?"
"MY MOM SAYS YOUR MOM TRIES WAY TOO HARD TO LOOK YOUNG."
WHEN I GOT INTO MY TEENS, I DIDN'T WANT PEOPLE TO KNOW WE WERE RELATED.
I HATED HER. I WOULD JUST IGNORE HER WHENEVER SHE TALKED TO ME.
...YOU KNOW MOM USED TO SNEAK AWAY INTO HER ROOM AND JUST CRY.
YEAH, I KNOW.
DAD TRIED TO TALK TO ME ABOUT IT, BUT I NEVER LISTENED...
I TREATED HER SO BADLY, BUT SHE NEVER GOT MAD AT ME.

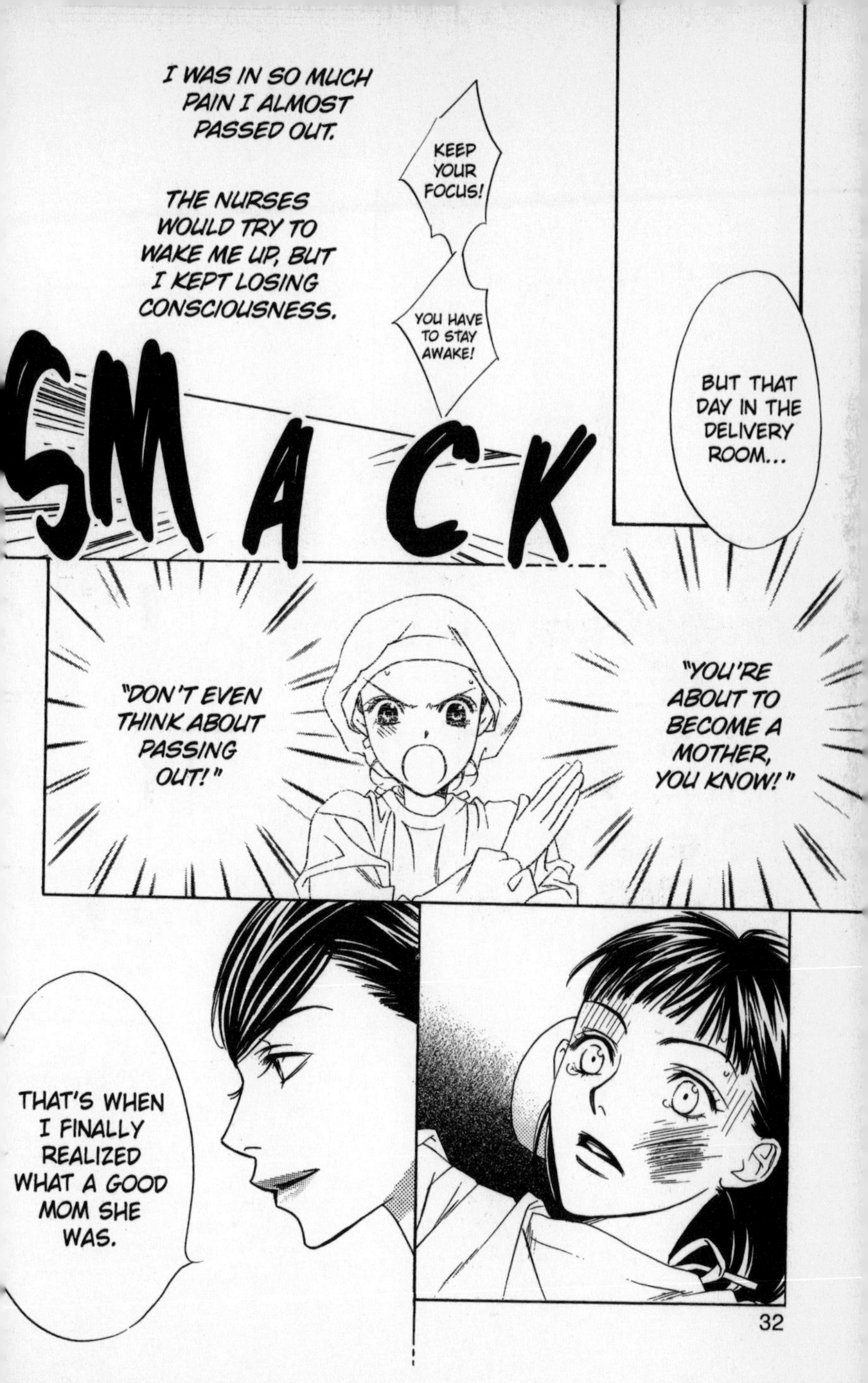
BUT THAT DAY IN THE DELIVERY ROOM...
I WAS IN SO MUCH PAIN I ALMOST PASSED OUT.
THE NURSES WOULD TRY TO WAKE ME UP, BUT I KEPT LOSING CONSCIOUSNESS.
KEEP YOUR FOCUS!
YOU HAVE TO STAY AWAKE!
SMACK
"YOU'RE ABOUT TO BECOME A MOTHER, YOU KNOW!"
"DON'T EVEN THINK ABOUT PASSING OUT!"
THAT'S WHEN I FINALLY REALIZED WHAT A GOOD MOM SHE WAS.

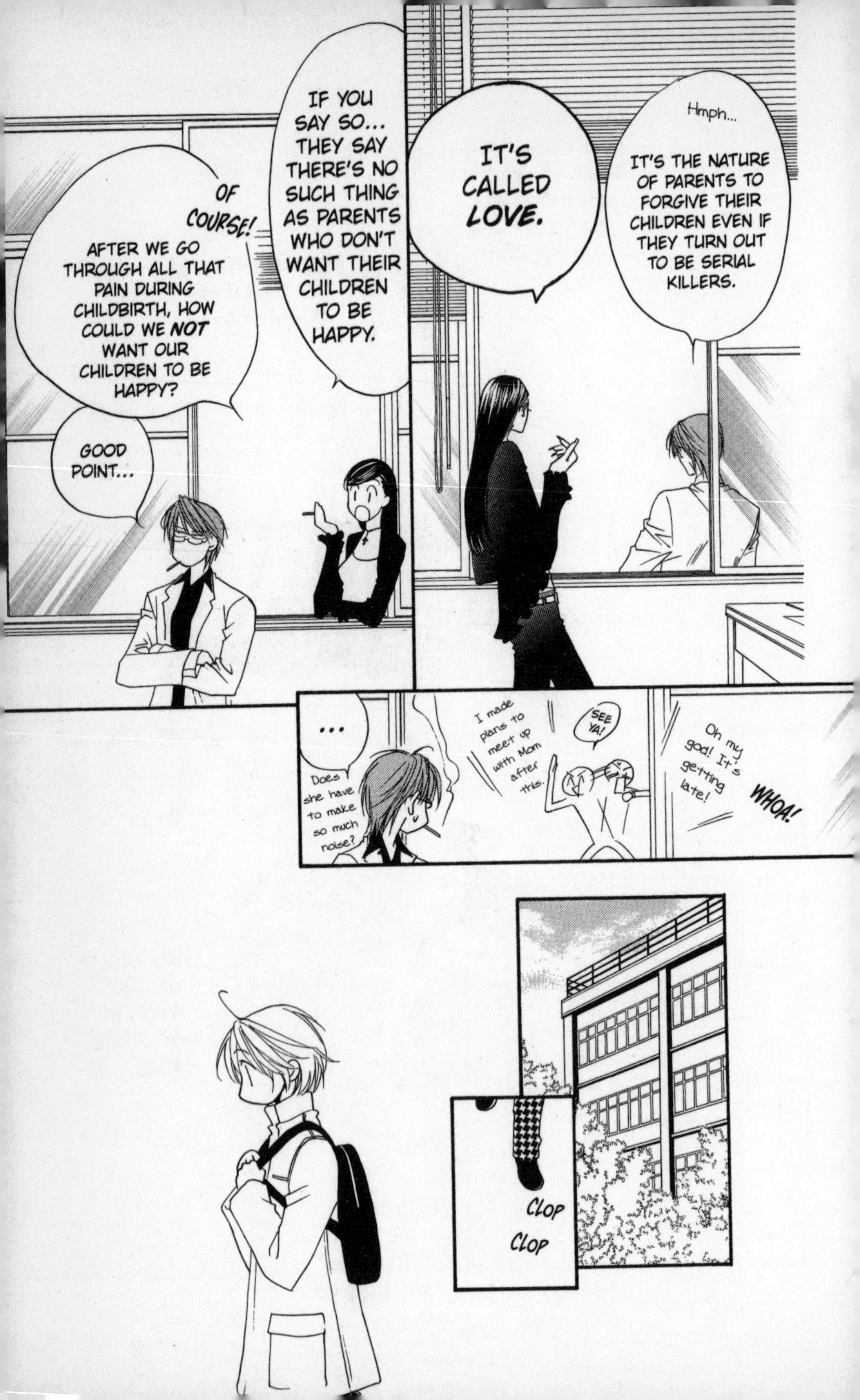
Hmph...
IT'S THE NATURE OF PARENTS TO FORGIVE THEIR CHILDREN EVEN IF THEY TURN OUT TO BE SERIAL KILLERS.
IT'S CALLED LOVE.
IF YOU SAY SO... THEY SAY THERE'S NO SUCH THING AS PARENTS WHO DON'T WANT THEIR CHILDREN TO BE HAPPY.
OF COURSE!
AFTER WE GO THROUGH ALL THAT PAIN DURING CHILDBIRTH, HOW COULD WE NOT WANT OUR CHILDREN TO BE HAPPY?
GOOD POINT...
WHOA!
Oh my god! It's getting late!
SEE YA!
I made plans to meet up with Mom after this.
...
Does she have to make so much noise?
CLOP
CLOP

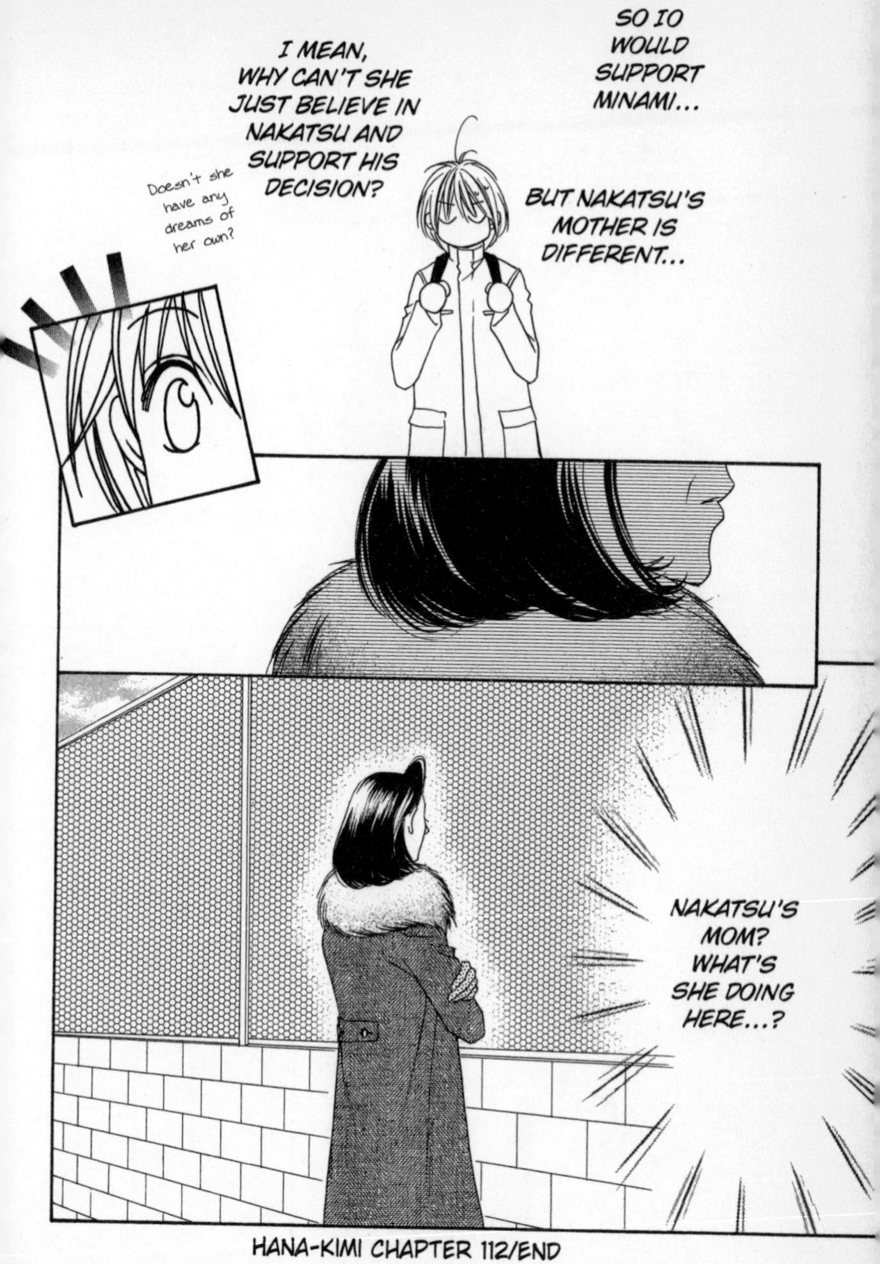
SO I'D WOULD SUPPORT MINAMI...
BUT NAKATSU'S MOTHER IS DIFFERENT...
I MEAN, WHY CAN'T SHE JUST BELIEVE IN NAKATSU AND SUPPORT HIS DECISION?
Doesn't she have any dreams of her own?
NAKATSU'S MOM? WHAT'S SHE DOING HERE...?

HANA-KIMI CHAPTER 112/END

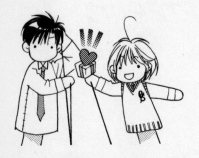

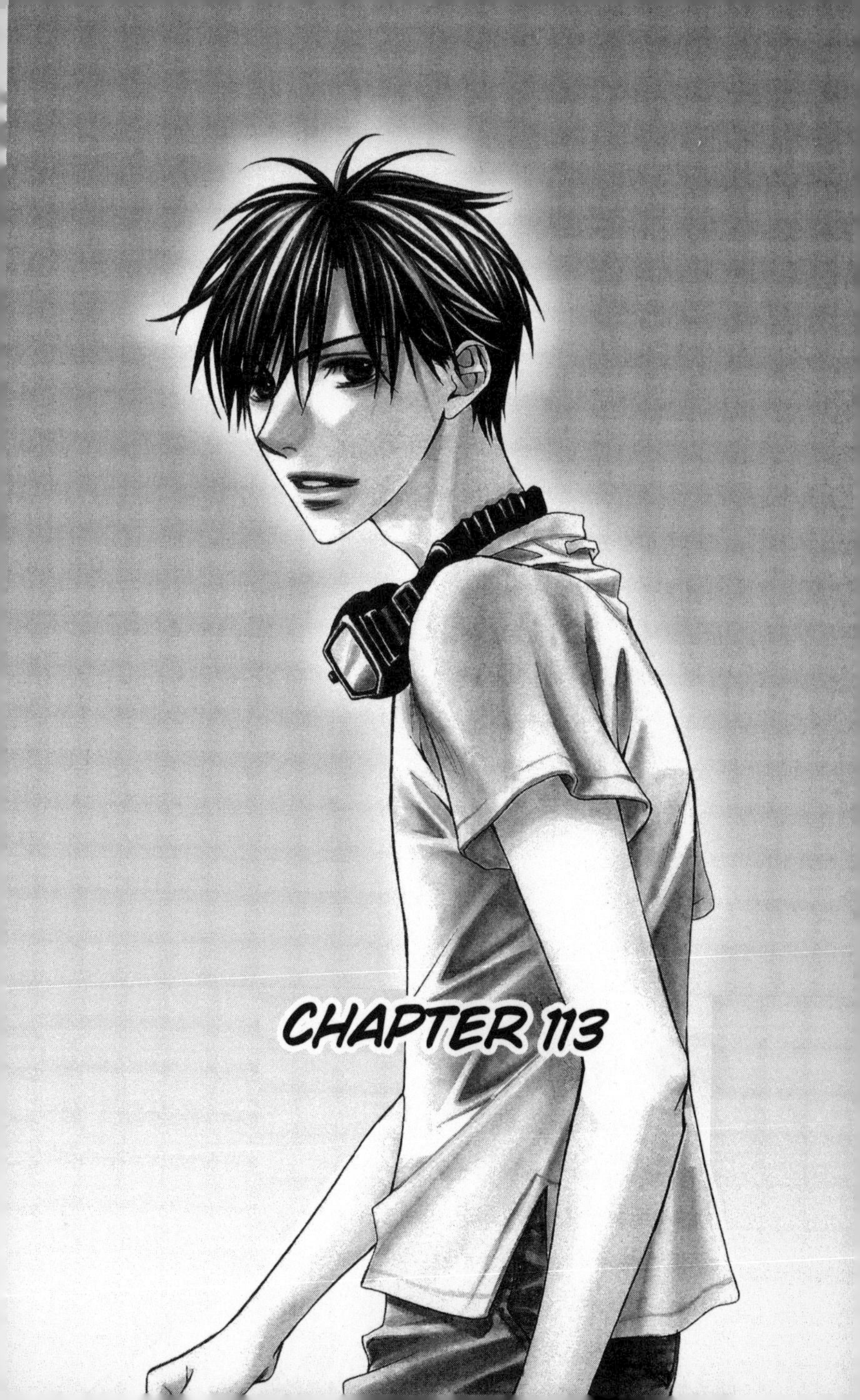
CHAPTER 113

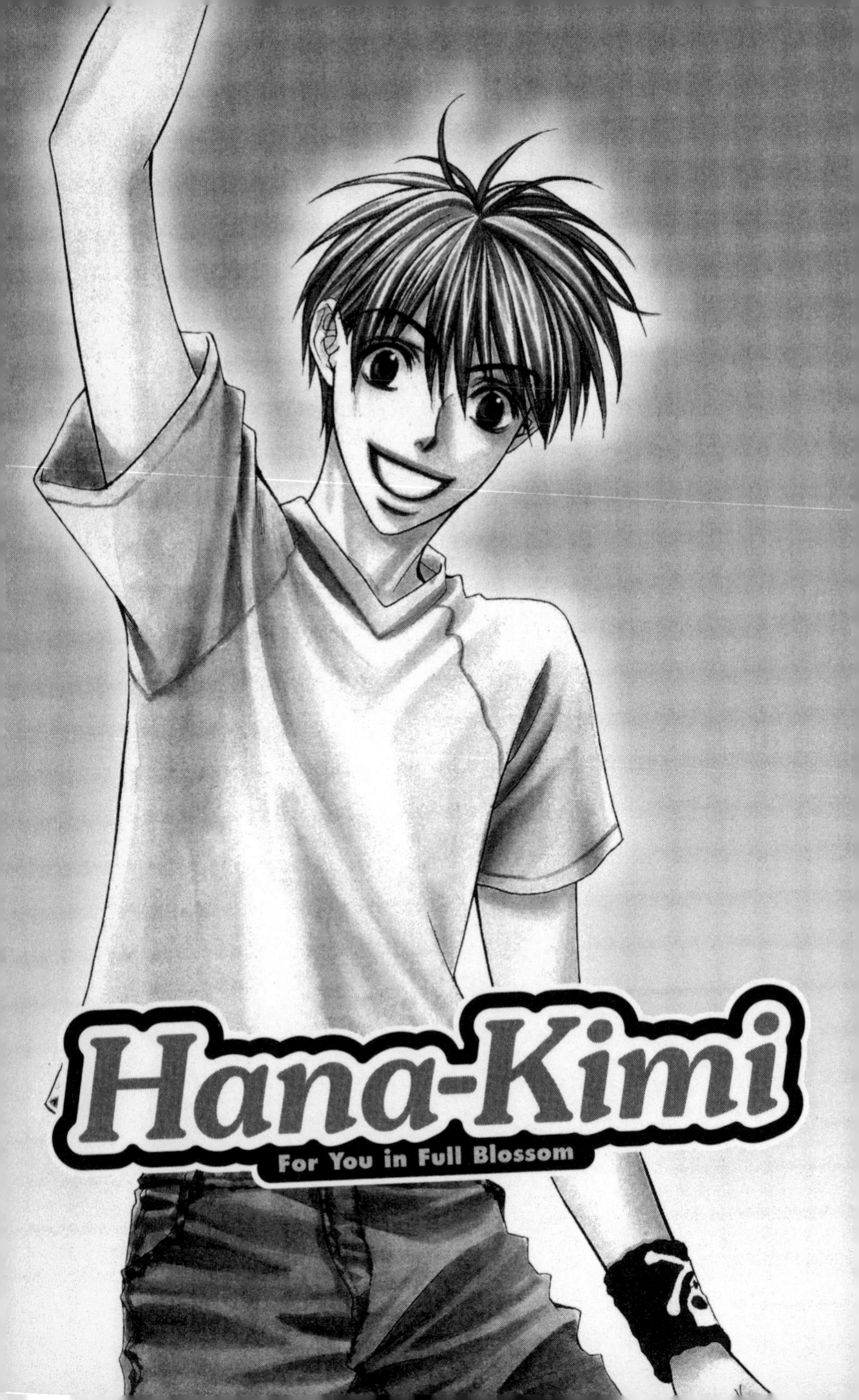
Hana-Kimi
For You in Full Blossom

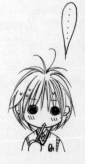

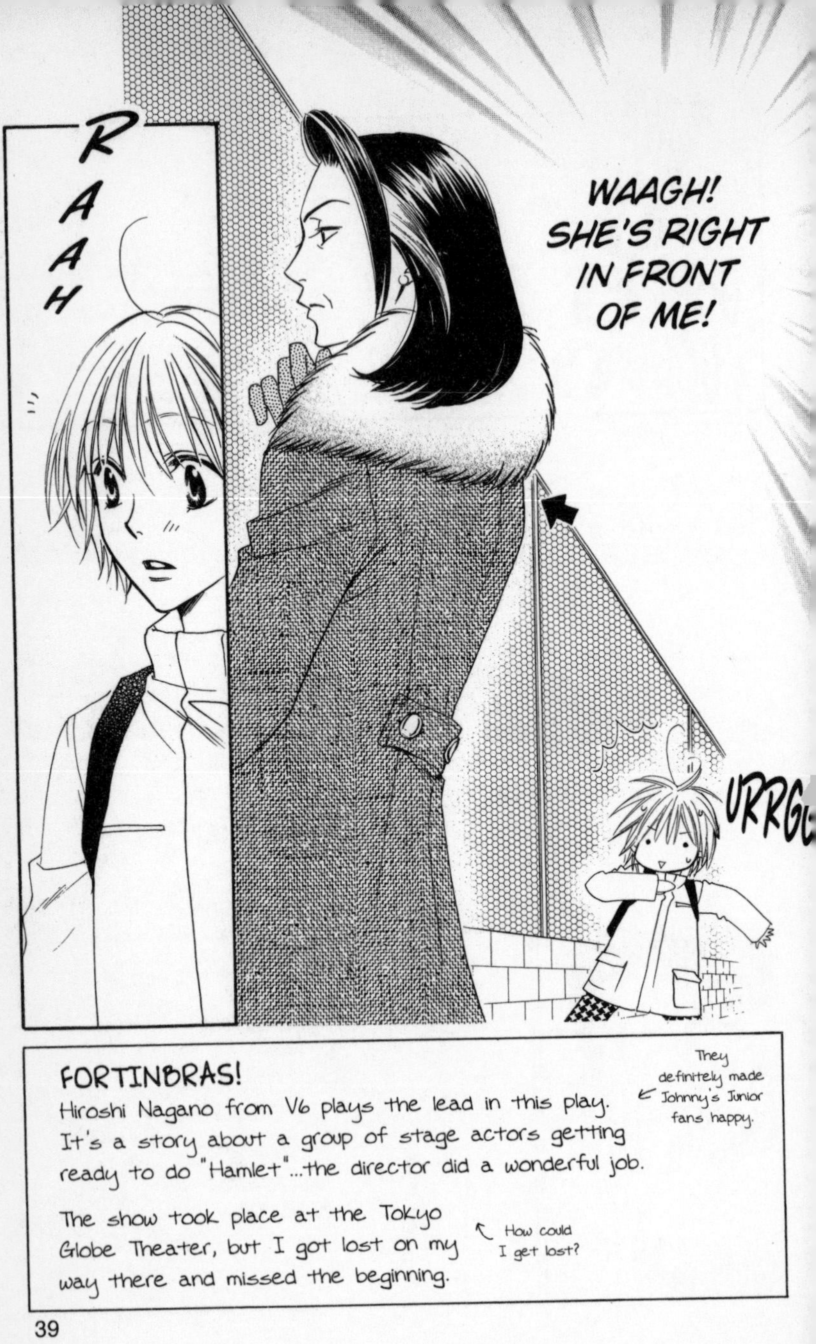
WAAGH! SHE'S RIGHT IN FRONT OF ME!
URRG
RAAAH

FORTINBRAS!

Hiroshi Nagano from V6 plays the lead in this play. It's a story about a group of stage actors getting ready to do "Hamlet"...the director did a wonderful job.

← They definitely made Johnny's Junior fans happy.

The show took place at the Tokyo Globe Theater, but I got lost on my way there and missed the beginning.

↖ How could I get lost?

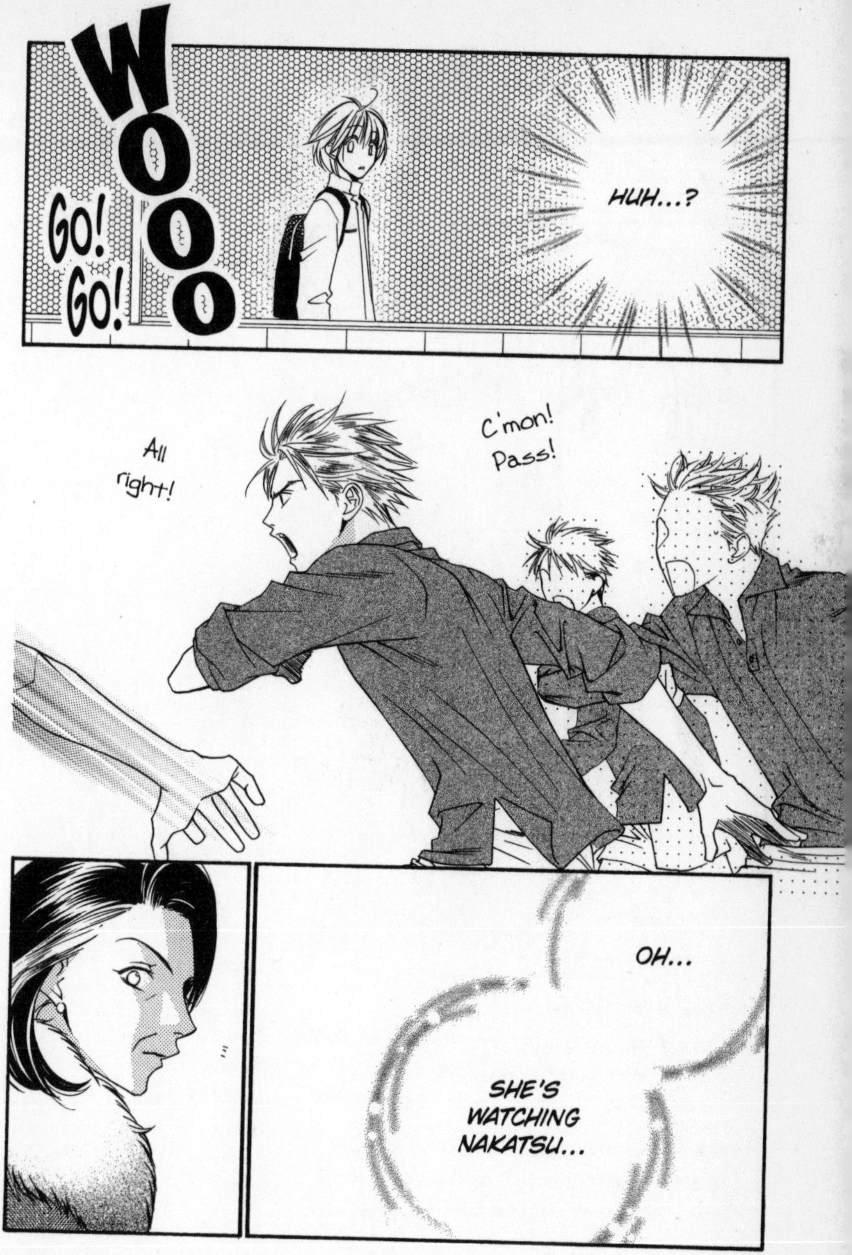
HUH...?
WOOO
GO! GO!
C'mon! Pass!
All right!
OH...
SHE'S WATCHING NAKATSU...

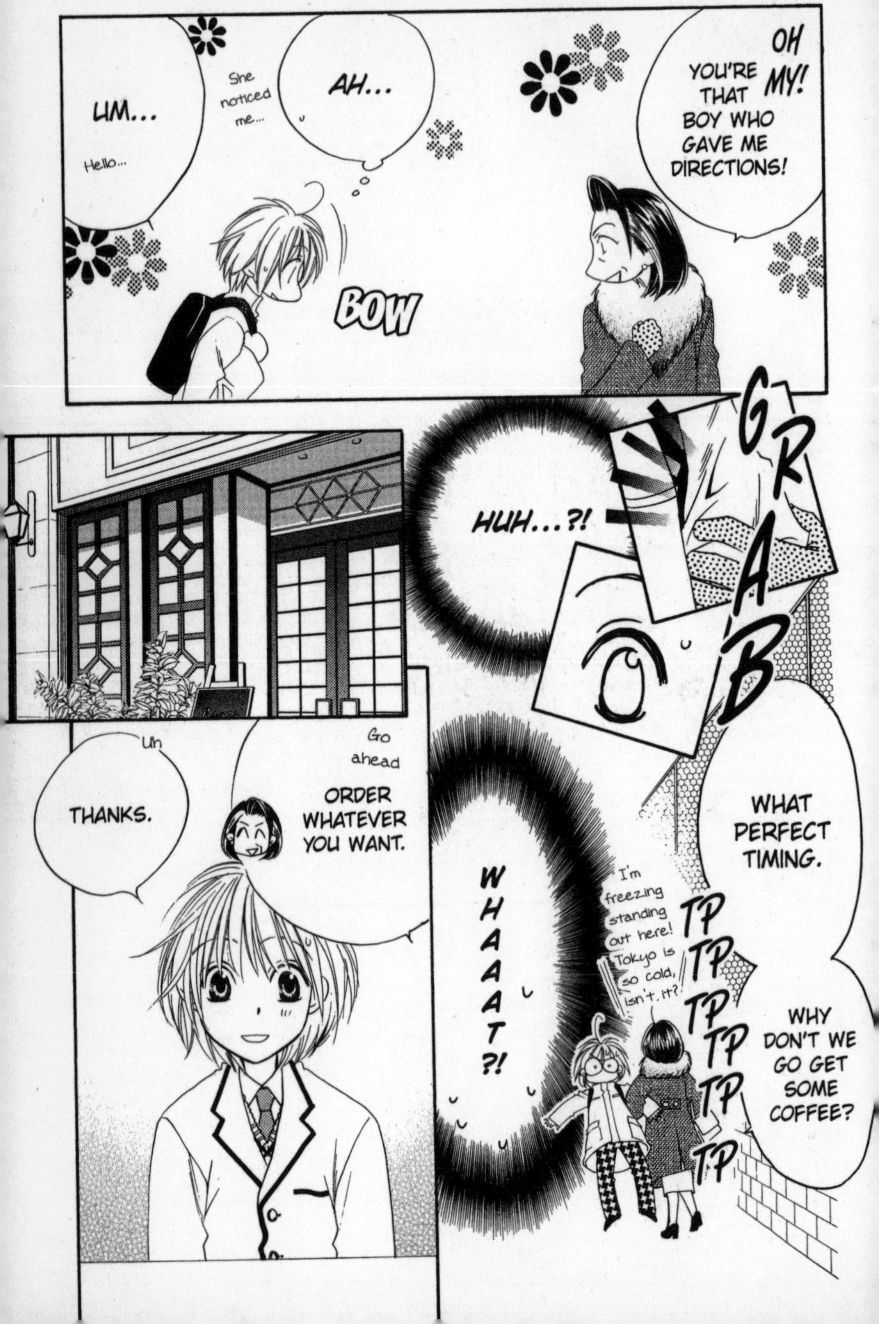
OH MY!
YOU'RE THAT BOY WHO GAVE ME DIRECTIONS!
AH...
She noticed me...
BOW
UM...
Hello...
GRAB
HUH...?!
WHAT PERFECT TIMING.
WHY DON'T WE GO GET SOME COFFEE?
I'm freezing standing out here! Tokyo is so cold, isn't it?
TP TP TP TP TP TP
WHAAAAT?!
Go ahead
ORDER WHATEVER YOU WANT.
Uh
THANKS.

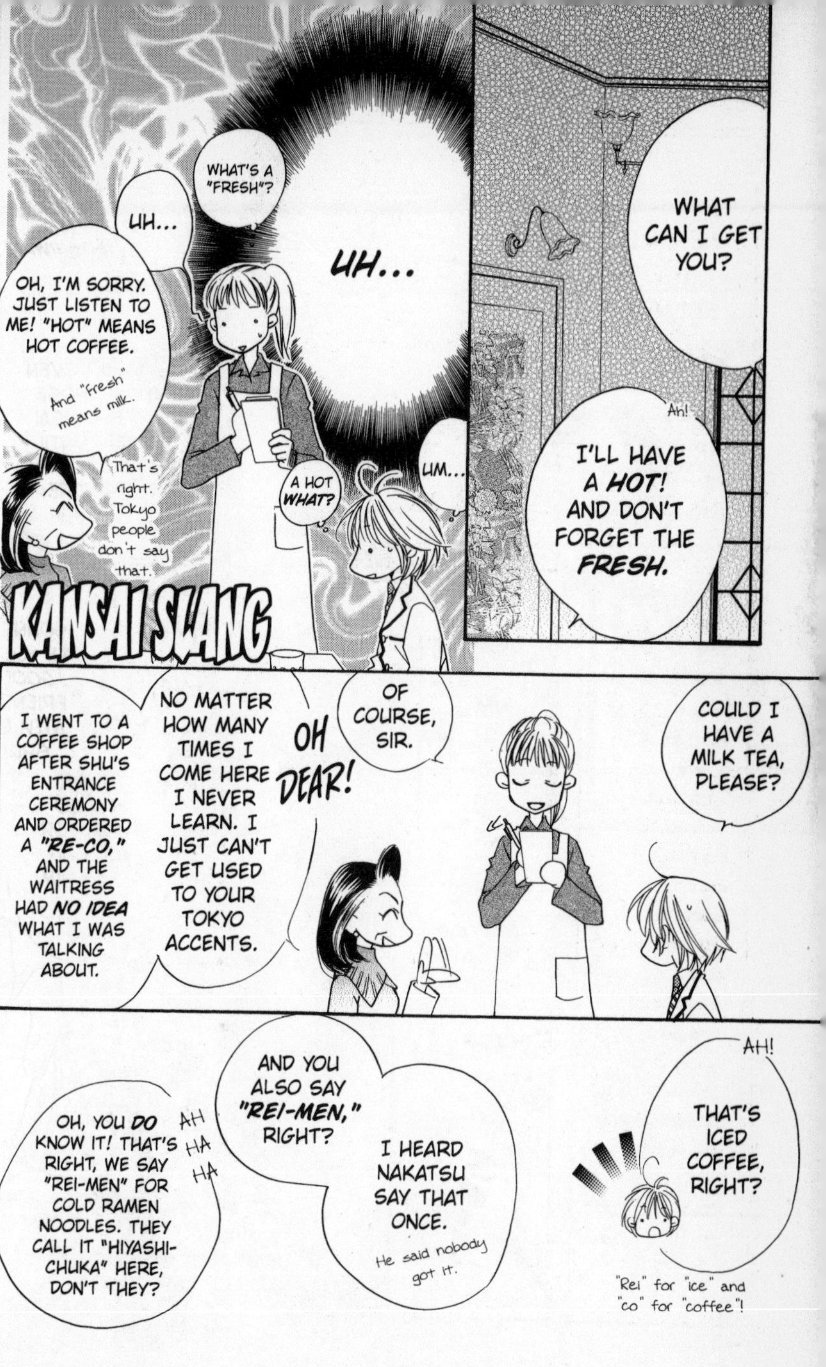
WHAT CAN I GET YOU?
Ah!
I'LL HAVE A *HOT*! AND DON'T FORGET THE *FRESH*.
UH...
WHAT'S A "FRESH"?
UH...
UM...
A HOT *WHAT?*
OH, I'M SORRY. JUST LISTEN TO ME! "HOT" MEANS HOT COFFEE.
And "fresh" means milk.
That's right. Tokyo people don't say that.
KANSAI SLANG
COULD I HAVE A MILK TEA, PLEASE?
OF COURSE, SIR.
OH DEAR!
NO MATTER HOW MANY TIMES I COME HERE I NEVER LEARN. I JUST CAN'T GET USED TO YOUR TOKYO ACCENTS.
I WENT TO A COFFEE SHOP AFTER SHU'S ENTRANCE CEREMONY AND ORDERED A *"RE-CO,"* AND THE WAITRESS HAD *NO IDEA* WHAT I WAS TALKING ABOUT.
AH!
THAT'S ICED COFFEE, RIGHT?
"Rei" for "ice" and "co" for "coffee"!
AND YOU ALSO SAY *"REI-MEN,"* RIGHT?
I HEARD NAKATSU SAY THAT ONCE.
He said nobody got it.
AH HA HA
OH, YOU *DO* KNOW IT! THAT'S RIGHT, WE SAY "REI-MEN" FOR COLD RAMEN NOODLES. THEY CALL IT "HIYASHI-CHUKA" HERE, DON'T THEY?

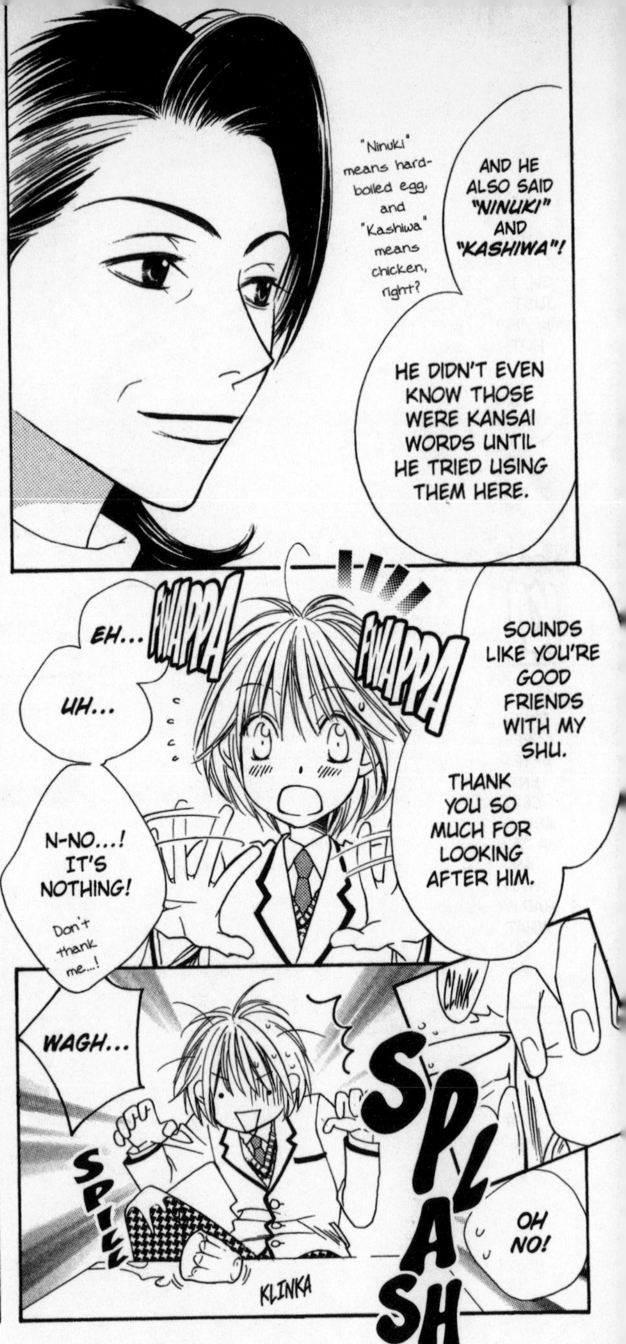
AND HE ALSO SAID "NINUKI" AND "KASHIWA"!
"Ninuki" means hard-boiled egg, and "Kashiwa" means chicken, right?
HE DIDN'T EVEN KNOW THOSE WERE KANSAI WORDS UNTIL HE TRIED USING THEM HERE.
SOUNDS LIKE YOU'RE GOOD FRIENDS WITH MY SHU.
THANK YOU SO MUCH FOR LOOKING AFTER HIM.
FWAPPA
FWAPPA
EH...
UH...
N-NO...! IT'S NOTHING!
Don't thank me...!
CLINK
SPLASH
OH NO!
WAGH...
SPILL
KLINKA

BEHIND THE SCENES

Nakatsu's silly childhood stories are based on my own experiences growing up in Kansai. The story about how he fell into a rice paddy actually happened to me when I was in kindergarten. I was half covered in mud. (As soon as I fell, my mom pulled me out.) I walked all the way to my grand-parents' house where my mom hosed me down in front of the house.

Actually, it was only about 100 meters.

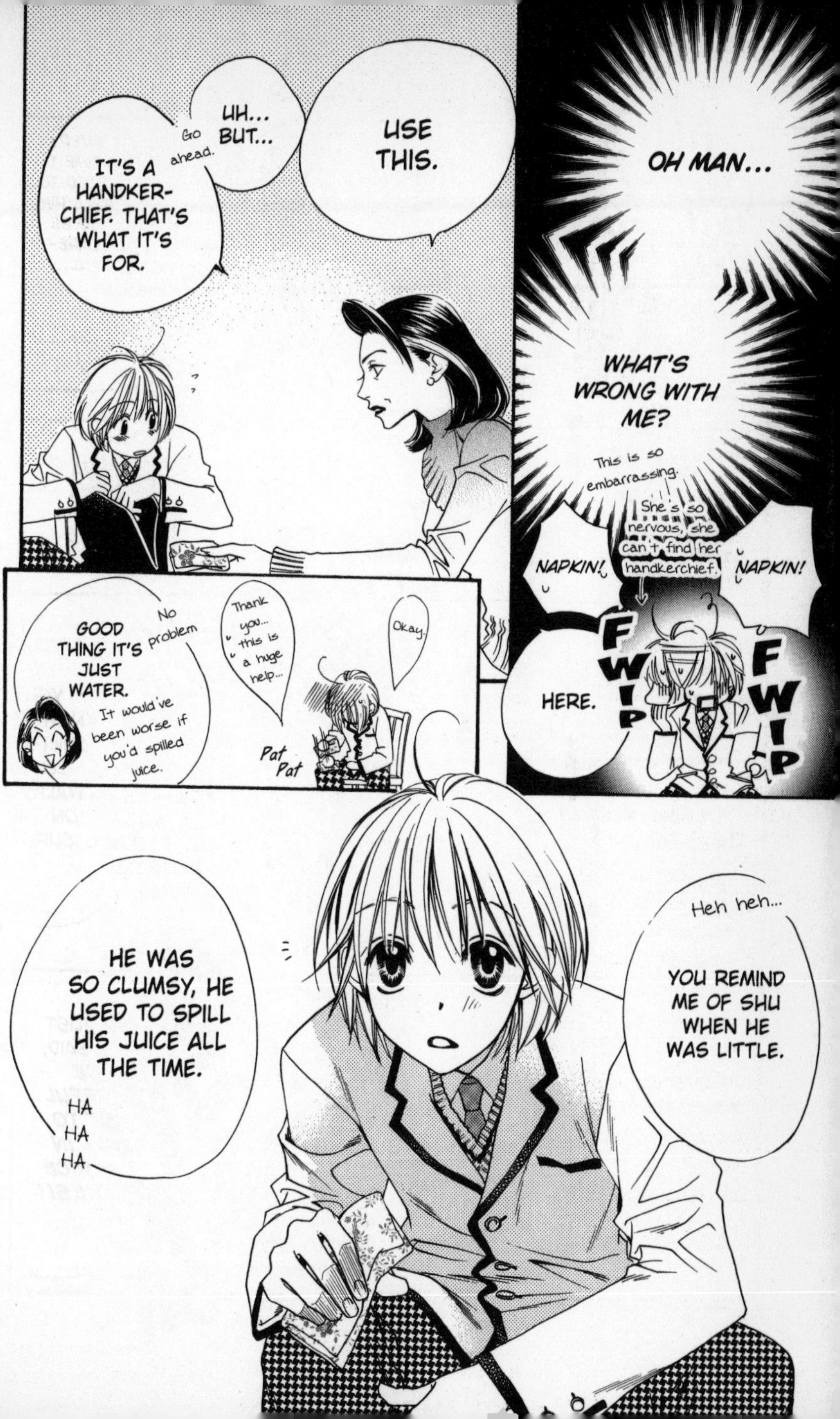
OH MAN...
WHAT'S WRONG WITH ME?
This is so embarrassing.
She's so nervous, she can't find her handkerchief.
NAPKIN!
NAPKIN!
FWIP
FWIP
HERE.
USE THIS.
UH... BUT...
Go ahead.
IT'S A HANDKERCHIEF. THAT'S WHAT IT'S FOR.
Okay.
Thank you... this is a huge help...
GOOD THING IT'S JUST WATER.
No problem
It would've been worse if you'd spilled juice.
Pat Pat
Heh heh...
YOU REMIND ME OF SHU WHEN HE WAS LITTLE.
HE WAS SO CLUMSY, HE USED TO SPILL HIS JUICE ALL THE TIME.
HA HA HA

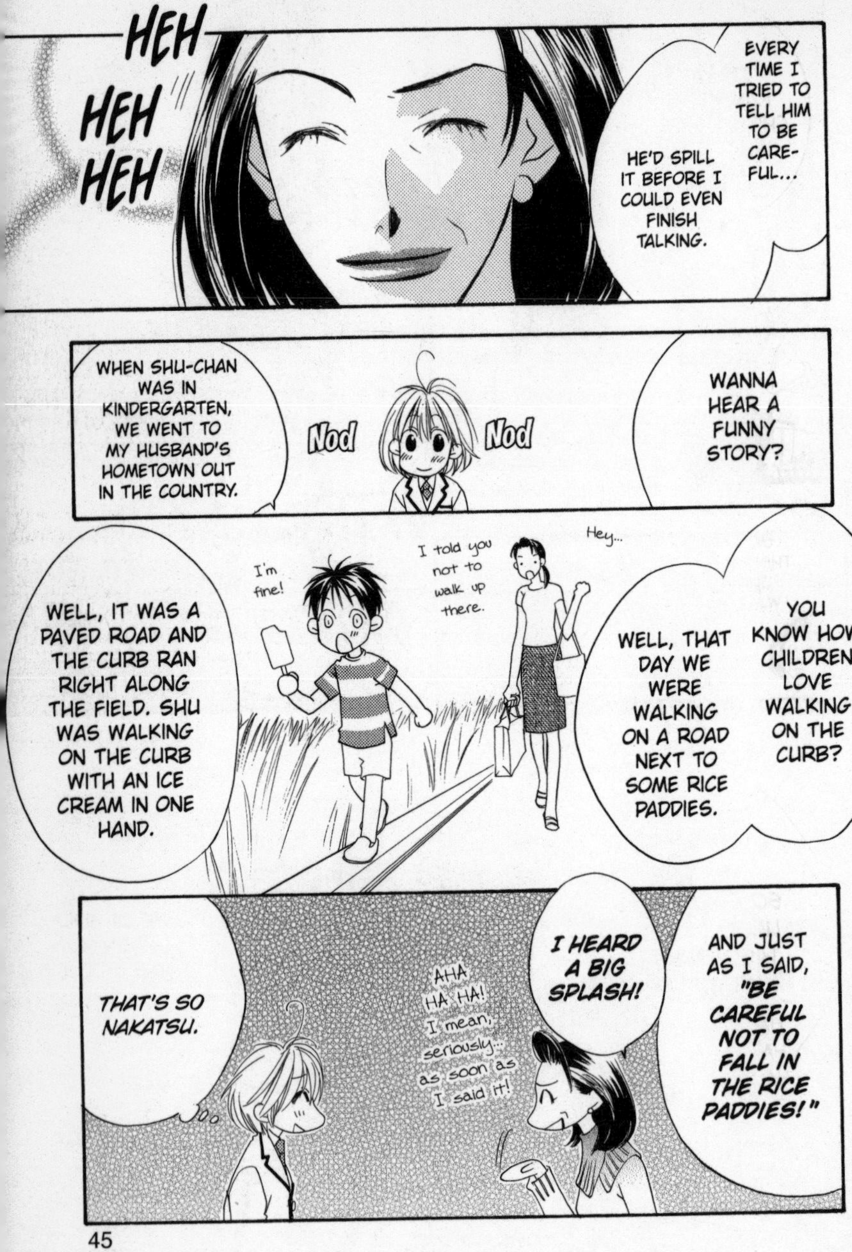
EVERY TIME I TRIED TO TELL HIM TO BE CAREFUL...
HE'D SPILL IT BEFORE I COULD EVEN FINISH TALKING.
HEH HEH HEH
WANNA HEAR A FUNNY STORY?
Nod Nod
WHEN SHU-CHAN WAS IN KINDERGARTEN, WE WENT TO MY HUSBAND'S HOMETOWN OUT IN THE COUNTRY.
YOU KNOW HOW CHILDREN LOVE WALKING ON THE CURB?
WELL, THAT DAY WE WERE WALKING ON A ROAD NEXT TO SOME RICE PADDIES.
Hey...
I told you not to walk up there.
I'm fine!
WELL, IT WAS A PAVED ROAD AND THE CURB RAN RIGHT ALONG THE FIELD. SHU WAS WALKING ON THE CURB WITH AN ICE CREAM IN ONE HAND.
AND JUST AS I SAID, "BE CAREFUL NOT TO FALL IN THE RICE PADDIES!"
I HEARD A BIG SPLASH!
AHA HA HA! I mean, seriously... as soon as I said it!
THAT'S SO NAKATSU.

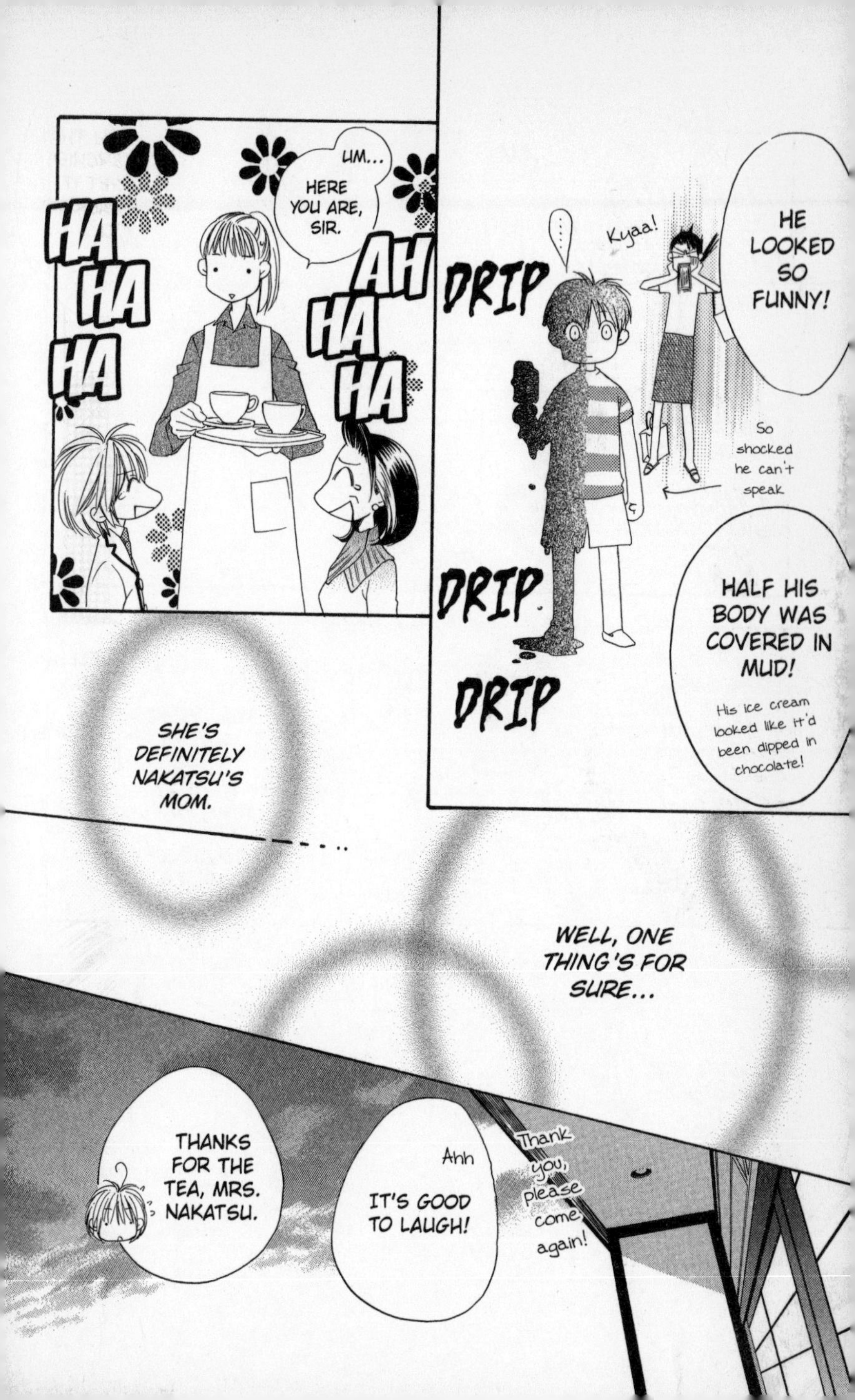
HE LOOKED SO FUNNY!
Kyaa!
So shocked he can't speak
. . . . .
DRIP
HALF HIS BODY WAS COVERED IN MUD!
His ice cream looked like it'd been dipped in chocolate!
DRIP
DRIP
UM...
HERE YOU ARE, SIR.
AH HA HA HA
HA HA HA
SHE'S DEFINITELY NAKATSU'S MOM.
WELL, ONE THING'S FOR SURE...
Thank you, please come again!
Ahh
IT'S GOOD TO LAUGH!
THANKS FOR THE TEA, MRS. NAKATSU.

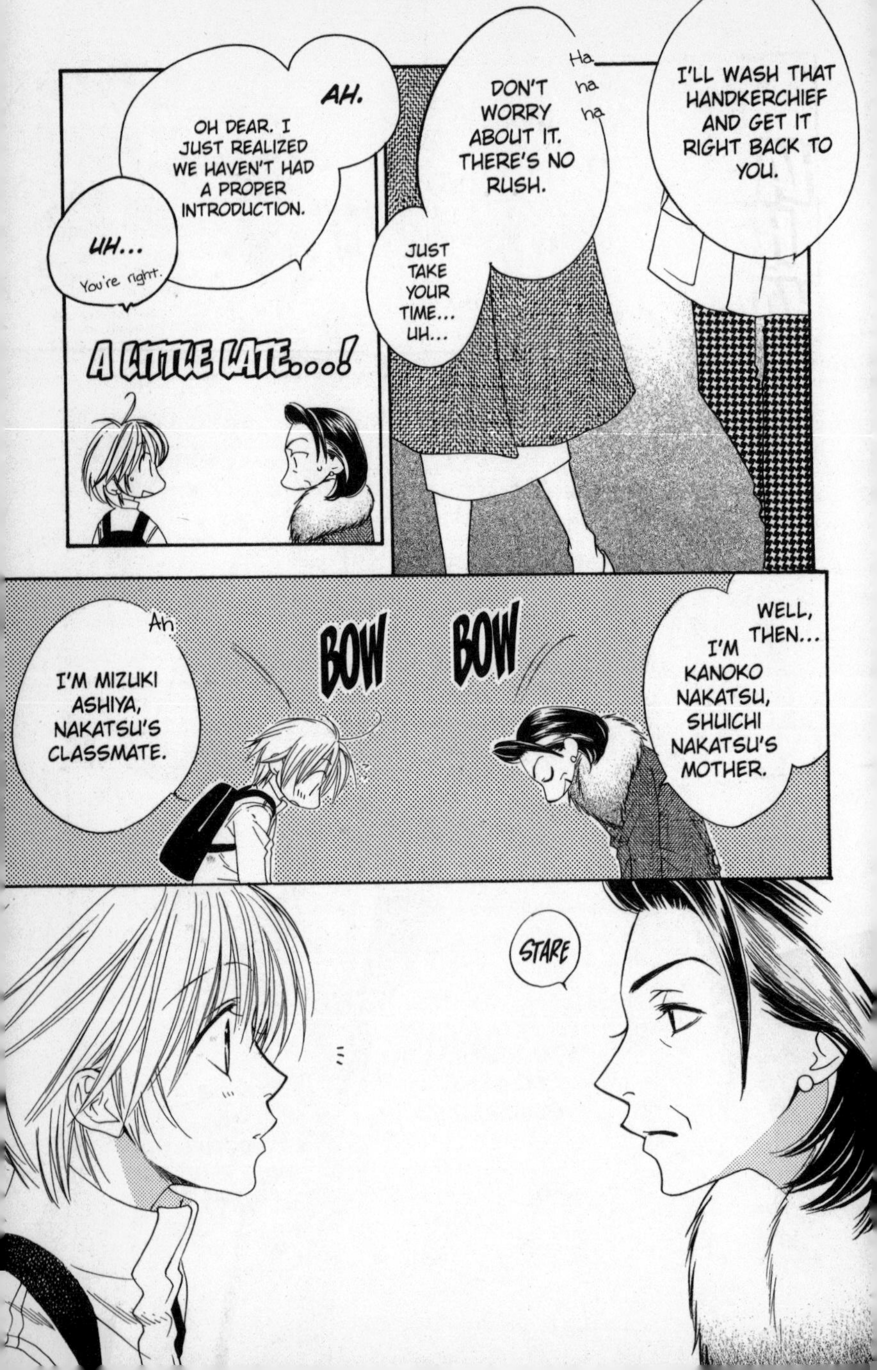
I'LL WASH THAT HANDKERCHIEF AND GET IT RIGHT BACK TO YOU.
DON'T WORRY ABOUT IT. THERE'S NO RUSH.
Ha ha ha
JUST TAKE YOUR TIME... UH...
AH. OH DEAR. I JUST REALIZED WE HAVEN'T HAD A PROPER INTRODUCTION.
UH... You're right.
A LITTLE LATE...!
WELL, THEN... I'M KANOKO NAKATSU, SHUICHI NAKATSU'S MOTHER.
BOW BOW
Ah I'M MIZUKI ASHIYA, NAKATSU'S CLASSMATE.
STARE

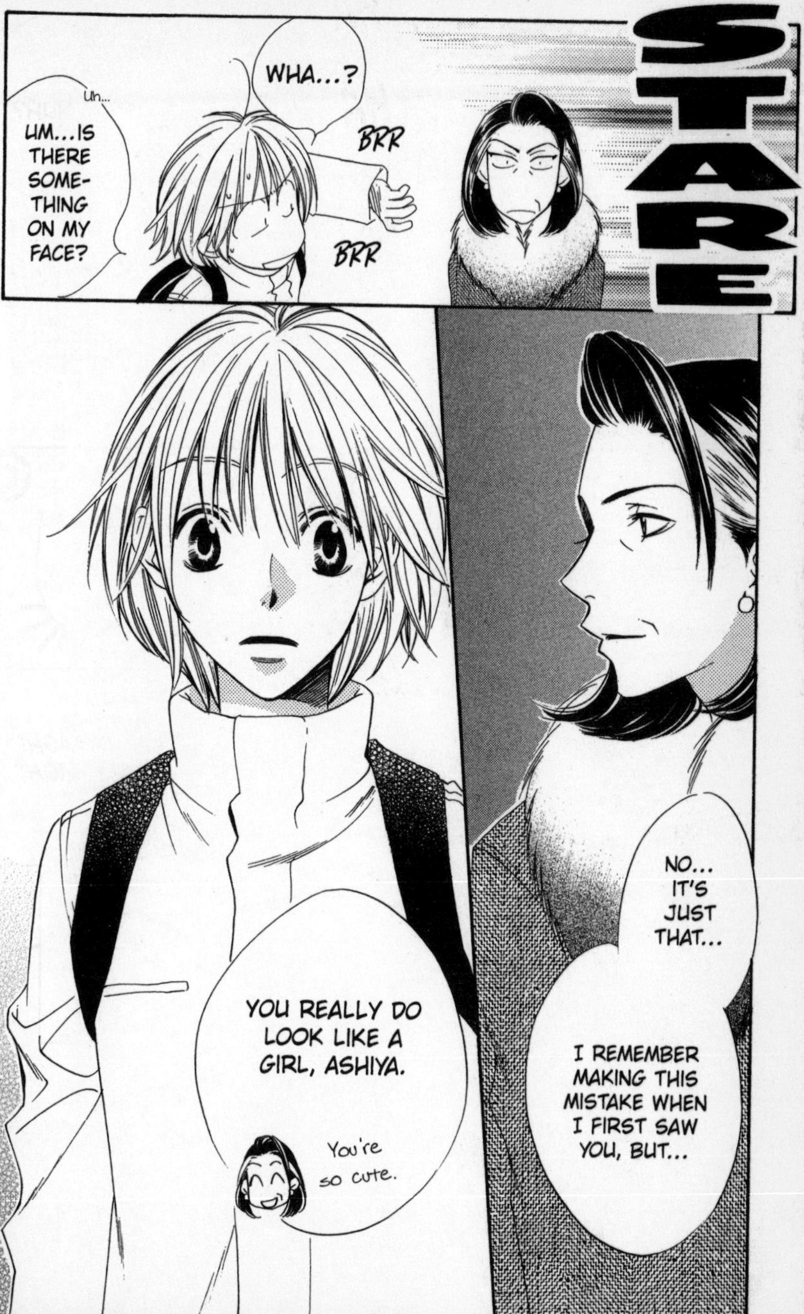
STARE
WHA...?
BRR
BRR
Uh...
UM...IS THERE SOME-THING ON MY FACE?
NO... IT'S JUST THAT...
I REMEMBER MAKING THIS MISTAKE WHEN I FIRST SAW YOU, BUT...
YOU REALLY DO LOOK LIKE A GIRL, ASHIYA.
You're so cute.

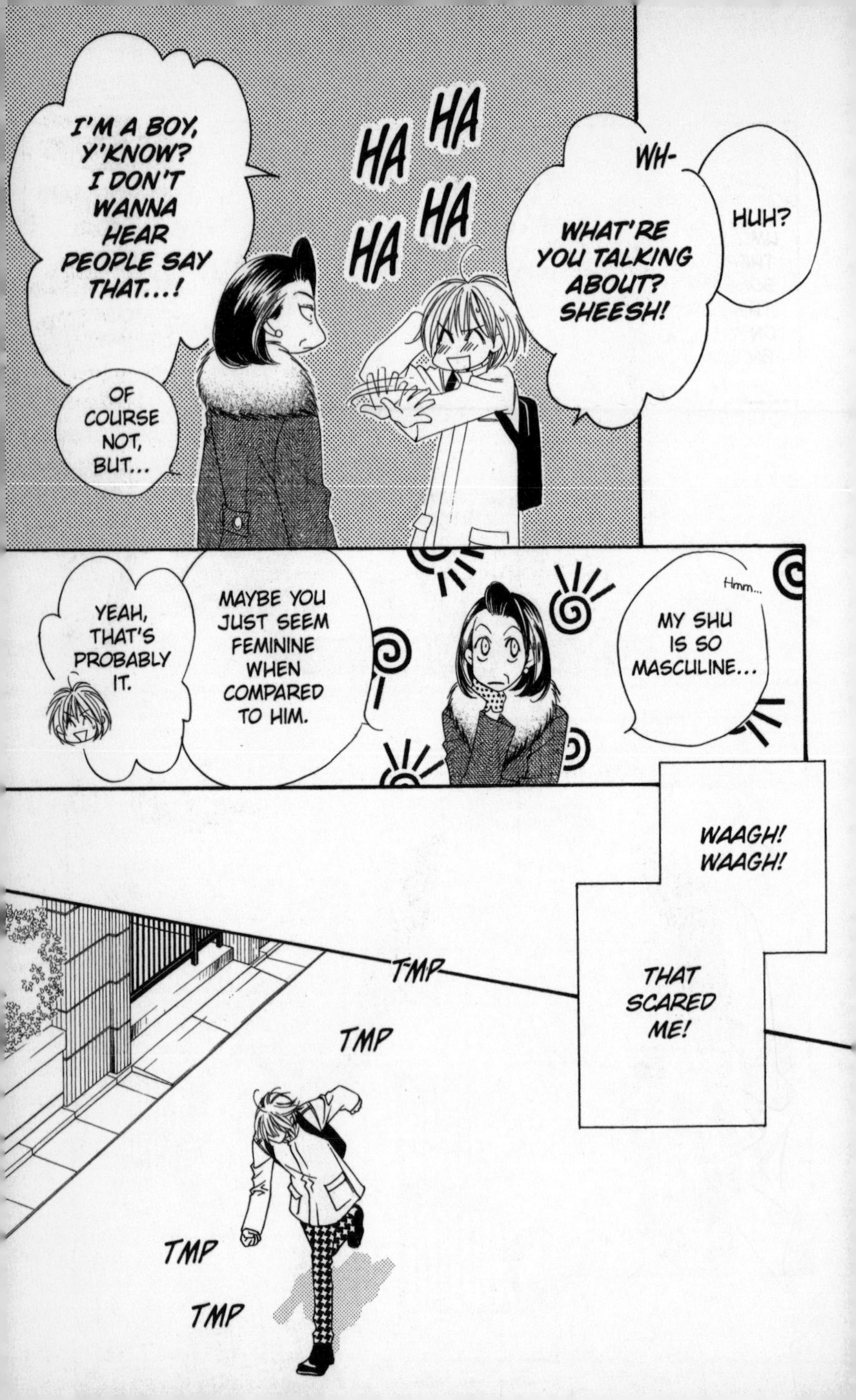
HUH?
WH-
WHAT'RE YOU TALKING ABOUT? SHEESH!
HA HA HA HA
I'M A BOY, Y'KNOW? I DON'T WANNA HEAR PEOPLE SAY THAT...!
OF COURSE NOT, BUT...
Hmm...
MY SHU IS SO MASCULINE...
MAYBE YOU JUST SEEM FEMININE WHEN COMPARED TO HIM.
YEAH, THAT'S PROBABLY IT.
WAAGH! WAAGH!
THAT SCARED ME!
TMP
TMP
TMP
TMP

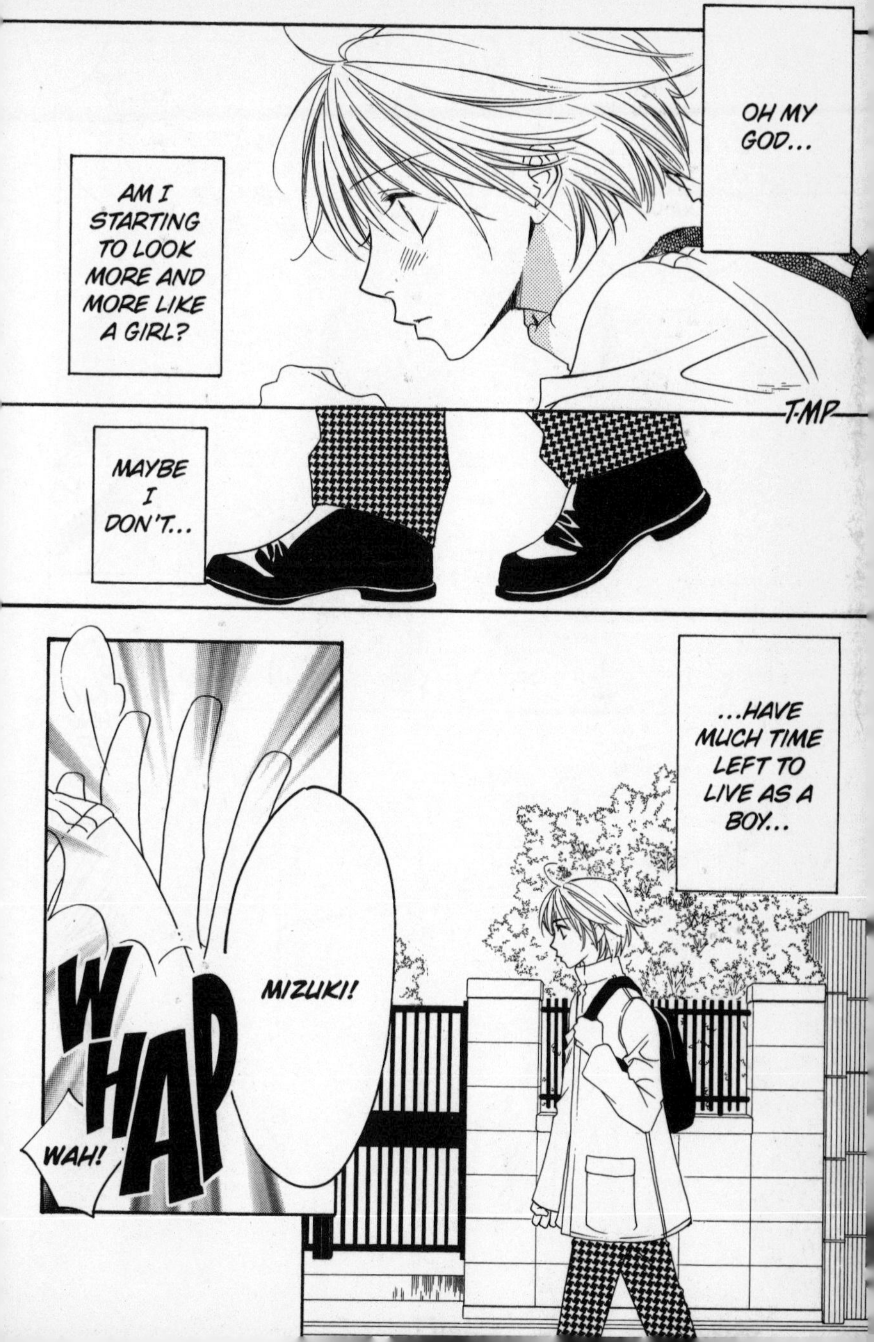
OH MY GOD...
AM I STARTING TO LOOK MORE AND MORE LIKE A GIRL?
T-MP
MAYBE I DON'T...
...HAVE MUCH TIME LEFT TO LIVE AS A BOY...
MIZUKI!
WHAP
WAH!

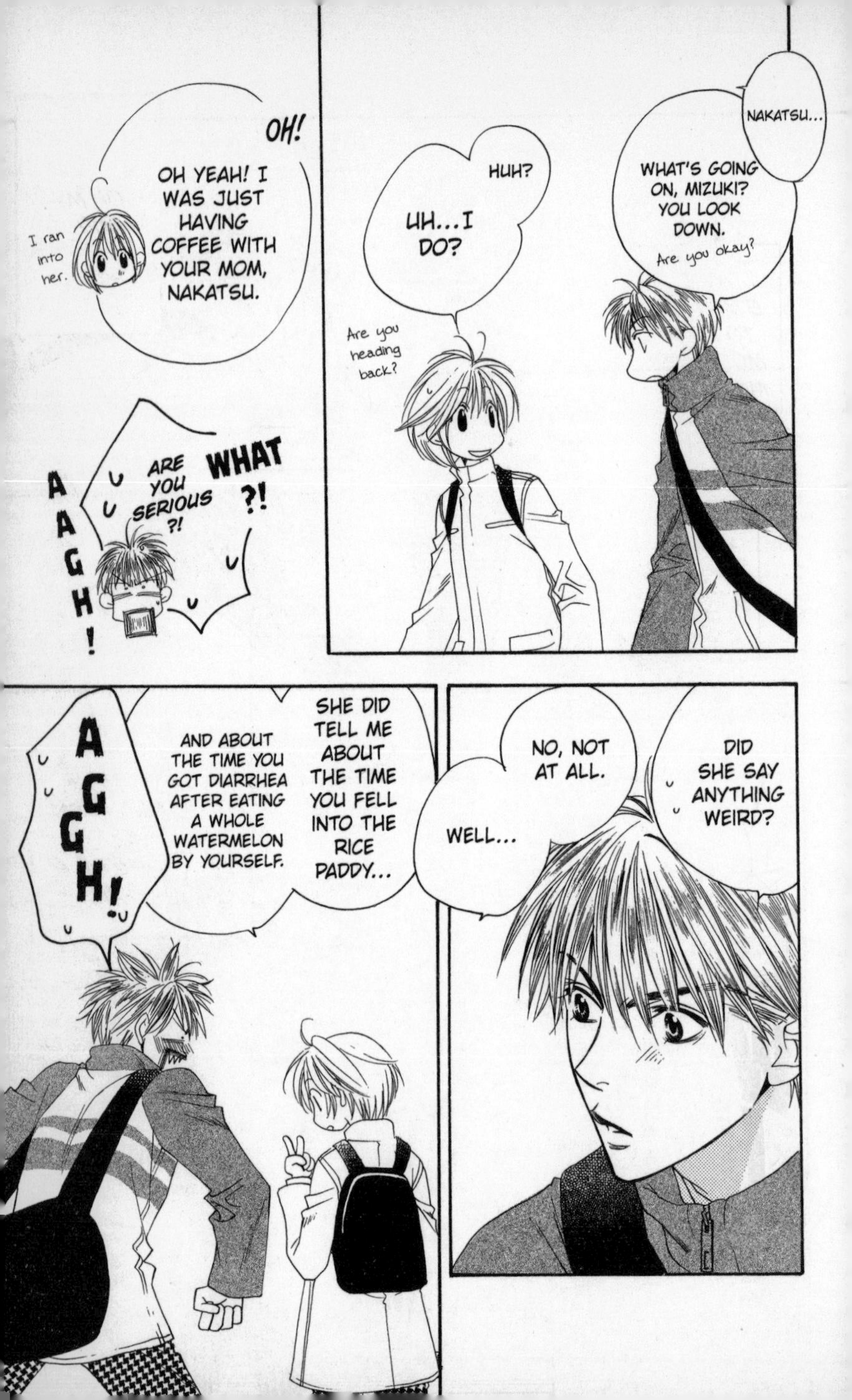
NAKATSU...
WHAT'S GOING ON, MIZUKI? YOU LOOK DOWN.
Are you okay?
HUH?
UH...I DO?
Are you heading back?
OH!
OH YEAH! I WAS JUST HAVING COFFEE WITH YOUR MOM, NAKATSU.
I ran into her.
WHAT ?!
ARE YOU SERIOUS ?!
AAGH!
DID SHE SAY ANYTHING WEIRD?
NO, NOT AT ALL.
WELL...
SHE DID TELL ME ABOUT THE TIME YOU FELL INTO THE RICE PADDY...
AND ABOUT THE TIME YOU GOT DIARRHEA AFTER EATING A WHOLE WATERMELON BY YOURSELF.
AGGH!

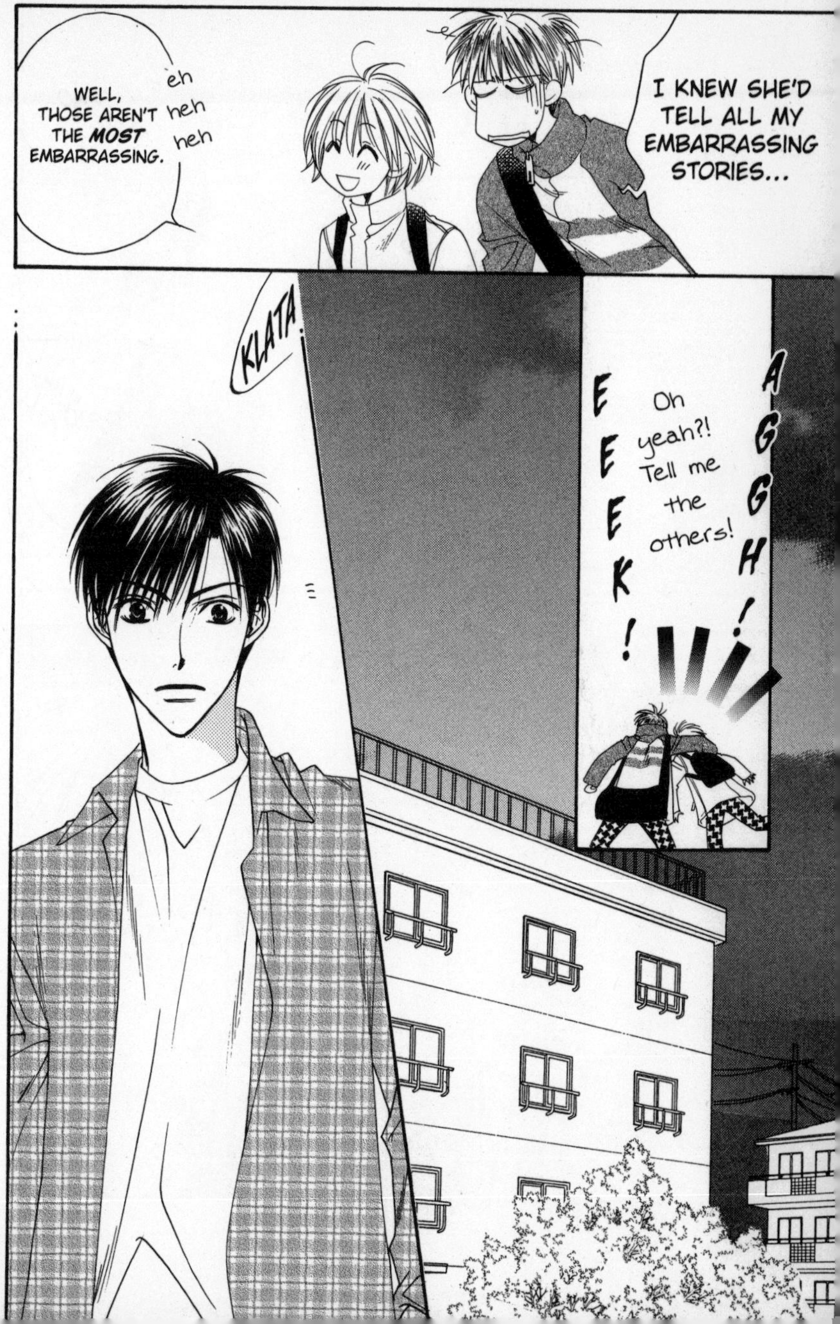
I KNEW SHE'D TELL ALL MY EMBARRASSING STORIES...
WELL, THOSE AREN'T THE **MOST** EMBARRASSING.
eh heh heh
AGGH!
Oh yeah?! Tell me the others!
EEEK!
KLATA

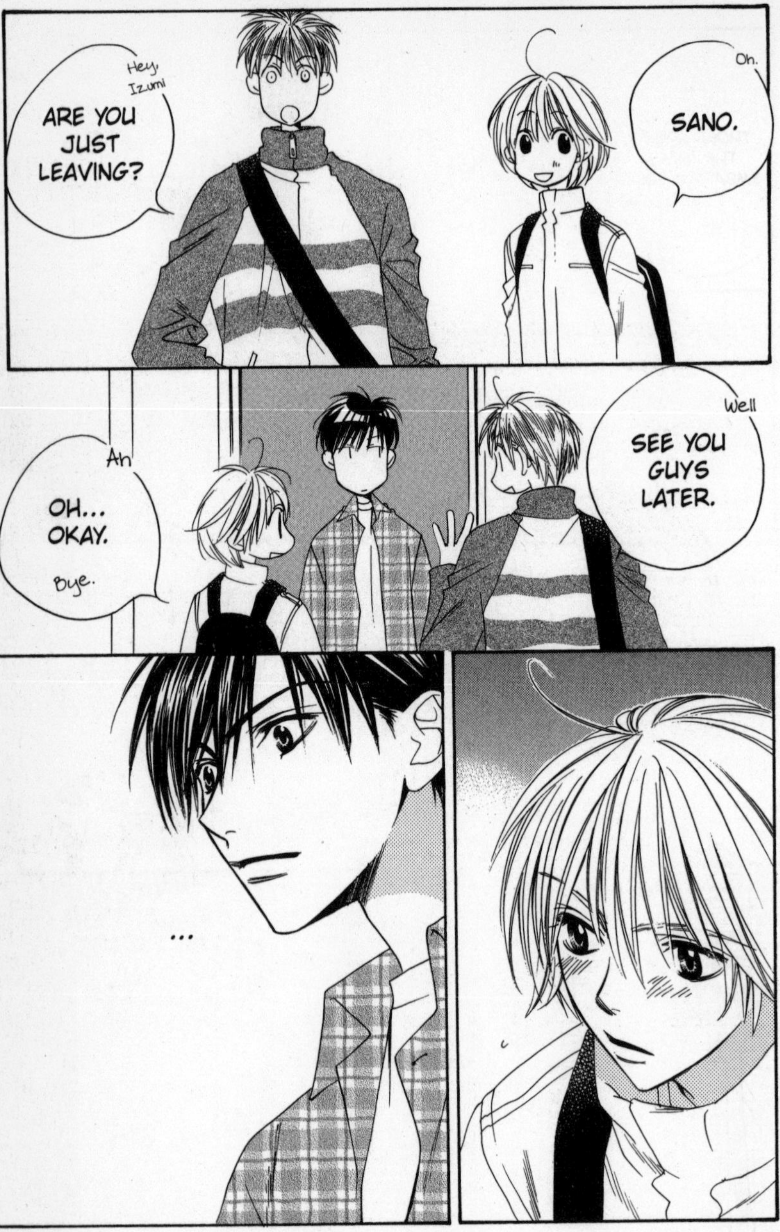
Oh.
SANO.
Hey, Izumi
ARE YOU JUST LEAVING?
Well
SEE YOU GUYS LATER.
Ah
OH... OKAY.
Bye.
...

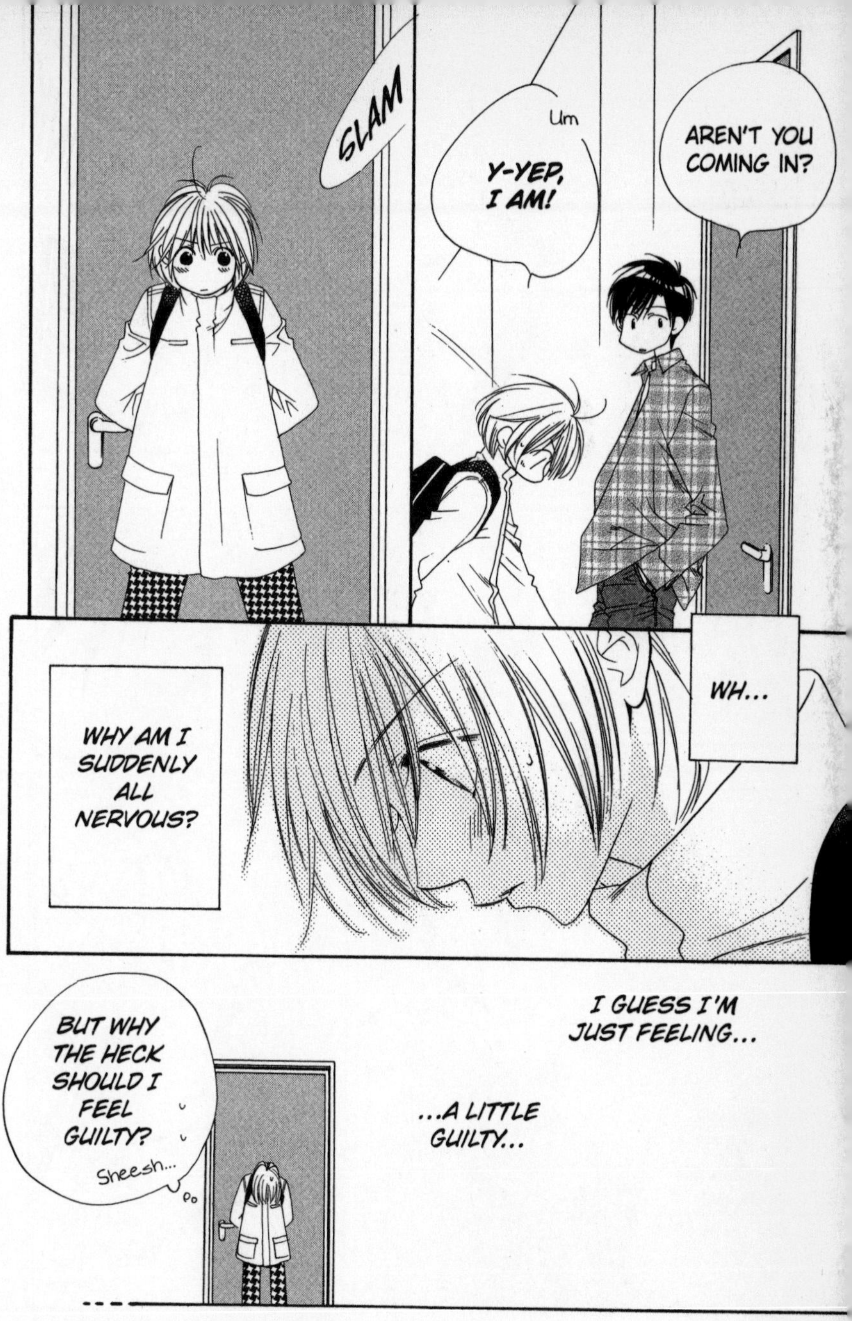
AREN'T YOU COMING IN?
Um
Y-YEP, I AM!
SLAM
WH...
WHY AM I SUDDENLY ALL NERVOUS?
I GUESS I'M JUST FEELING...
...A LITTLE GUILTY...
BUT WHY THE HECK SHOULD I FEEL GUILTY?
Sheesh...

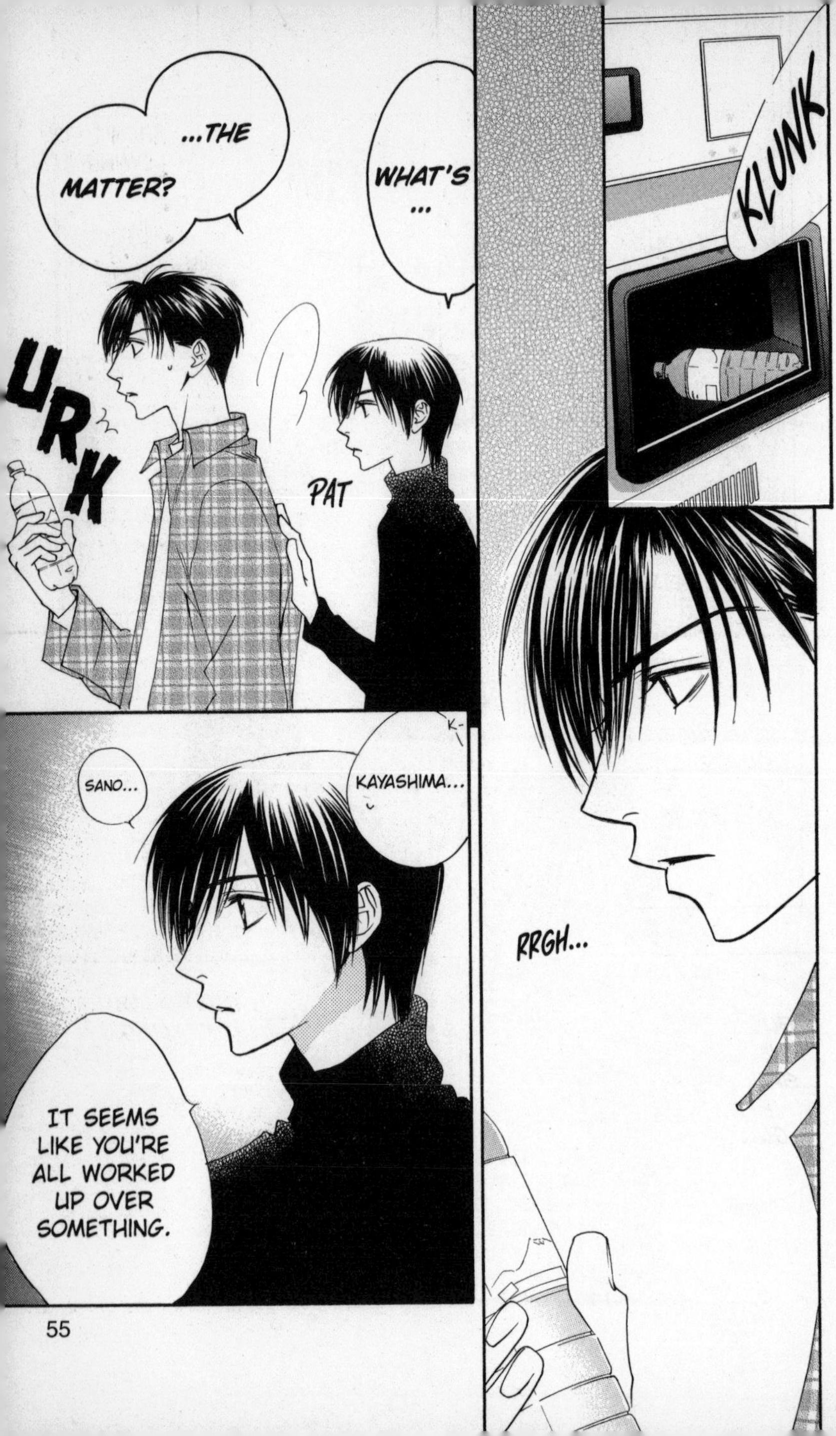
KLUNK
RRGH...
WHAT'S ...
...THE MATTER?
URK
PAT
K-
KAYASHIMA...
SANO...
IT SEEMS LIKE YOU'RE ALL WORKED UP OVER SOMETHING.

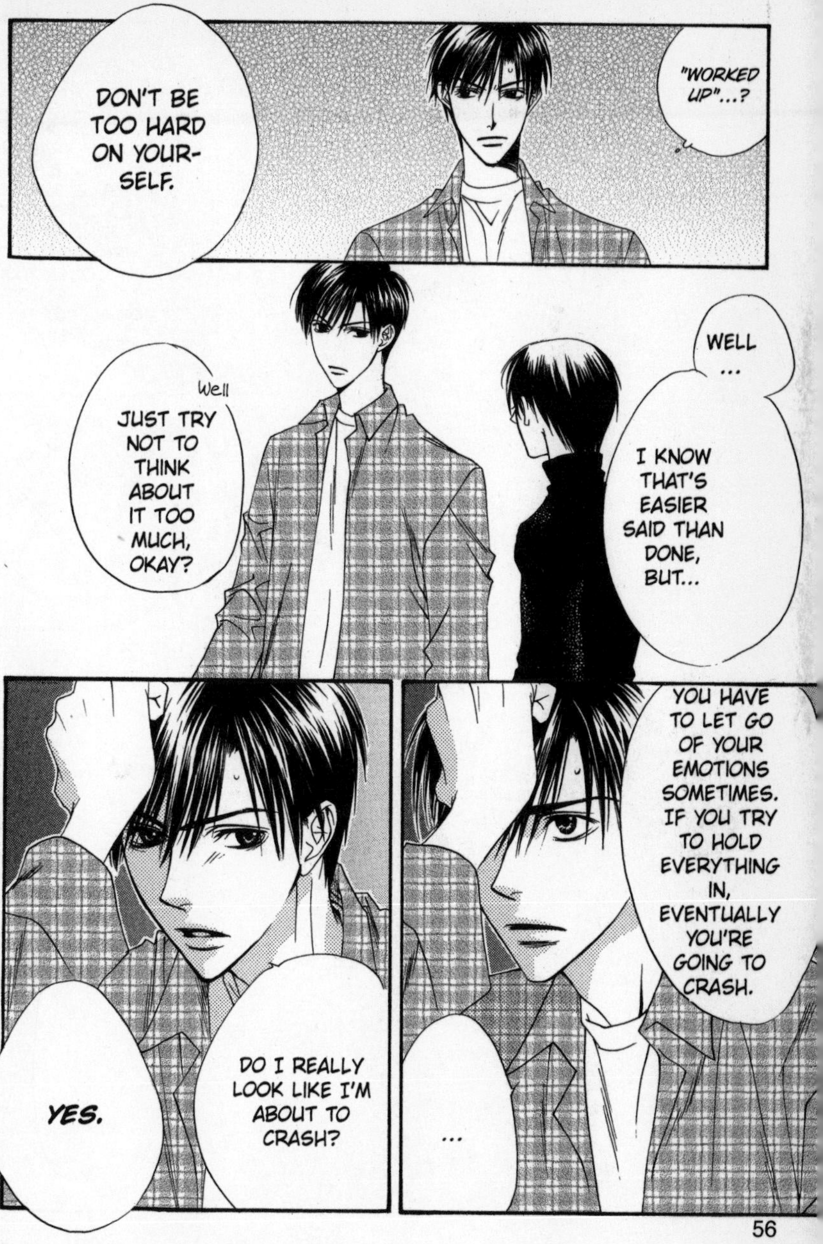
"WORKED UP"...?
DON'T BE TOO HARD ON YOUR-SELF.
WELL...
I KNOW THAT'S EASIER SAID THAN DONE, BUT...
Well
JUST TRY NOT TO THINK ABOUT IT TOO MUCH, OKAY?
YOU HAVE TO LET GO OF YOUR EMOTIONS SOMETIMES. IF YOU TRY TO HOLD EVERYTHING IN, EVENTUALLY YOU'RE GOING TO CRASH.
...
DO I REALLY LOOK LIKE I'M ABOUT TO CRASH?
YES.

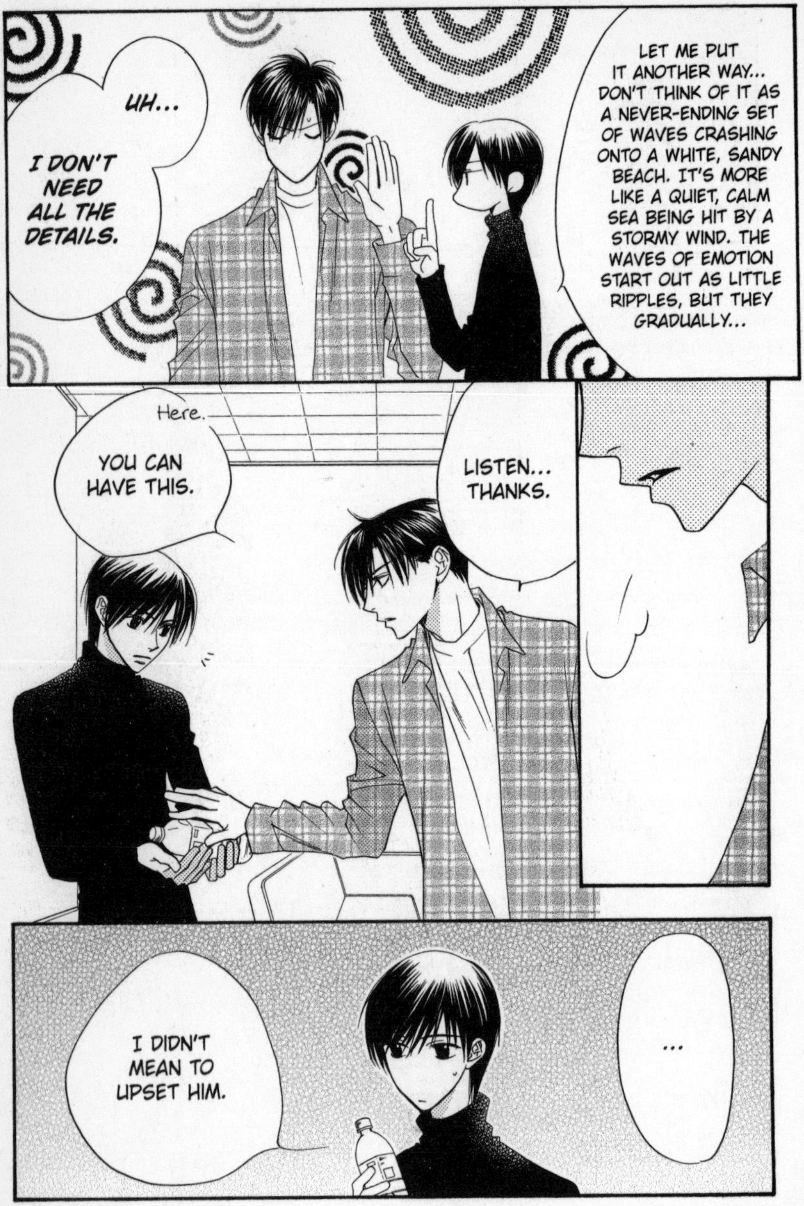
LET ME PUT IT ANOTHER WAY... DON'T THINK OF IT AS A NEVER-ENDING SET OF WAVES CRASHING ONTO A WHITE, SANDY BEACH. IT'S MORE LIKE A QUIET, CALM SEA BEING HIT BY A STORMY WIND. THE WAVES OF EMOTION START OUT AS LITTLE RIPPLES, BUT THEY GRADUALLY...
UH...
I DON'T NEED ALL THE DETAILS.
LISTEN... THANKS.
Here.
YOU CAN HAVE THIS.
...
I DIDN'T MEAN TO UPSET HIM.

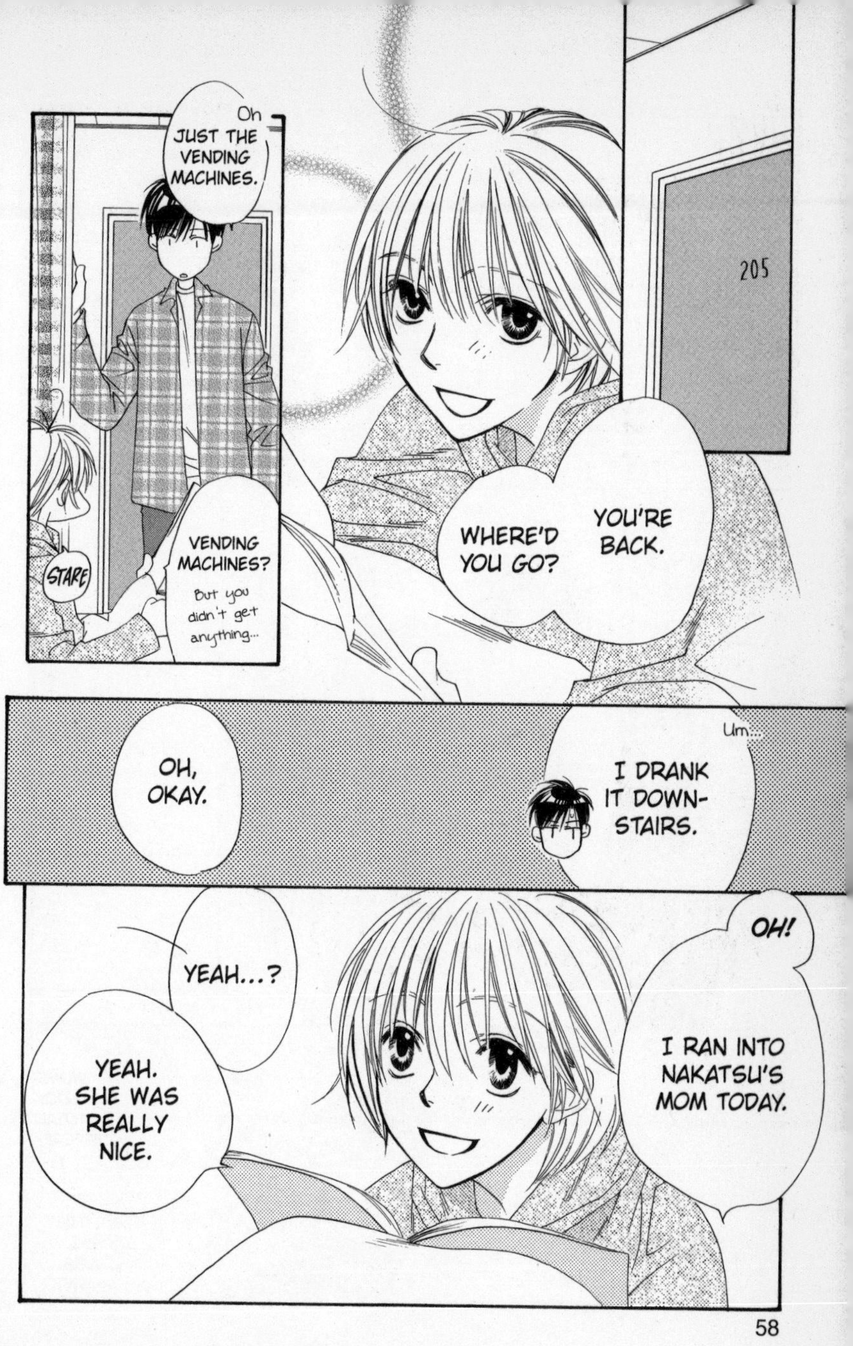
205
YOU'RE BACK.
WHERE'D YOU GO?
Oh
JUST THE VENDING MACHINES.
VENDING MACHINES?
But you didn't get anything...
STARE
Um...
I DRANK IT DOWN-STAIRS.
OH, OKAY.
OH!
I RAN INTO NAKATSU'S MOM TODAY.
YEAH...?
YEAH. SHE WAS REALLY NICE.

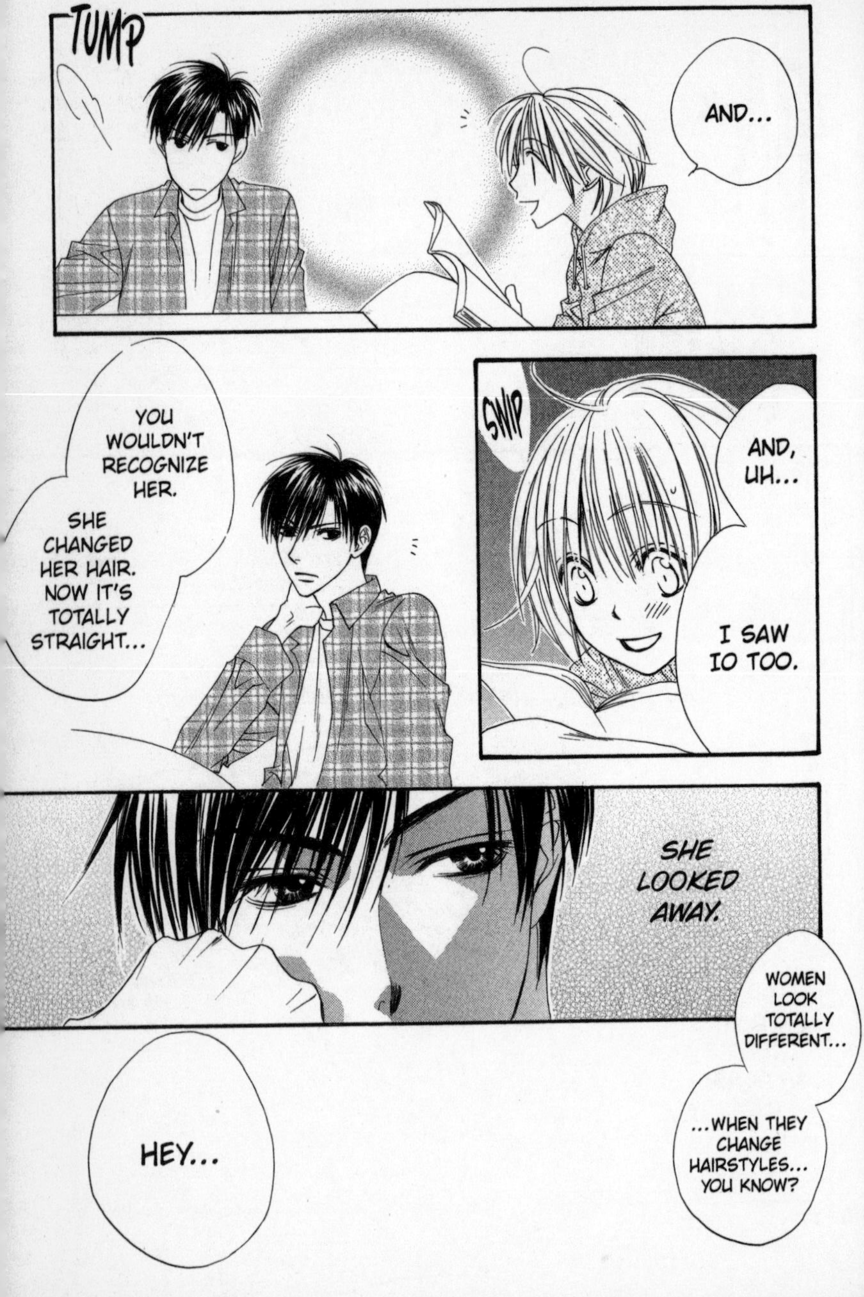
TUMP
AND...
SWIP
AND, UH...
I SAW IO TOO.
YOU WOULDN'T RECOGNIZE HER.
SHE CHANGED HER HAIR. NOW IT'S TOTALLY STRAIGHT...
SHE LOOKED AWAY.
WOMEN LOOK TOTALLY DIFFERENT...
...WHEN THEY CHANGE HAIRSTYLES... YOU KNOW?
HEY...

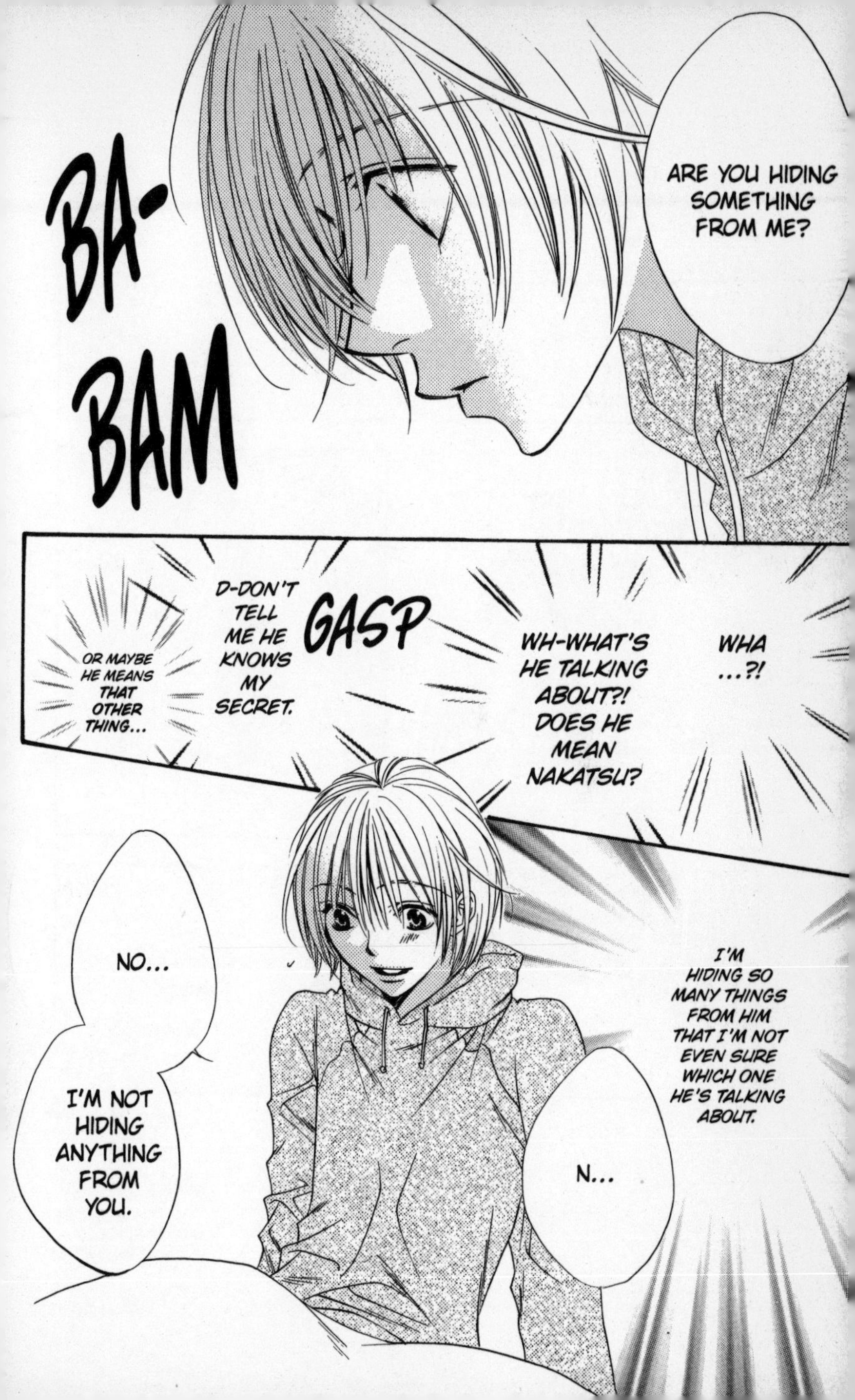
ARE YOU HIDING SOMETHING FROM ME?
BA-BAM
WHA ...?!
WH-WHAT'S HE TALKING ABOUT?! DOES HE MEAN NAKATSU?
GASP
D-DON'T TELL ME HE KNOWS MY SECRET.
OR MAYBE HE MEANS THAT OTHER THING...
I'M HIDING SO MANY THINGS FROM HIM THAT I'M NOT EVEN SURE WHICH ONE HE'S TALKING ABOUT.
N...
NO...
I'M NOT HIDING ANYTHING FROM YOU.

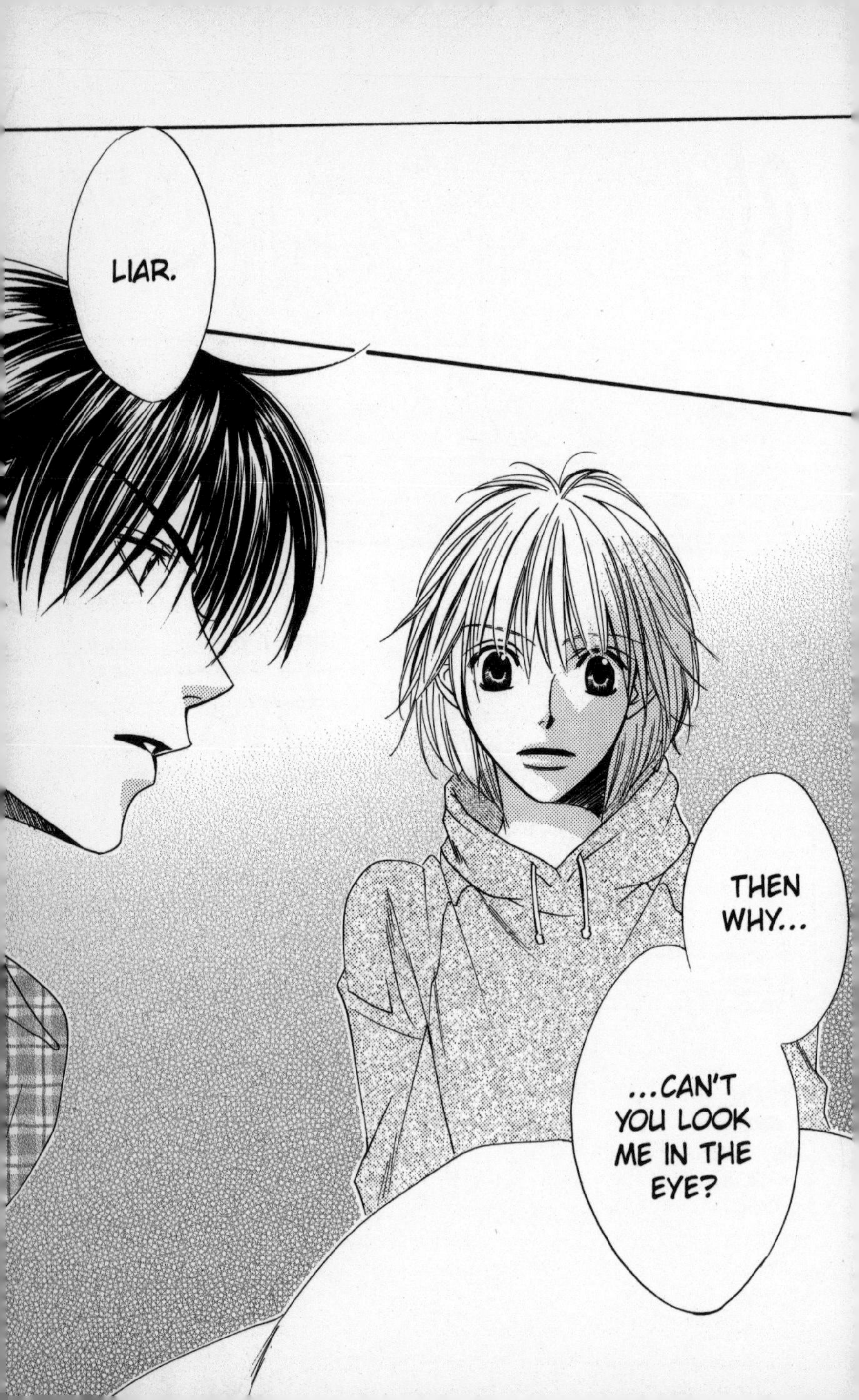
LIAR.
THEN WHY...
...CAN'T YOU LOOK ME IN THE EYE?

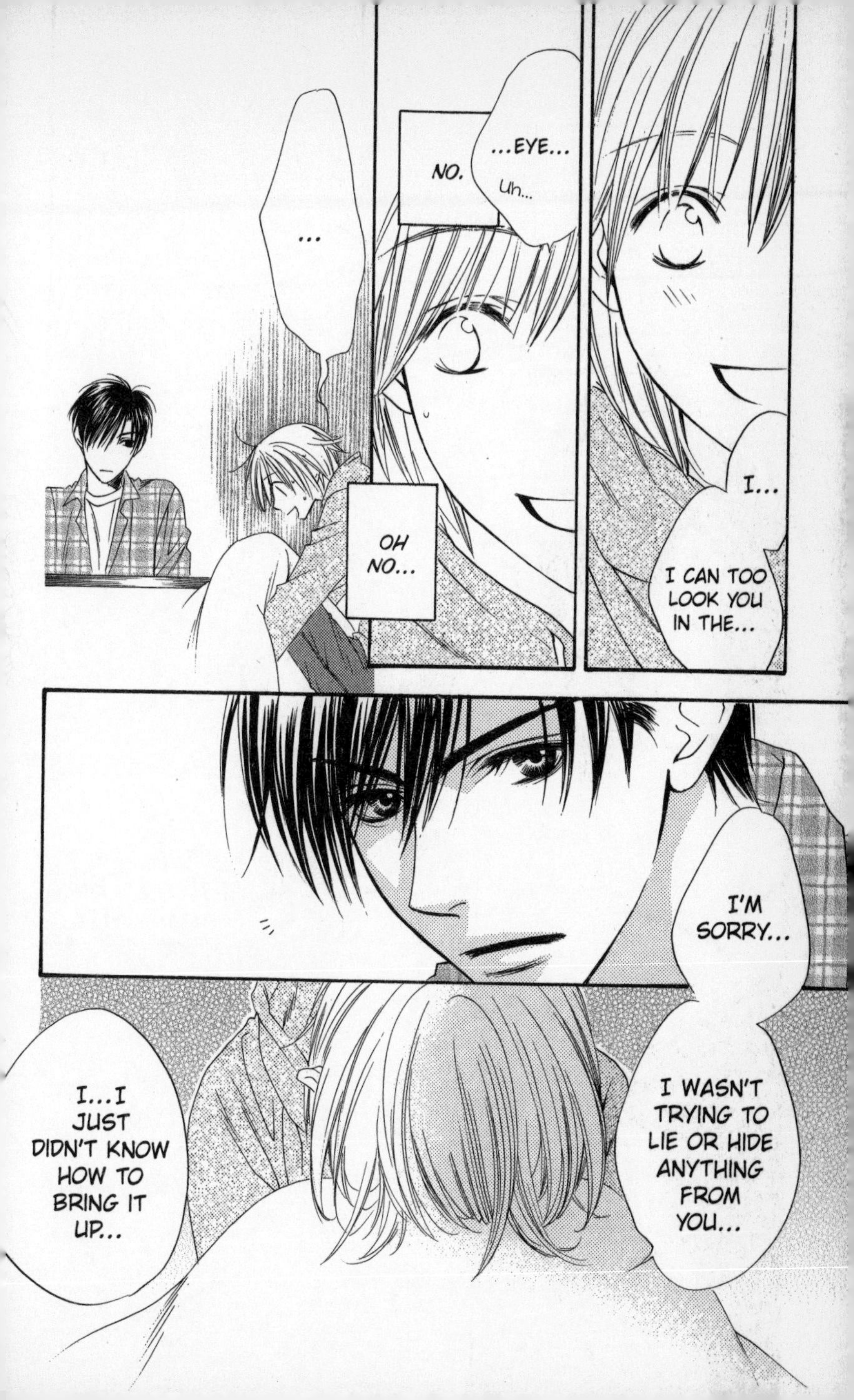
I...
I CAN TOO LOOK YOU IN THE...
...EYE...
Uh...
NO.
OH NO...
...
I'M SORRY...
I WASN'T TRYING TO LIE OR HIDE ANYTHING FROM YOU...
I...I JUST DIDN'T KNOW HOW TO BRING IT UP...

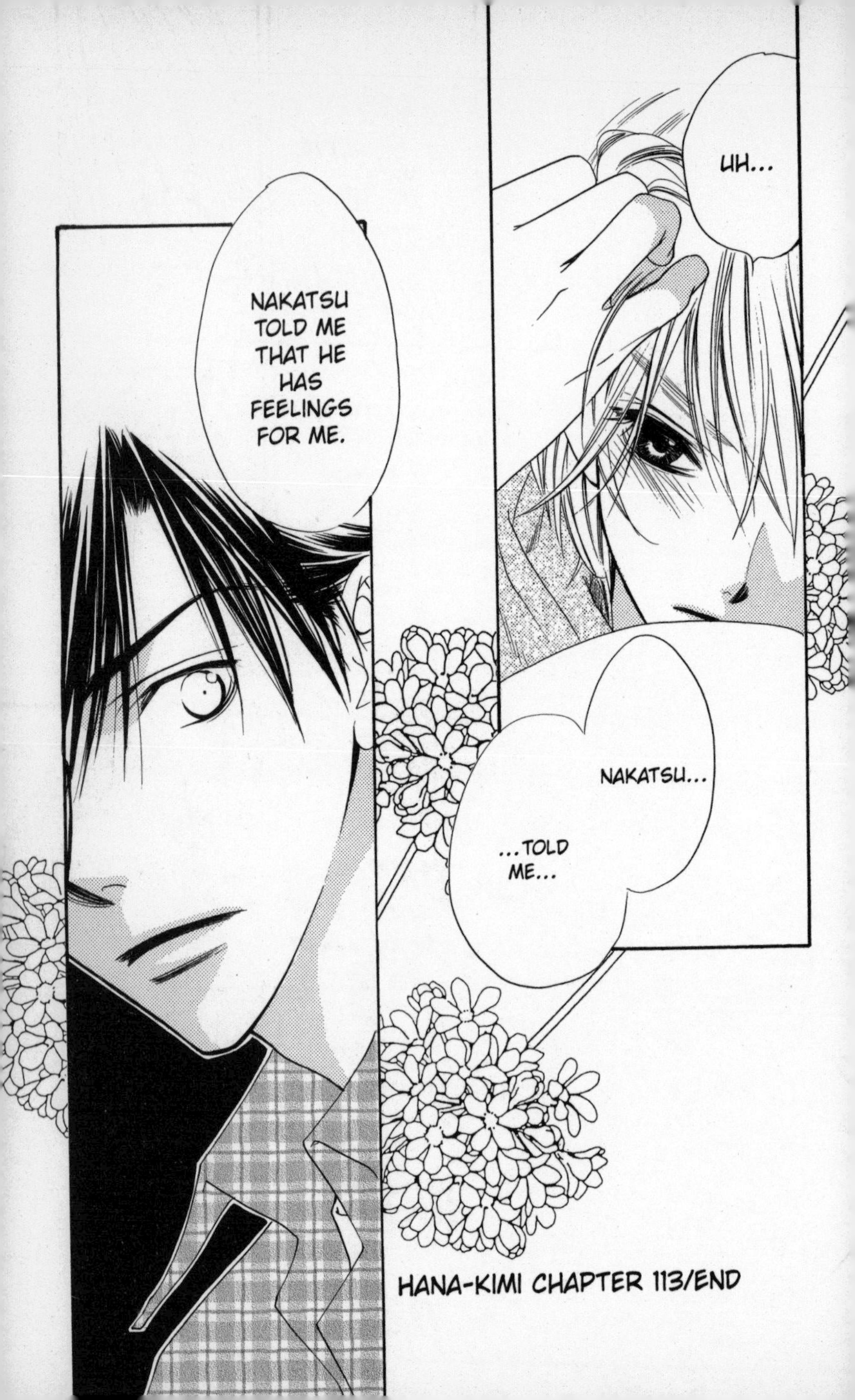
UH...
NAKATSU...
...TOLD ME...
NAKATSU TOLD ME THAT HE HAS FEELINGS FOR ME.

HANA-KIMI CHAPTER 113/END

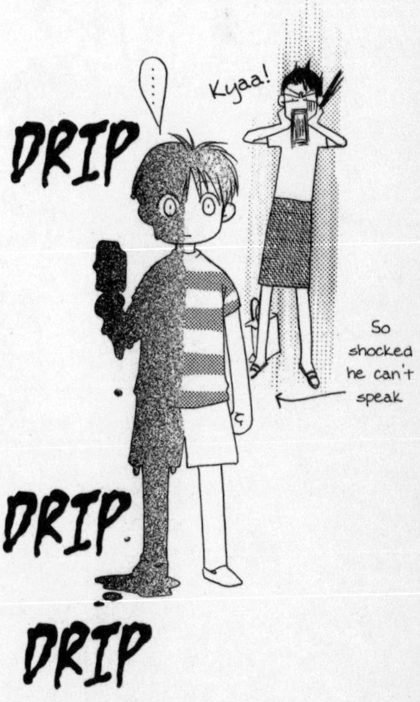

Kyaa!
DRIP
...!
So shocked he can't speak
DRIP
DRIP

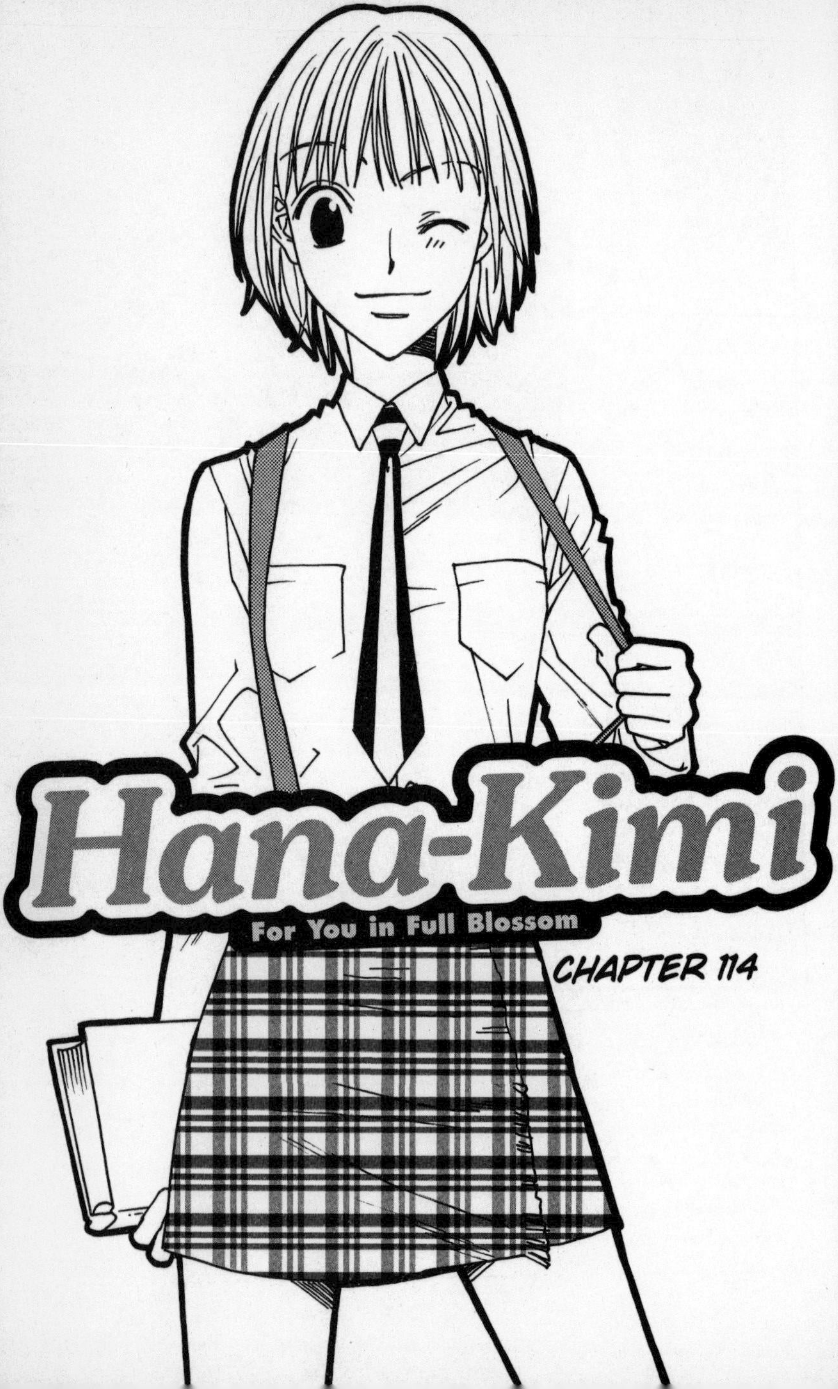
Hana-Kimi
For You in Full Blossom
CHAPTER 114

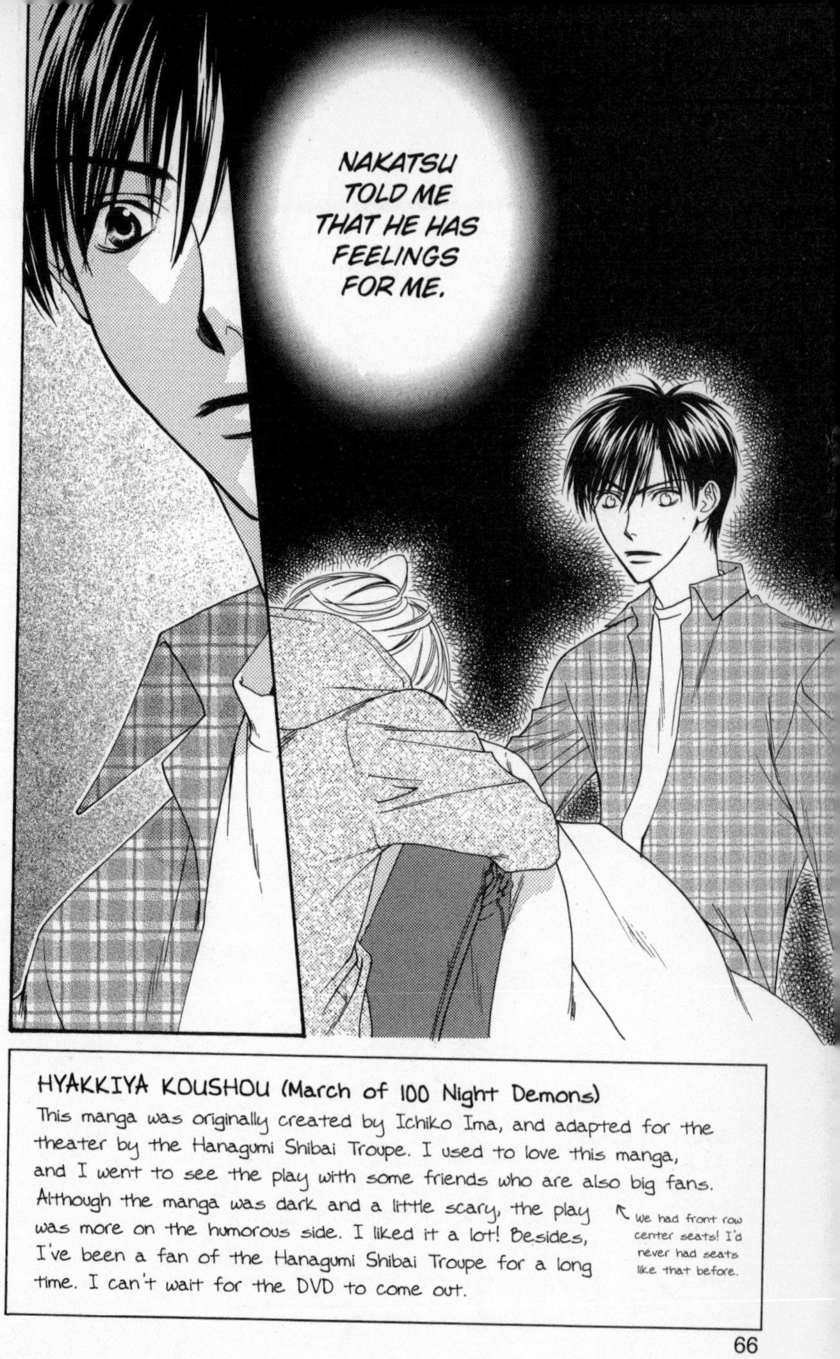
NAKATSU TOLD ME THAT HE HAS FEELINGS FOR ME.

HYAKKIYA KOUSHOU (March of 100 Night Demons)

This manga was originally created by Ichiko Ima, and adapted for the theater by the Hanagumi Shibai Troupe. I used to love this manga, and I went to see the play with some friends who are also big fans. Although the manga was dark and a little scary, the play was more on the humorous side. I liked it a lot! Besides, I've been a fan of the Hanagumi Shibai Troupe for a long time. I can't wait for the DVD to come out.

↖ We had front row center seats! I'd never had seats like that before.

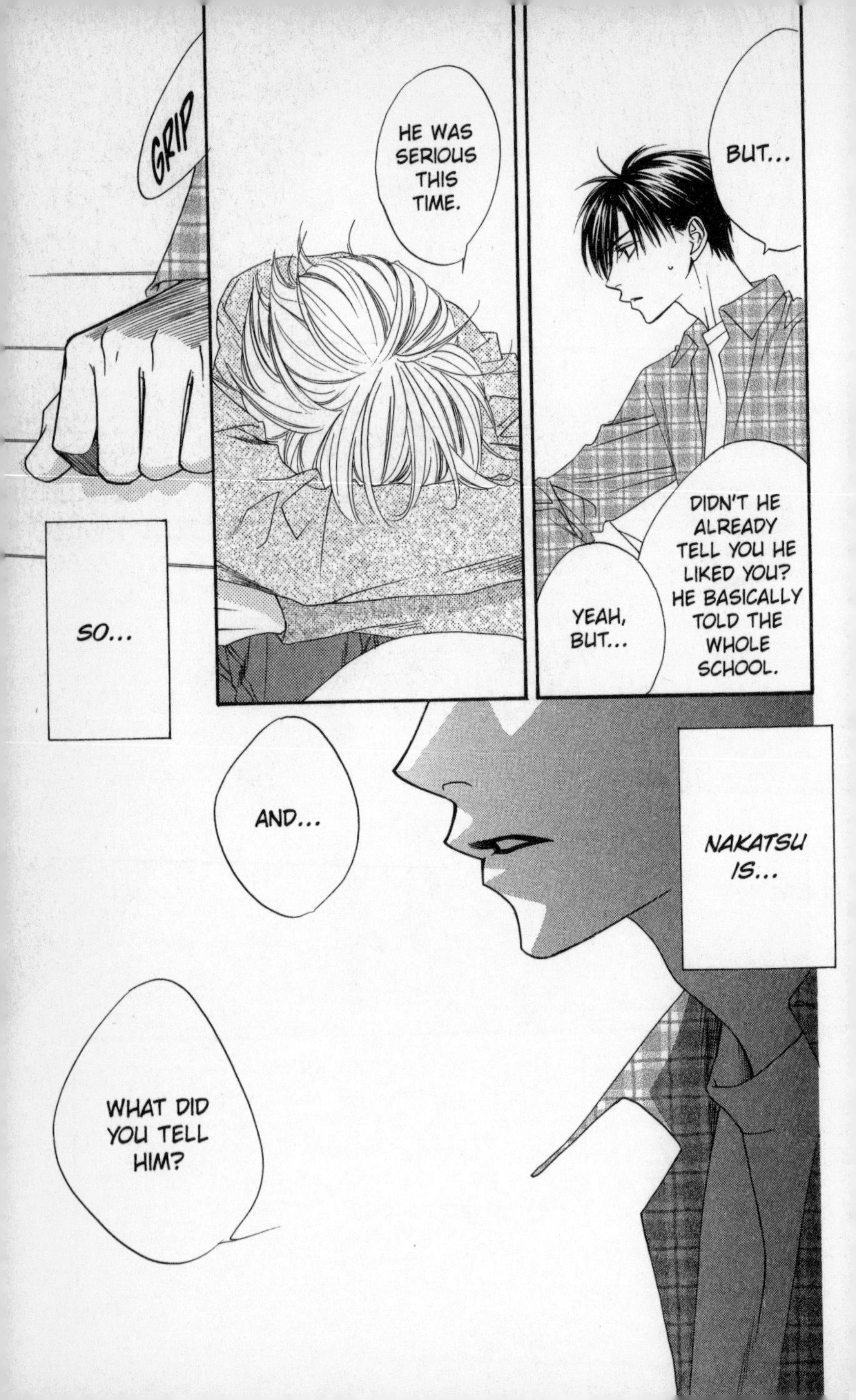
BUT...
DIDN'T HE ALREADY TELL YOU HE LIKED YOU? HE BASICALLY TOLD THE WHOLE SCHOOL.
YEAH, BUT...
HE WAS SERIOUS THIS TIME.
GRIP
SO...
NAKATSU IS...
AND...
WHAT DID YOU TELL HIM?

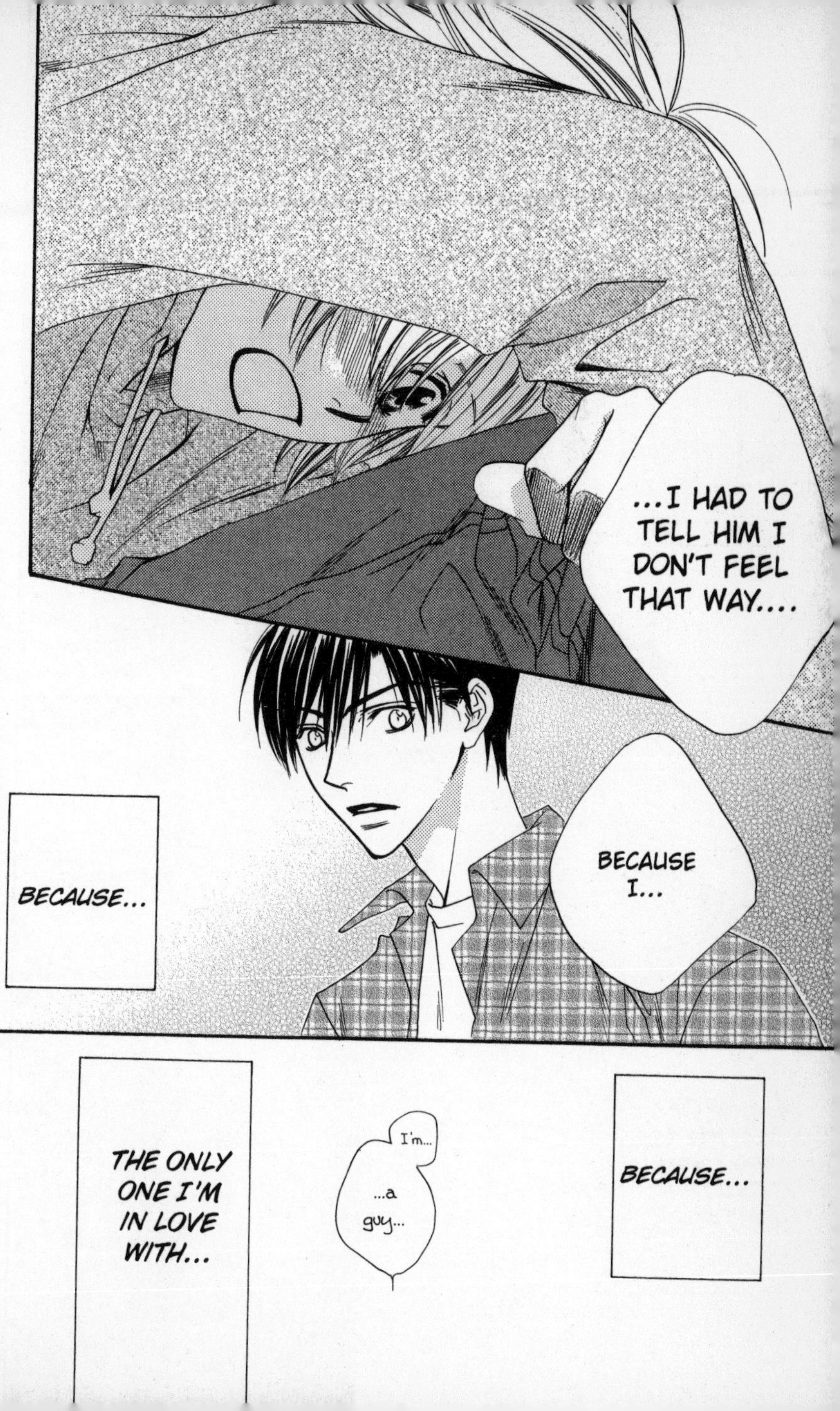
...I HAD TO TELL HIM I DON'T FEEL THAT WAY....
BECAUSE I...
BECAUSE...
BECAUSE...
I'm... ...a guy...
THE ONLY ONE I'M IN LOVE WITH...

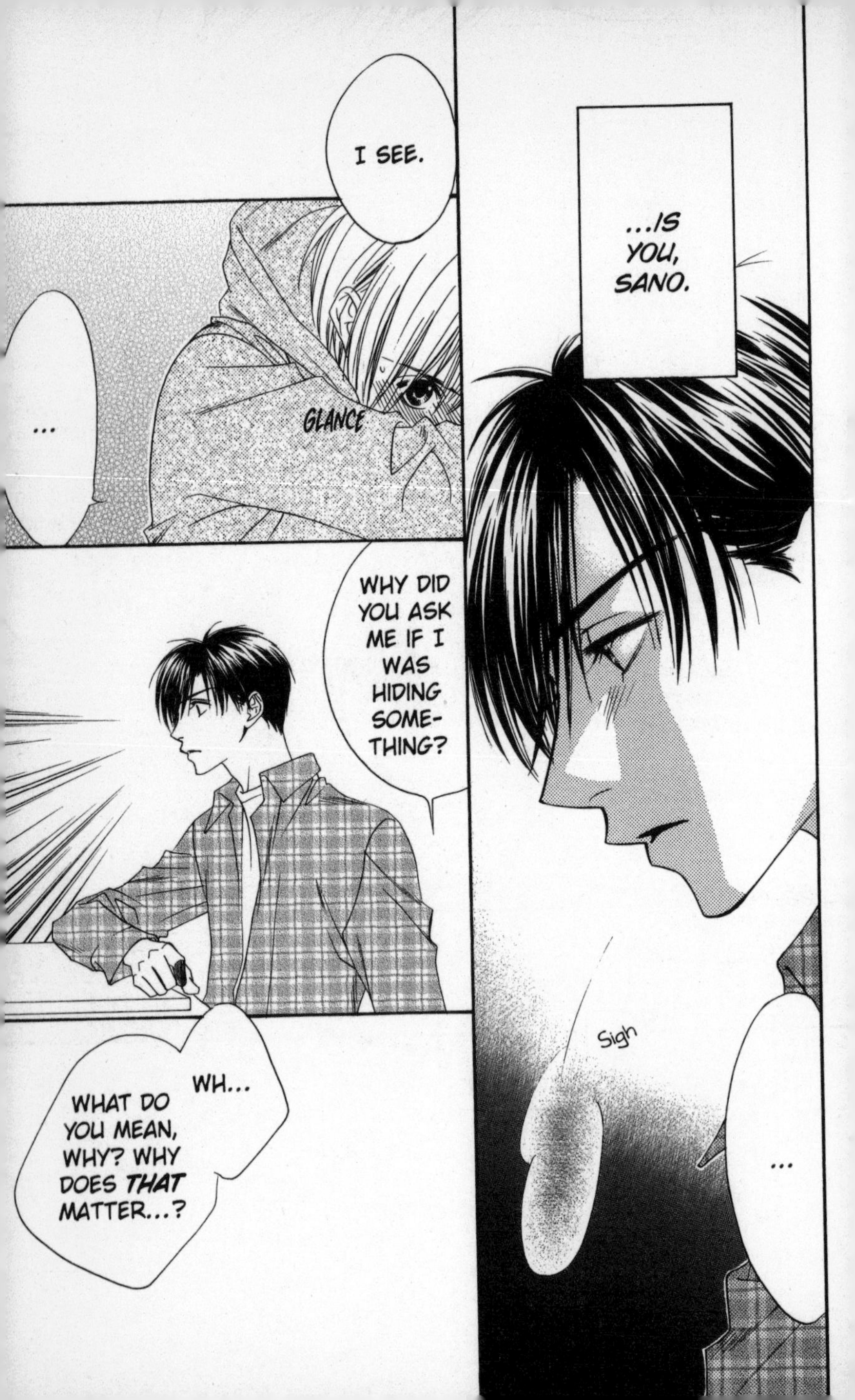
...IS YOU, SANO.
Sigh
...
I SEE.
...
GLANCE
WHY DID YOU ASK ME IF I WAS HIDING SOME-THING?
WH...
WHAT DO YOU MEAN, WHY? WHY DOES *THAT* MATTER...?

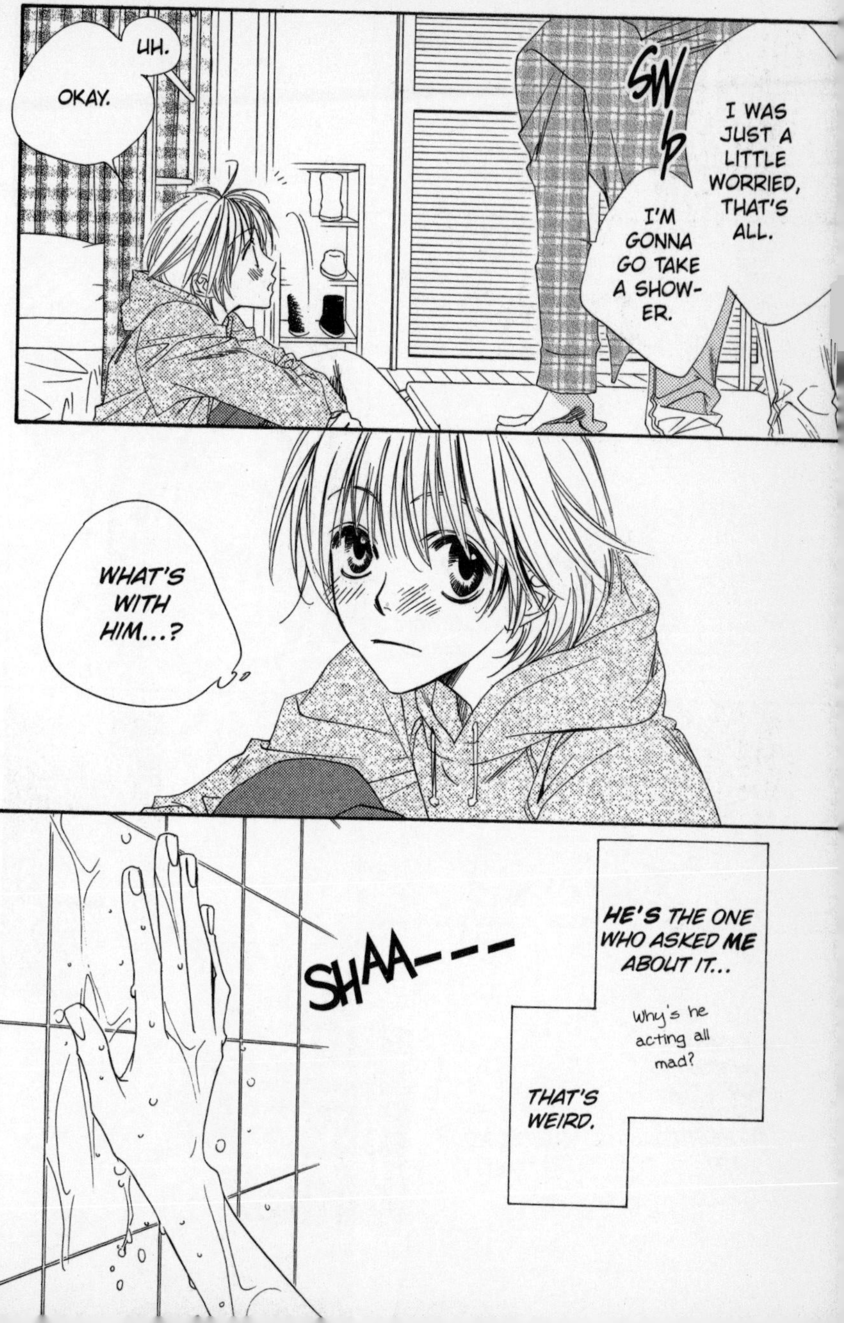
I WAS JUST A LITTLE WORRIED, THAT'S ALL.
SWP
I'M GONNA GO TAKE A SHOW-ER.
UH.
OKAY.
WHAT'S WITH HIM...?
HE'S THE ONE WHO ASKED ME ABOUT IT...
Why's he acting all mad?
THAT'S WEIRD.
SHAA---

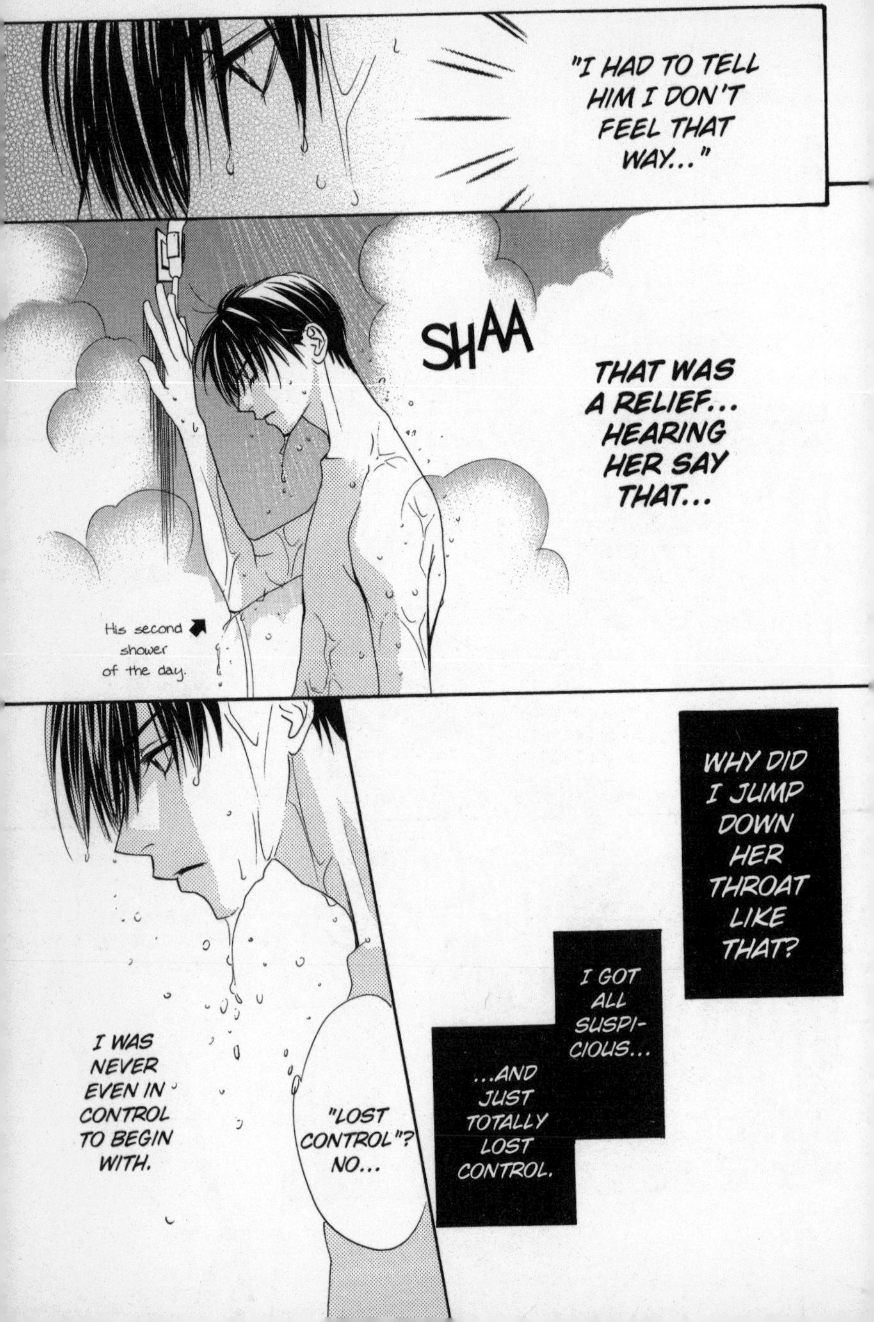
"I HAD TO TELL HIM I DON'T FEEL THAT WAY..."
SHAA
THAT WAS A RELIEF... HEARING HER SAY THAT...
His second shower of the day.
WHY DID I JUMP DOWN HER THROAT LIKE THAT?
I GOT ALL SUSPICIOUS...
...AND JUST TOTALLY LOST CONTROL.
"LOST CONTROL"? NO...
I WAS NEVER EVEN IN CONTROL TO BEGIN WITH.

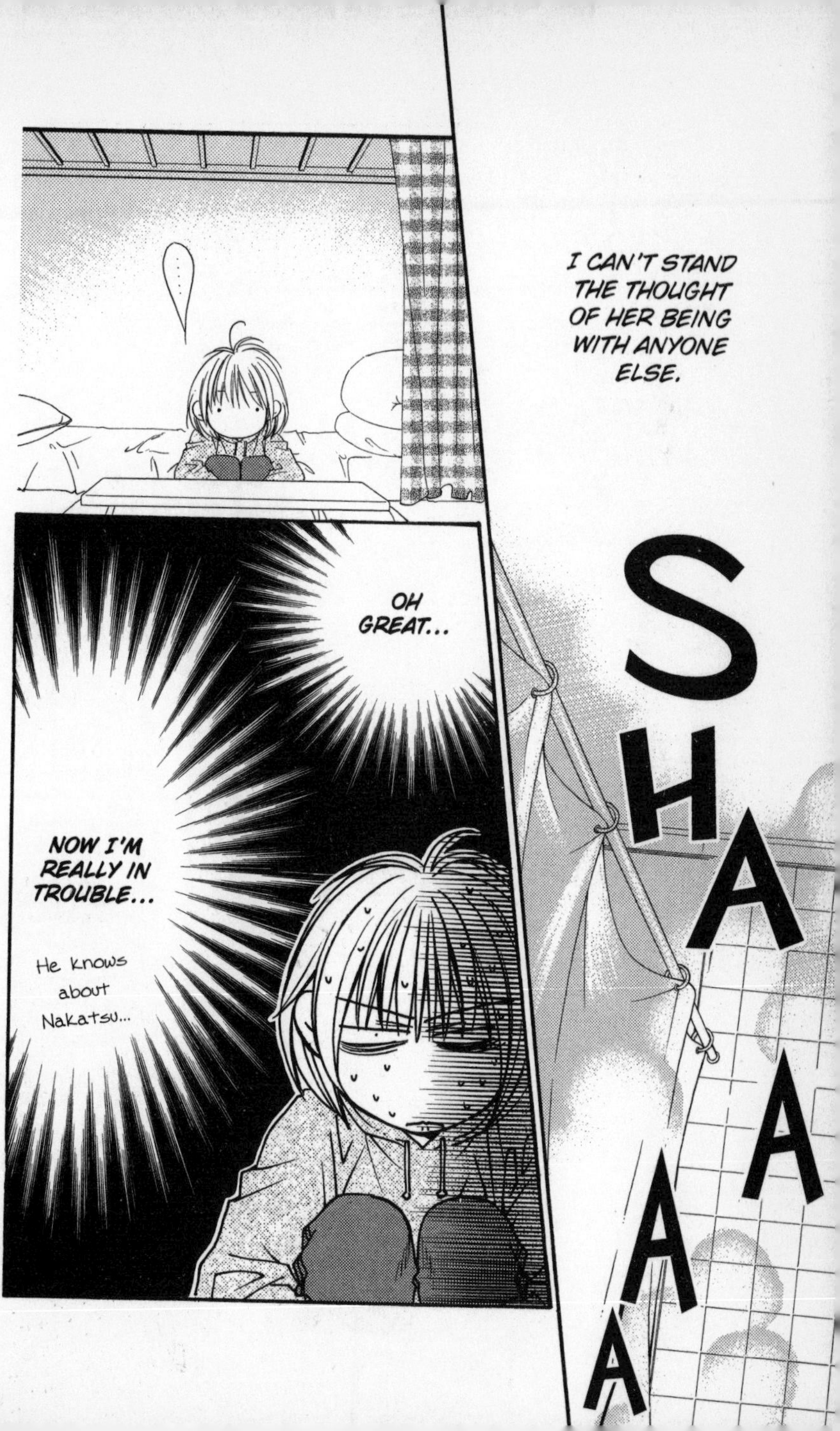
I CAN'T STAND THE THOUGHT OF HER BEING WITH ANYONE ELSE.
SHAAAAA
...!
OH GREAT...
NOW I'M REALLY IN TROUBLE...
He knows about Nakatsu...

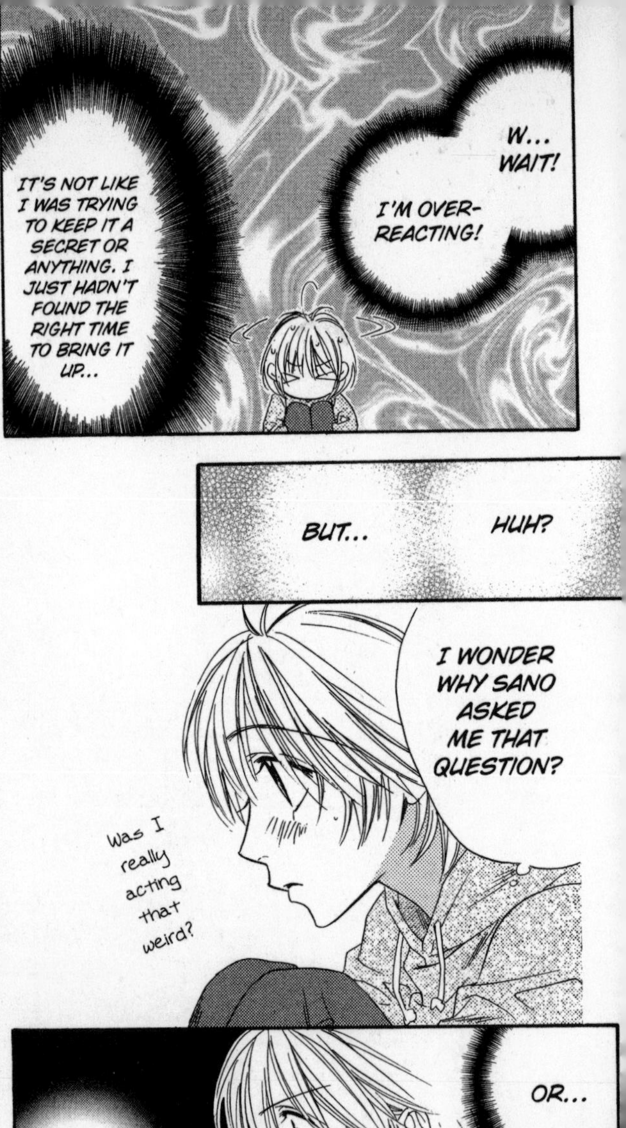
W... WAIT!
I'M OVER-REACTING!
IT'S NOT LIKE I WAS TRYING TO KEEP IT A SECRET OR ANYTHING. I JUST HADN'T FOUND THE RIGHT TIME TO BRING IT UP...
HUH?
BUT...
I WONDER WHY SANO ASKED ME THAT QUESTION?
Was I really acting that weird?
OR...
OH NO...

BEHIND THE SCENES 2

I love watermelon, but unfortunately, it brings back some bad memories. You know how some people get the urge to eat a whole cake by themselves? Well I always wanted to eat a whole watermelon by myself.... just kidding, but actually...Back when I was in first or second grade, I got in trouble and I'm pretty sure my mom made me eat a whole watermelon as punishment. Of course, it's impossible to eat a whole watermelon, so somewhere around the tenth bite, I gave up and apologized.

I mean, of course I tried to apologize right from the start, but when my mom gets mad, she never misses an opportunity to give me a lecture. One time, I had to listen to her for 3 hours straight.

My mom was really strict... I can only eat one piece of cake...it's too sweet.

Looking back on it, I don't think I ever did anything to deserve that kind of punishment.

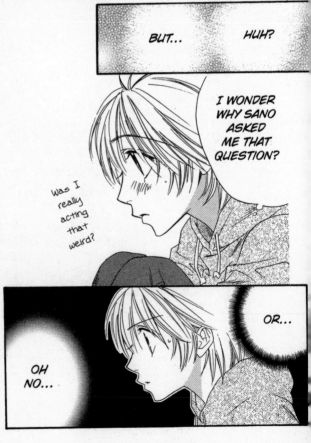

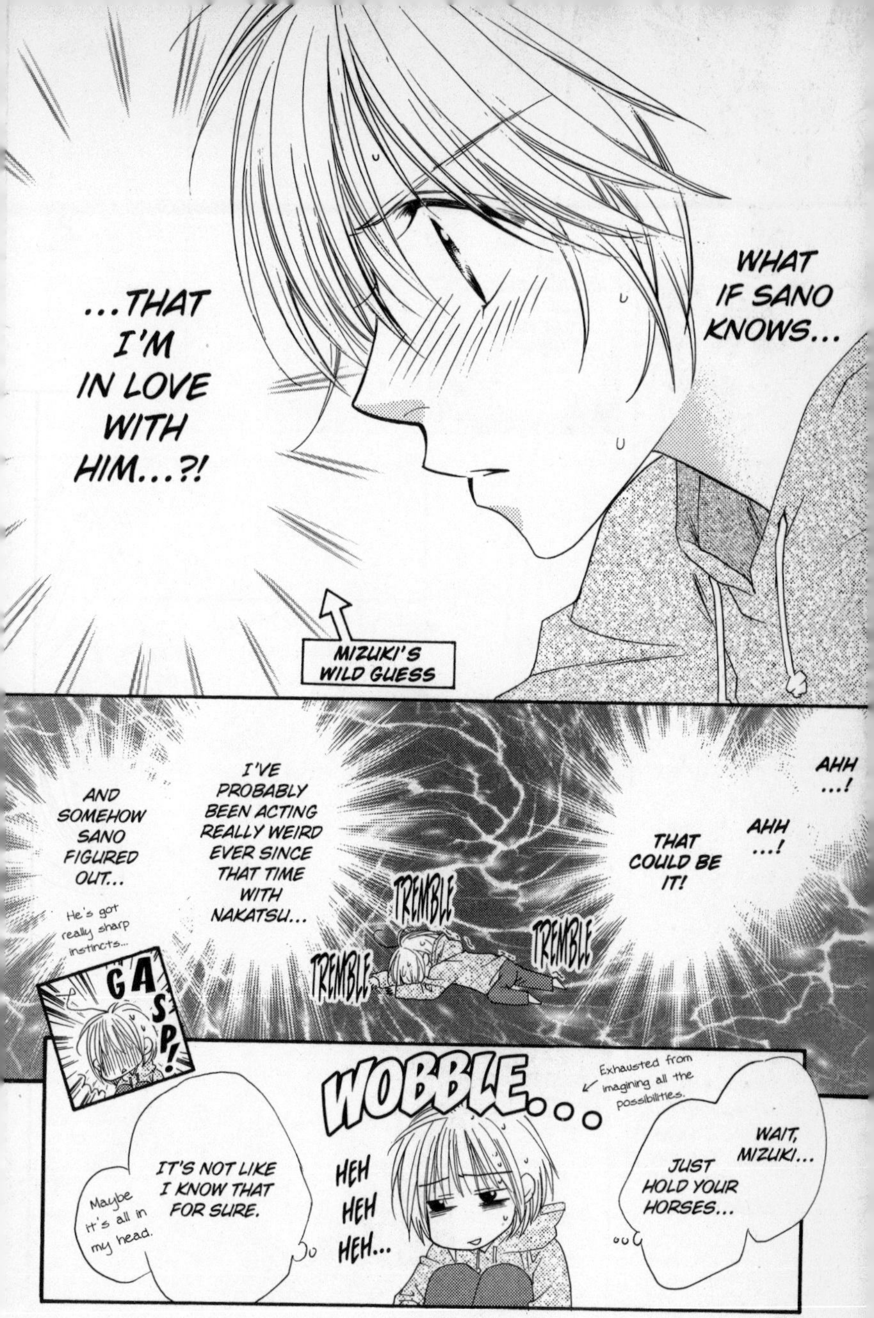
WHAT IF SANO KNOWS...
...THAT I'M IN LOVE WITH HIM...?!
MIZUKI'S WILD GUESS
AHH ...!
AHH ...!
THAT COULD BE IT!
TREMBLE
TREMBLE
TREMBLE
I'VE PROBABLY BEEN ACTING REALLY WEIRD EVER SINCE THAT TIME WITH NAKATSU...
AND SOMEHOW SANO FIGURED OUT...
He's got really sharp instincts...
GASP!
WAIT, MIZUKI...
JUST HOLD YOUR HORSES...
Exhausted from imagining all the possibilities.
WOBBLE...
HEH HEH HEH...
IT'S NOT LIKE I KNOW THAT FOR SURE.
Maybe it's all in my head.

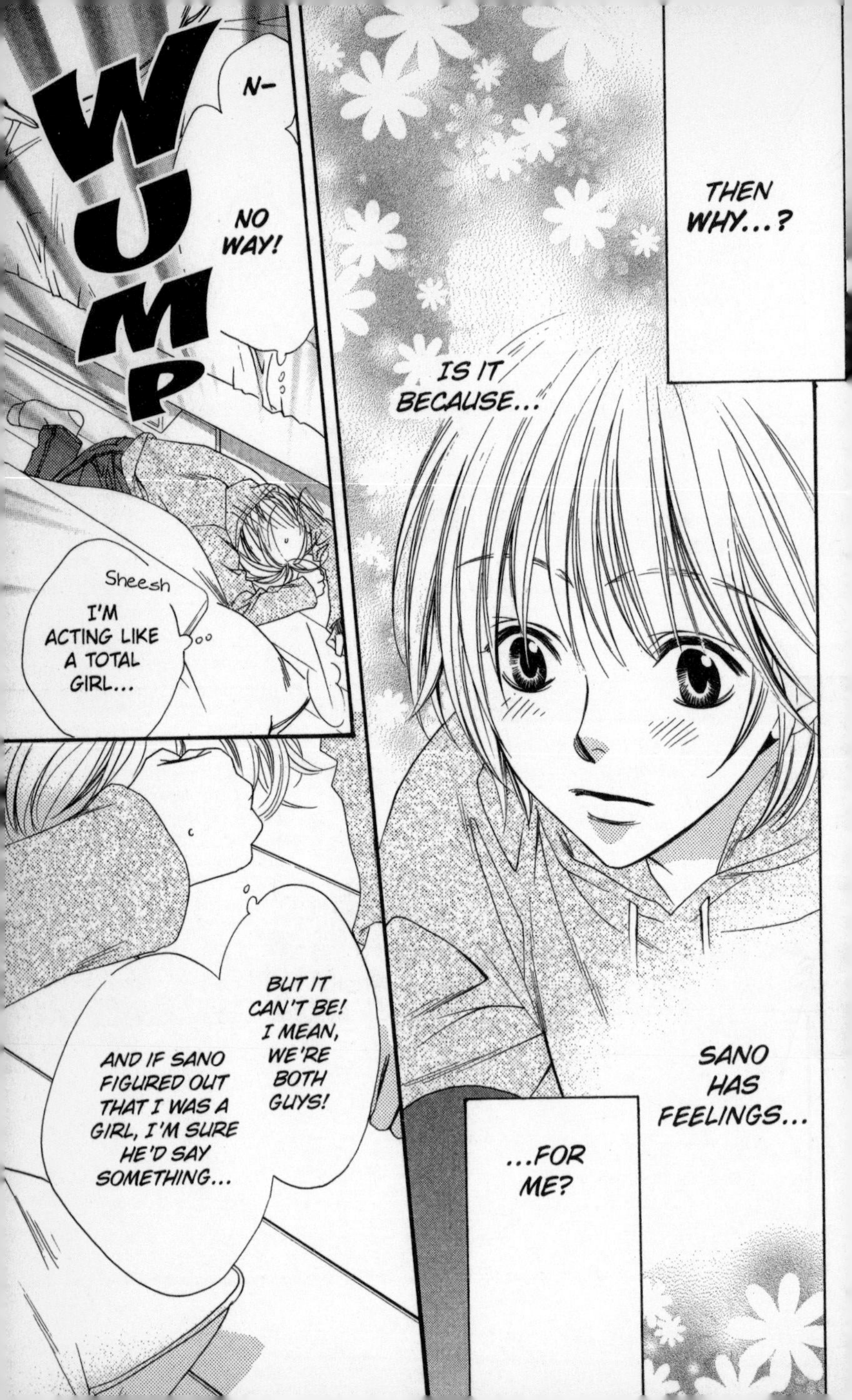

THEN WHY...?
IS IT BECAUSE...
SANO HAS FEELINGS...
...FOR ME?
N-
NO WAY!
WUMP
Sheesh
I'M ACTING LIKE A TOTAL GIRL...
BUT IT CAN'T BE! I MEAN, WE'RE BOTH GUYS!
AND IF SANO FIGURED OUT THAT I WAS A GIRL, I'M SURE HE'D SAY SOMETHING...

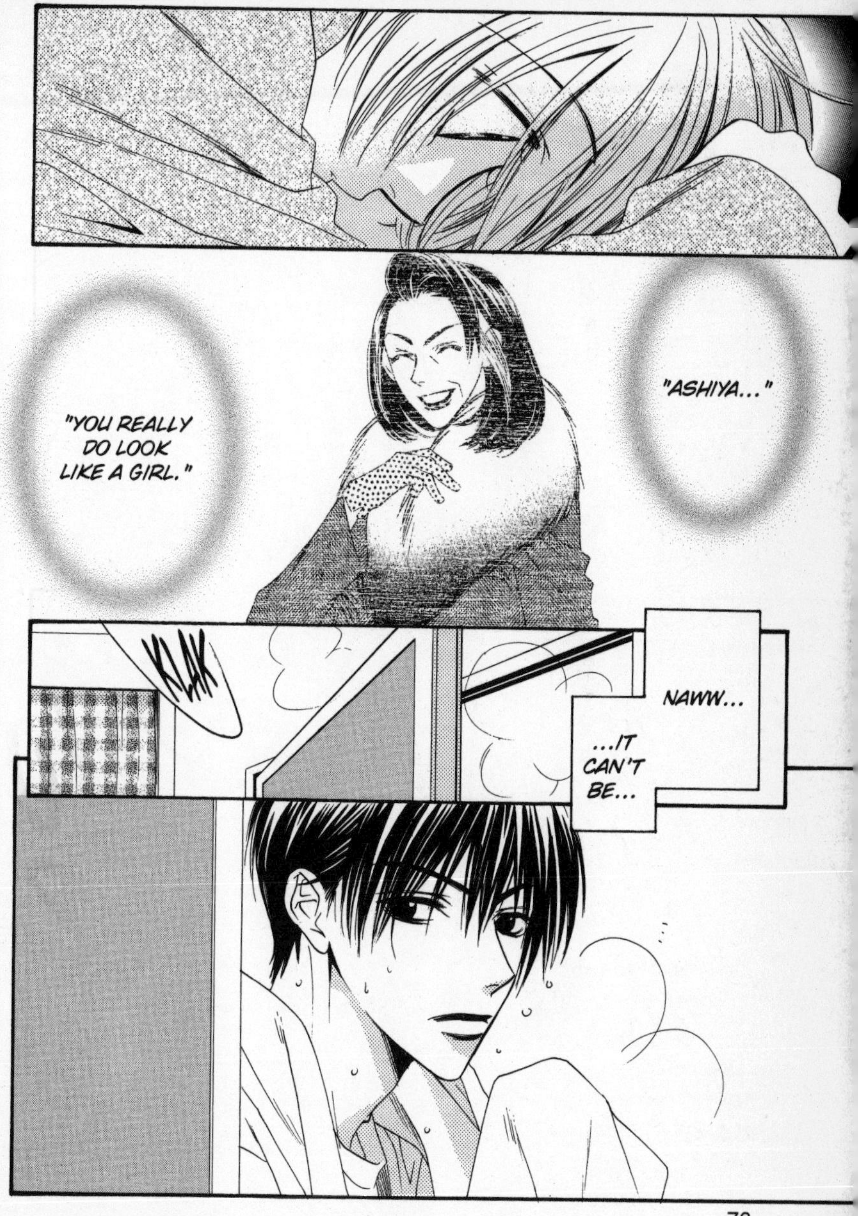
"ASHIYA..."
"YOU REALLY DO LOOK LIKE A GIRL."
NAWW...
...IT CAN'T BE...
KLAK

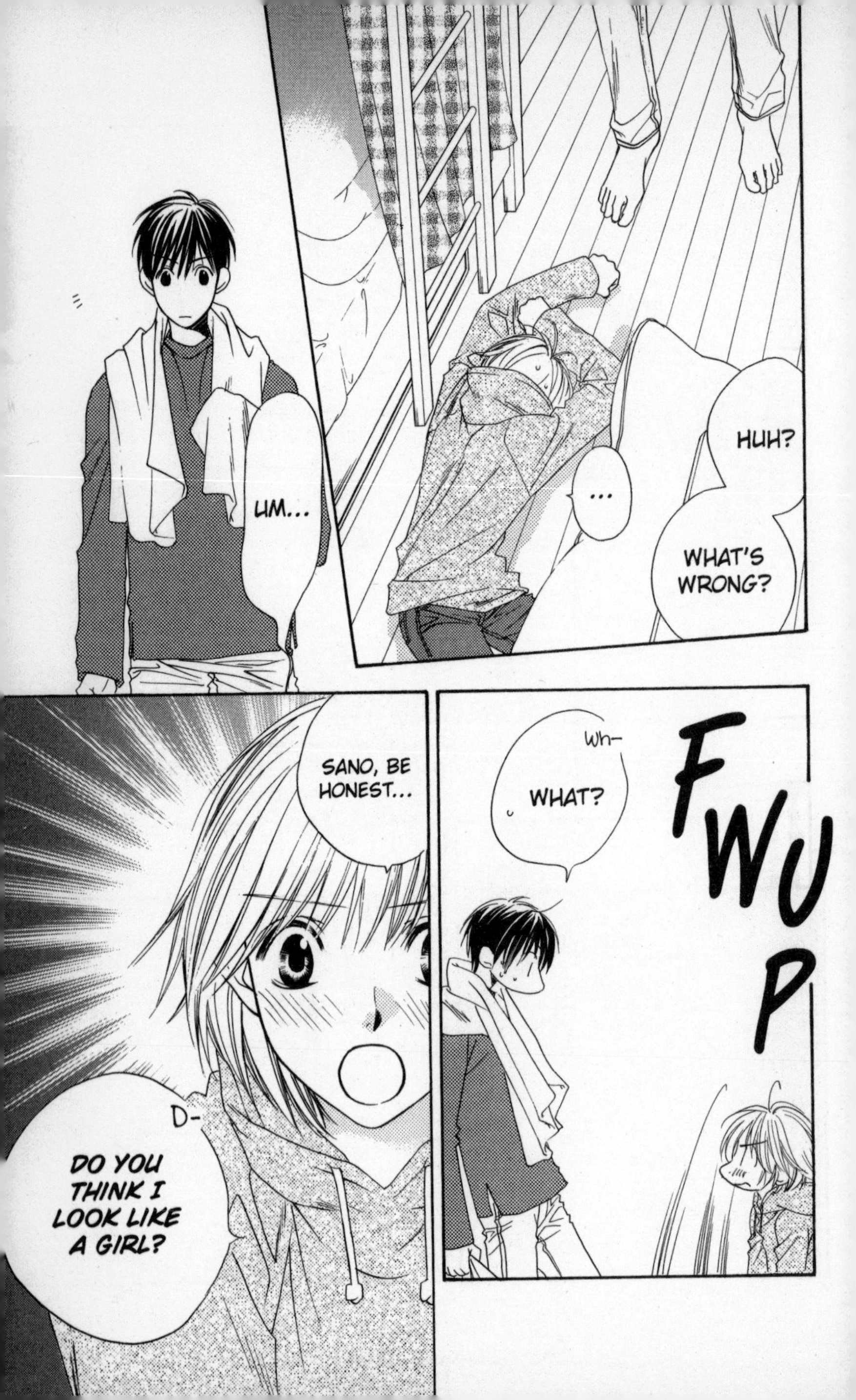
HUH?
WHAT'S WRONG?
...
UM...
FWUP
Wh- WHAT?
SANO, BE HONEST...
D- DO YOU THINK I LOOK LIKE A GIRL?

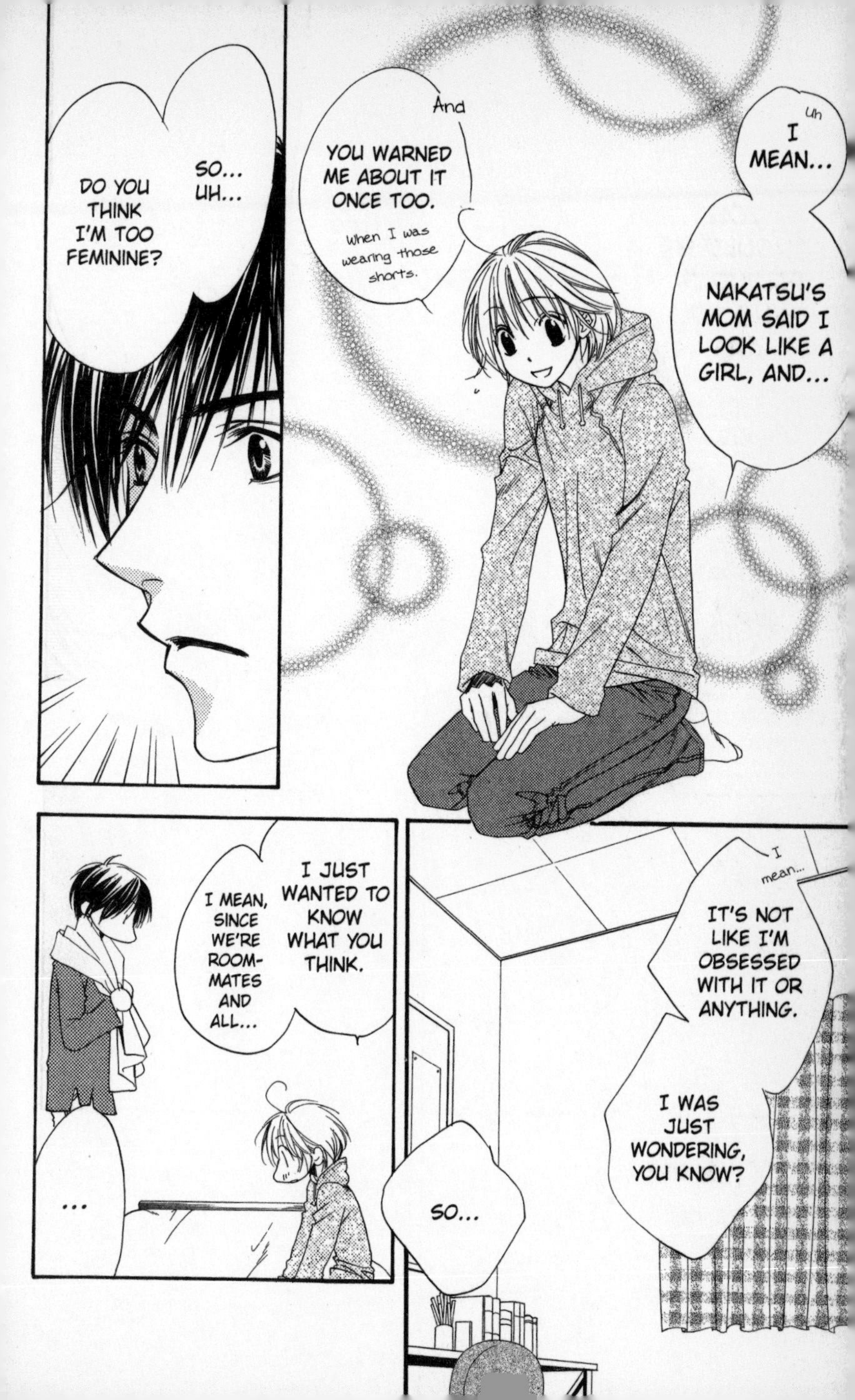
Uh
I MEAN...
NAKATSU'S MOM SAID I LOOK LIKE A GIRL, AND...
And
YOU WARNED ME ABOUT IT ONCE TOO.
When I was wearing those shorts.
SO... UH...
DO YOU THINK I'M TOO FEMININE?
I mean...
IT'S NOT LIKE I'M OBSESSED WITH IT OR ANYTHING.
I WAS JUST WONDERING, YOU KNOW?
SO...
I JUST WANTED TO KNOW WHAT YOU THINK.
I MEAN, SINCE WE'RE ROOM-MATES AND ALL...
...

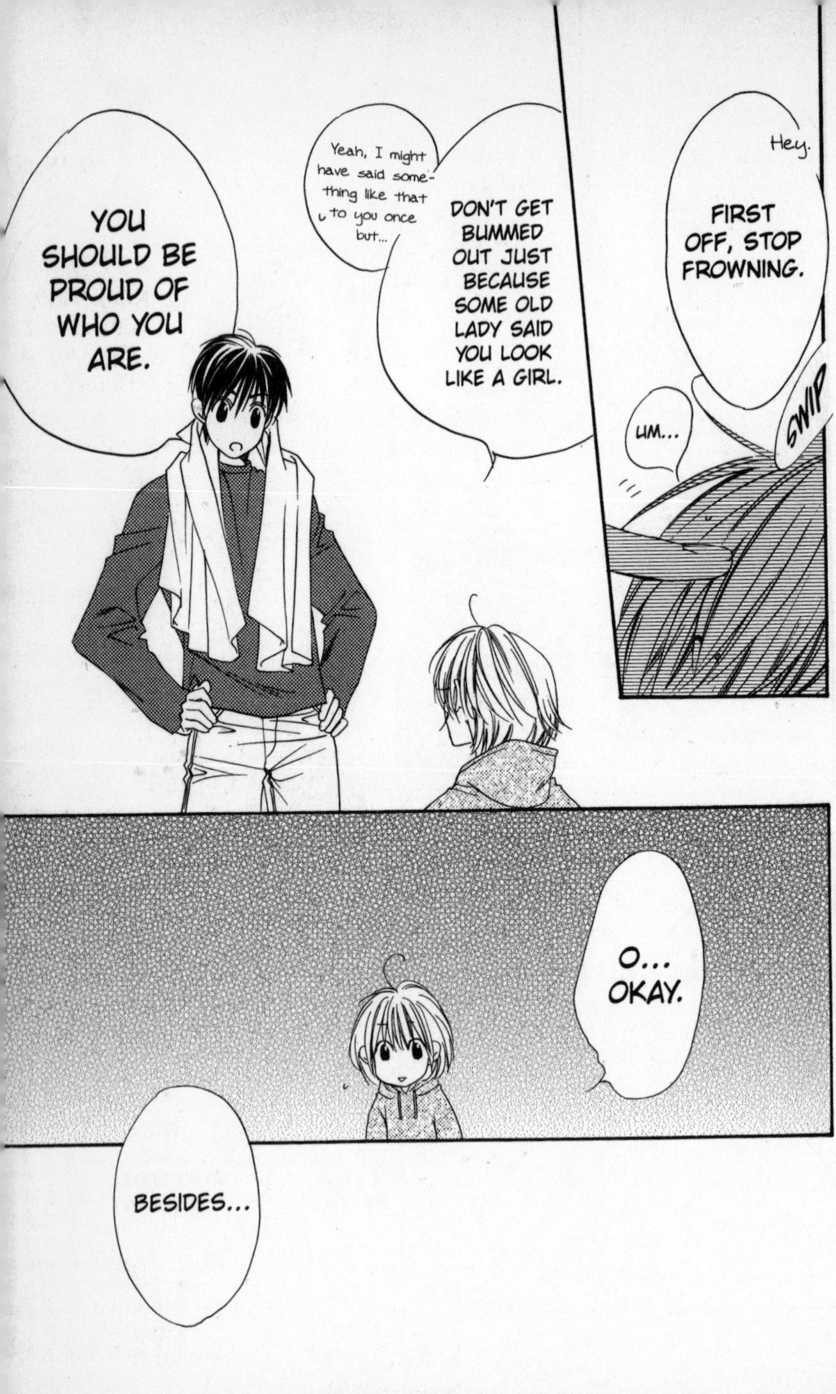
Hey.
FIRST OFF, STOP FROWNING.
SWIP
UM...
DON'T GET BUMMED OUT JUST BECAUSE SOME OLD LADY SAID YOU LOOK LIKE A GIRL.
Yeah, I might have said something like that to you once but...
YOU SHOULD BE PROUD OF WHO YOU ARE.
O... OKAY.
BESIDES...

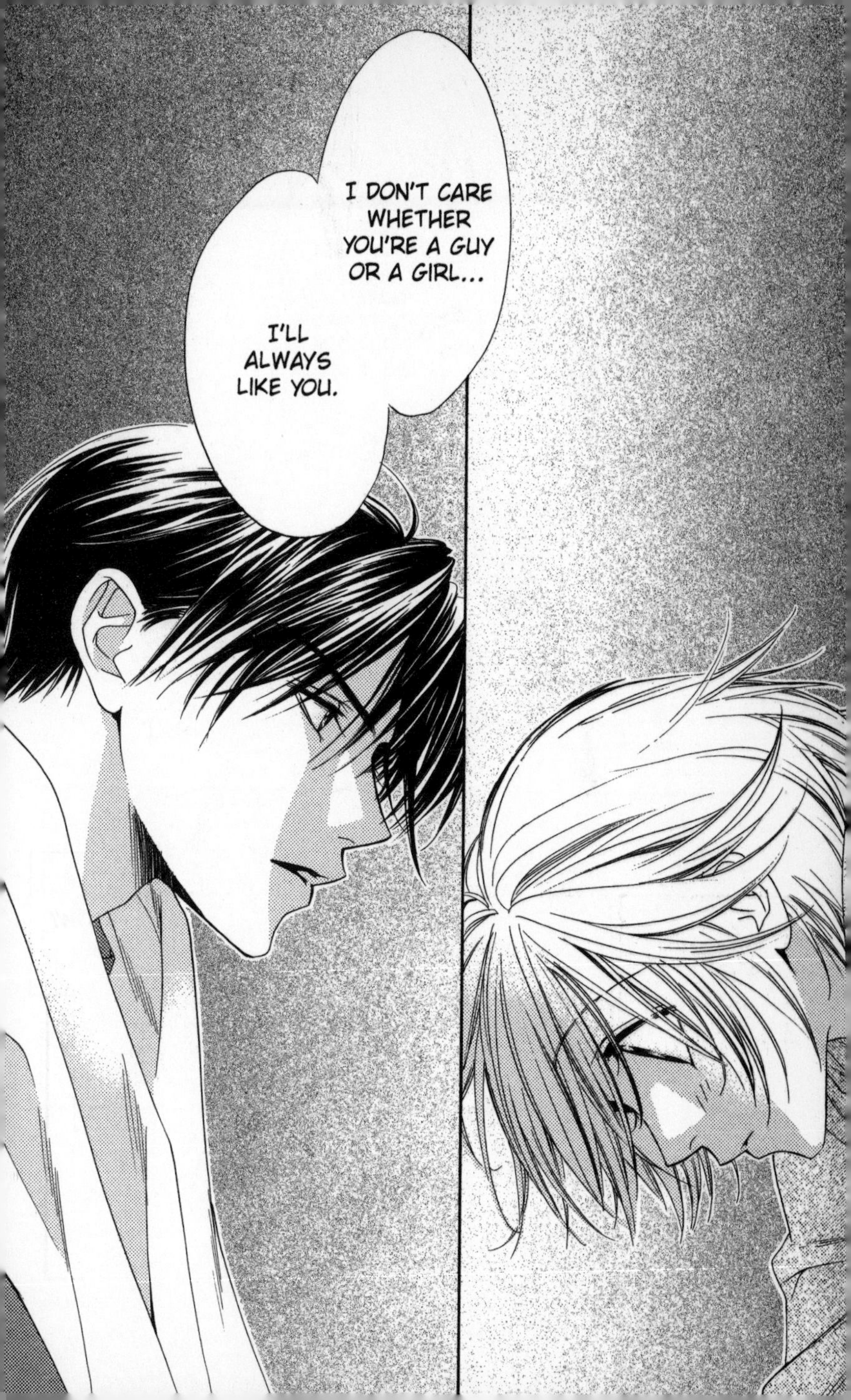
I DON'T CARE WHETHER YOU'RE A GUY OR A GIRL...
I'LL ALWAYS LIKE YOU.

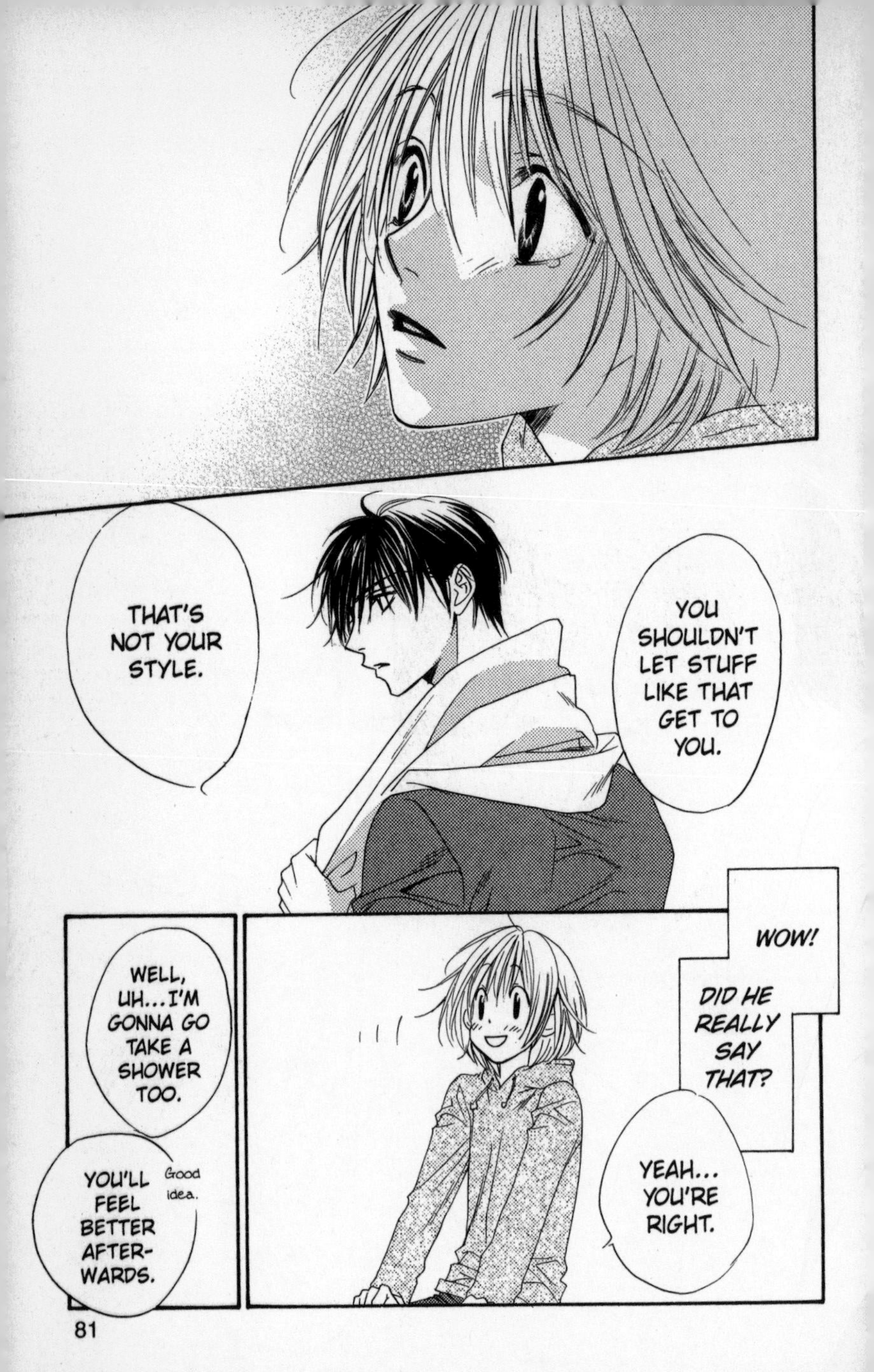
YOU SHOULDN'T LET STUFF LIKE THAT GET TO YOU.
THAT'S NOT YOUR STYLE.
WOW!
DID HE REALLY SAY THAT?
YEAH... YOU'RE RIGHT.
WELL, UH...I'M GONNA GO TAKE A SHOWER TOO.
YOU'LL FEEL BETTER AFTER-WARDS.
Good idea.

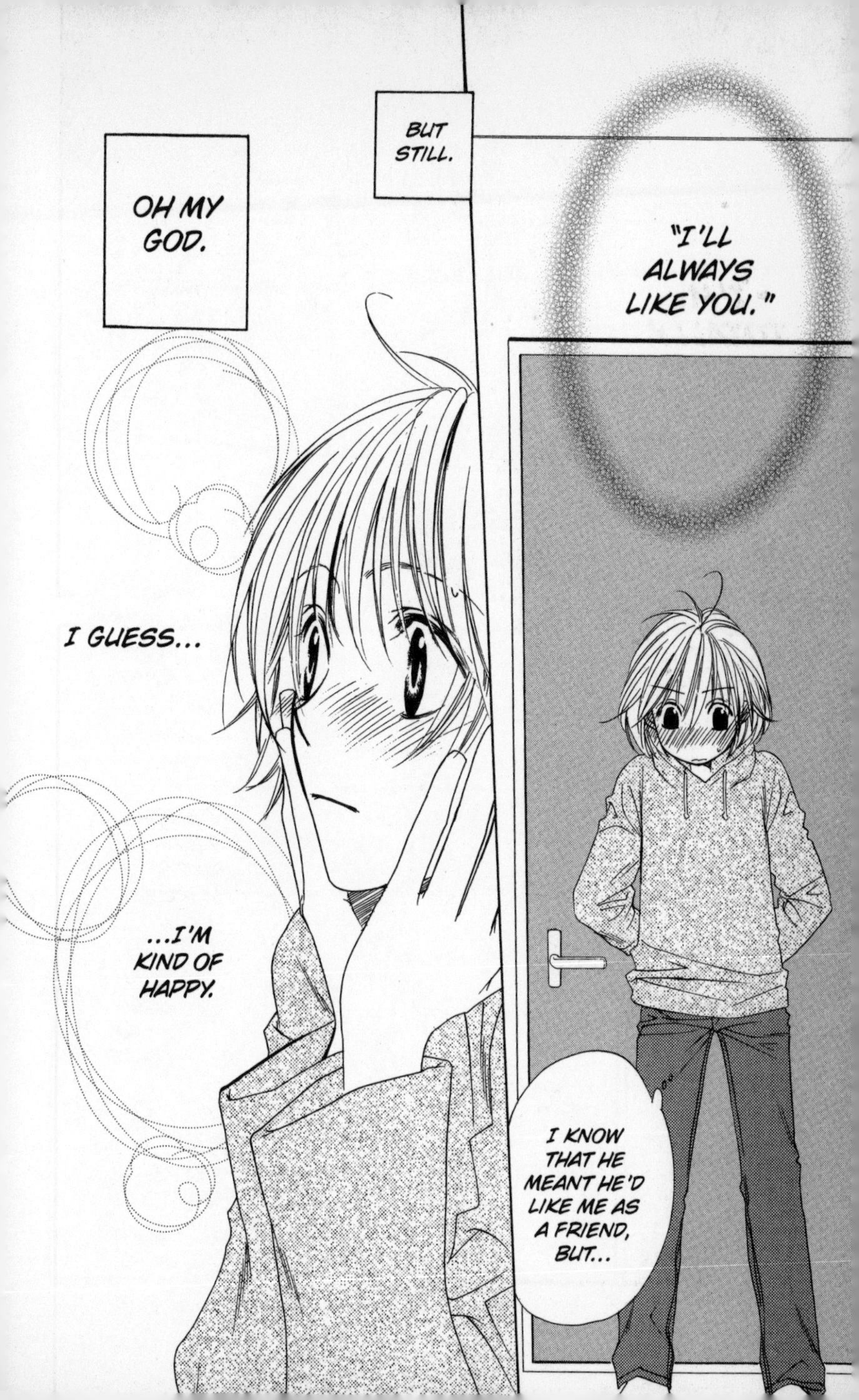
"I'LL ALWAYS LIKE YOU."
I KNOW THAT HE MEANT HE'D LIKE ME AS A FRIEND, BUT...
BUT STILL.
OH MY GOD.
I GUESS...
...I'M KIND OF HAPPY.

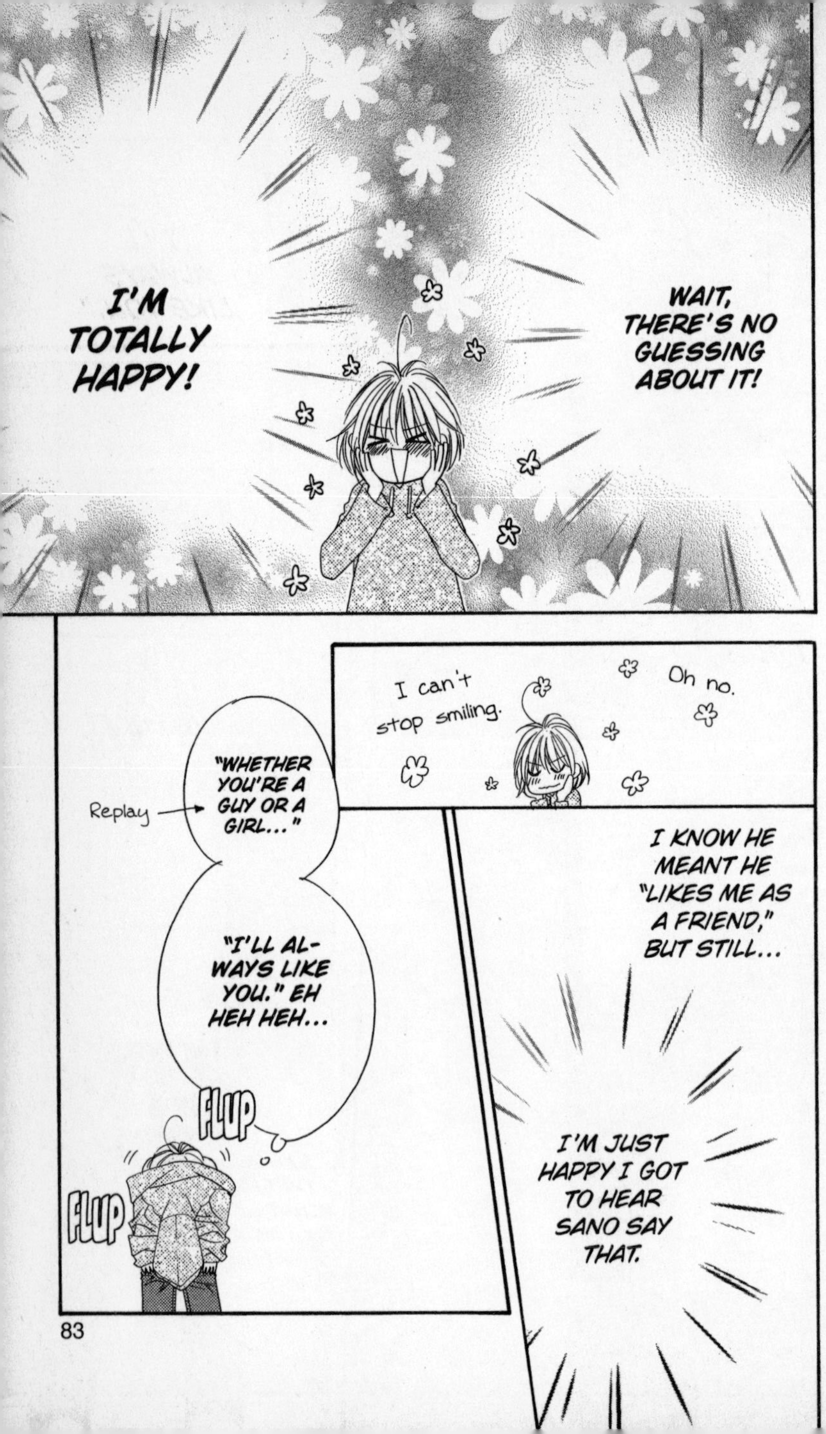
WAIT, THERE'S NO GUESSING ABOUT IT!
I'M TOTALLY HAPPY!
Oh no.
I can't stop smiling.
I KNOW HE MEANT HE "LIKES ME AS A FRIEND," BUT STILL...
I'M JUST HAPPY I GOT TO HEAR SANO SAY THAT.
"WHETHER YOU'RE A GUY OR A GIRL..."
Replay
"I'LL AL- WAYS LIKE YOU." EH HEH HEH...
FLUP
FLUP

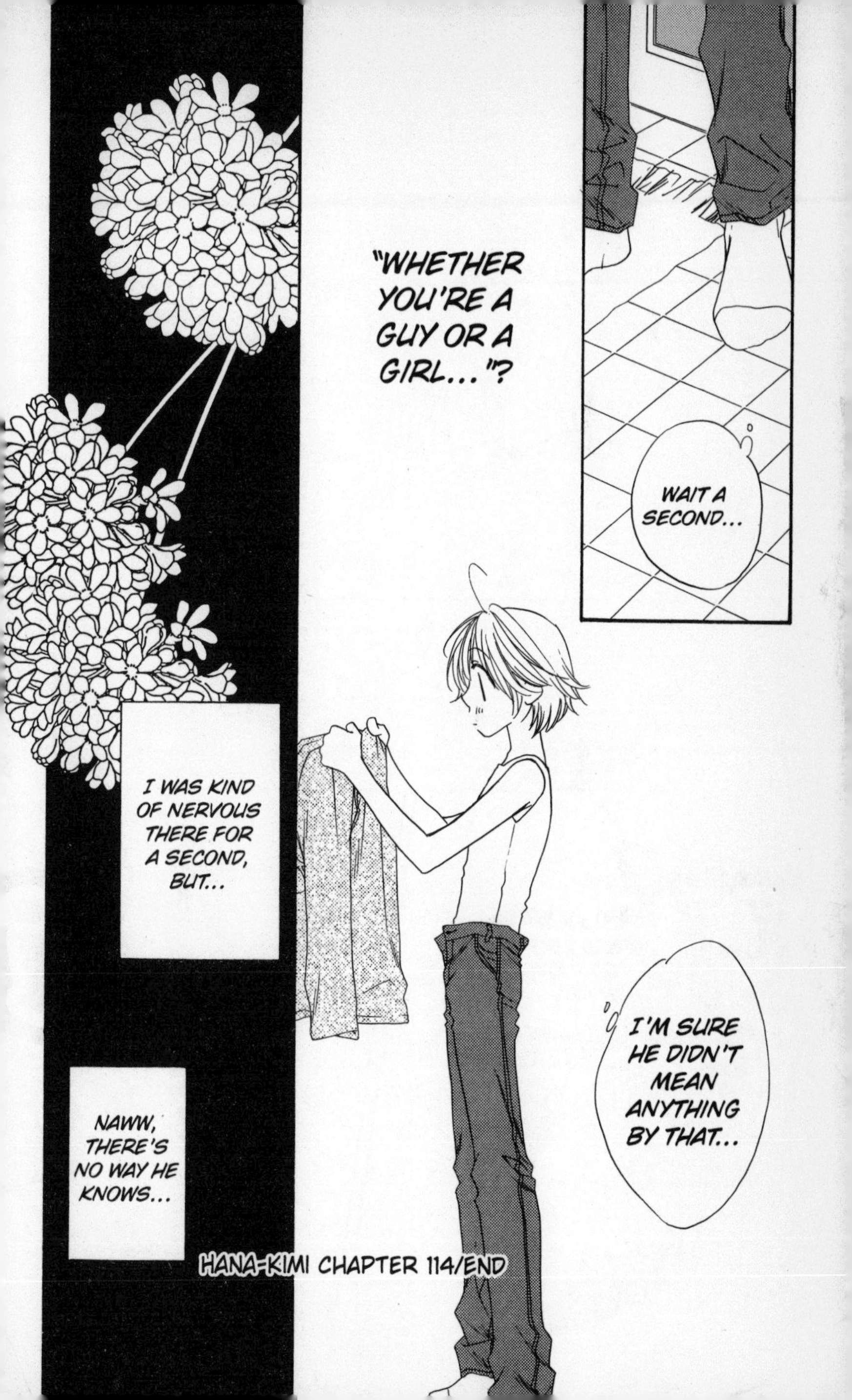
WAIT A SECOND...
"WHETHER YOU'RE A GUY OR A GIRL..."?
I'M SURE HE DIDN'T MEAN ANYTHING BY THAT...
I WAS KIND OF NERVOUS THERE FOR A SECOND, BUT...
NAWW, THERE'S NO WAY HE KNOWS...
HANA-KIMI CHAPTER 114/END

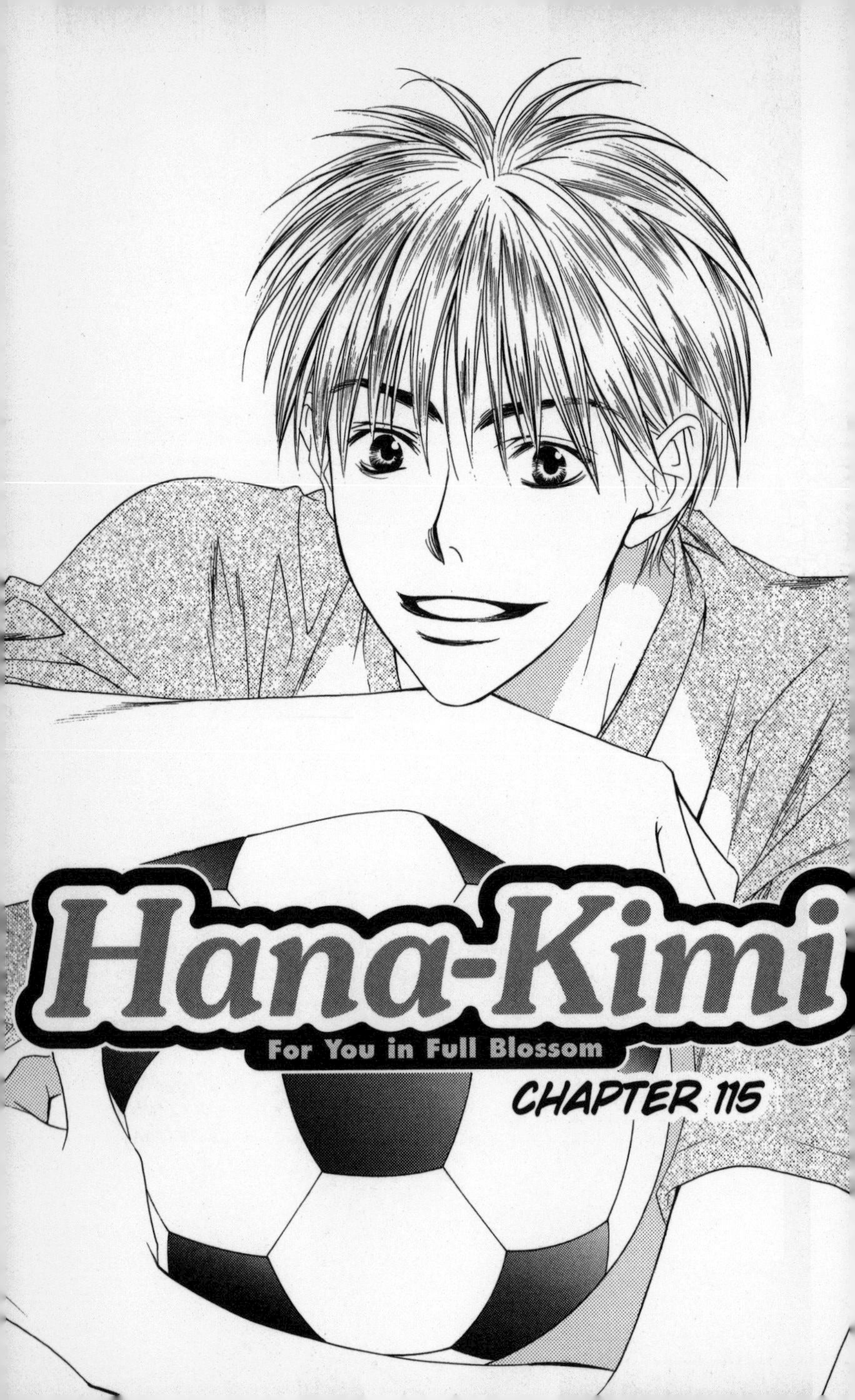
Hana-Kimi
For You in Full Blossom
CHAPTER 115

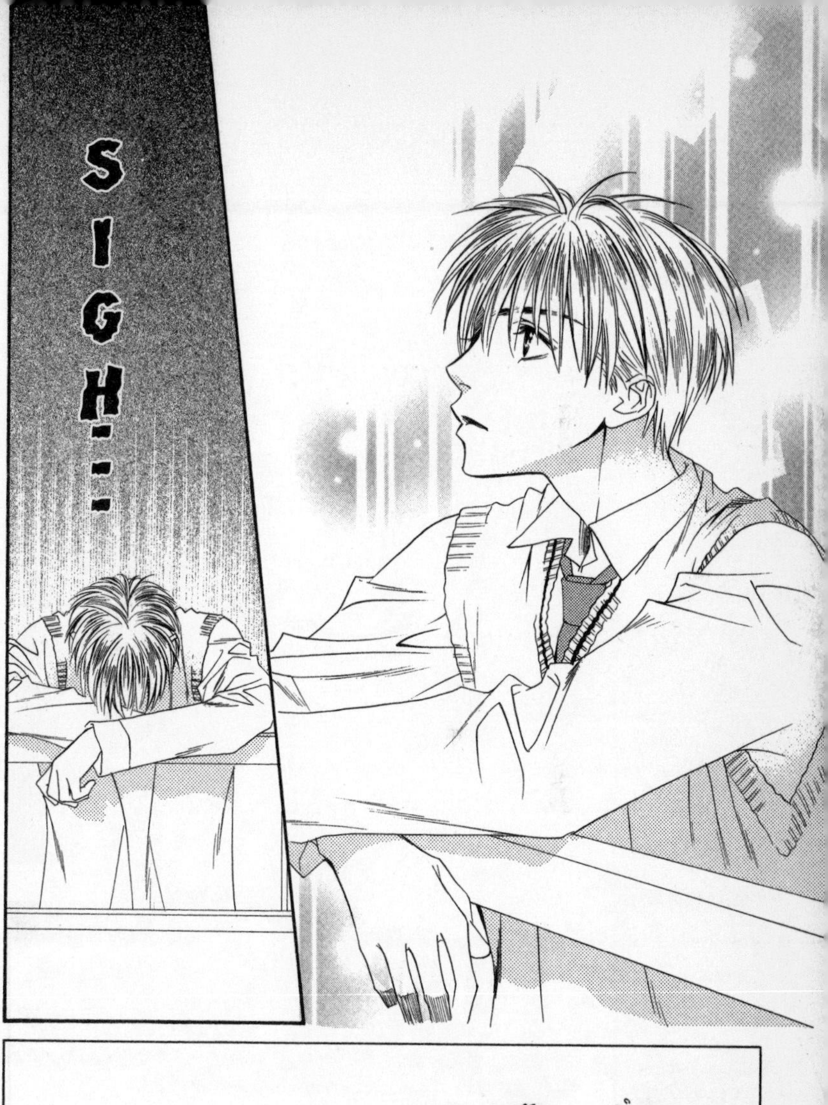
SIGH...

WHAT I'M INTO THESE DAYS

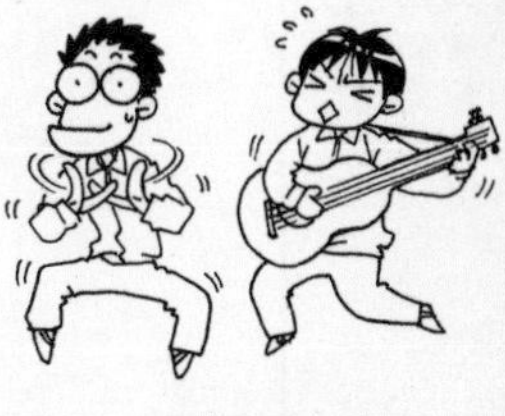

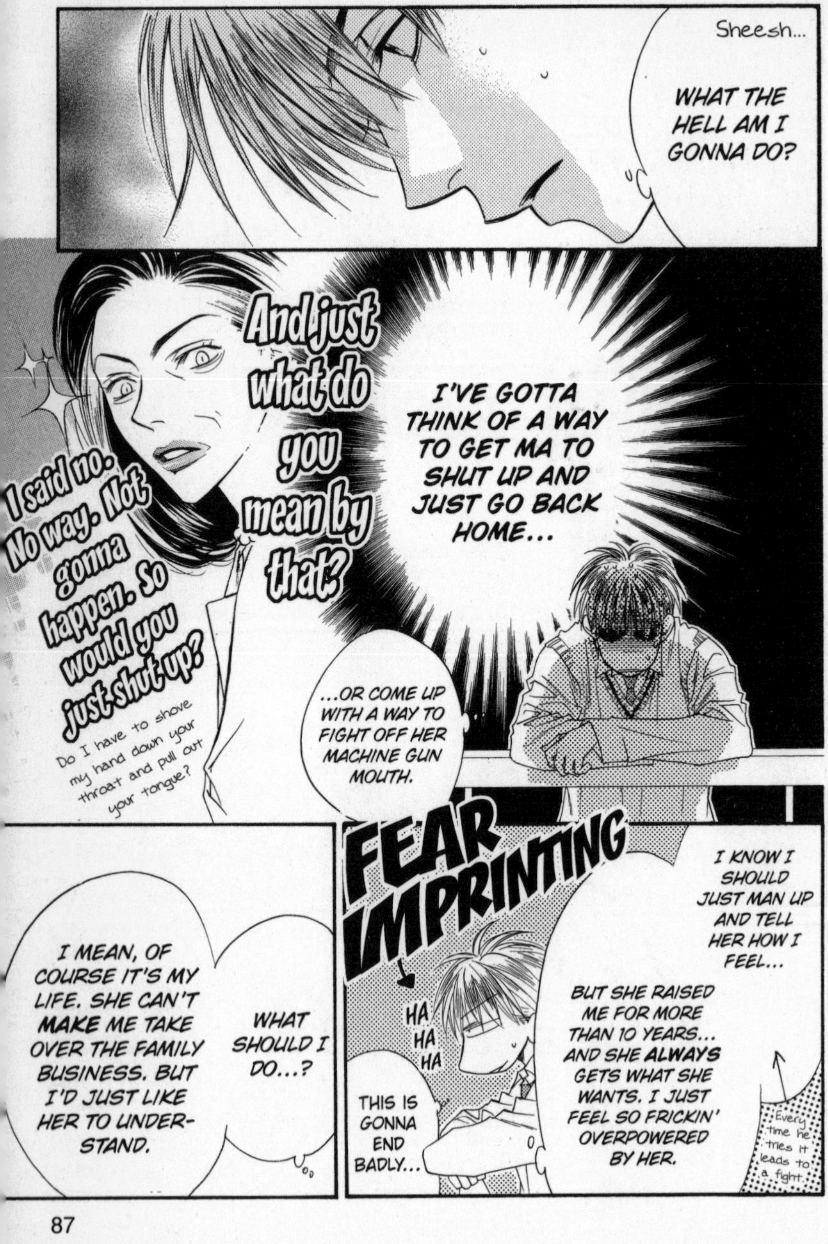
Sheesh...
WHAT THE HELL AM I GONNA DO?
I'VE GOTTA THINK OF A WAY TO GET MA TO SHUT UP AND JUST GO BACK HOME...
...OR COME UP WITH A WAY TO FIGHT OFF HER MACHINE GUN MOUTH.
And just what do you mean by that?
I said no. No way. Not gonna happen. So would you just shut up?
Do I have to shove my hand down your throat and pull out your tongue?
FEAR IMPRINTING
I KNOW I SHOULD JUST MAN UP AND TELL HER HOW I FEEL...
Every time he tries it leads to a fight.
BUT SHE RAISED ME FOR MORE THAN 10 YEARS... AND SHE ALWAYS GETS WHAT SHE WANTS. I JUST FEEL SO FRICKIN' OVERPOWERED BY HER.
HA HA HA
THIS IS GONNA END BADLY...
WHAT SHOULD I DO...?
I MEAN, OF COURSE IT'S MY LIFE. SHE CAN'T MAKE ME TAKE OVER THE FAMILY BUSINESS. BUT I'D JUST LIKE HER TO UNDERSTAND.

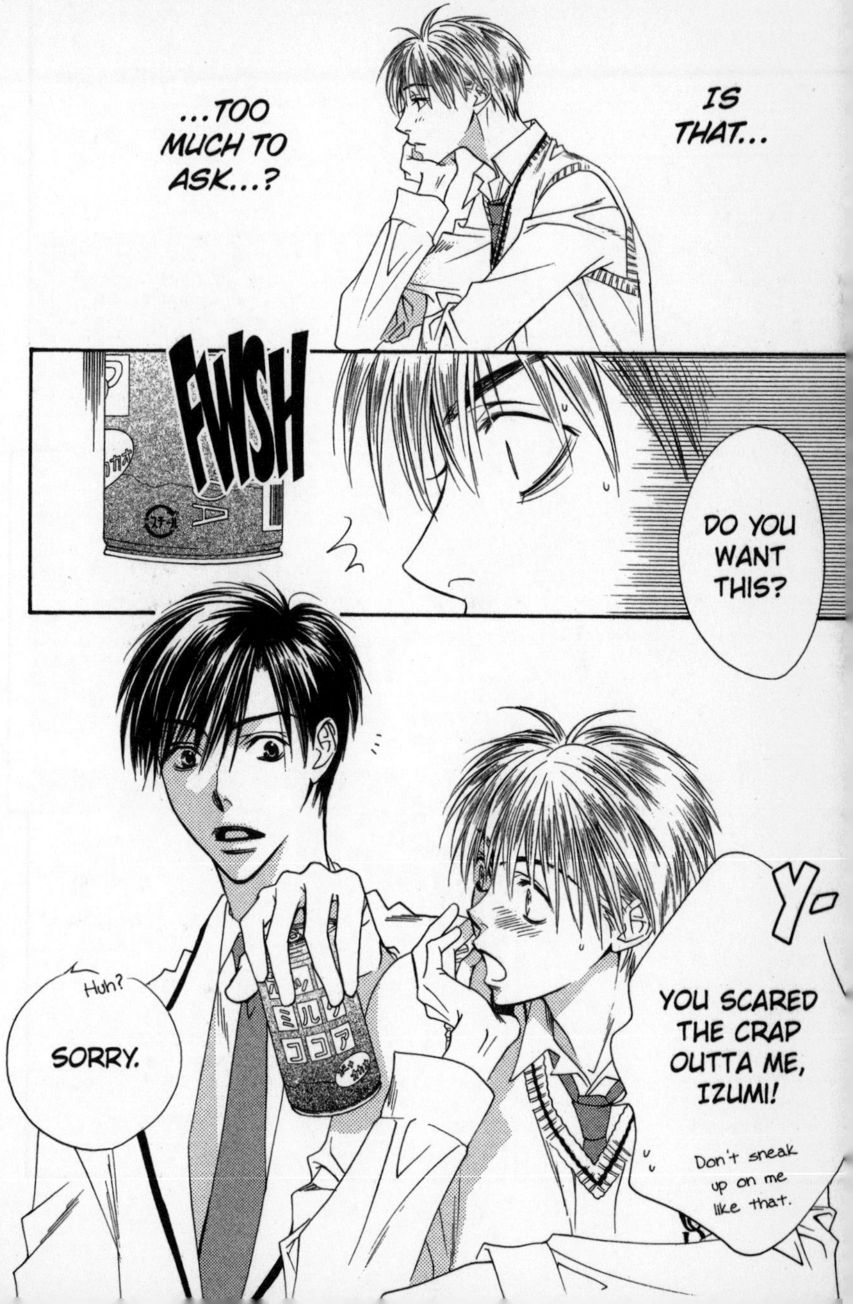
IS THAT...
...TOO MUCH TO ASK...?
FWISH
DO YOU WANT THIS?
Y-
YOU SCARED THE CRAP OUTTA ME, IZUMI!
Don't sneak up on me like that.
Huh?
SORRY.

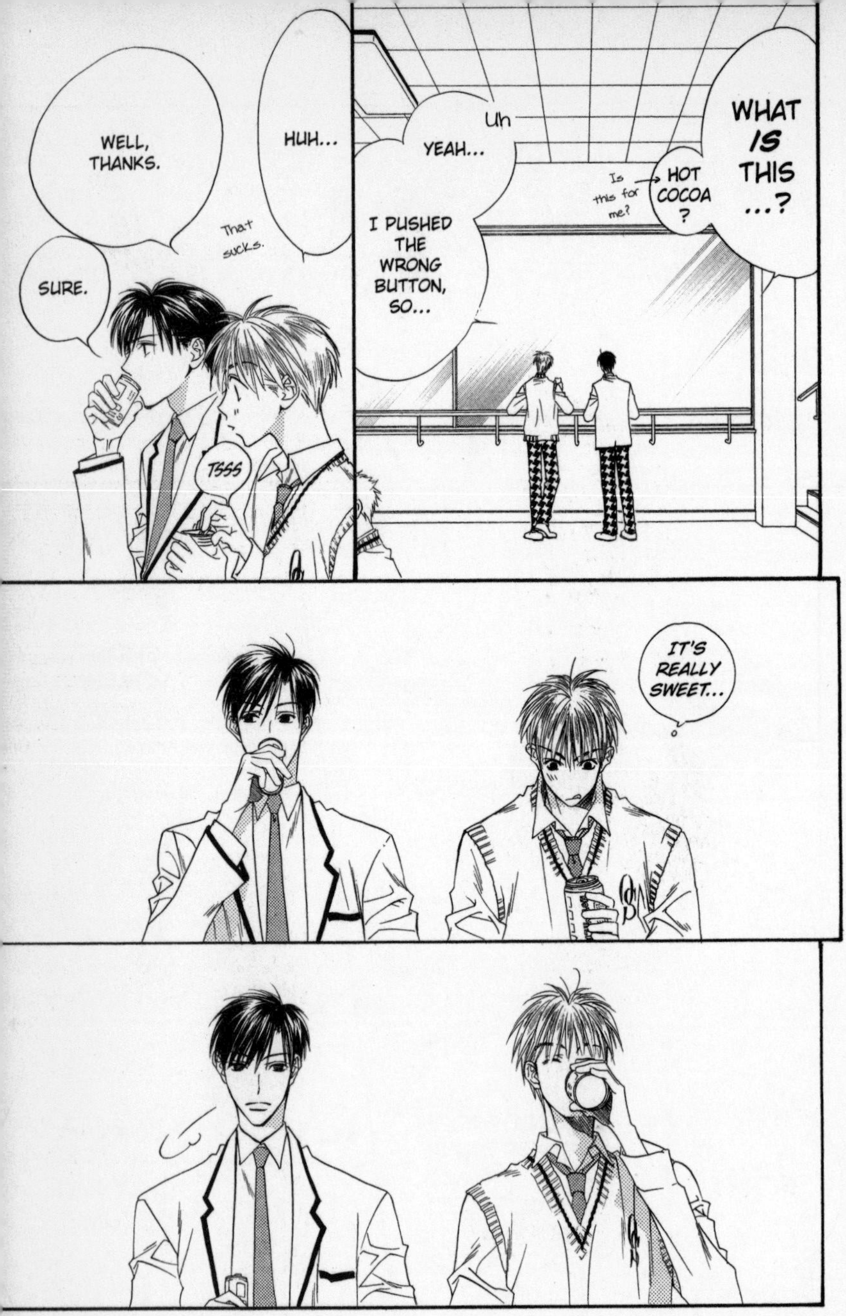
WHAT IS THIS ...?
HOT COCOA?
Is this for me?
Uh
YEAH...
I PUSHED THE WRONG BUTTON, SO...
HUH...
That sucks.
WELL, THANKS.
SURE.
TSSS
IT'S REALLY SWEET...

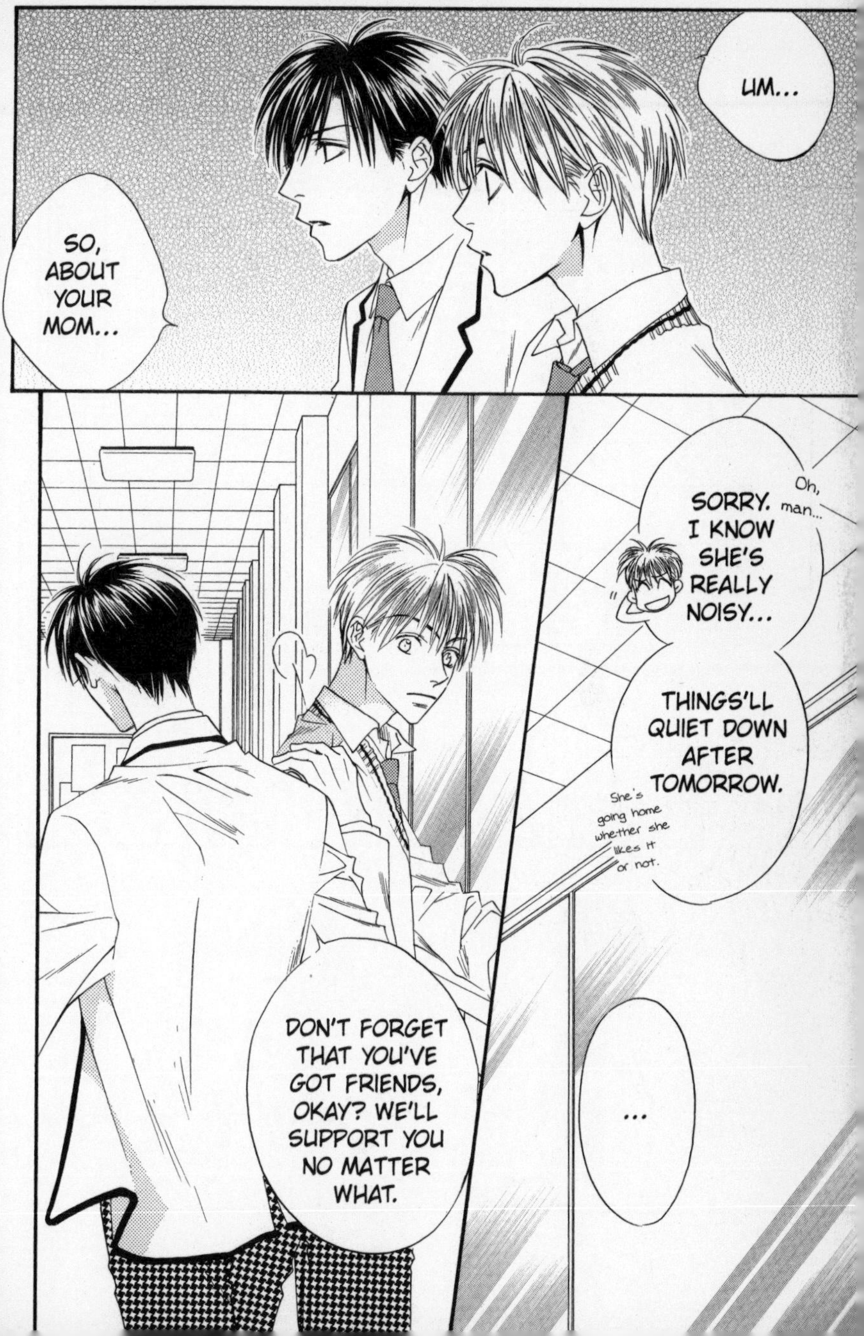
UM...
SO, ABOUT YOUR MOM...
Oh, man...
SORRY. I KNOW SHE'S REALLY NOISY...
THINGS'LL QUIET DOWN AFTER TOMORROW.
She's going home whether she likes it or not.
...
DON'T FORGET THAT YOU'VE GOT FRIENDS, OKAY? WE'LL SUPPORT YOU NO MATTER WHAT.

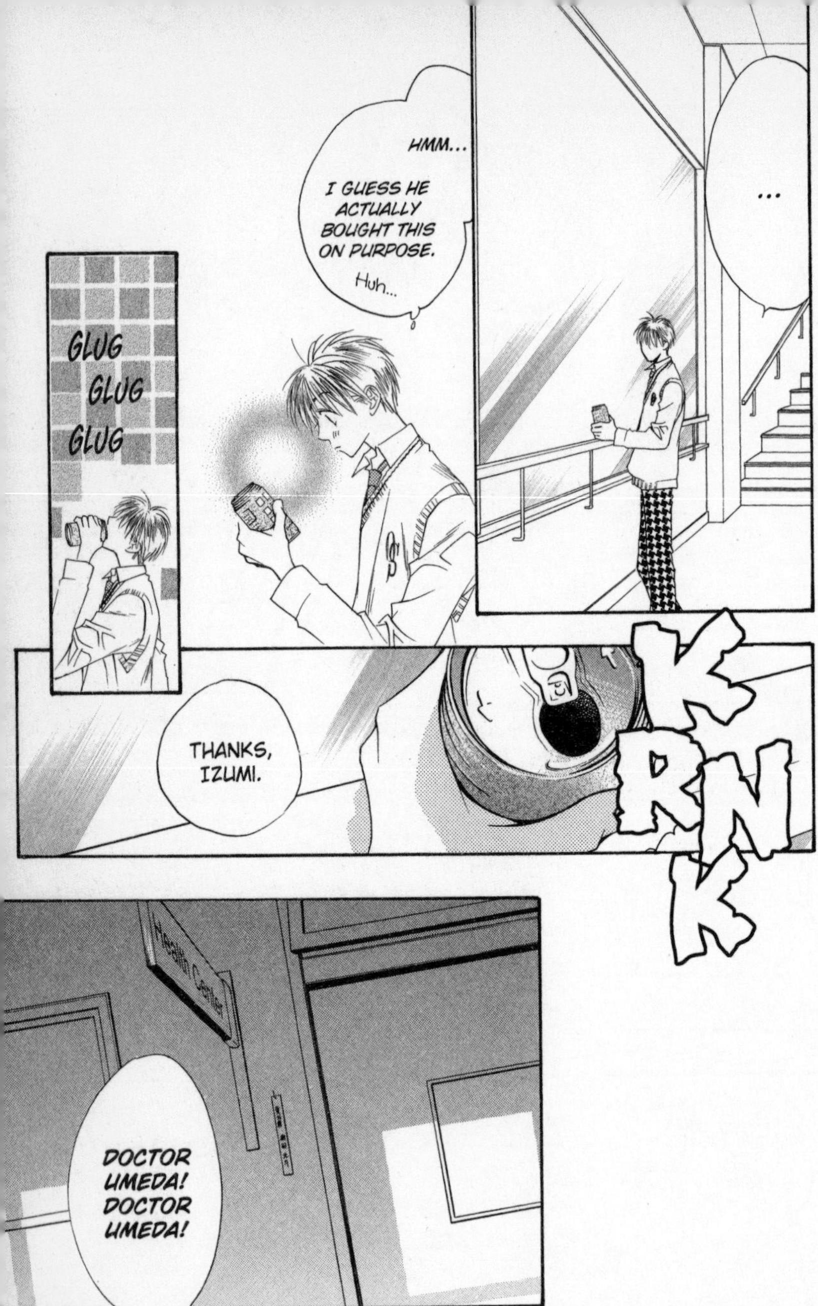
...
HMM...
I GUESS HE ACTUALLY BOUGHT THIS ON PURPOSE.
Huh...
GLUG GLUG GLUG
KRNK
THANKS, IZUMI.
Health Center
DOCTOR UMEDA! DOCTOR UMEDA!

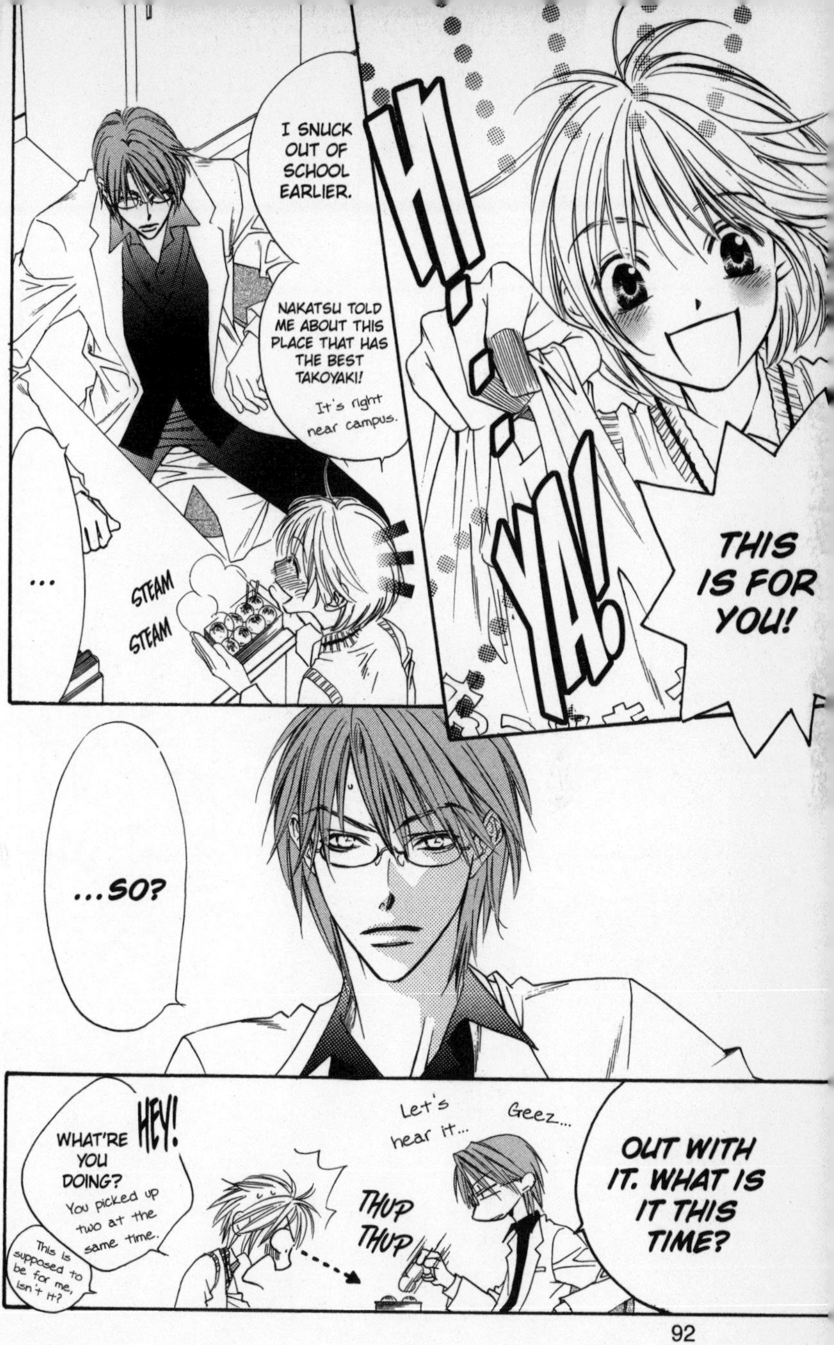
HI!
YA!
THIS IS FOR YOU!
I SNUCK OUT OF SCHOOL EARLIER.
NAKATSU TOLD ME ABOUT THIS PLACE THAT HAS THE BEST TAKOYAKI!
It's right near campus.
...
STEAM
STEAM
...SO?
OUT WITH IT. WHAT IS IT THIS TIME?
Geez...
Let's hear it...
THUP THUP
HEY!
WHAT'RE YOU DOING?
You picked up two at the same time.
This is supposed to be for me, isn't it?

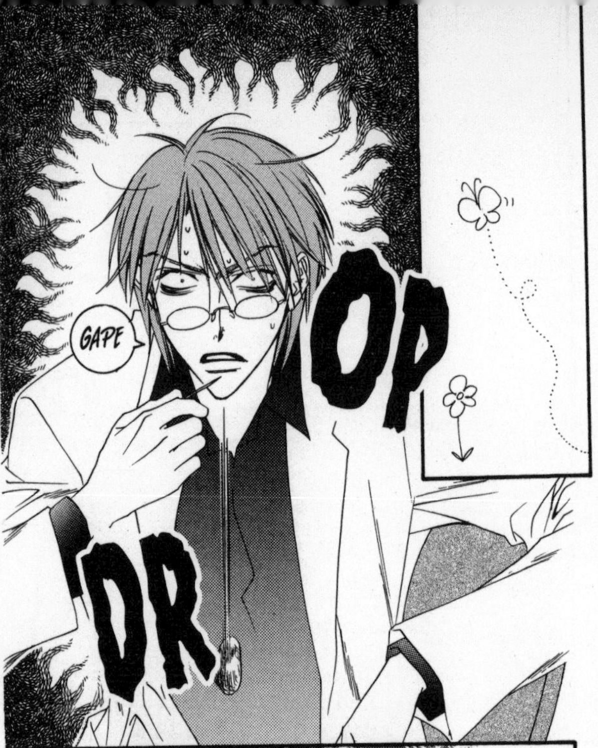
GAPE
DR
OP

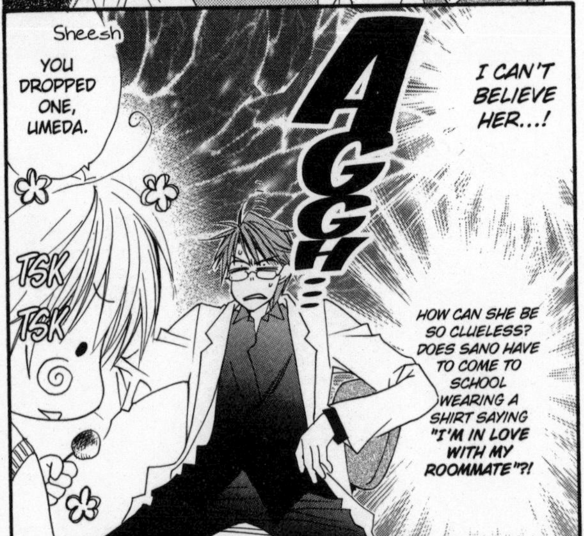
I CAN'T BELIEVE HER...!
AGGH...
HOW CAN SHE BE SO CLUELESS? DOES SANO HAVE TO COME TO SCHOOL WEARING A SHIRT SAYING "I'M IN LOVE WITH MY ROOMMATE"?!
YOU DROPPED ONE, UMEDA.
Sheesh
TSK
TSK

MY CAT

My second cat is named Leon... he's actually Sue's brother. (They both have the same parents, so they really are brother and sister) And it turns out that Leon is super smart... (Well, maybe I'm exaggerating because he's my cat, but...) He always watches what people are doing and learns how to do stuff on his own. He learned how to turn the doorknob, and he can open the VCR cabinet's glass door. He studies Sue too, and he never makes the same mistakes Sue makes. He's a good listener, and he understands Japanese. (At least it seems like he does.) He's got good manners and he's friendly too.

This is important stuff.

He's like the typical younger sibling.

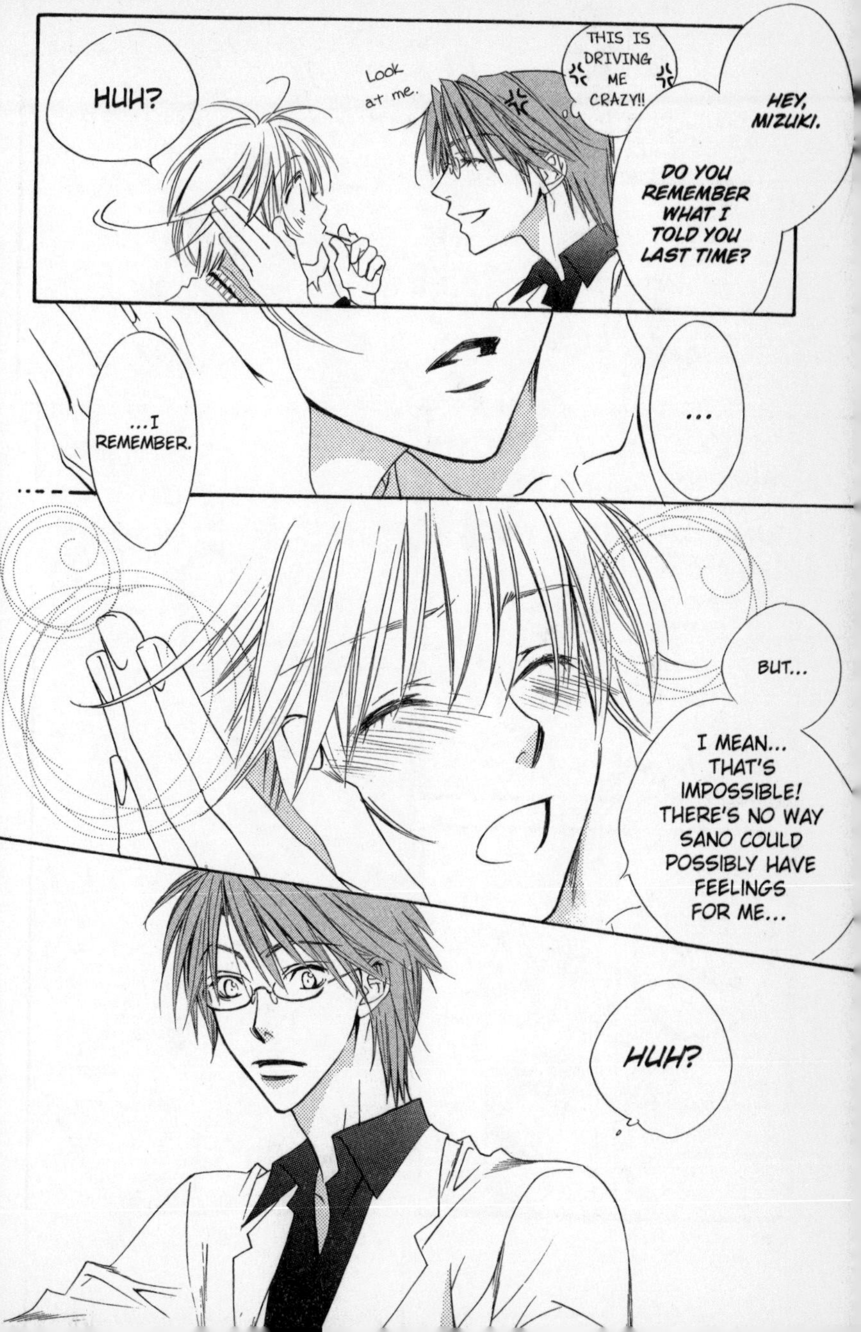
HEY, MIZUKI.
DO YOU REMEMBER WHAT I TOLD YOU LAST TIME?
THIS IS DRIVING ME CRAZY!!
Look at me.
HUH?
...
...I REMEMBER.
BUT...
I MEAN... THAT'S IMPOSSIBLE! THERE'S NO WAY SANO COULD POSSIBLY HAVE FEELINGS FOR ME...
HUH?

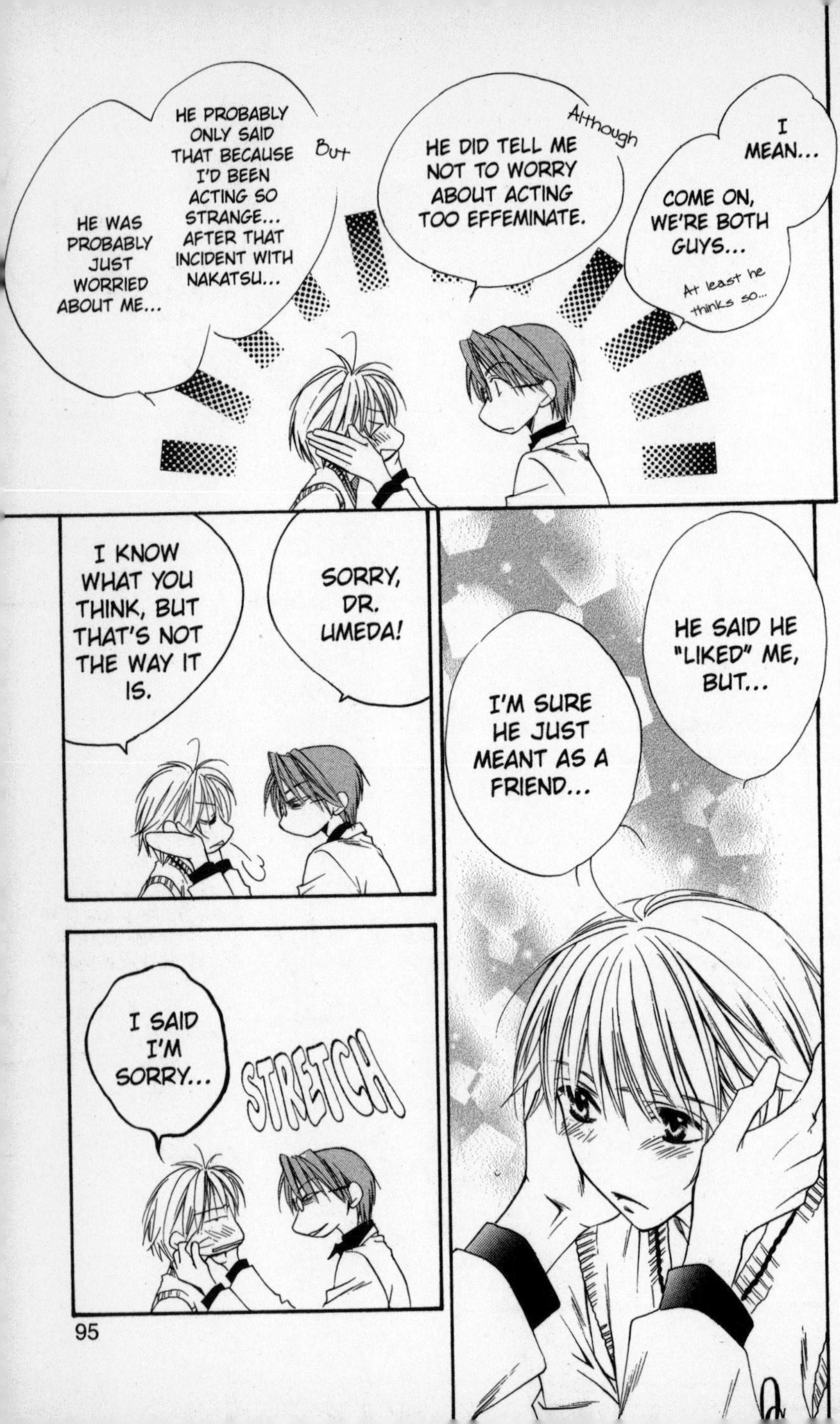
I MEAN...
COME ON, WE'RE BOTH GUYS...
At least he thinks so...
Although
HE DID TELL ME NOT TO WORRY ABOUT ACTING TOO EFFEMINATE.
But
HE PROBABLY ONLY SAID THAT BECAUSE I'D BEEN ACTING SO STRANGE... AFTER THAT INCIDENT WITH NAKATSU...
HE WAS PROBABLY JUST WORRIED ABOUT ME...
HE SAID HE "LIKED" ME, BUT...
I'M SURE HE JUST MEANT AS A FRIEND...
SORRY, DR. UMEDA!
I KNOW WHAT YOU THINK, BUT THAT'S NOT THE WAY IT IS.
I SAID I'M SORRY...
STRETCH

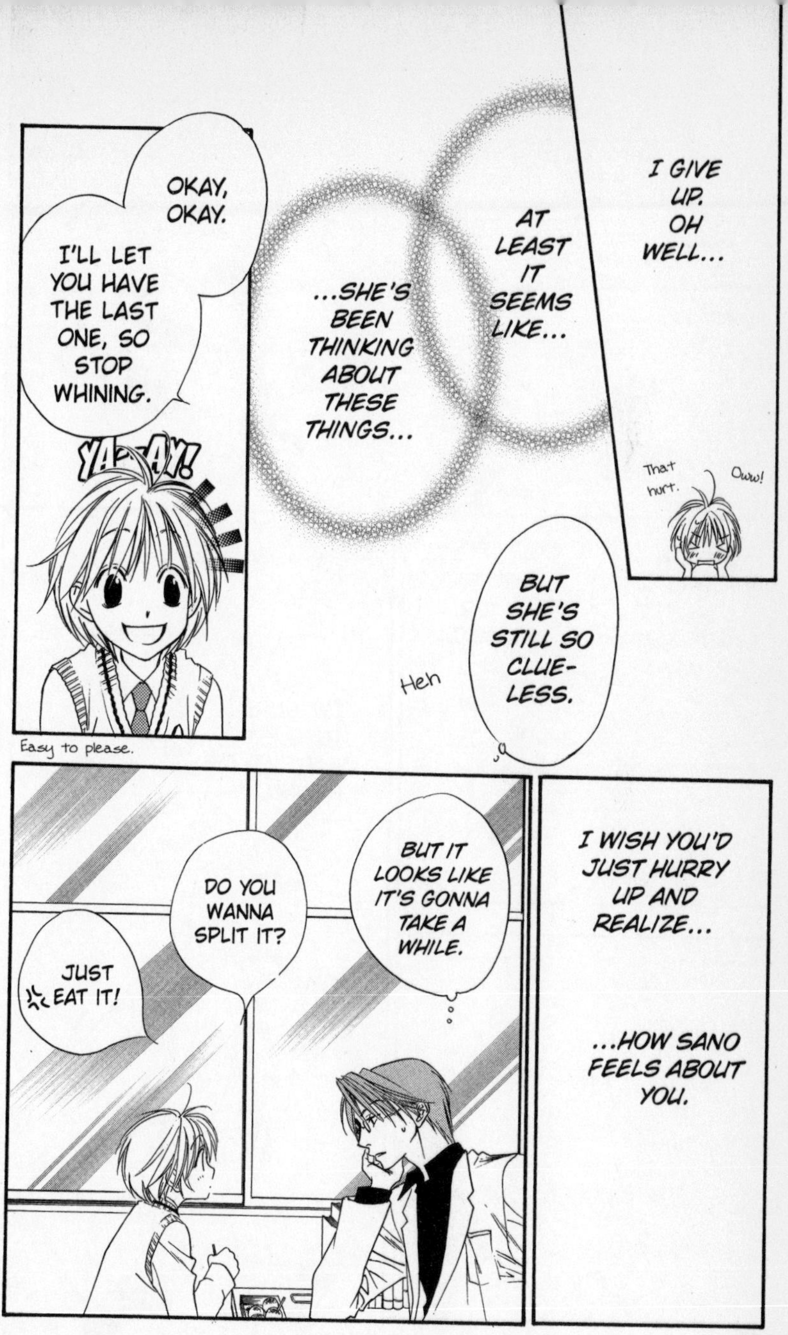
I GIVE UP. OH WELL...
That hurt.
Oww!
AT LEAST IT SEEMS LIKE...
...SHE'S BEEN THINKING ABOUT THESE THINGS...
OKAY, OKAY.
I'LL LET YOU HAVE THE LAST ONE, SO STOP WHINING.
BUT SHE'S STILL SO CLUELESS.
Heh
Easy to please.
I WISH YOU'D JUST HURRY UP AND REALIZE...
...HOW SANO FEELS ABOUT YOU.
BUT IT LOOKS LIKE IT'S GONNA TAKE A WHILE.
DO YOU WANNA SPLIT IT?
JUST EAT IT!

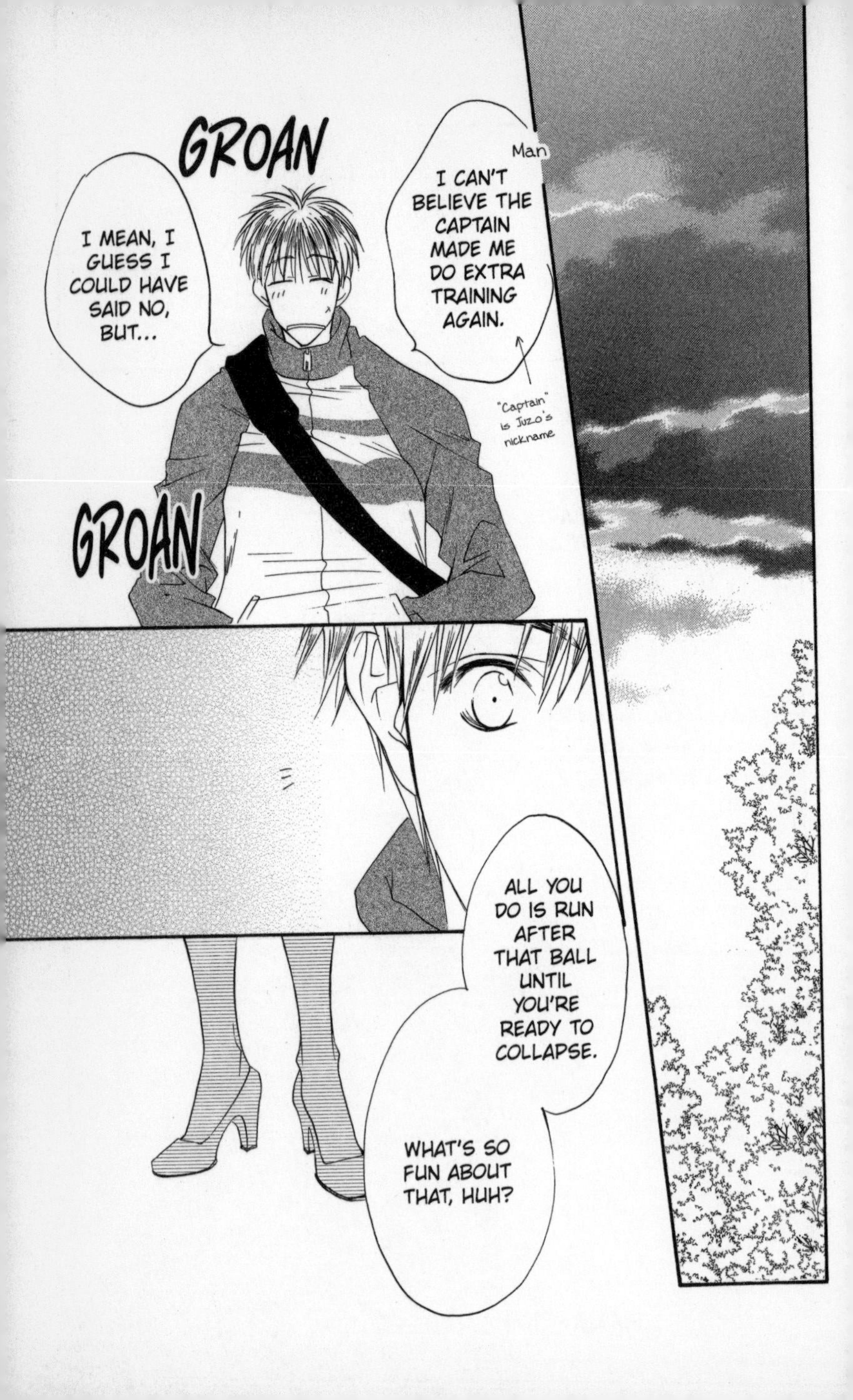
Man
I CAN'T BELIEVE THE CAPTAIN MADE ME DO EXTRA TRAINING AGAIN.
"Captain" is Juzo's nickname
GROAN
I MEAN, I GUESS I COULD HAVE SAID NO, BUT...
GROAN
ALL YOU DO IS RUN AFTER THAT BALL UNTIL YOU'RE READY TO COLLAPSE.
WHAT'S SO FUN ABOUT THAT, HUH?

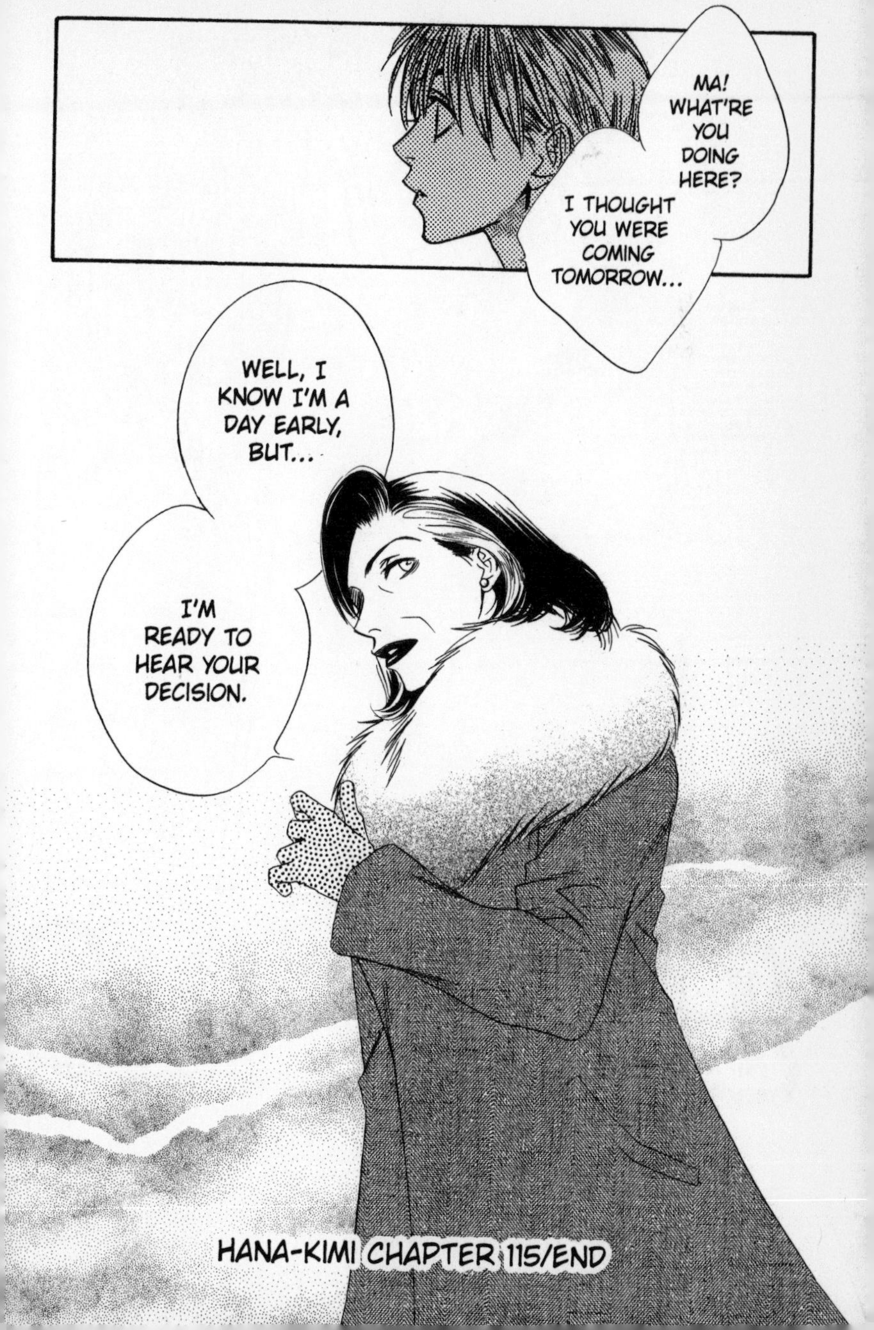
MA! WHAT'RE YOU DOING HERE?
I THOUGHT YOU WERE COMING TOMORROW...
WELL, I KNOW I'M A DAY EARLY, BUT...
I'M READY TO HEAR YOUR DECISION.
HANA-KIMI CHAPTER 115/END

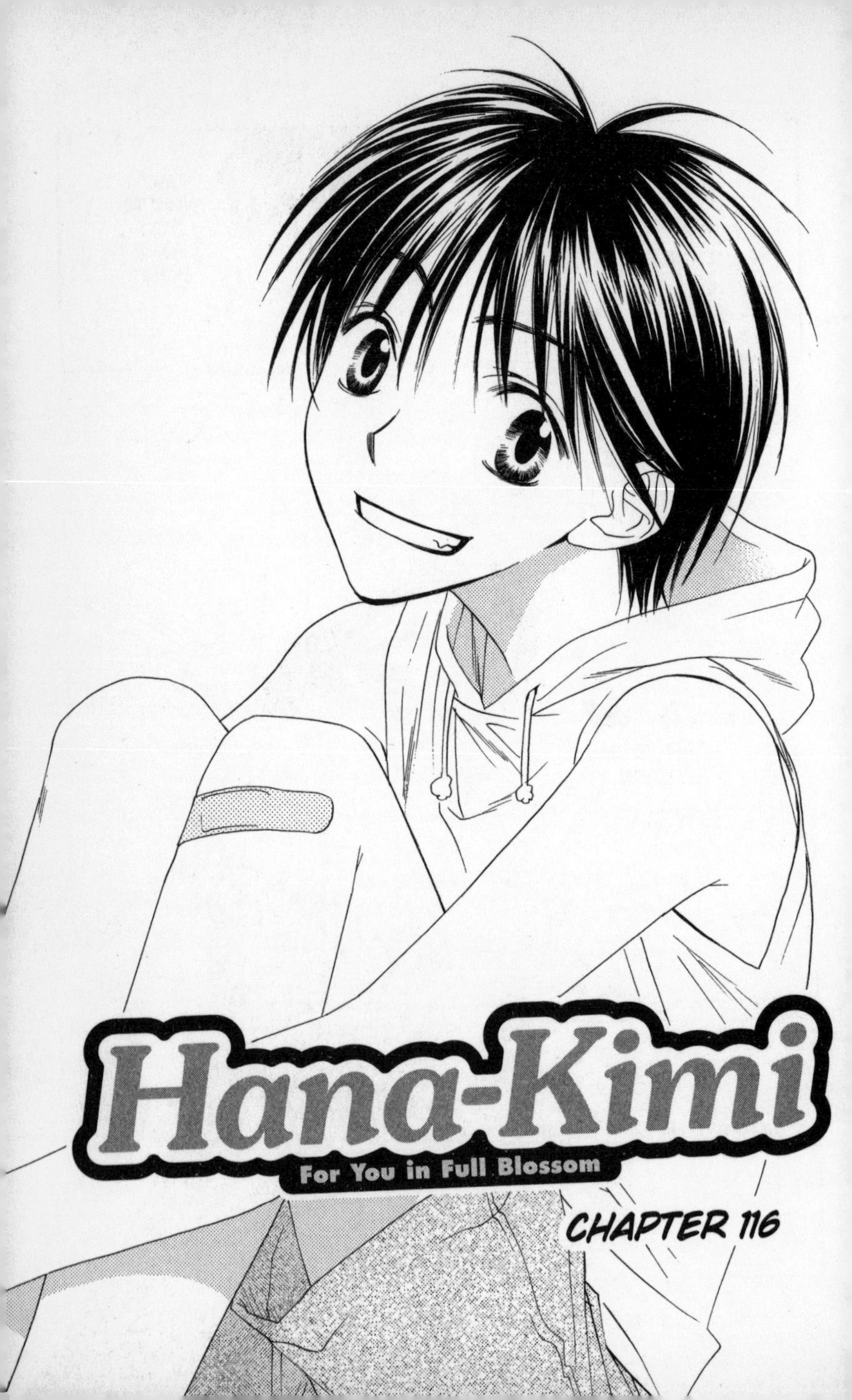
Hana-Kimi
For You in Full Blossom
CHAPTER 116

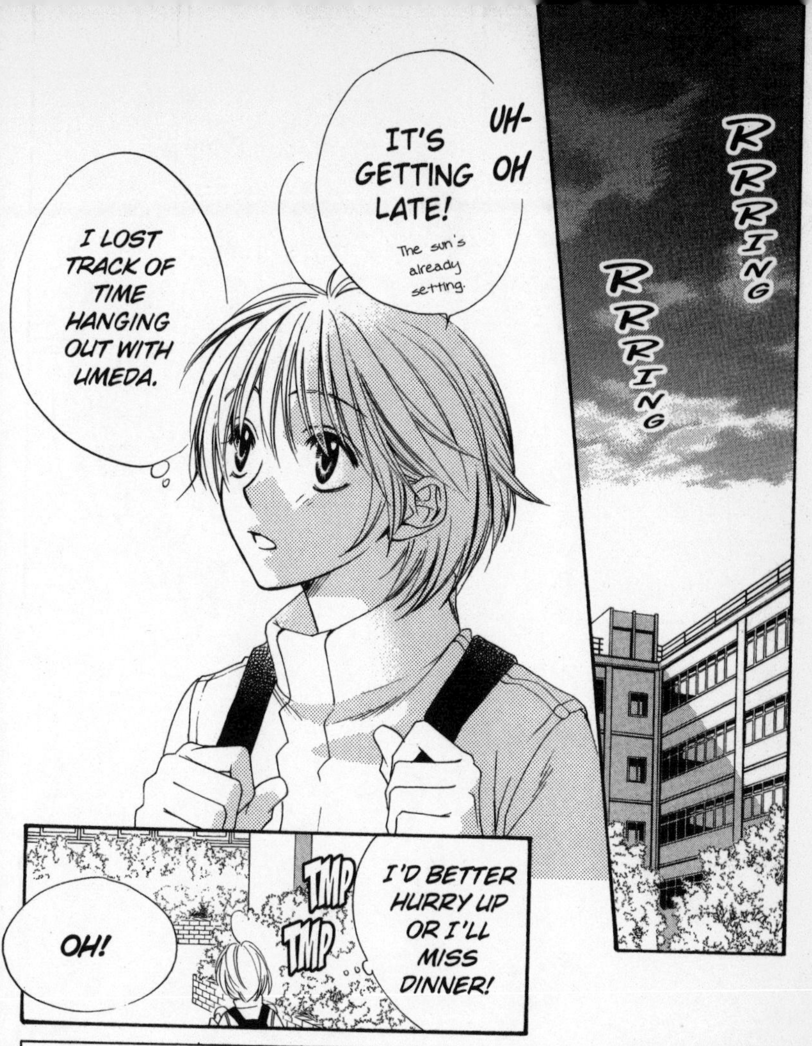
RRRING
RRRING
UH-OH
IT'S GETTING LATE!
The sun's already setting.
I LOST TRACK OF TIME HANGING OUT WITH UMEDA.
I'D BETTER HURRY UP OR I'LL MISS DINNER!
TMP
TMP
OH!

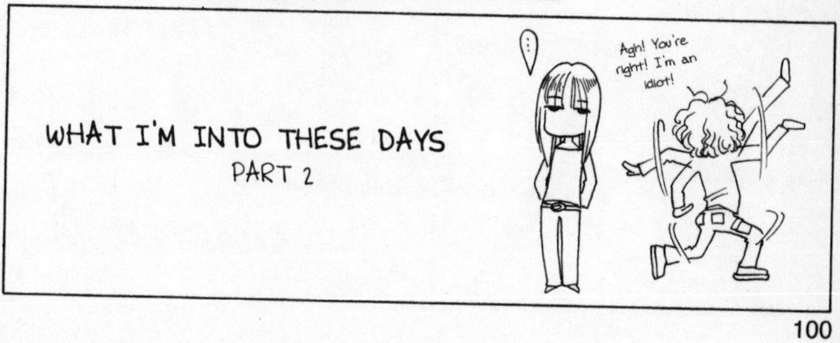
Agh! You're right! I'm an idiot!
WHAT I'M INTO THESE DAYS
PART 2

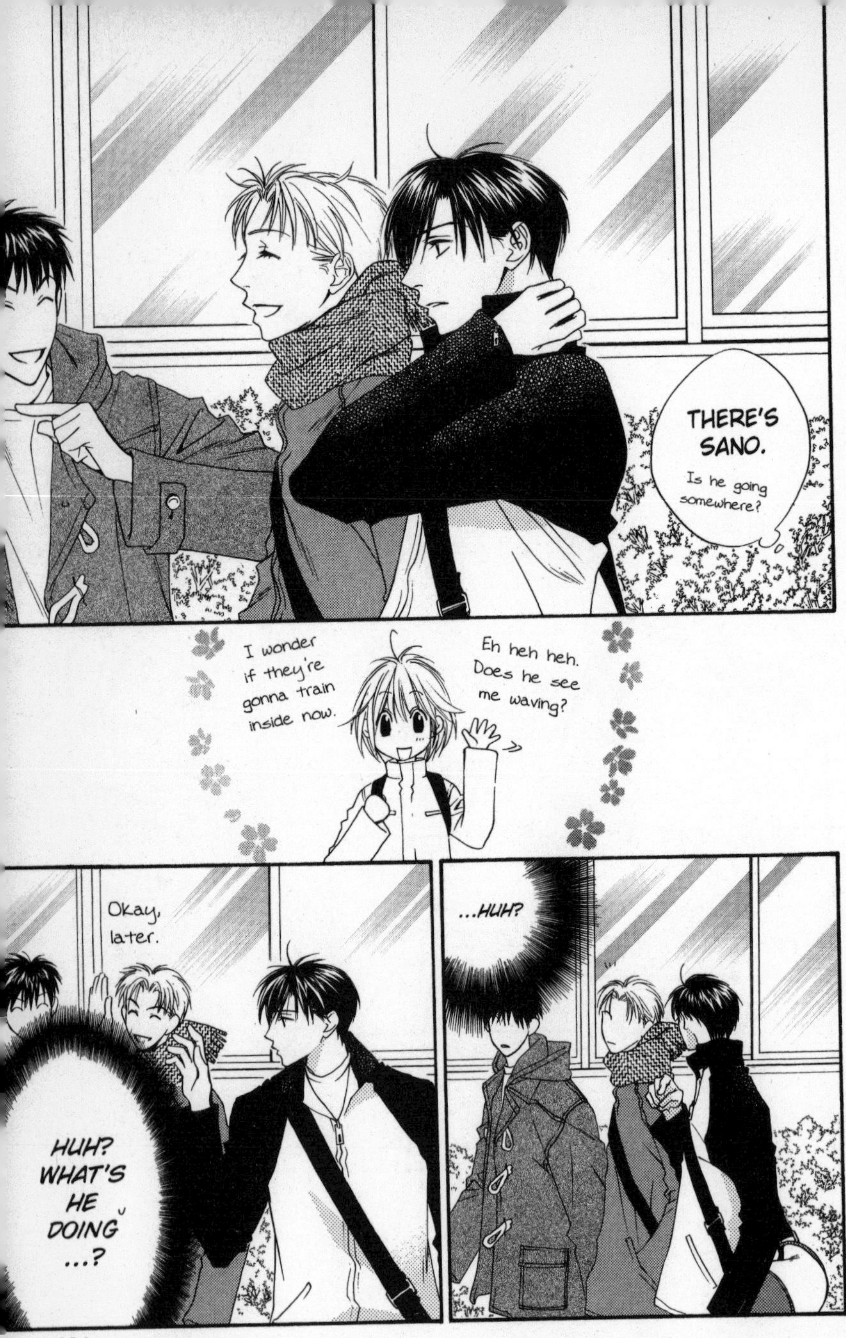
THERE'S SANO.
Is he going somewhere?
Eh heh heh. Does he see me waving?
I wonder if they're gonna train inside now.
...HUH?
Okay, later.
HUH? WHAT'S HE DOING ...?

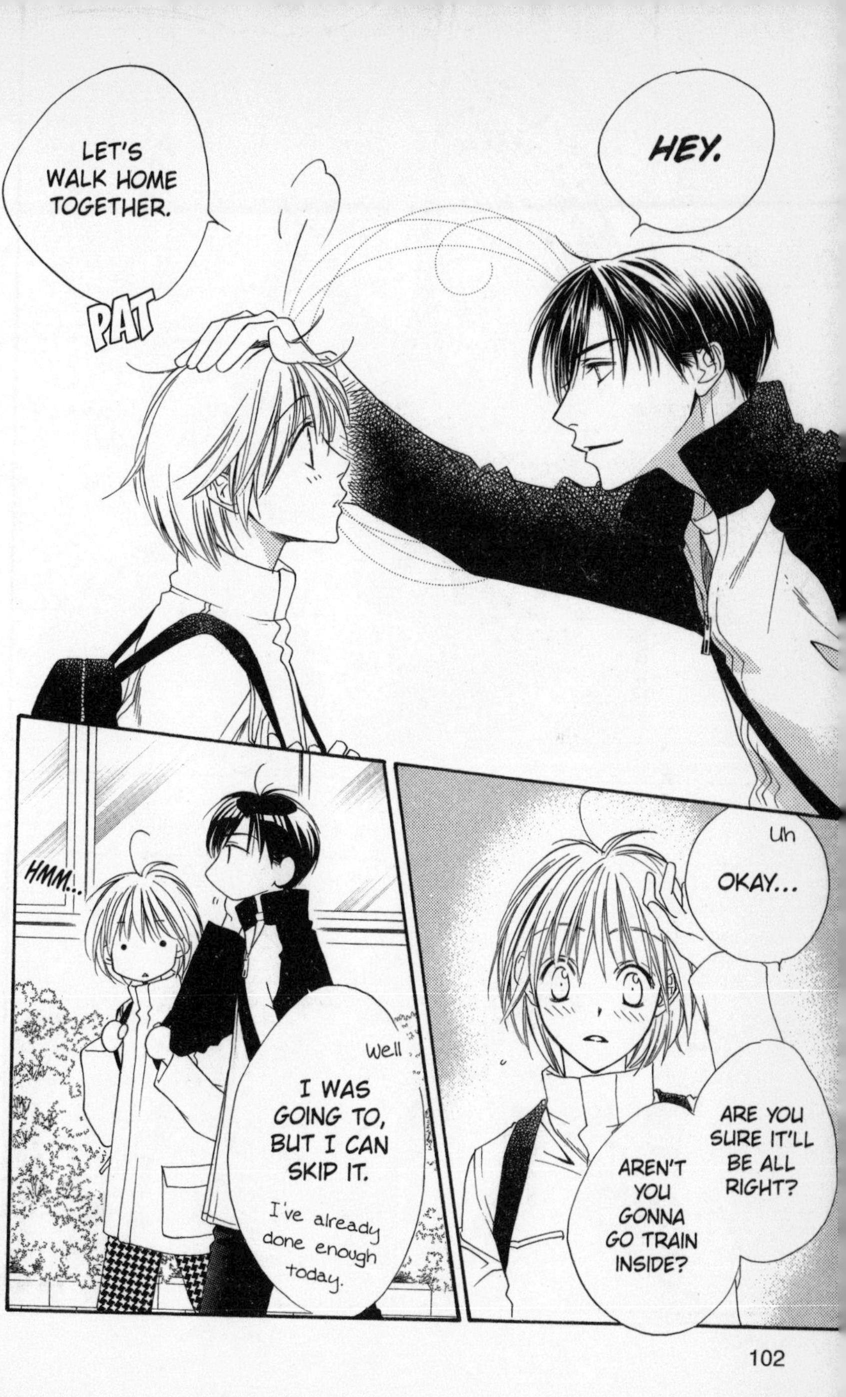
HEY.
LET'S WALK HOME TOGETHER.
PAT
Uh
OKAY...
ARE YOU SURE IT'LL BE ALL RIGHT?
AREN'T YOU GONNA GO TRAIN INSIDE?
HMM...
Well
I WAS GOING TO, BUT I CAN SKIP IT.
I've already done enough today.

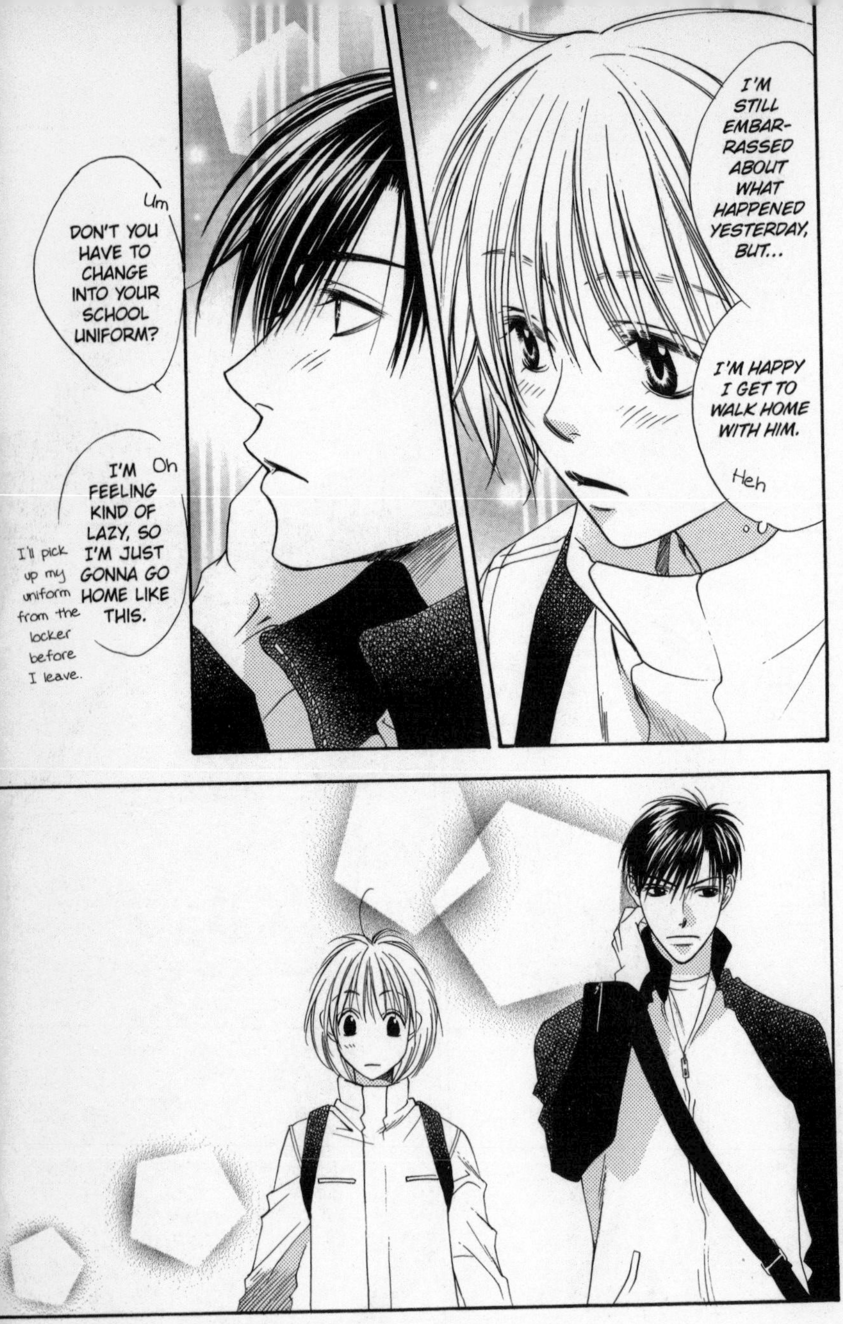
I'M STILL EMBARRASSED ABOUT WHAT HAPPENED YESTERDAY, BUT...
I'M HAPPY I GET TO WALK HOME WITH HIM.
Heh
Um
DON'T YOU HAVE TO CHANGE INTO YOUR SCHOOL UNIFORM?
Oh
I'M FEELING KIND OF LAZY, SO I'M JUST GONNA GO HOME LIKE THIS.
I'll pick up my uniform from the locker before I leave.

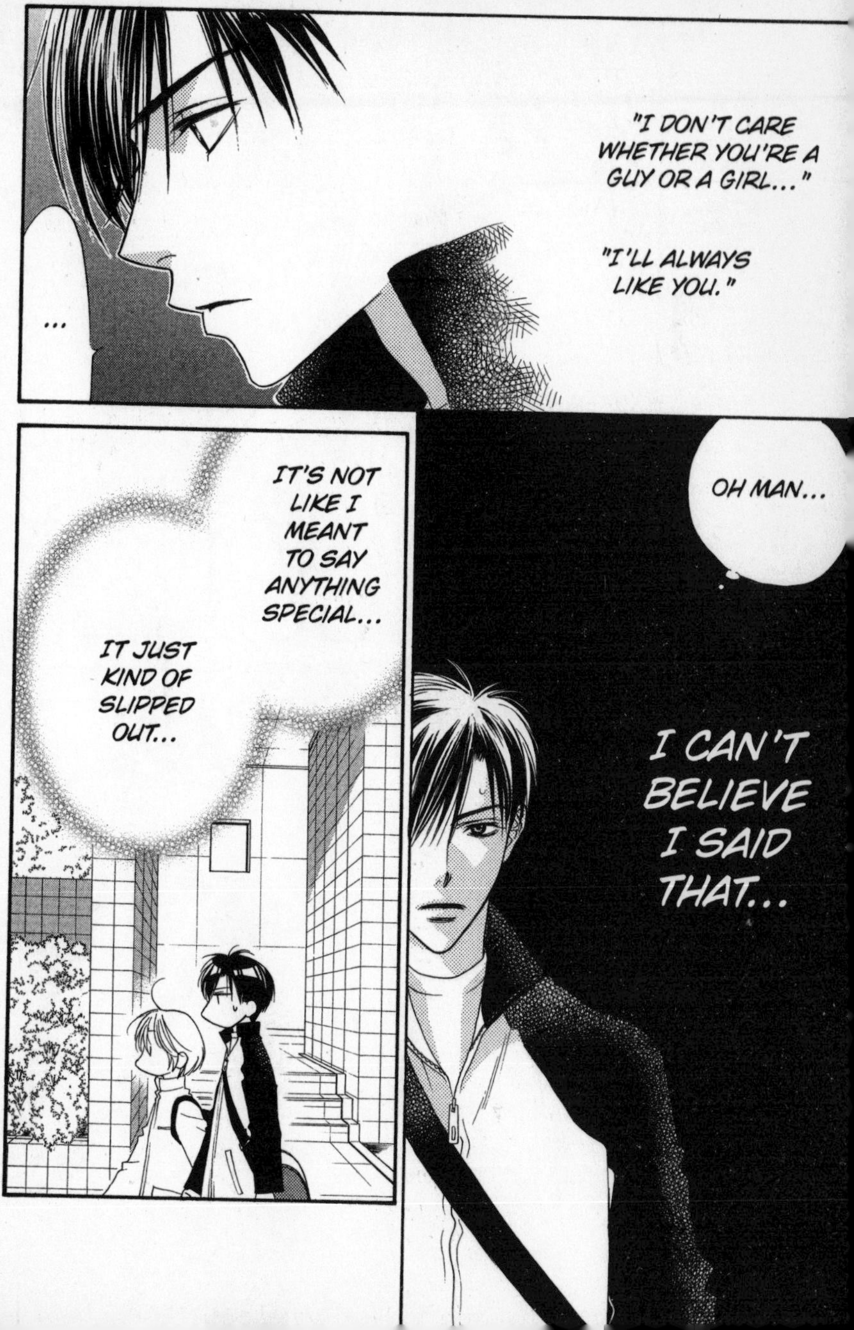
"I DON'T CARE WHETHER YOU'RE A GUY OR A GIRL..."
"I'LL ALWAYS LIKE YOU."
...
OH MAN...
I CAN'T BELIEVE I SAID THAT...
IT'S NOT LIKE I MEANT TO SAY ANYTHING SPECIAL...
IT JUST KIND OF SLIPPED OUT...

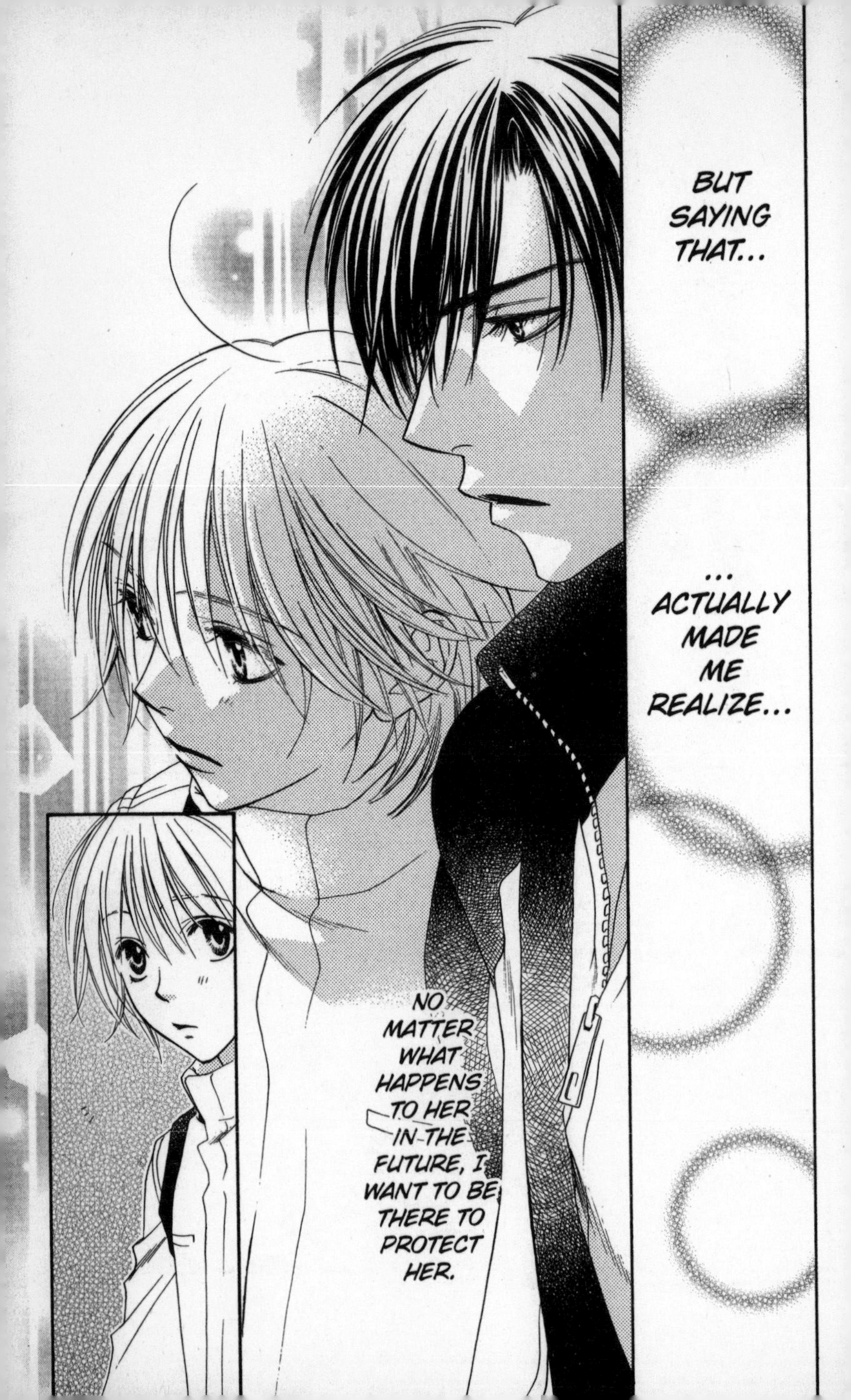
BUT SAYING THAT...
...ACTUALLY MADE ME REALIZE...
NO MATTER WHAT HAPPENS TO HER IN THE FUTURE, I WANT TO BE THERE TO PROTECT HER.

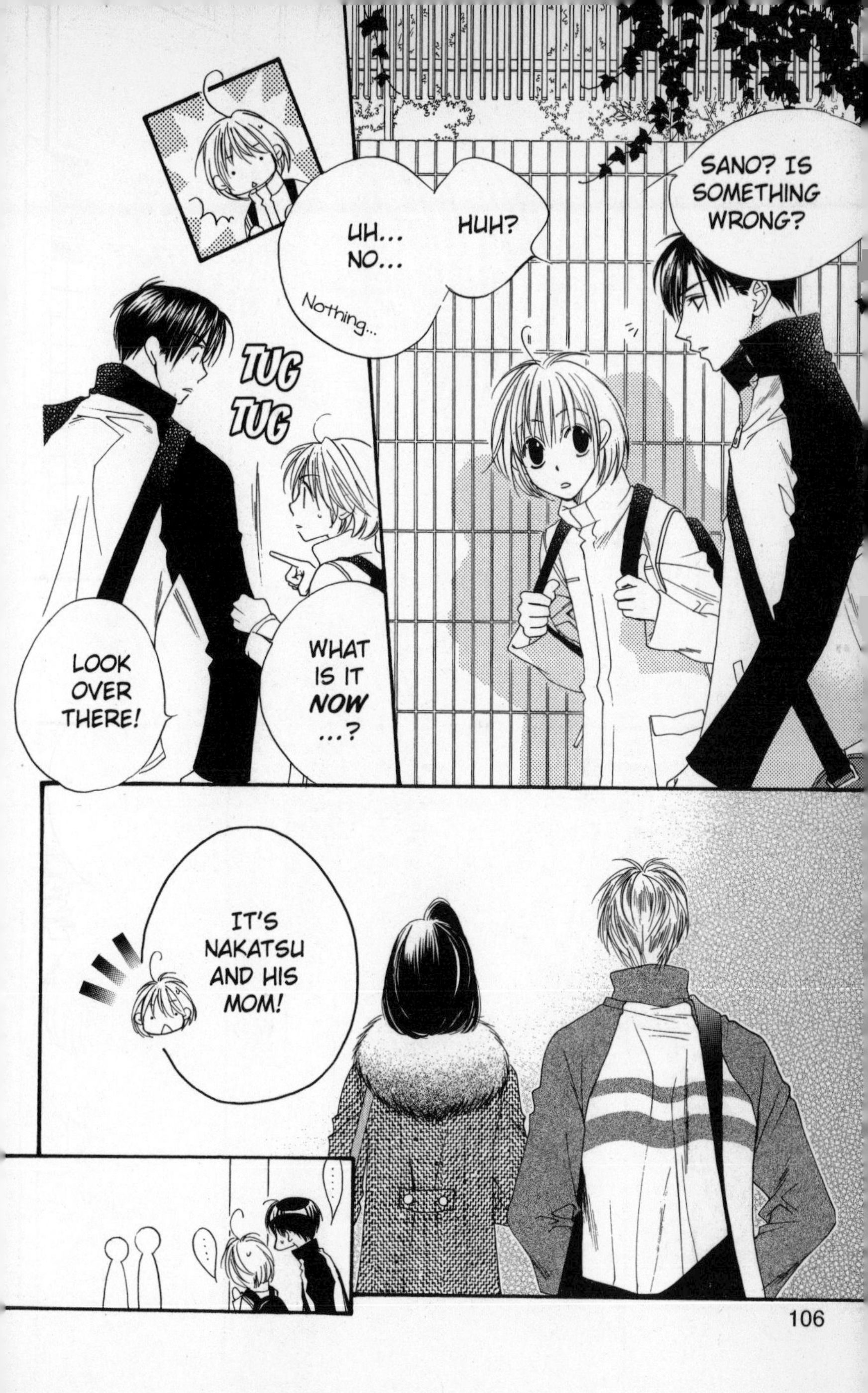
SANO? IS SOMETHING WRONG?
HUH?
UH... NO...
Nothing...
TUG TUG
WHAT IS IT NOW ...?
LOOK OVER THERE!
IT'S NAKATSU AND HIS MOM!

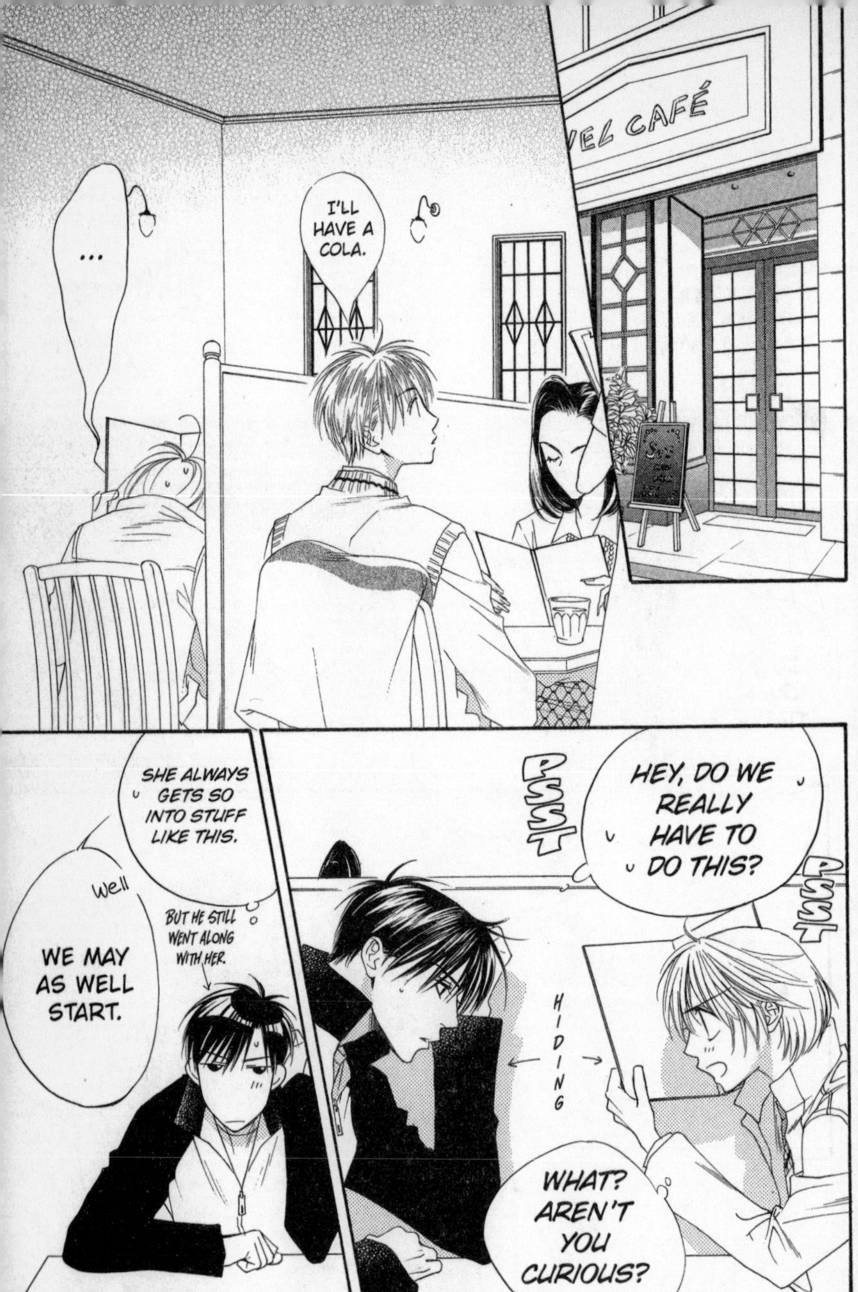
VEL CAFÉ
I'LL HAVE A COLA.
...
PSST
HEY, DO WE REALLY HAVE TO DO THIS?
PSST
HIDING
WHAT? AREN'T YOU CURIOUS?
SHE ALWAYS GETS SO INTO STUFF LIKE THIS.
BUT HE STILL WENT ALONG WITH HER.
Well
WE MAY AS WELL START.

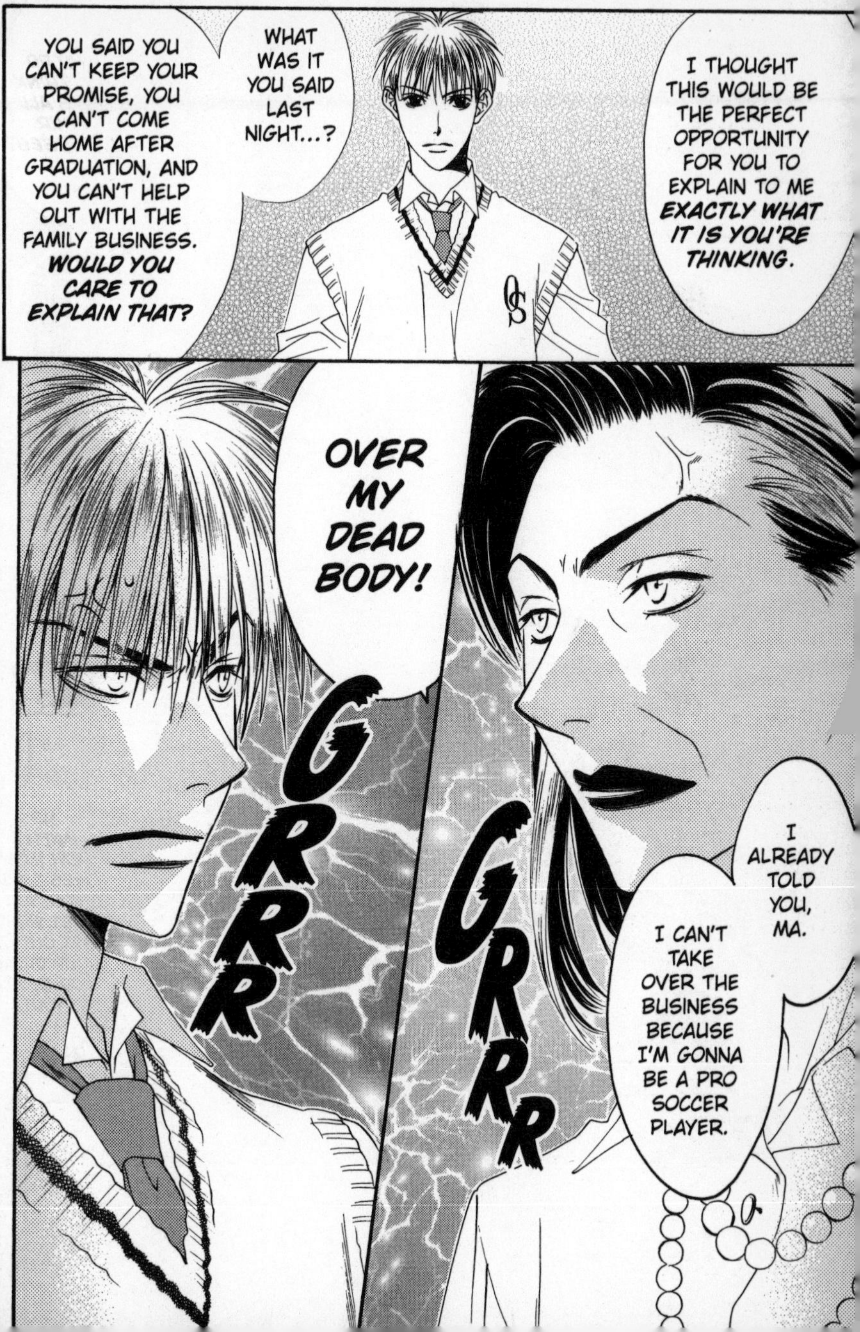
I THOUGHT THIS WOULD BE THE PERFECT OPPORTUNITY FOR YOU TO EXPLAIN TO ME ***EXACTLY WHAT IT IS YOU'RE THINKING.***
WHAT WAS IT YOU SAID LAST NIGHT...?
YOU SAID YOU CAN'T KEEP YOUR PROMISE, YOU CAN'T COME HOME AFTER GRADUATION, AND YOU CAN'T HELP OUT WITH THE FAMILY BUSINESS. ***WOULD YOU CARE TO EXPLAIN THAT?***
I ALREADY TOLD YOU, MA.
I CAN'T TAKE OVER THE BUSINESS BECAUSE I'M GONNA BE A PRO SOCCER PLAYER.
GRRR
OVER MY DEAD BODY!
GRRR

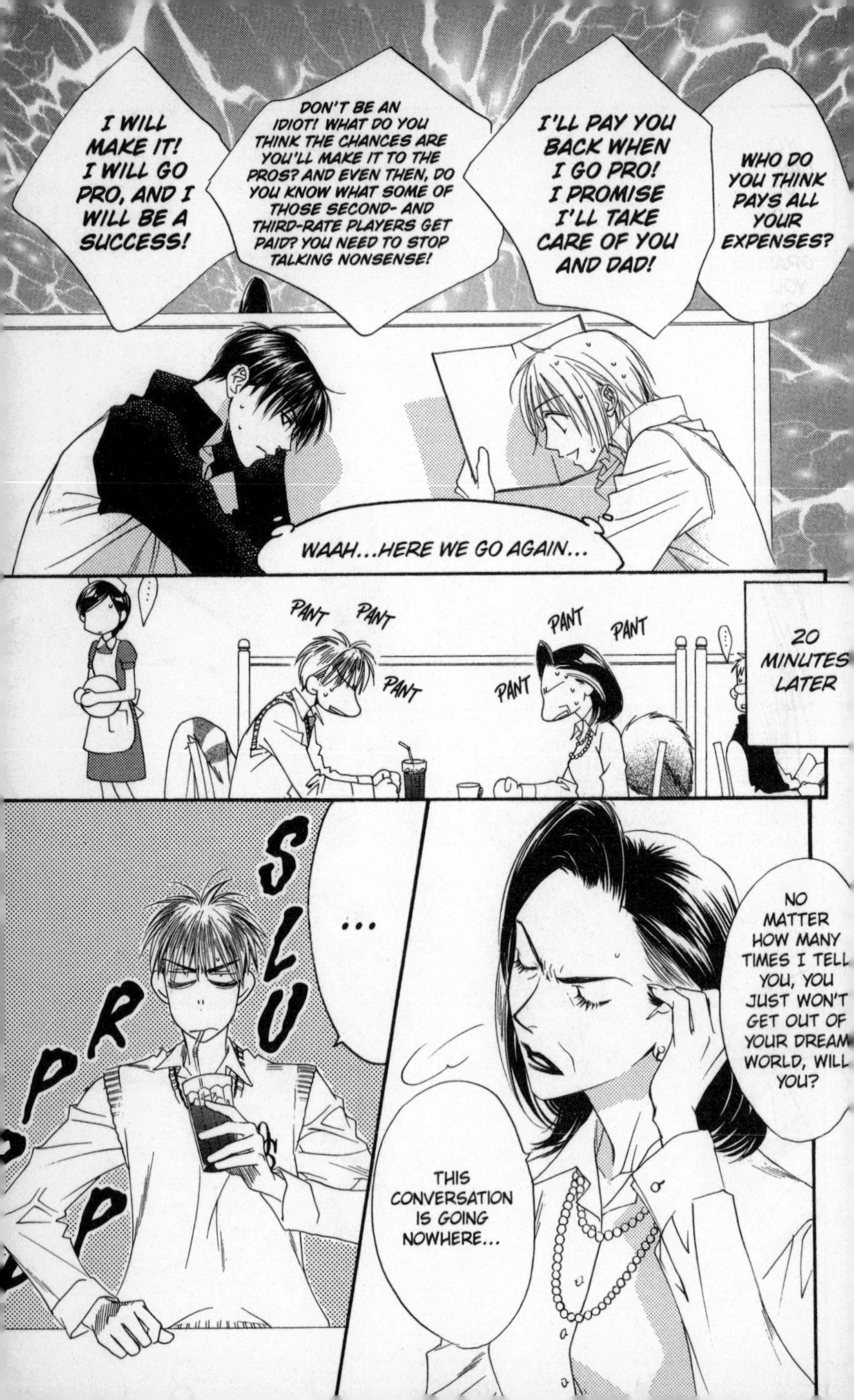

WHO DO YOU THINK PAYS ALL YOUR EXPENSES?
I'LL PAY YOU BACK WHEN I GO PRO! I PROMISE I'LL TAKE CARE OF YOU AND DAD!
DON'T BE AN IDIOT! WHAT DO YOU THINK THE CHANCES ARE YOU'LL MAKE IT TO THE PROS? AND EVEN THEN, DO YOU KNOW WHAT SOME OF THOSE SECOND- AND THIRD-RATE PLAYERS GET PAID? YOU NEED TO STOP TALKING NONSENSE!
I WILL MAKE IT! I WILL GO PRO, AND I WILL BE A SUCCESS!
WAAH...HERE WE GO AGAIN...
20 MINUTES LATER
PANT PANT
PANT
PANT PANT
PANT
NO MATTER HOW MANY TIMES I TELL YOU, YOU JUST WON'T GET OUT OF YOUR DREAM WORLD, WILL YOU?
THIS CONVERSATION IS GOING NOWHERE...
...
SLURPP

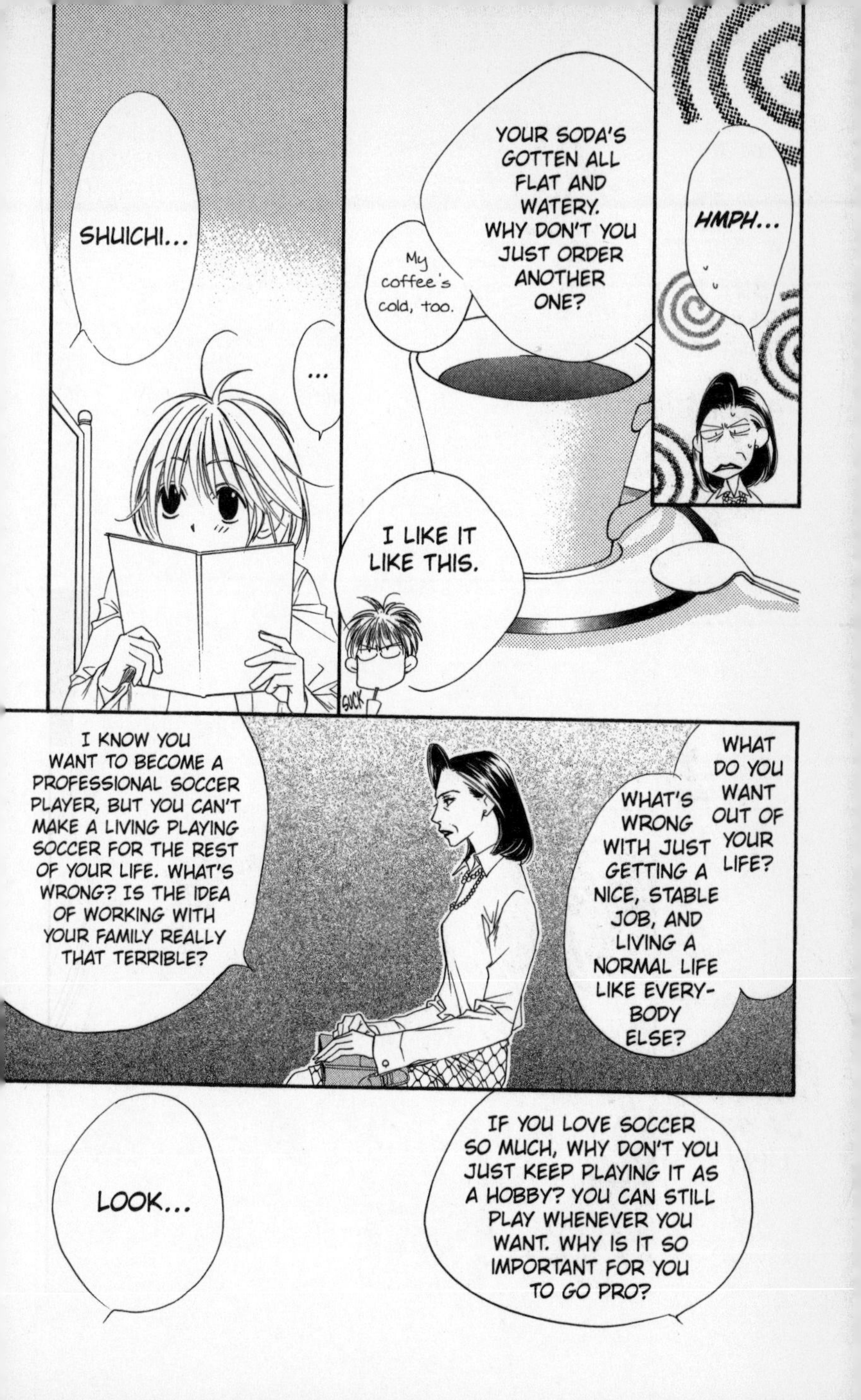
HMPH...
YOUR SODA'S GOTTEN ALL FLAT AND WATERY. WHY DON'T YOU JUST ORDER ANOTHER ONE?
My coffee's cold, too.
I LIKE IT LIKE THIS.
SUCK
SHUICHI...
...
WHAT DO YOU WANT OUT OF YOUR LIFE?
WHAT'S WRONG WITH JUST GETTING A NICE, STABLE JOB, AND LIVING A NORMAL LIFE LIKE EVERY-BODY ELSE?
I KNOW YOU WANT TO BECOME A PROFESSIONAL SOCCER PLAYER, BUT YOU CAN'T MAKE A LIVING PLAYING SOCCER FOR THE REST OF YOUR LIFE. WHAT'S WRONG? IS THE IDEA OF WORKING WITH YOUR FAMILY REALLY THAT TERRIBLE?
IF YOU LOVE SOCCER SO MUCH, WHY DON'T YOU JUST KEEP PLAYING IT AS A HOBBY? YOU CAN STILL PLAY WHENEVER YOU WANT. WHY IS IT SO IMPORTANT FOR YOU TO GO PRO?
LOOK...

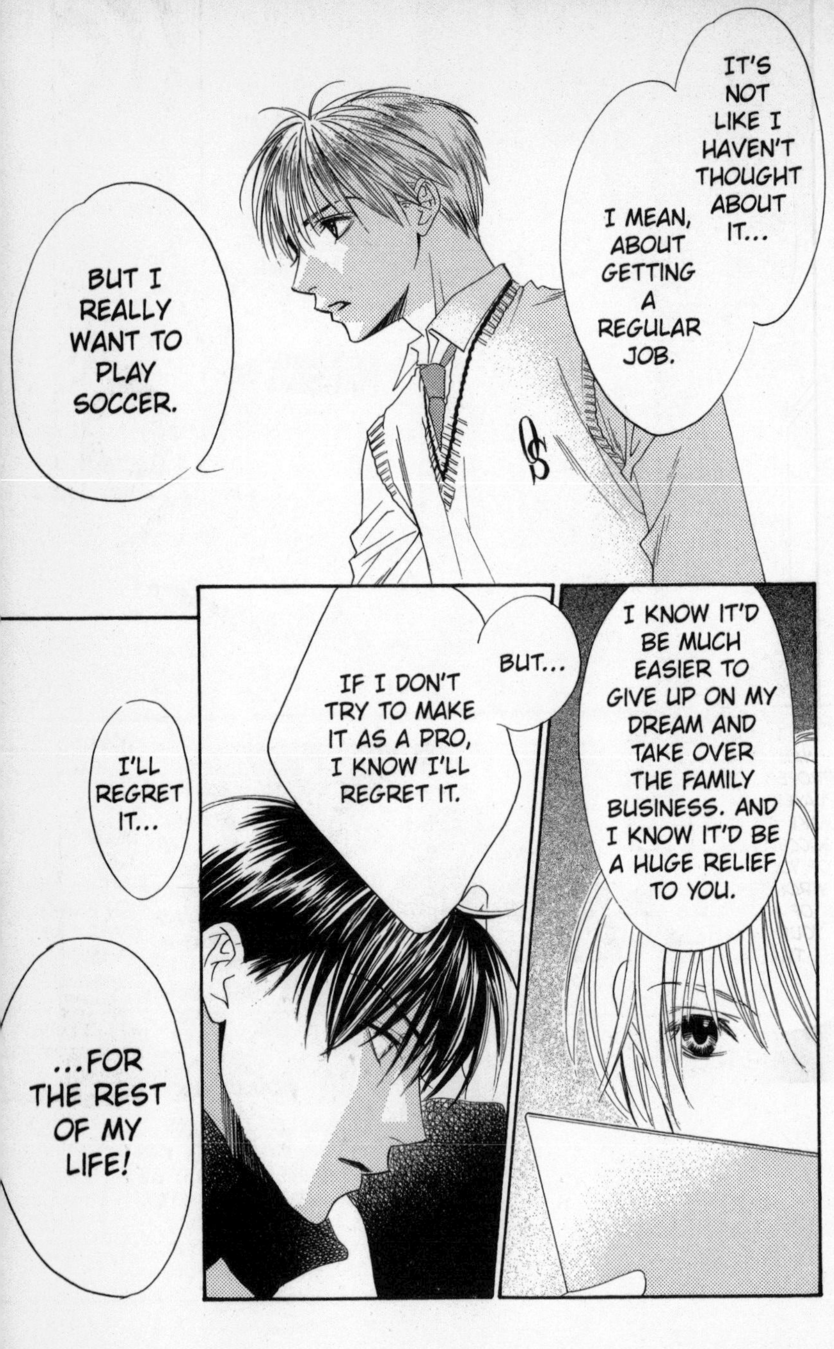
IT'S NOT LIKE I HAVEN'T THOUGHT ABOUT IT...
I MEAN, ABOUT GETTING A REGULAR JOB.
BUT I REALLY WANT TO PLAY SOCCER.
I KNOW IT'D BE MUCH EASIER TO GIVE UP ON MY DREAM AND TAKE OVER THE FAMILY BUSINESS. AND I KNOW IT'D BE A HUGE RELIEF TO YOU.
BUT...
IF I DON'T TRY TO MAKE IT AS A PRO, I KNOW I'LL REGRET IT.
I'LL REGRET IT...
...FOR THE REST OF MY LIFE!

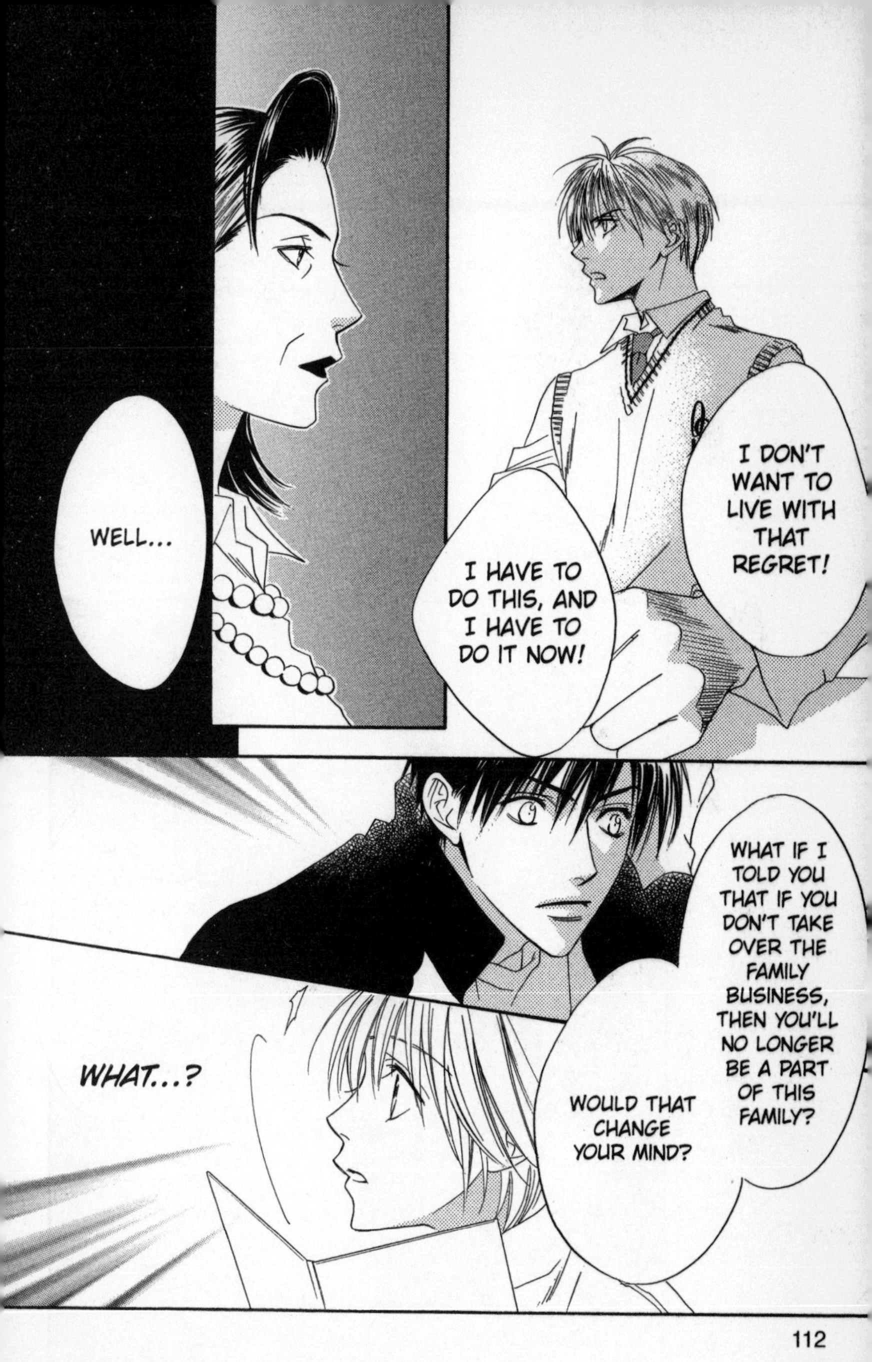
I DON'T WANT TO LIVE WITH THAT REGRET!
I HAVE TO DO THIS, AND I HAVE TO DO IT NOW!
WELL...
WHAT IF I TOLD YOU THAT IF YOU DON'T TAKE OVER THE FAMILY BUSINESS, THEN YOU'LL NO LONGER BE A PART OF THIS FAMILY?
WOULD THAT CHANGE YOUR MIND?
WHAT...?

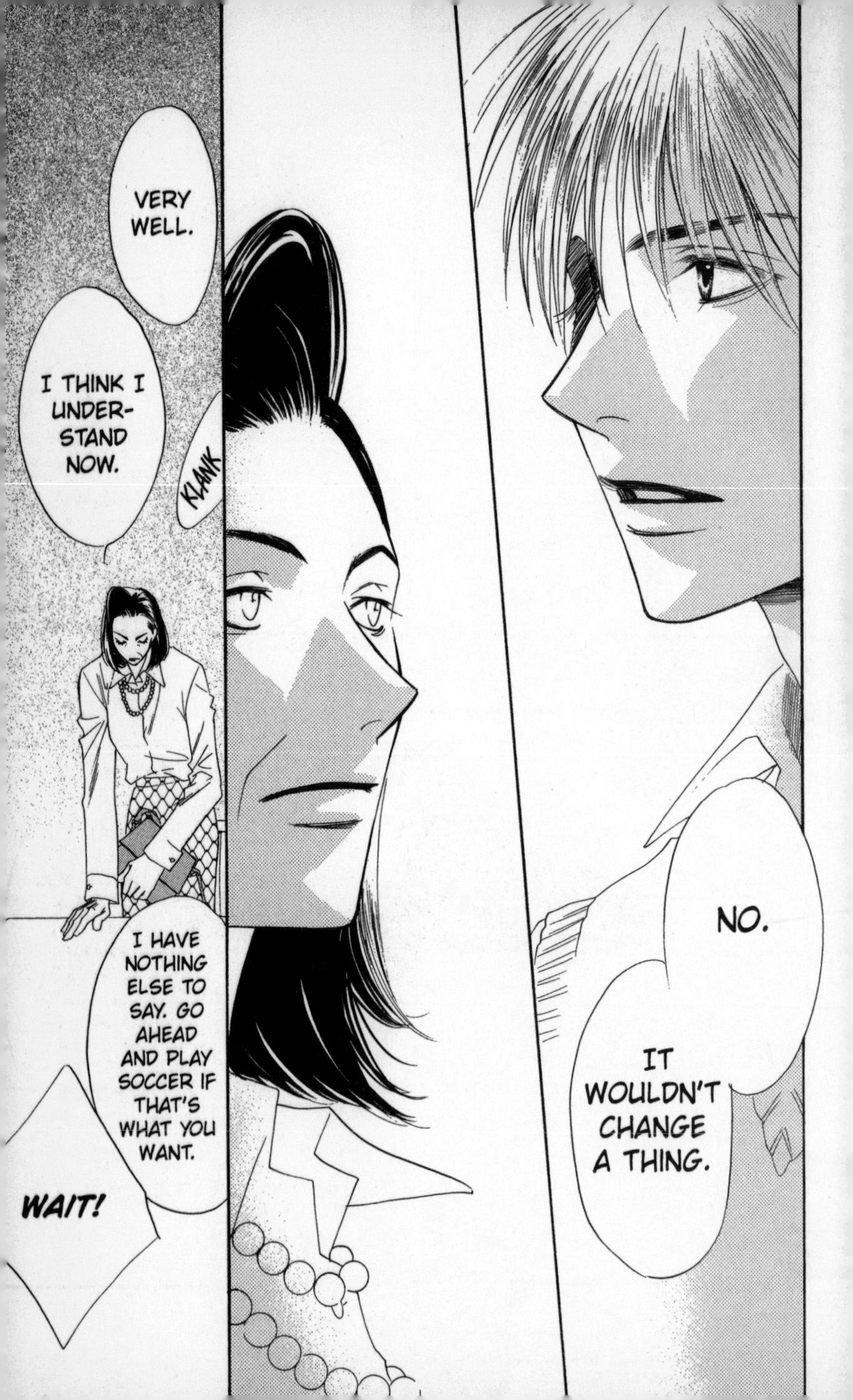
NO.
IT WOULDN'T CHANGE A THING.
VERY WELL.
I THINK I UNDERSTAND NOW.
KLANK
I HAVE NOTHING ELSE TO SAY. GO AHEAD AND PLAY SOCCER IF THAT'S WHAT YOU WANT.
WAIT!

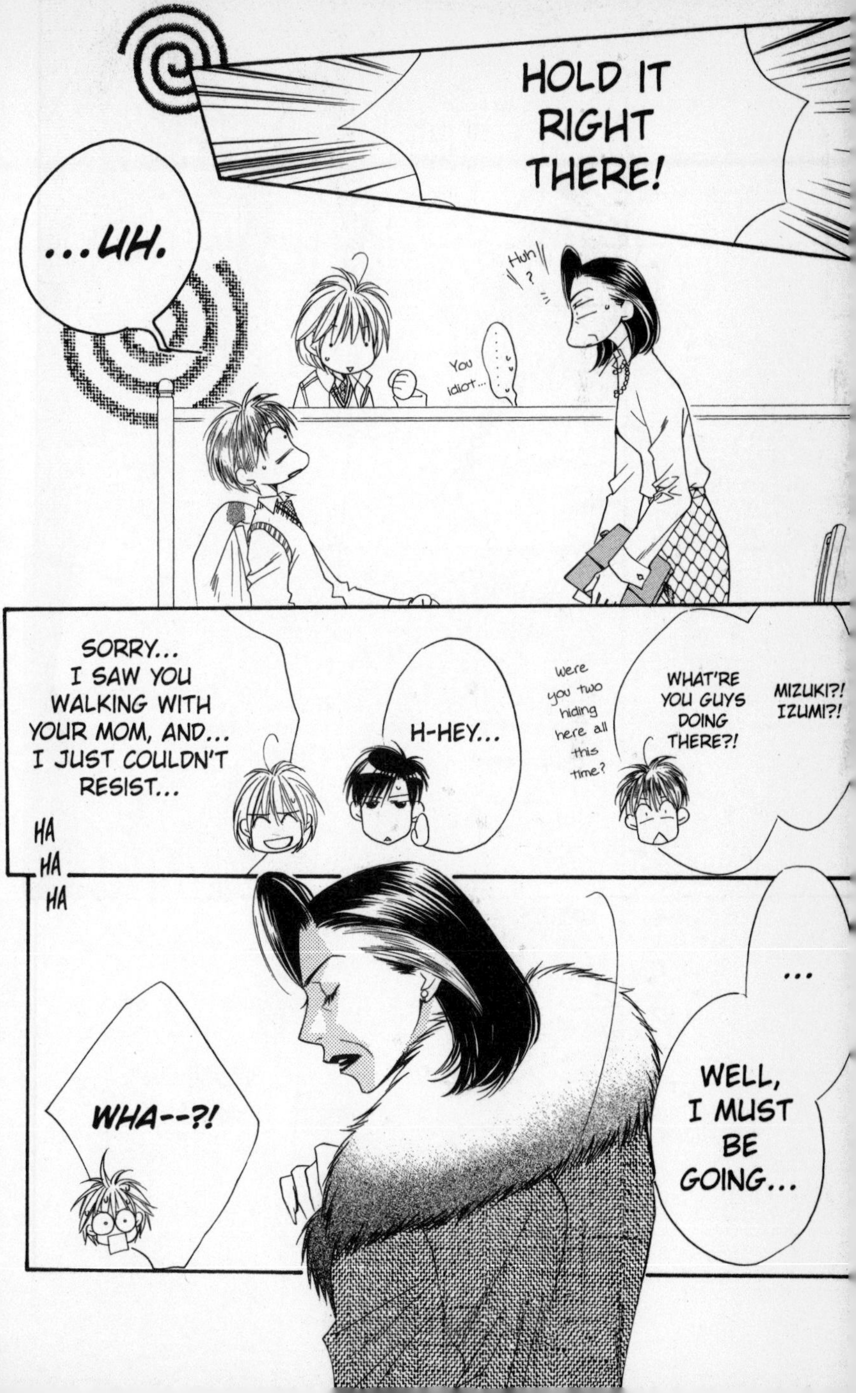
HOLD IT RIGHT THERE!
Huh?
...
You idiot...
...UH.
MIZUKI?! IZUMI?!
WHAT'RE YOU GUYS DOING THERE?!
Were you two hiding here all this time?
H-HEY...
SORRY... I SAW YOU WALKING WITH YOUR MOM, AND... I JUST COULDN'T RESIST...
HA HA HA
...
WELL, I MUST BE GOING...
WHA--?!

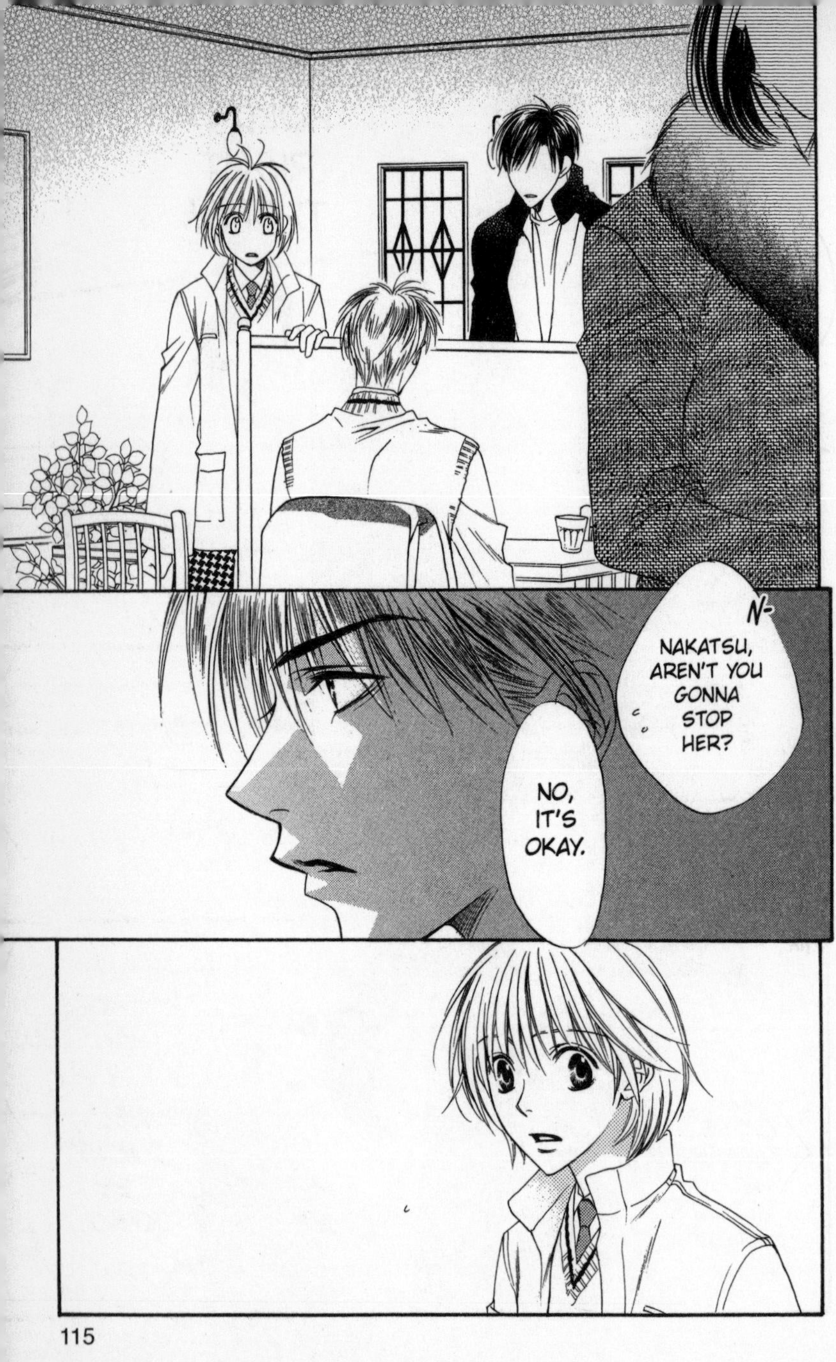
N-
NAKATSU, AREN'T YOU GONNA STOP HER?
NO, IT'S OKAY.

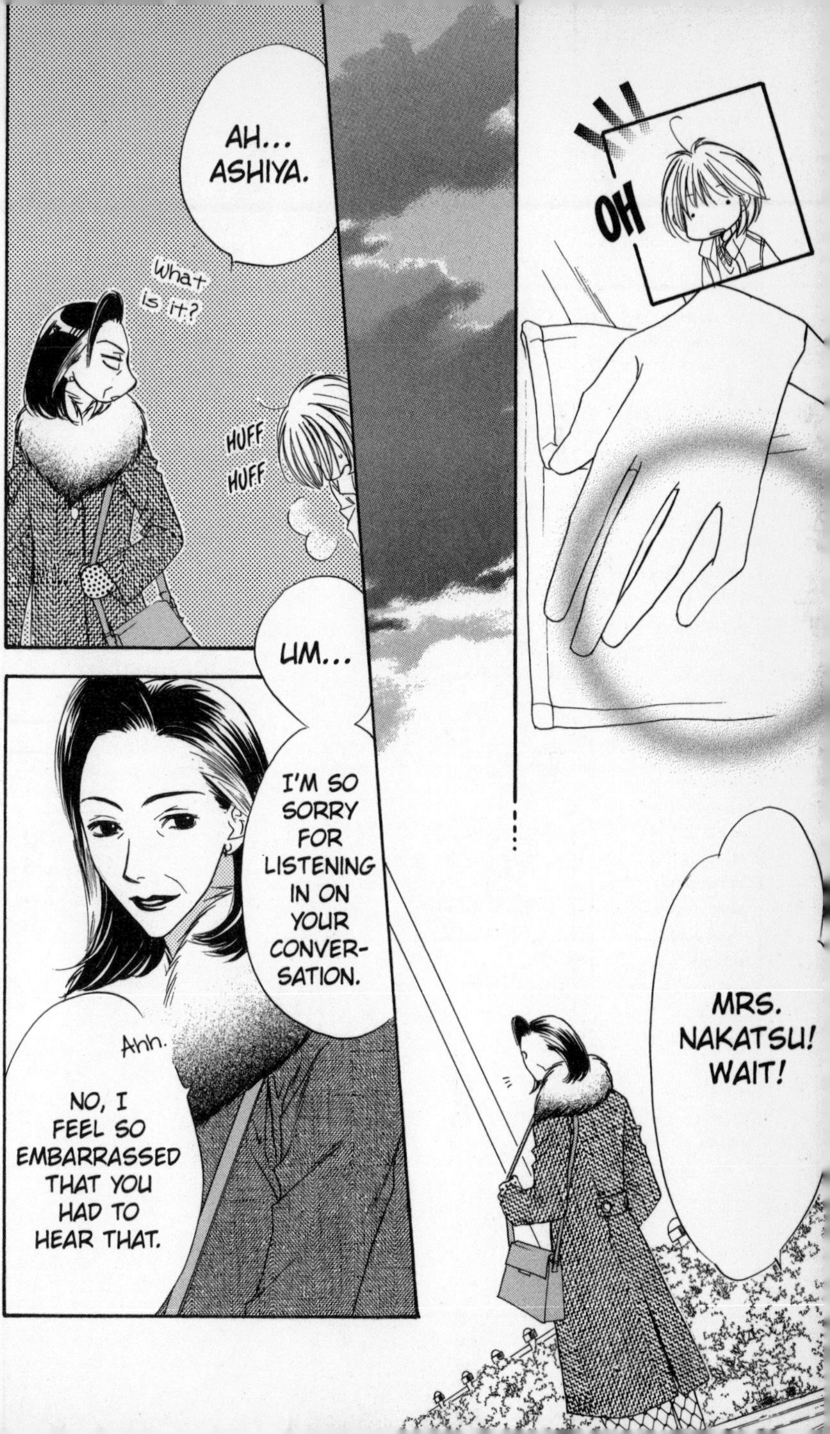
OH
MRS. NAKATSU! WAIT!
AH... ASHIYA.
What is it?
HUFF HUFF
UM...
I'M SO SORRY FOR LISTENING IN ON YOUR CONVER-SATION.
Anh.
NO, I FEEL SO EMBARRASSED THAT YOU HAD TO HEAR THAT.

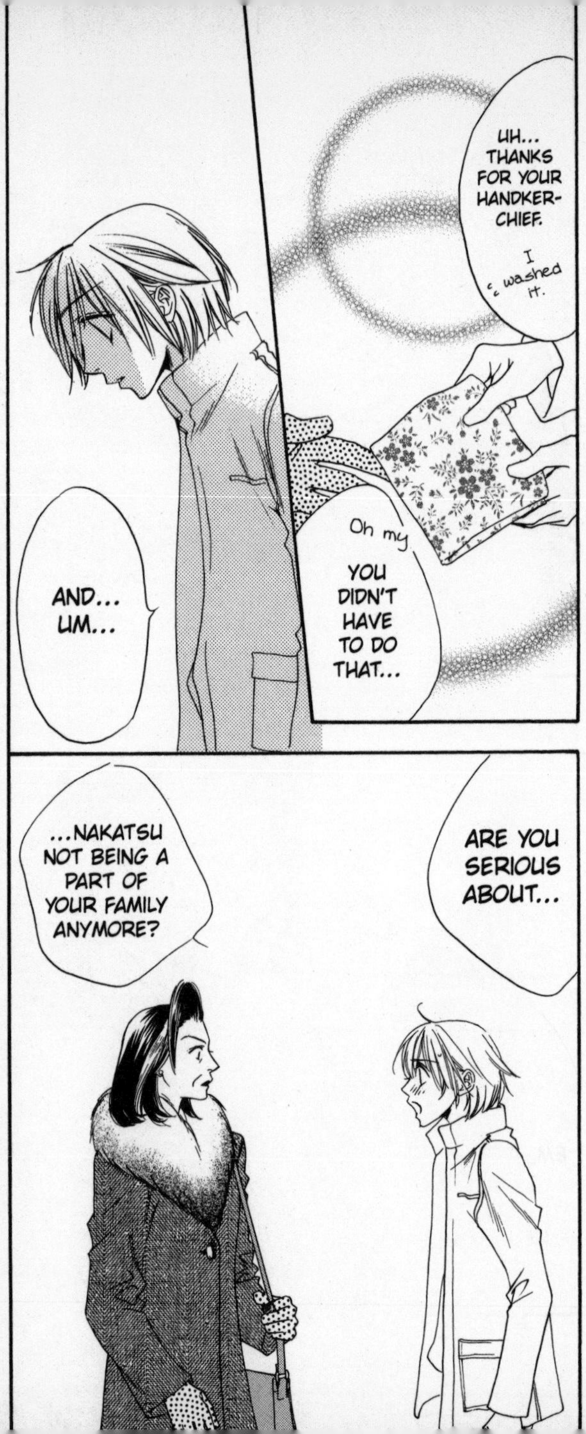
UH... THANKS FOR YOUR HANDKER-CHIEF.
I washed it.
Oh my
YOU DIDN'T HAVE TO DO THAT...
AND... UM...
ARE YOU SERIOUS ABOUT...
...NAKATSU NOT BEING A PART OF YOUR FAMILY ANYMORE?

MY CAT: Part 2

Leon is such a good boy, but he has one problem... He's **terrible** at covering his pee in the litter box. (Ha ha!) Cats normally put sand over their pee when they use the litter box, but all Leon does is scratch the side of the box. The pee starts smelling bad, so Leon tries really hard to put the sand on, but he just keeps scratching the side. I have two litter boxes. Leon uses one when he pees, and uses the other one when he poops...but he always makes a mess. I wonder why. [laughs]

Compared to Sue who's such a handful.

Sometimes I have to give him a hand, and put sand over his pee for him.

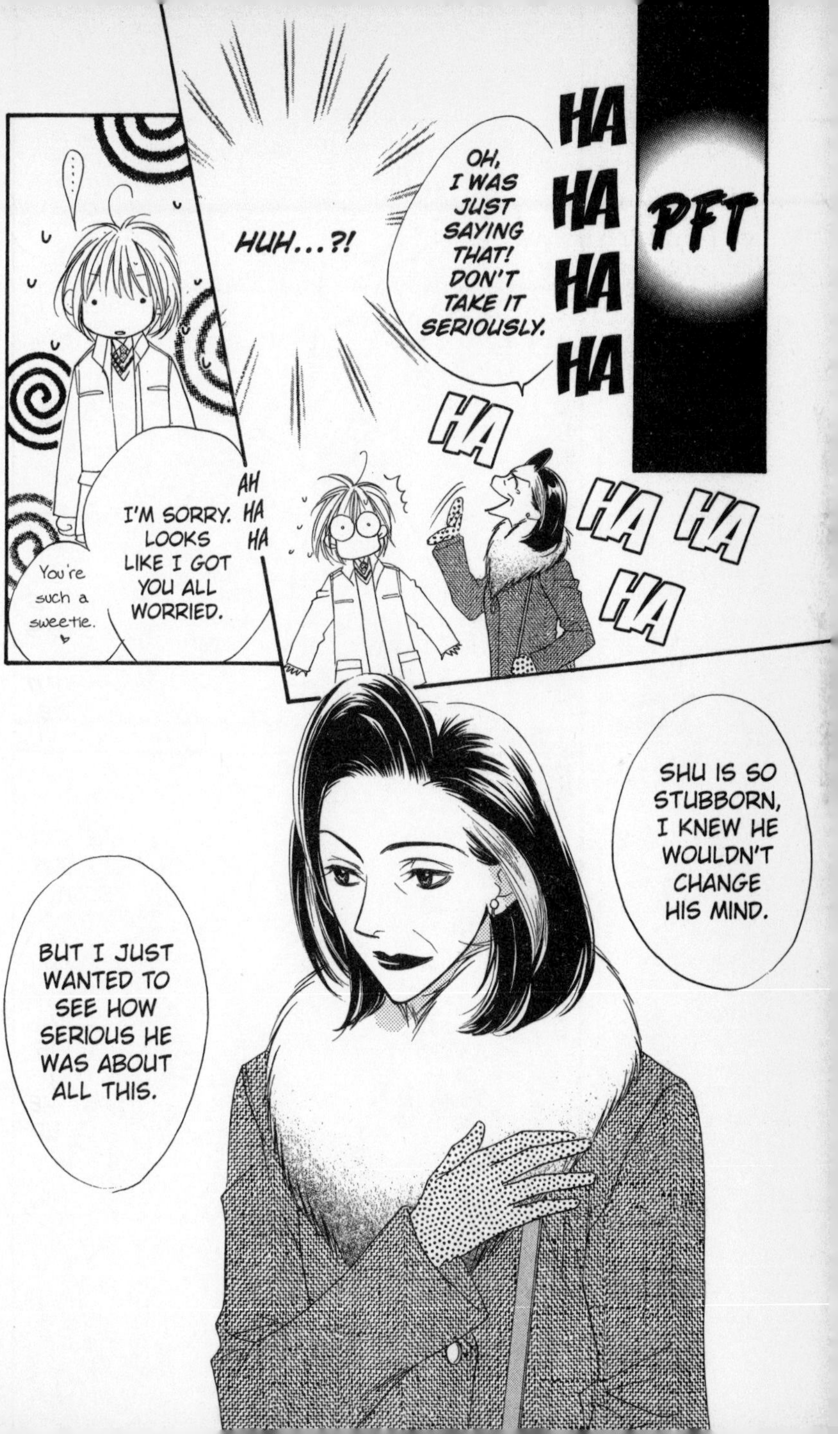
PFT
HA HA HA HA
OH, I WAS JUST SAYING THAT! DON'T TAKE IT SERIOUSLY.
HUH...?!
HA
HA HA HA
...
AH HA HA
I'M SORRY. LOOKS LIKE I GOT YOU ALL WORRIED.
You're such a sweetie.
SHU IS SO STUBBORN, I KNEW HE WOULDN'T CHANGE HIS MIND.
BUT I JUST WANTED TO SEE HOW SERIOUS HE WAS ABOUT ALL THIS.

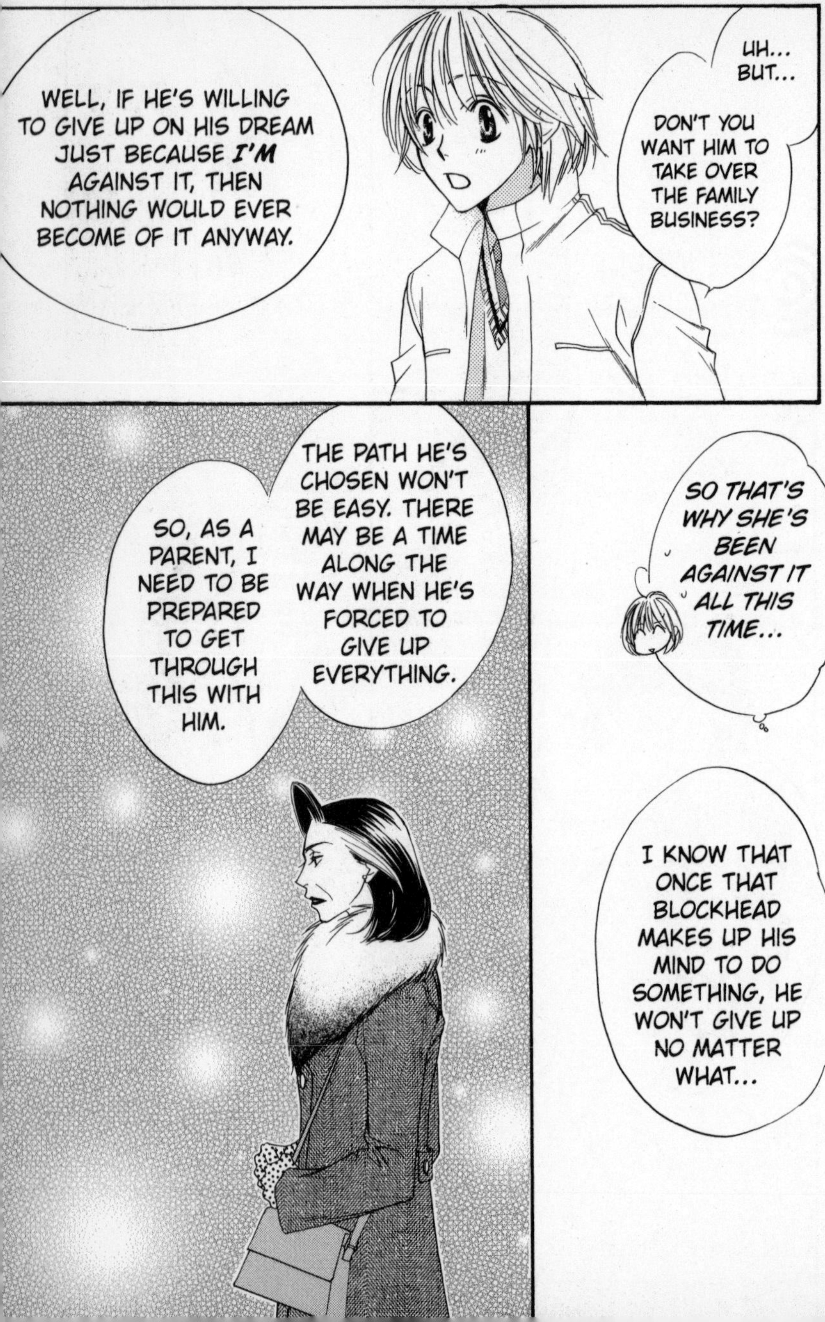
UH... BUT...
DON'T YOU WANT HIM TO TAKE OVER THE FAMILY BUSINESS?
WELL, IF HE'S WILLING TO GIVE UP ON HIS DREAM JUST BECAUSE *I'M* AGAINST IT, THEN NOTHING WOULD EVER BECOME OF IT ANYWAY.
SO THAT'S WHY SHE'S BEEN AGAINST IT ALL THIS TIME...
I KNOW THAT ONCE THAT BLOCKHEAD MAKES UP HIS MIND TO DO SOMETHING, HE WON'T GIVE UP NO MATTER WHAT...
THE PATH HE'S CHOSEN WON'T BE EASY. THERE MAY BE A TIME ALONG THE WAY WHEN HE'S FORCED TO GIVE UP EVERYTHING.
SO, AS A PARENT, I NEED TO BE PREPARED TO GET THROUGH THIS WITH HIM.

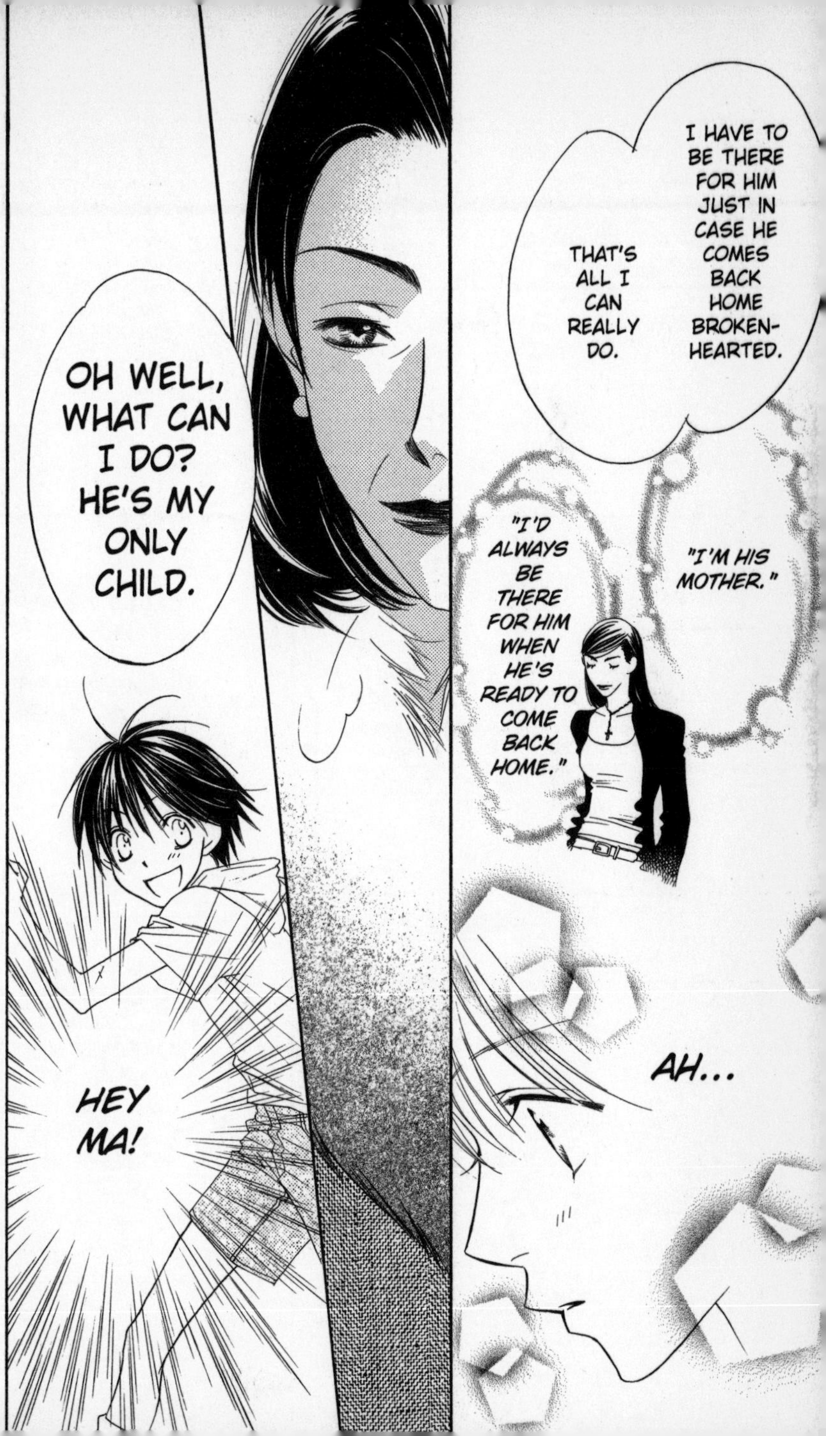
I HAVE TO BE THERE FOR HIM JUST IN CASE HE COMES BACK HOME BROKEN-HEARTED.
THAT'S ALL I CAN REALLY DO.
"I'M HIS MOTHER."
"I'D ALWAYS BE THERE FOR HIM WHEN HE'S READY TO COME BACK HOME."
AH...
OH WELL, WHAT CAN I DO? HE'S MY ONLY CHILD.
HEY MA!

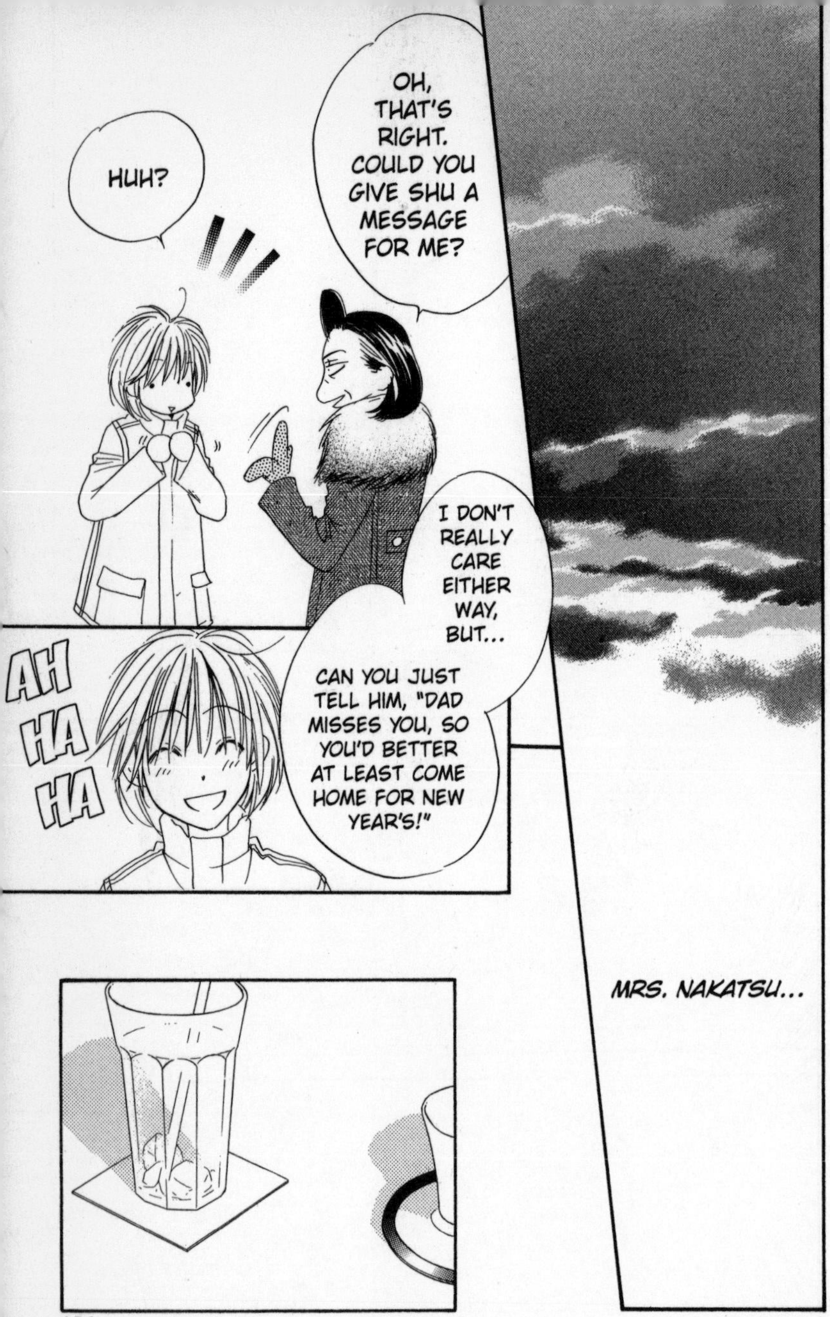

MRS. NAKATSU...
OH, THAT'S RIGHT. COULD YOU GIVE SHU A MESSAGE FOR ME?
HUH?
I DON'T REALLY CARE EITHER WAY, BUT...
CAN YOU JUST TELL HIM, "DAD MISSES YOU, SO YOU'D BETTER AT LEAST COME HOME FOR NEW YEAR'S!"
AH HA HA

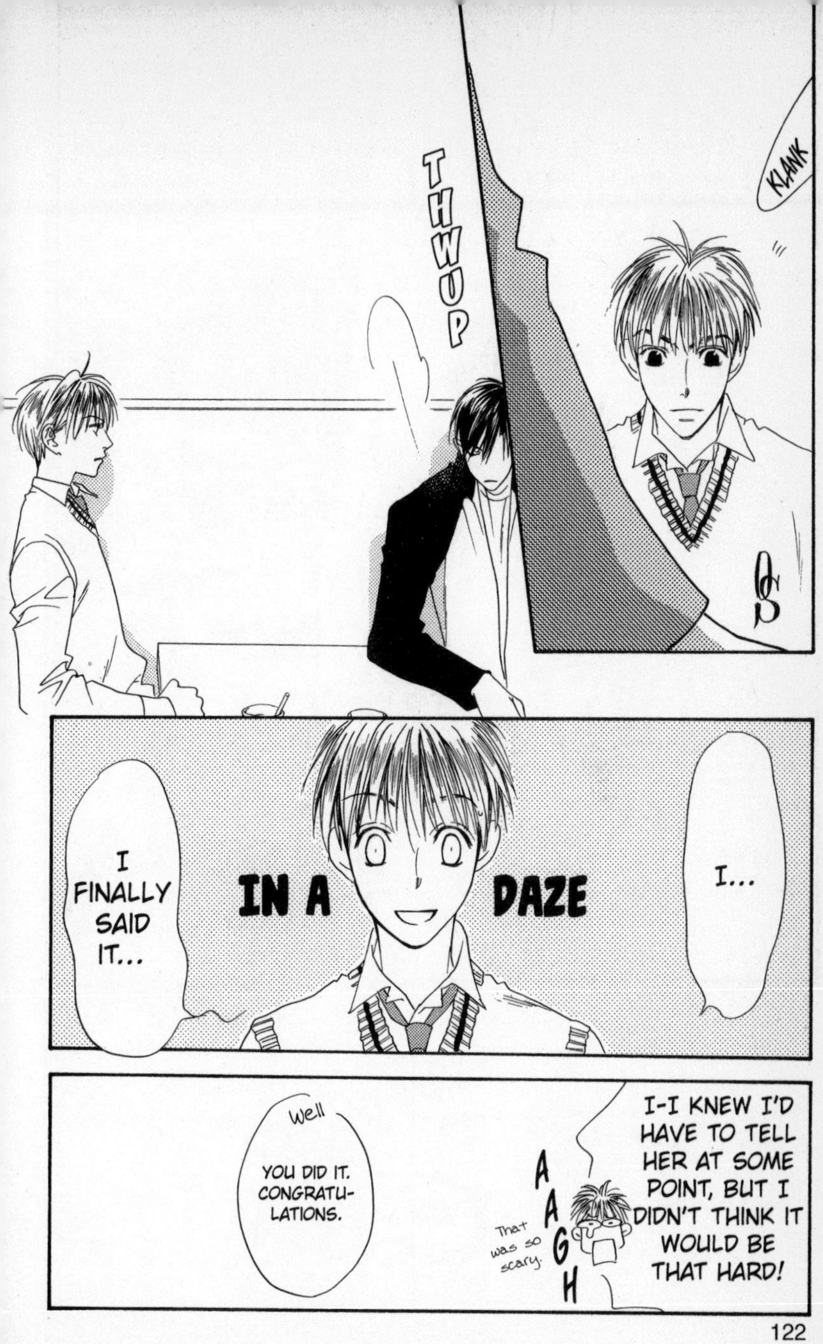
KLANK
THWUP
I...
IN A DAZE
I FINALLY SAID IT...
I-I KNEW I'D HAVE TO TELL HER AT SOME POINT, BUT I DIDN'T THINK IT WOULD BE THAT HARD!
AAGH
That was so scary.
Well
YOU DID IT. CONGRATULATIONS.

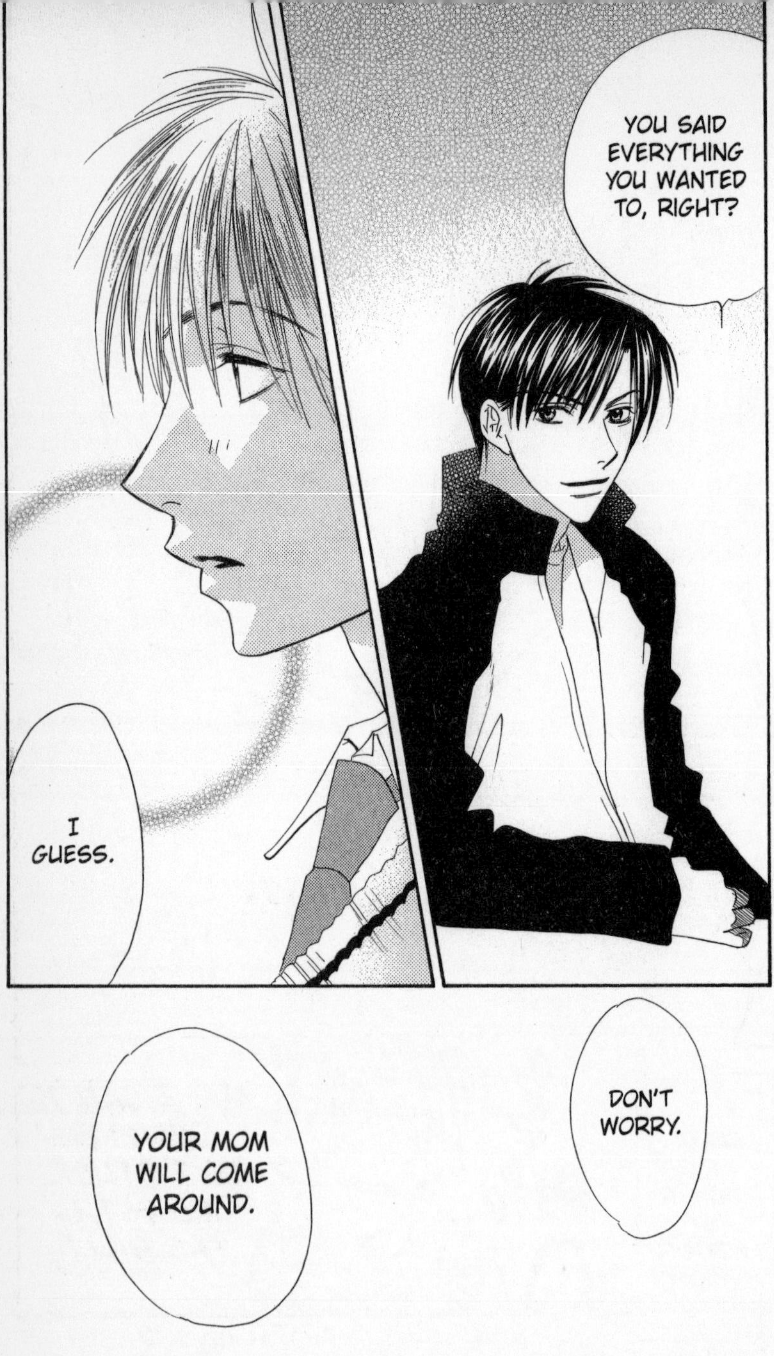
YOU SAID EVERYTHING YOU WANTED TO, RIGHT?
I GUESS.
DON'T WORRY.
YOUR MOM WILL COME AROUND.

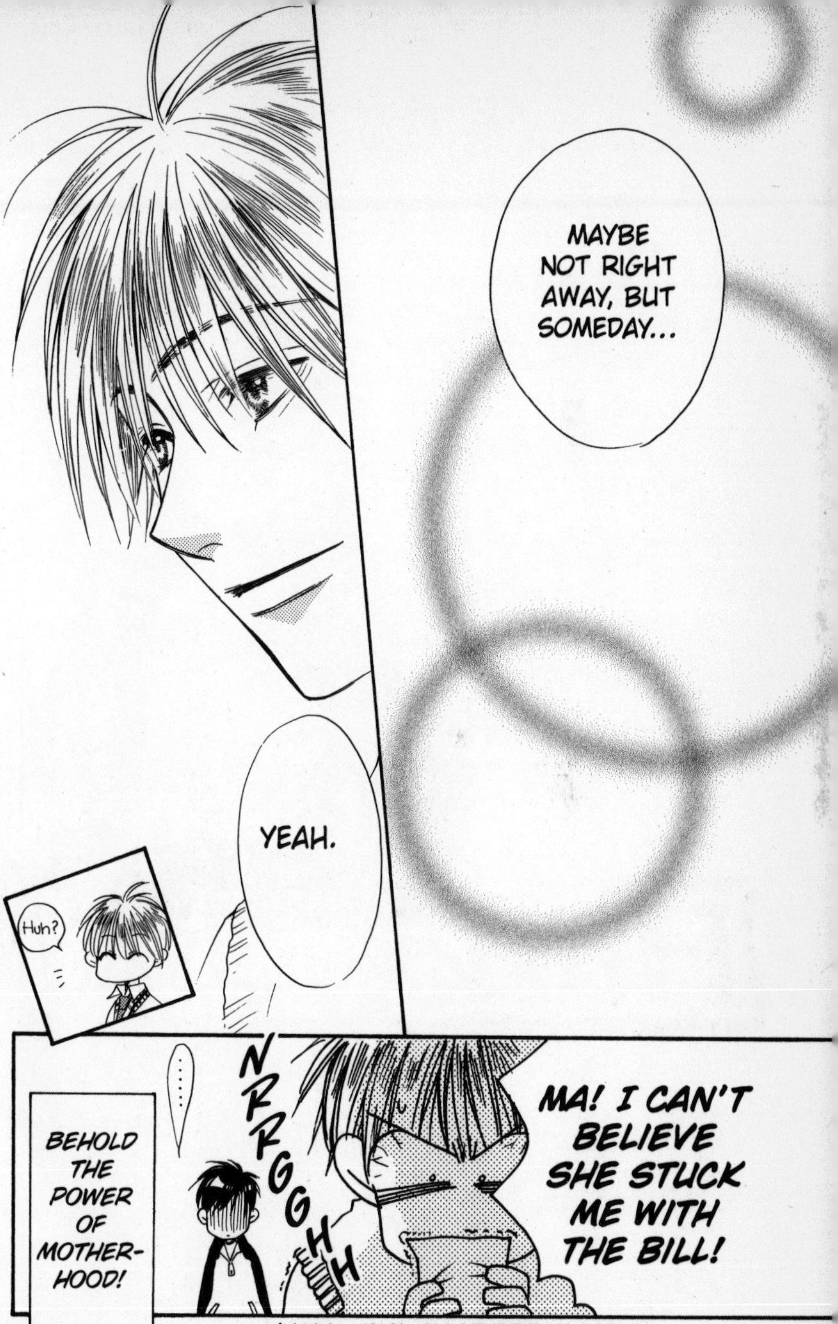
MAYBE NOT RIGHT AWAY, BUT SOMEDAY...
YEAH.
Huh?
MA! I CAN'T BELIEVE SHE STUCK ME WITH THE BILL!
NRRGGHHH
......
BEHOLD THE POWER OF MOTHER-HOOD!

HANA-KIMI CHAPTER 116/END

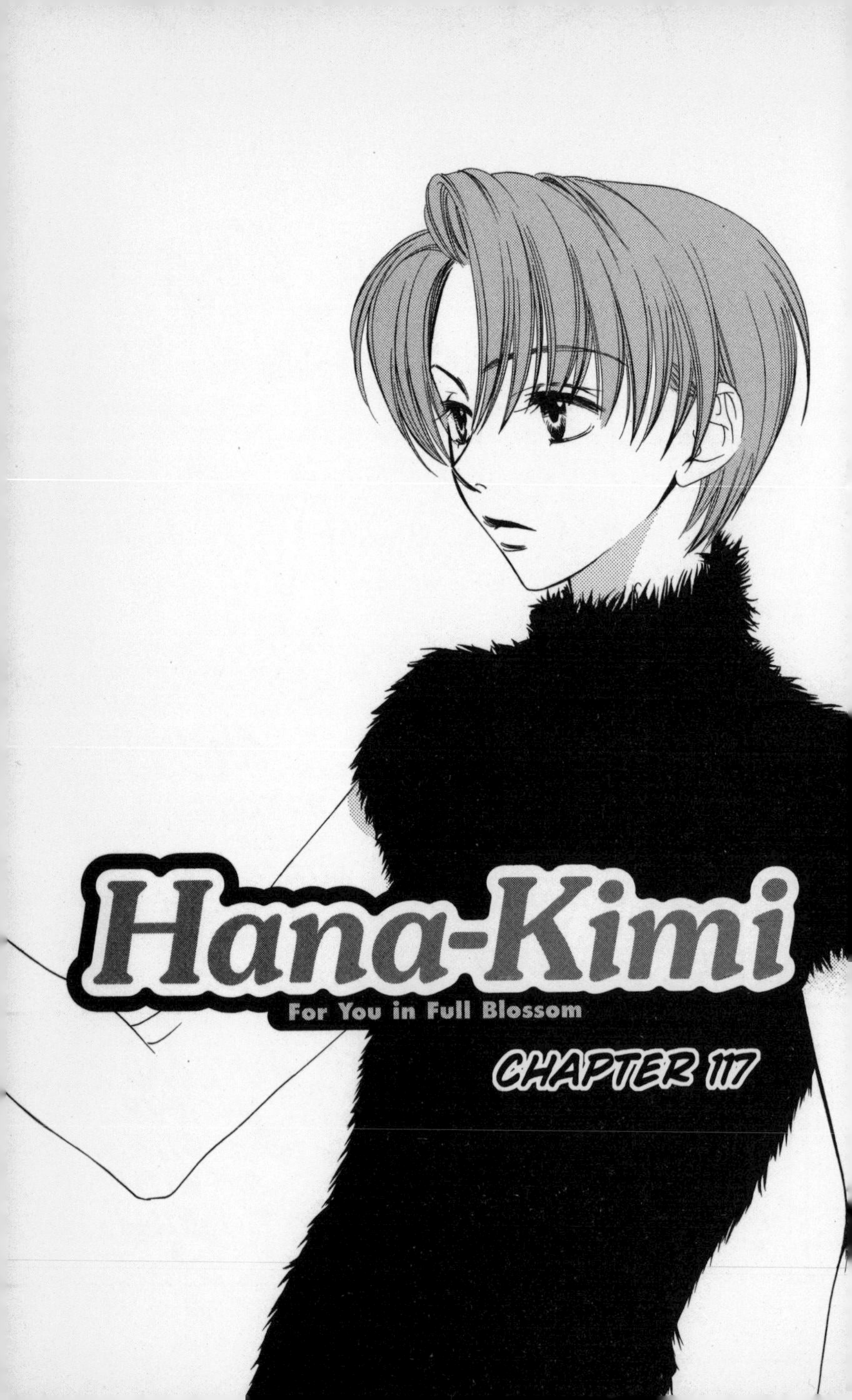
Hana-Kimi
For You in Full Blossom
CHAPTER 117

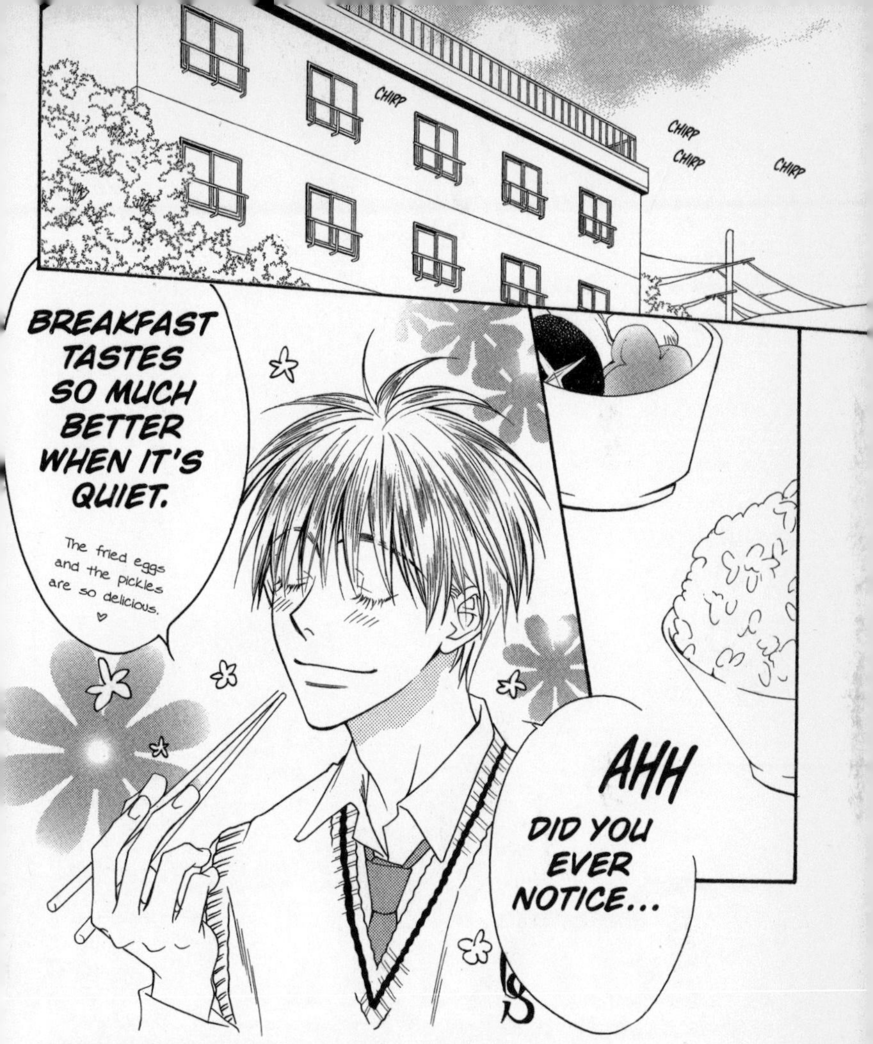
CHIRP
CHIRP
CHIRP
CHIRP
AHH
DID YOU EVER NOTICE...
BREAKFAST TASTES SO MUCH BETTER WHEN IT'S QUIET.
The fried eggs and the pickles are so delicious. ♡

WHAT I'M INTO THESE DAYS

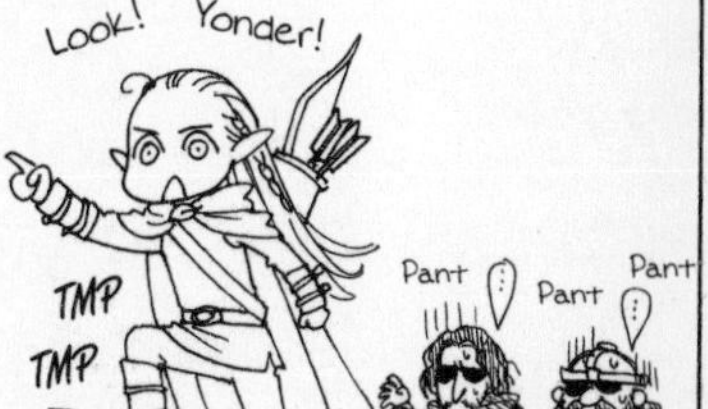
Look! Yonder!
TMP
TMP
Pant
Pant
Pant

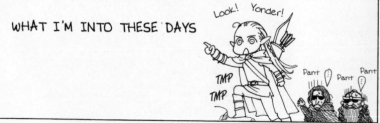

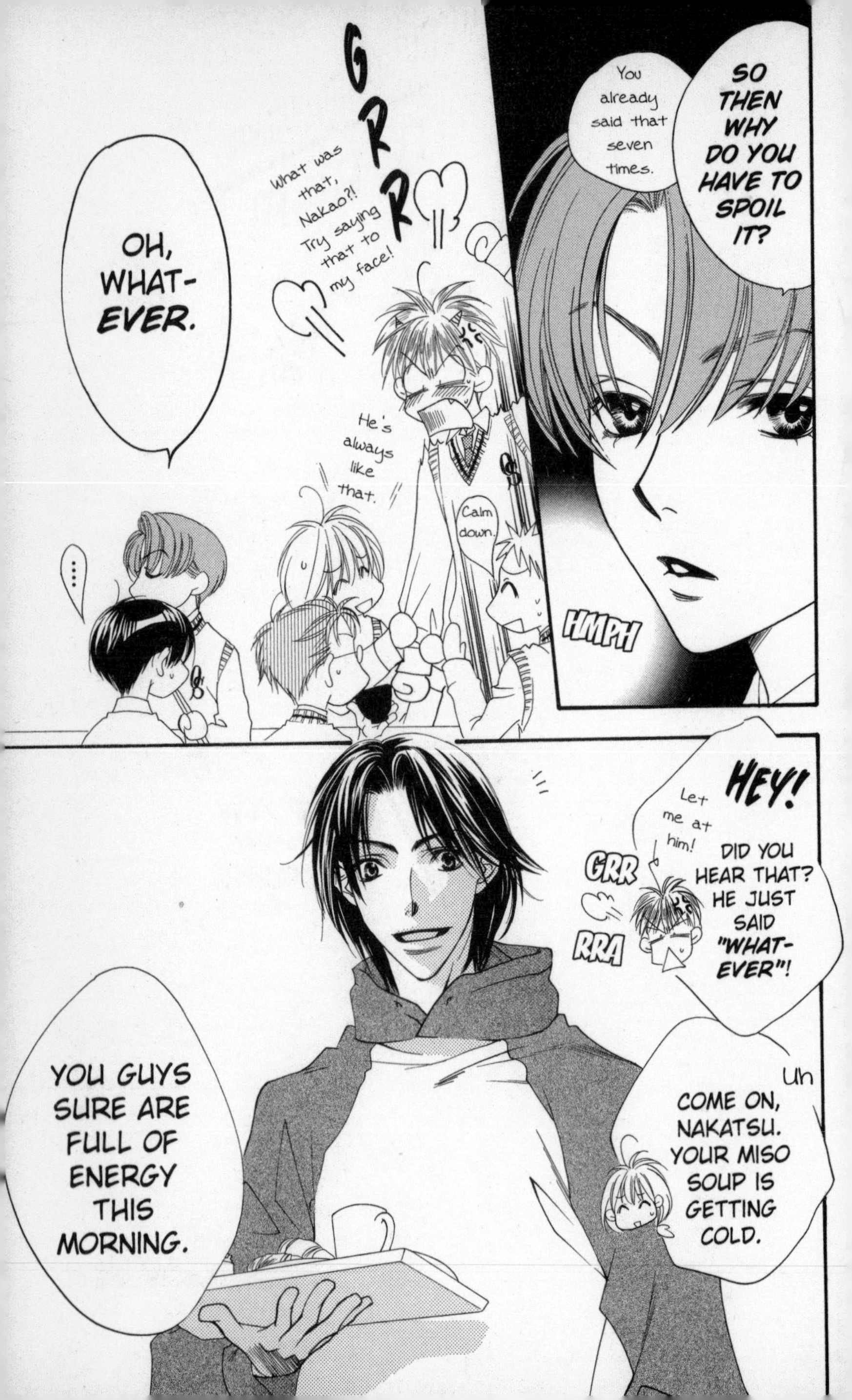
SO THEN WHY DO YOU HAVE TO SPOIL IT?
You already said that seven times.
HMPH
OH, WHAT-EVER.
GRRR
What was that, Nakao?! Try saying that to my face!
He's always like that.
Calm down.
....
HEY!
DID YOU HEAR THAT? HE JUST SAID "WHAT-EVER"!
Let me at him!
GRR
RRA
Uh
COME ON, NAKATSU. YOUR MISO SOUP IS GETTING COLD.
YOU GUYS SURE ARE FULL OF ENERGY THIS MORNING.

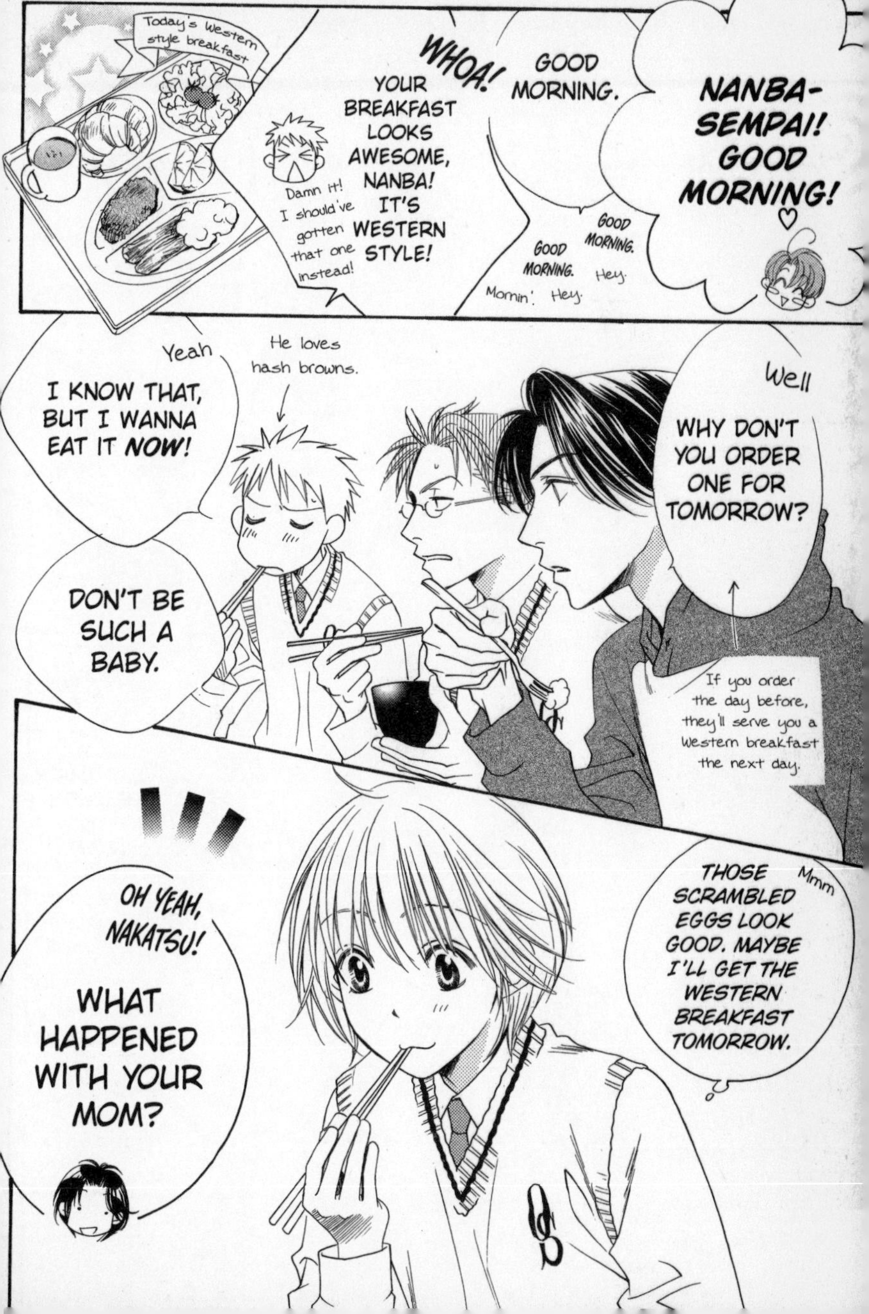
NANBA-SEMPAI! GOOD MORNING!
GOOD MORNING.
GOOD MORNING.
GOOD MORNING.
Hey.
Mornin'. Hey.
WHOA!
YOUR BREAKFAST LOOKS AWESOME, NANBA! IT'S WESTERN STYLE!
Damn it! I should've gotten that one instead!
Today's Western style breakfast
Well
WHY DON'T YOU ORDER ONE FOR TOMORROW?
If you order the day before, they'll serve you a Western breakfast the next day.
He loves hash browns.
Yeah
I KNOW THAT, BUT I WANNA EAT IT *NOW*!
DON'T BE SUCH A BABY.
THOSE SCRAMBLED EGGS LOOK GOOD. MAYBE I'LL GET THE WESTERN BREAKFAST TOMORROW.
Mmm
OH YEAH, NAKATSU!
WHAT HAPPENED WITH YOUR MOM?

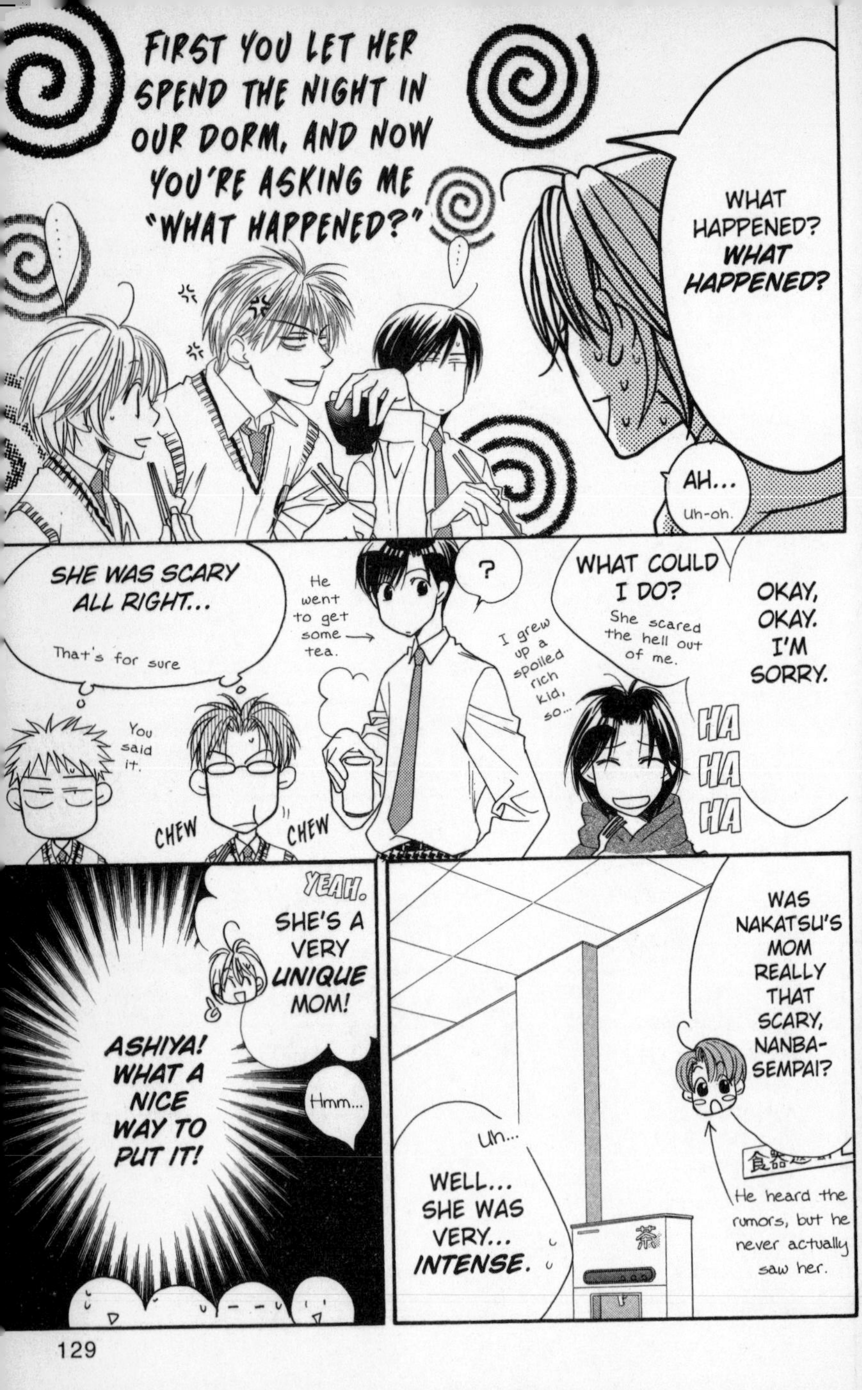
WHAT HAPPENED? WHAT HAPPENED?
FIRST YOU LET HER SPEND THE NIGHT IN OUR DORM, AND NOW YOU'RE ASKING ME "WHAT HAPPENED?"
AH... Uh-oh.
OKAY, OKAY. I'M SORRY.
HA HA HA
WHAT COULD I DO? She scared the hell out of me.
I grew up a spoiled rich kid, so...
?
He went to get some tea.
SHE WAS SCARY ALL RIGHT... That's for sure
You said it.
CHEW CHEW
WAS NAKATSU'S MOM REALLY THAT SCARY, NANBA-SEMPAI?
He heard the rumors, but he never actually saw her.
Uh...
WELL... SHE WAS VERY... INTENSE.
YEAH. SHE'S A VERY UNIQUE MOM!
Hmm...
ASHIYA! WHAT A NICE WAY TO PUT IT!

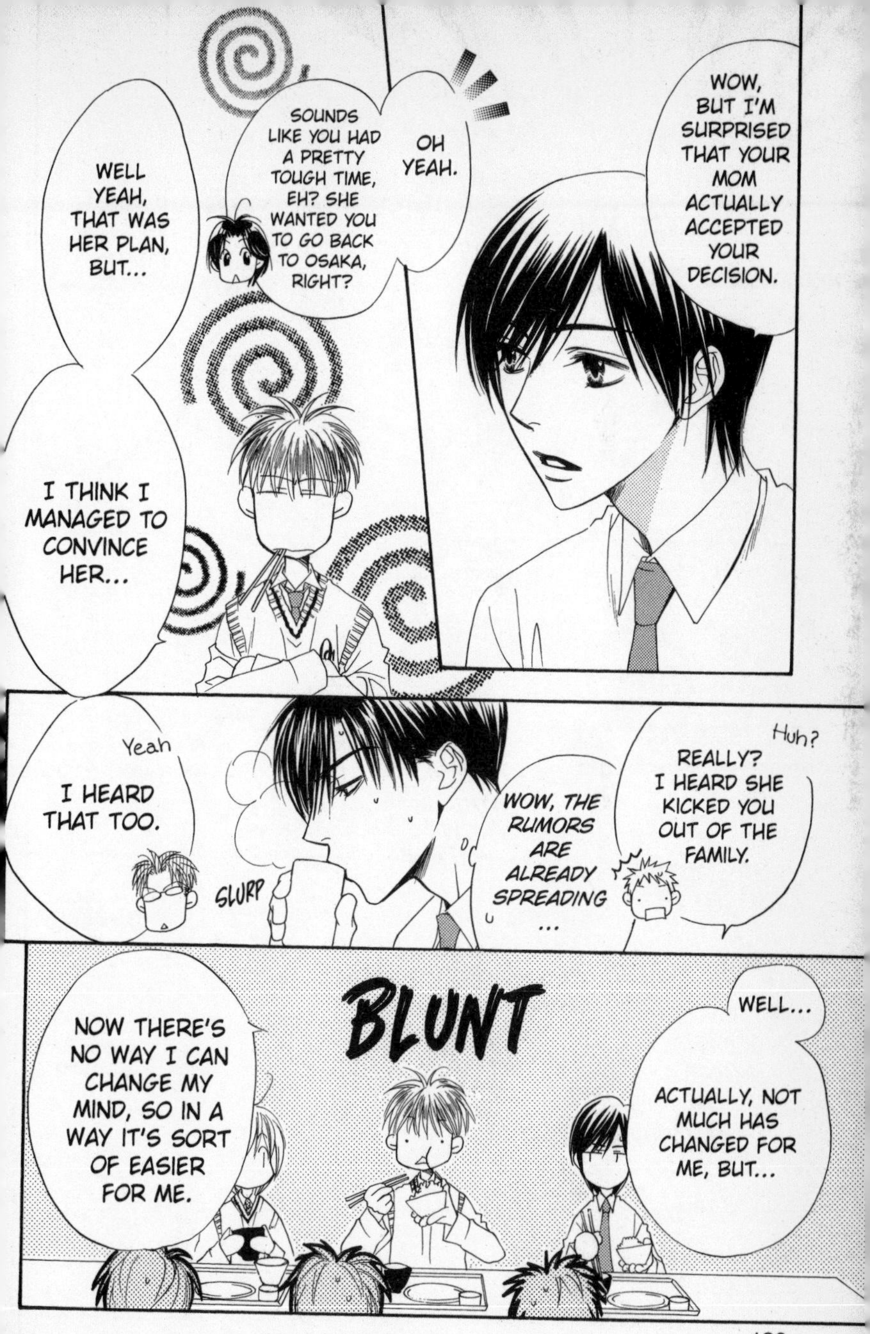
WOW, BUT I'M SURPRISED THAT YOUR MOM ACTUALLY ACCEPTED YOUR DECISION.
OH YEAH.
SOUNDS LIKE YOU HAD A PRETTY TOUGH TIME, EH? SHE WANTED YOU TO GO BACK TO OSAKA, RIGHT?
WELL YEAH, THAT WAS HER PLAN, BUT...
I THINK I MANAGED TO CONVINCE HER...
Huh?
REALLY? I HEARD SHE KICKED YOU OUT OF THE FAMILY.
WOW, THE RUMORS ARE ALREADY SPREADING...
SLURP
Yeah
I HEARD THAT TOO.
WELL...
ACTUALLY, NOT MUCH HAS CHANGED FOR ME, BUT...
BLUNT
NOW THERE'S NO WAY I CAN CHANGE MY MIND, SO IN A WAY IT'S SORT OF EASIER FOR ME.

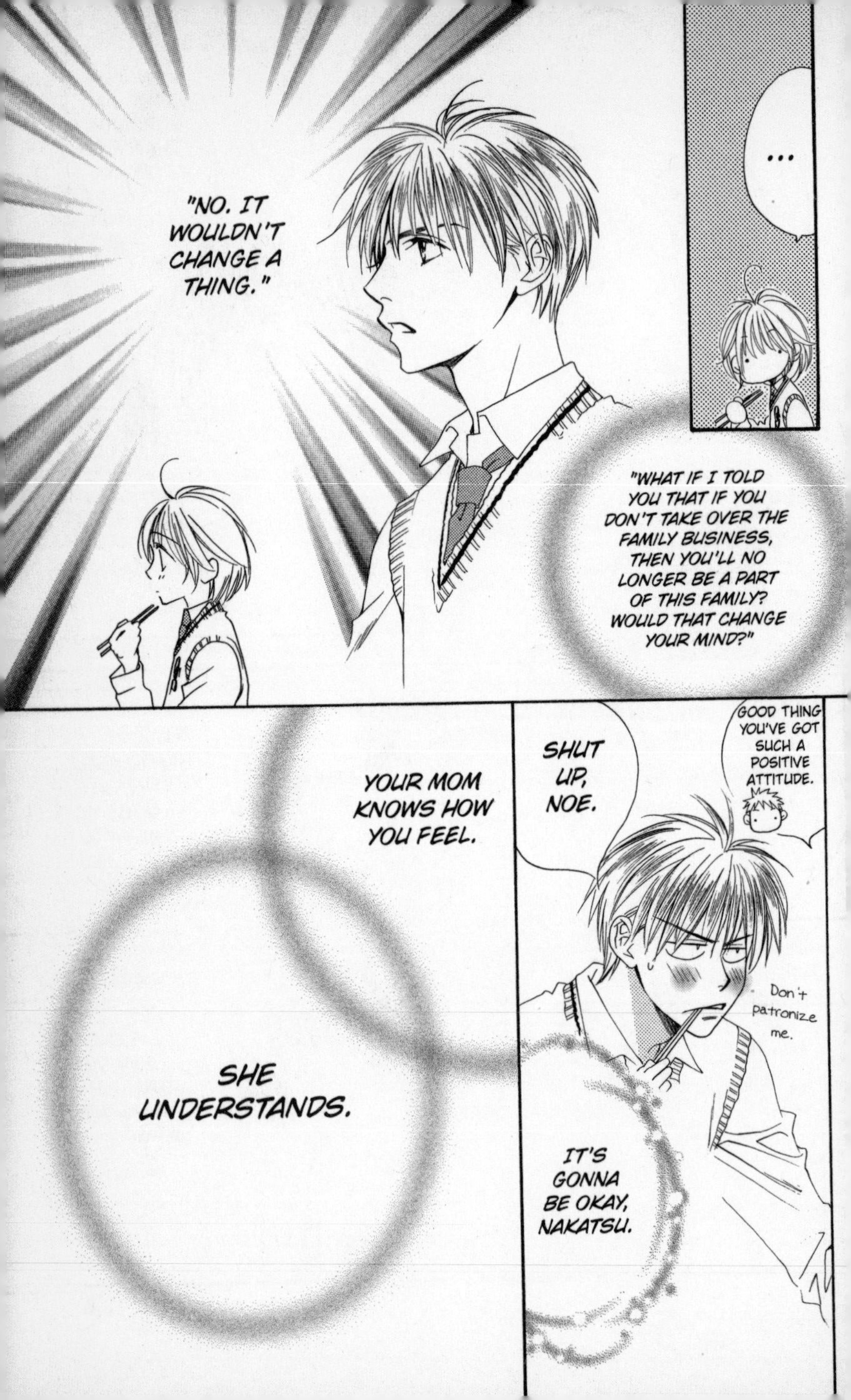
...
"WHAT IF I TOLD YOU THAT IF YOU DON'T TAKE OVER THE FAMILY BUSINESS, THEN YOU'LL NO LONGER BE A PART OF THIS FAMILY? WOULD THAT CHANGE YOUR MIND?"
"NO. IT WOULDN'T CHANGE A THING."
GOOD THING YOU'VE GOT SUCH A POSITIVE ATTITUDE.
SHUT UP, NOE.
Don't patronize me.
IT'S GONNA BE OKAY, NAKATSU.
YOUR MOM KNOWS HOW YOU FEEL.
SHE UNDERSTANDS.

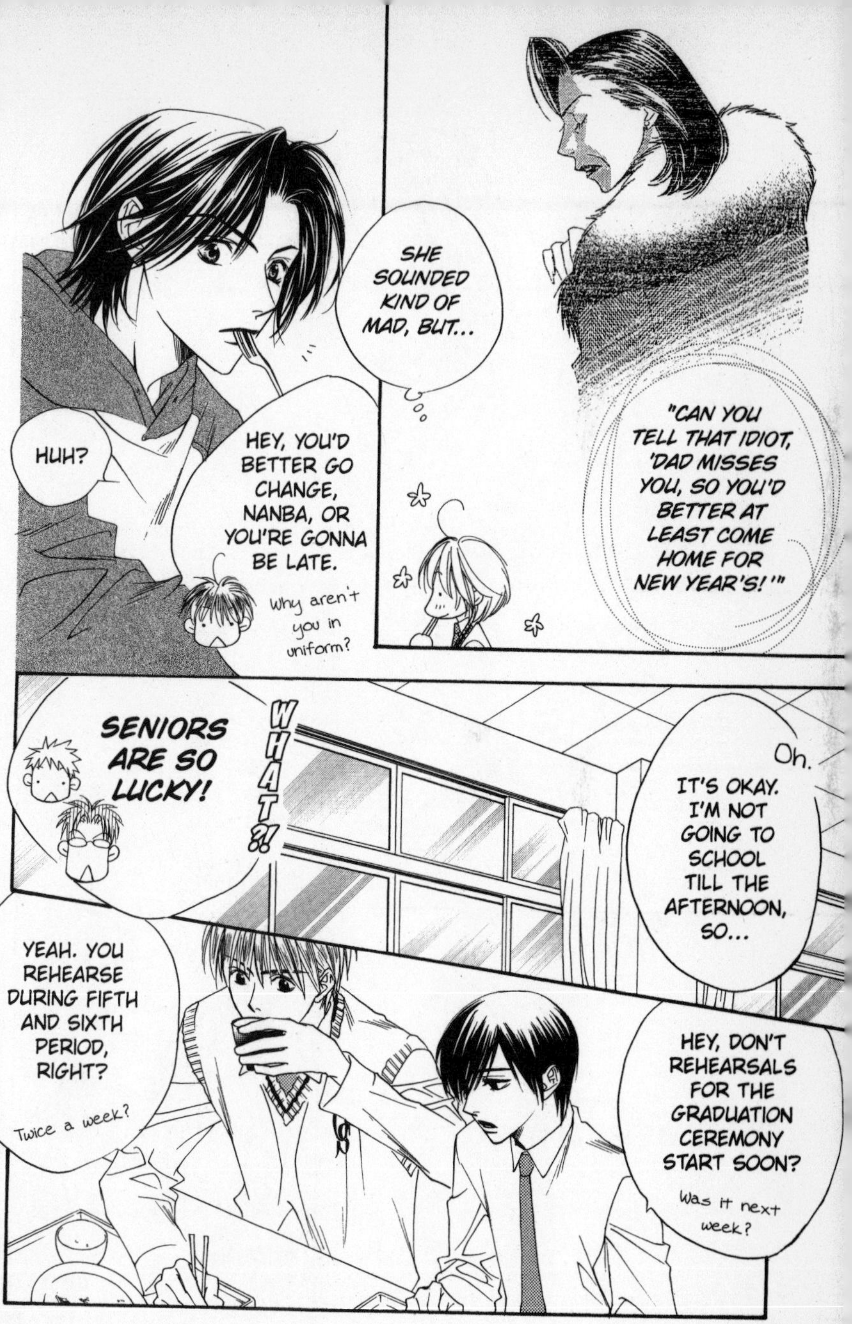
"CAN YOU TELL THAT IDIOT, 'DAD MISSES YOU, SO YOU'D BETTER AT LEAST COME HOME FOR NEW YEAR'S!'"
SHE SOUNDED KIND OF MAD, BUT...
HEY, YOU'D BETTER GO CHANGE, NANBA, OR YOU'RE GONNA BE LATE.
Why aren't you in uniform?
HUH?
Oh.
IT'S OKAY. I'M NOT GOING TO SCHOOL TILL THE AFTERNOON, SO...
WHAT?!
SENIORS ARE SO LUCKY!
HEY, DON'T REHEARSALS FOR THE GRADUATION CEREMONY START SOON?
Was it next week?
YEAH. YOU REHEARSE DURING FIFTH AND SIXTH PERIOD, RIGHT?
Twice a week?

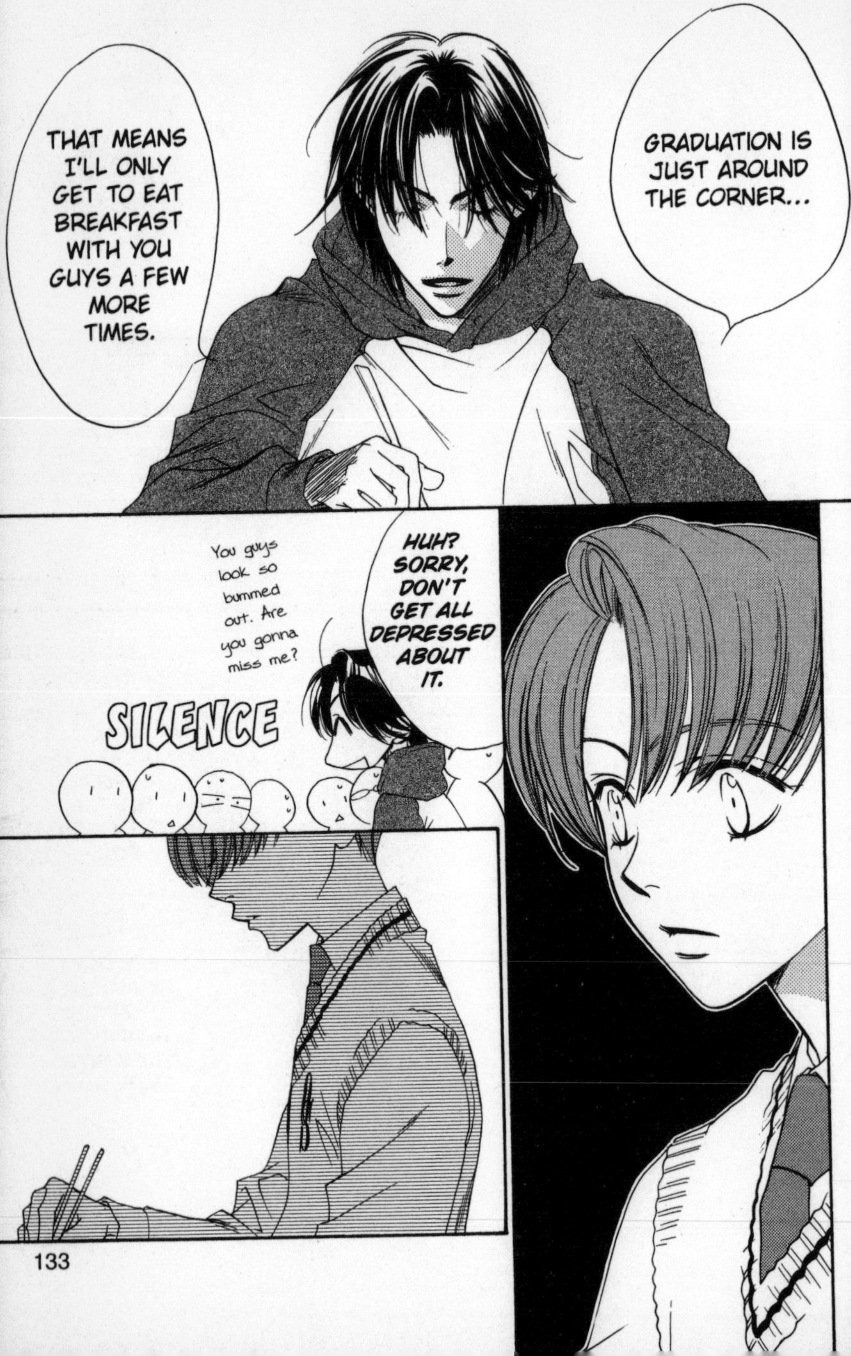

GRADUATION IS JUST AROUND THE CORNER...
THAT MEANS I'LL ONLY GET TO EAT BREAKFAST WITH YOU GUYS A FEW MORE TIMES.
HUH? SORRY, DON'T GET ALL DEPRESSED ABOUT IT.
You guys look so bummed out. Are you gonna miss me?
SILENCE

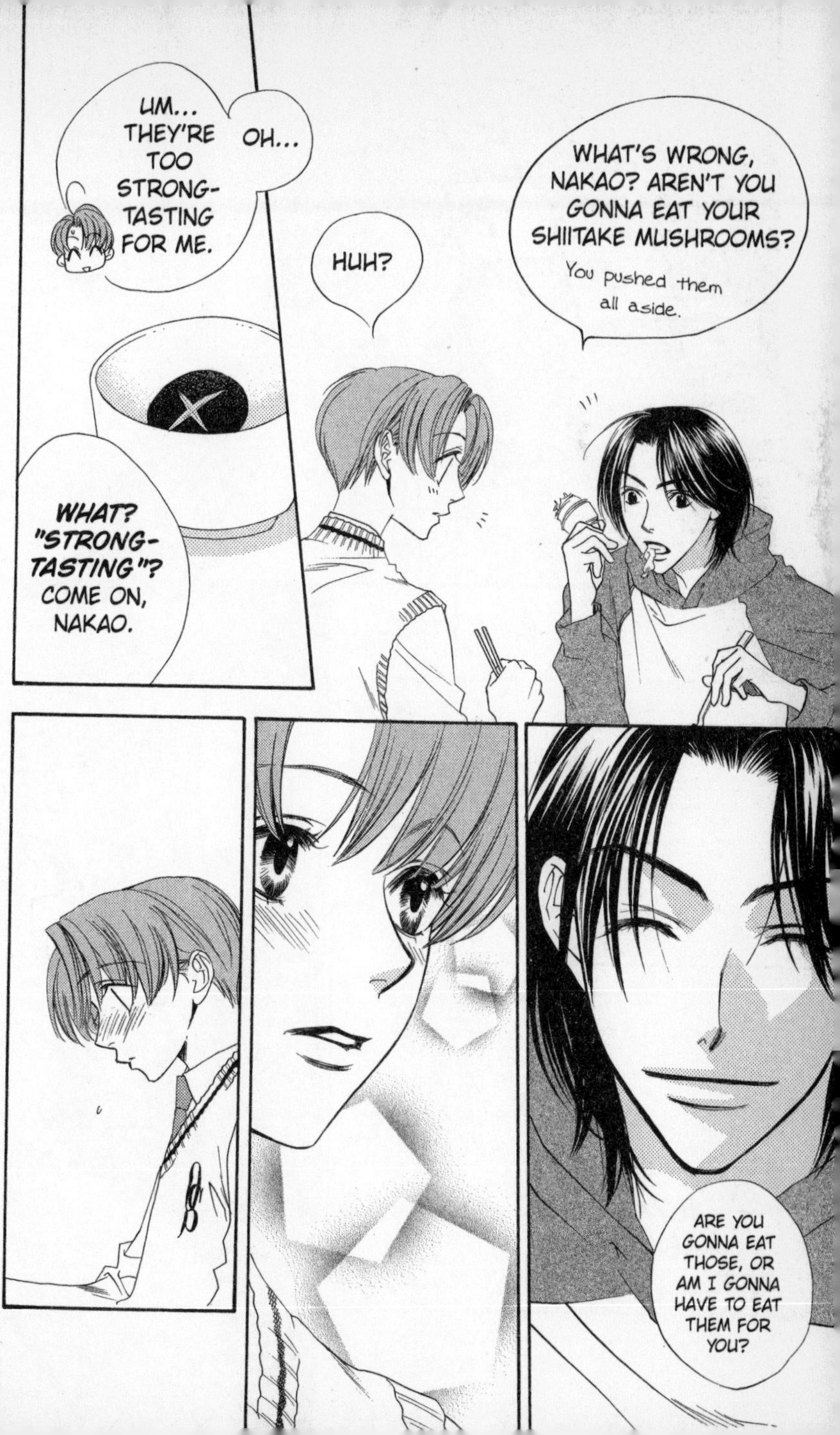
WHAT'S WRONG, NAKAO? AREN'T YOU GONNA EAT YOUR SHIITAKE MUSHROOMS?
You pushed them all aside.
HUH?
UM... THEY'RE TOO STRONG-TASTING FOR ME.
OH...
WHAT? "STRONG-TASTING"? COME ON, NAKAO.
ARE YOU GONNA EAT THOSE, OR AM I GONNA HAVE TO EAT THEM FOR YOU?

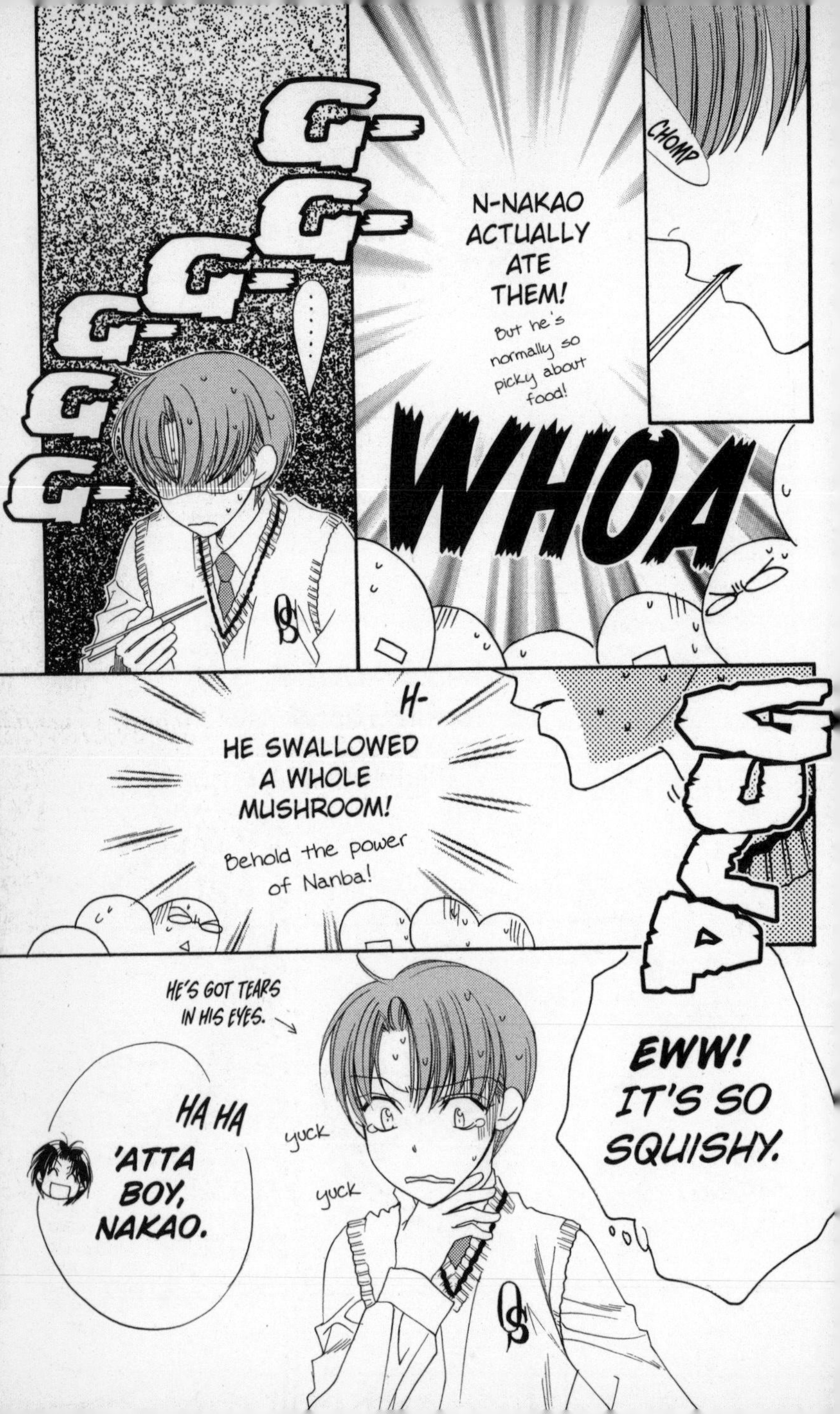
CHOMP
N-NAKAO ACTUALLY ATE THEM!
But he's normally so picky about food!
WHOA
G-G-G-G-G-G-
......
GULP
H-
HE SWALLOWED A WHOLE MUSHROOM!
Behold the power of Nanba!
EWW! IT'S SO SQUISHY.
HE'S GOT TEARS IN HIS EYES.
yuck
yuck
HA HA
'ATTA BOY, NAKAO.

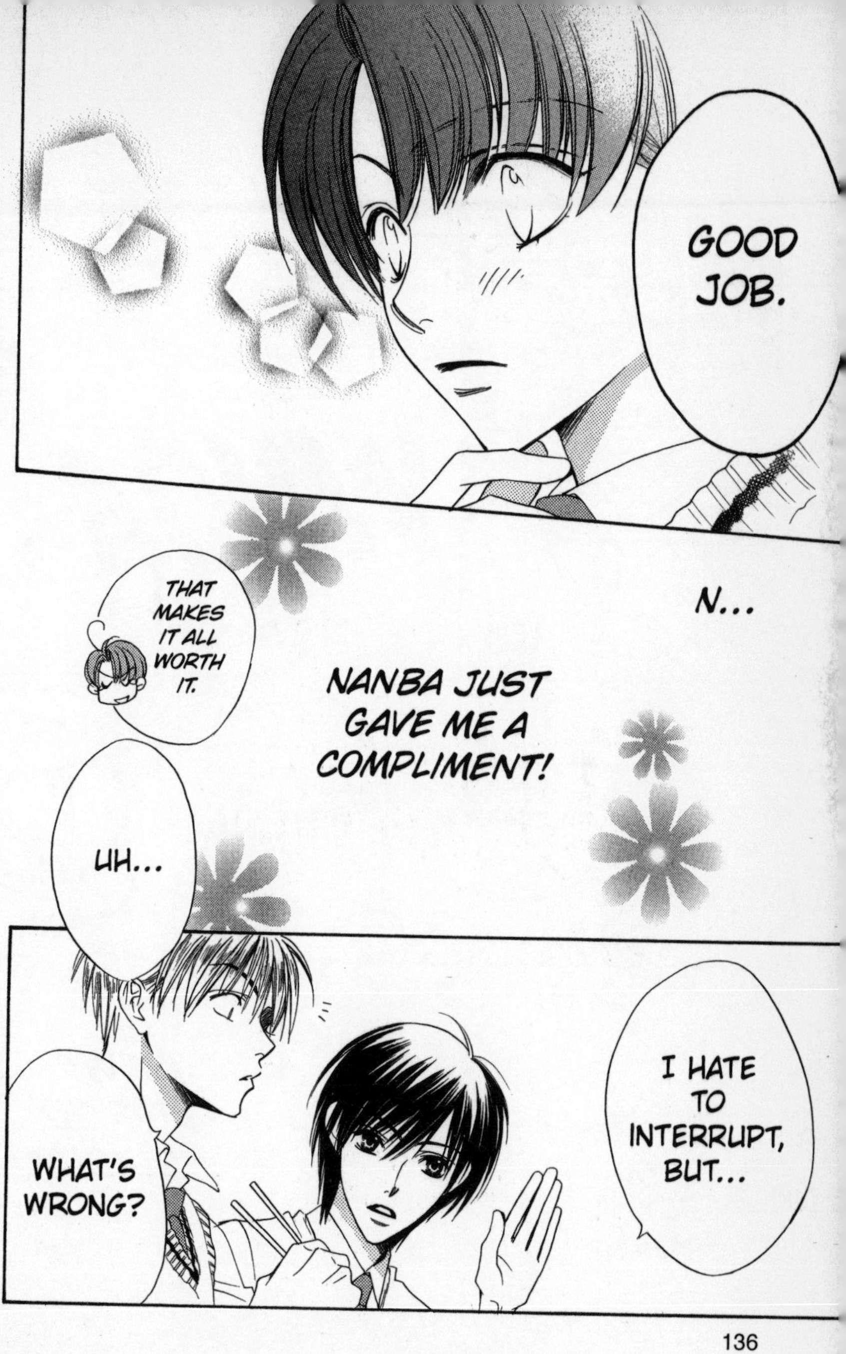
GOOD JOB.
N...
NANBA JUST GAVE ME A COMPLIMENT!
THAT MAKES IT ALL WORTH IT.
UH...
I HATE TO INTERRUPT, BUT...
WHAT'S WRONG?

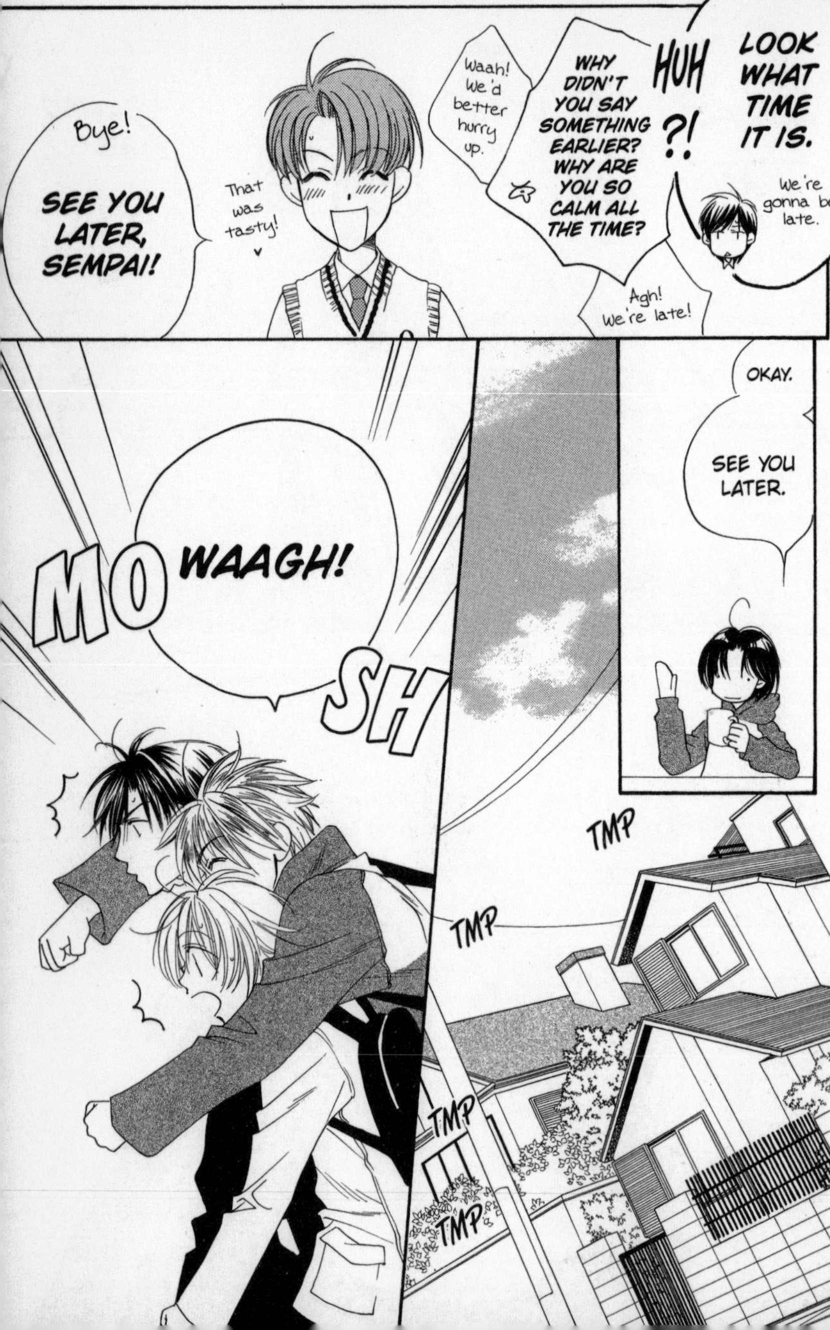
LOOK WHAT TIME IT IS.
We're gonna be late.
HUH ?!
WHY DIDN'T YOU SAY SOMETHING EARLIER? WHY ARE YOU SO CALM ALL THE TIME?
Agh! We're late!
Waah! We'd better hurry up.
That was tasty!
Bye!
SEE YOU LATER, SEMPAI!
OKAY.
SEE YOU LATER.
TMP
TMP
TMP
TMP
MOSH
WAAGH!

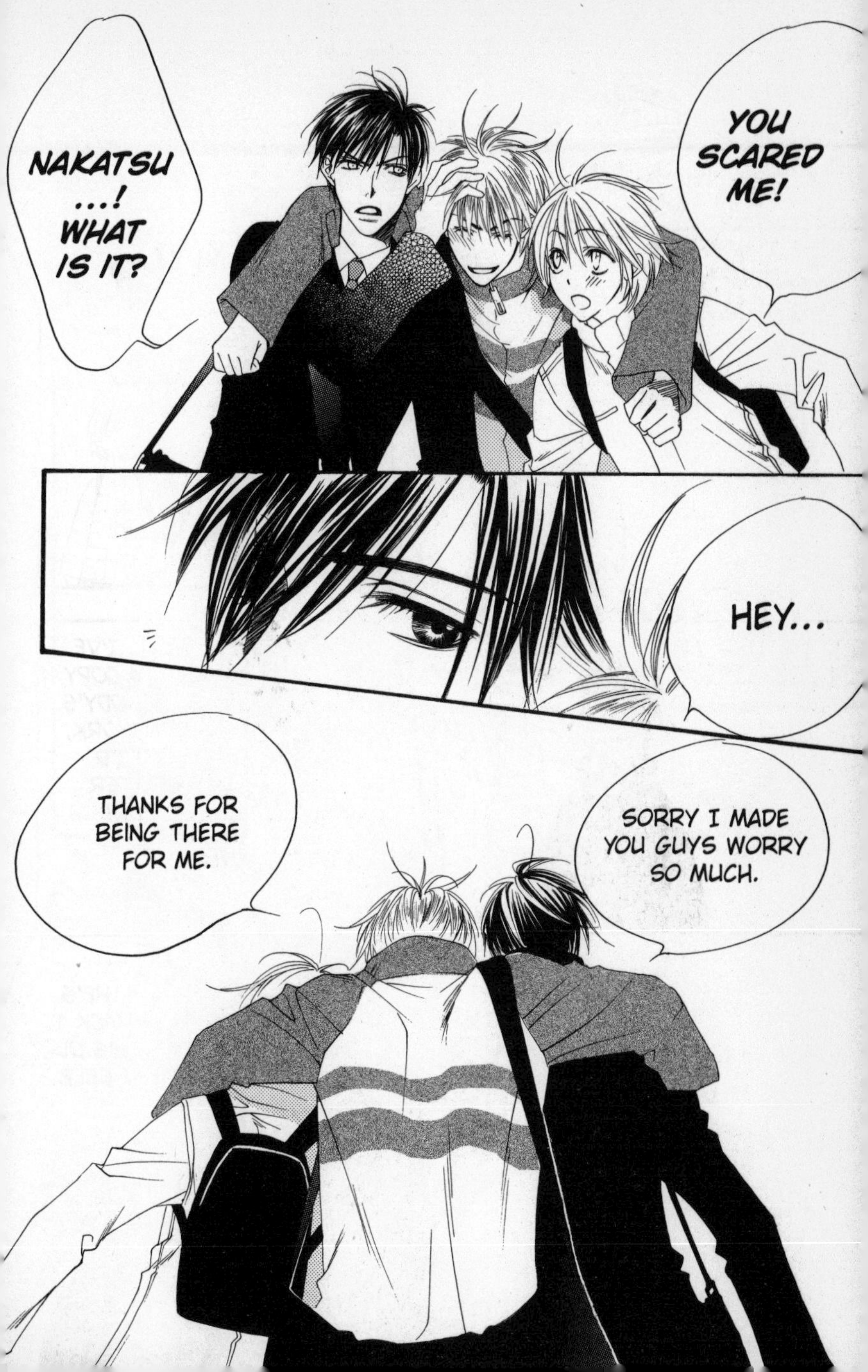
YOU SCARED ME!
NAKATSU ...! WHAT IS IT?
HEY...
SORRY I MADE YOU GUYS WORRY SO MUCH.
THANKS FOR BEING THERE FOR ME.

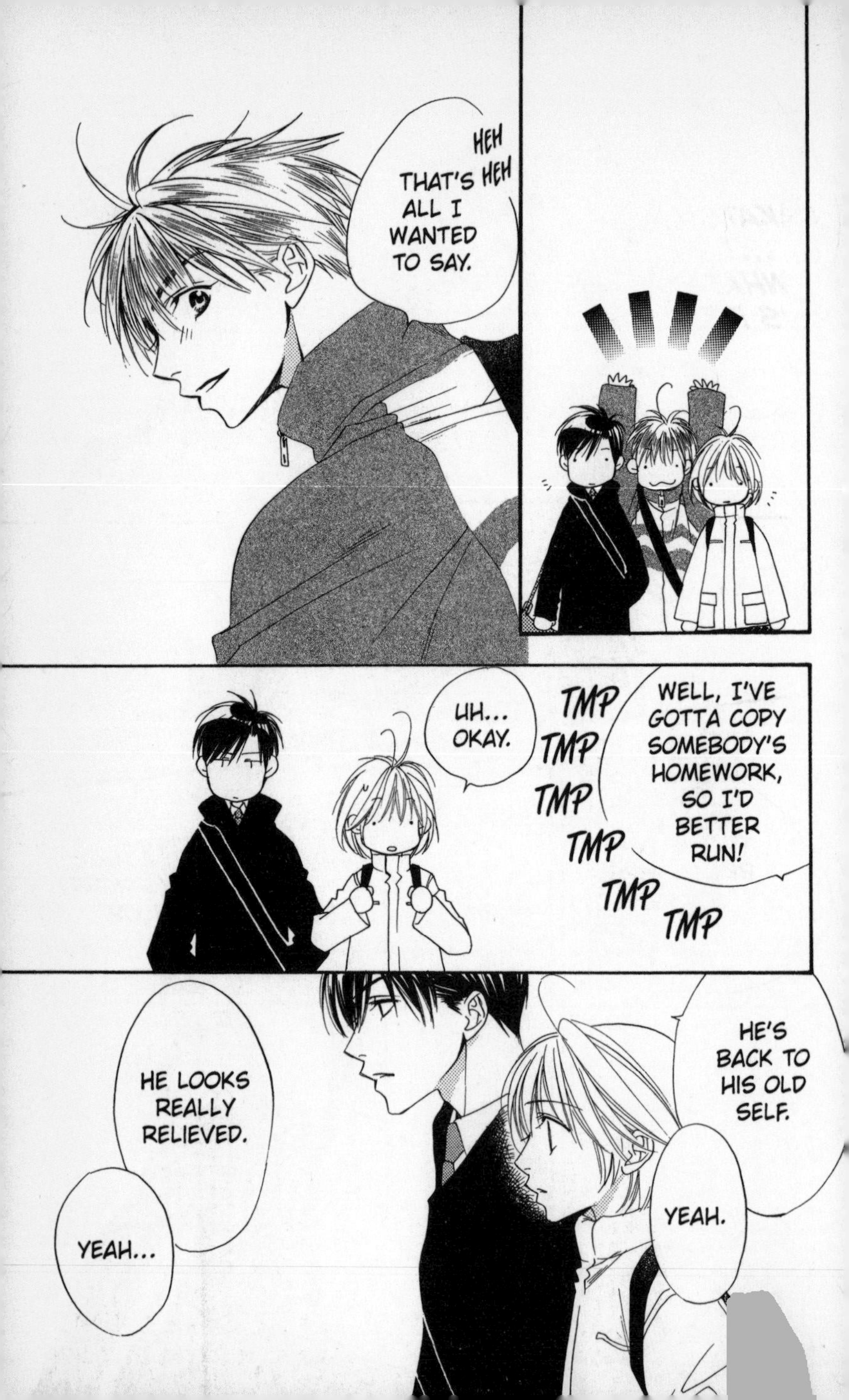
HEH HEH
THAT'S ALL I WANTED TO SAY.
WELL, I'VE GOTTA COPY SOMEBODY'S HOMEWORK, SO I'D BETTER RUN!
TMP TMP TMP TMP TMP TMP
UH... OKAY.
HE'S BACK TO HIS OLD SELF.
YEAH.
HE LOOKS REALLY RELIEVED.
YEAH...

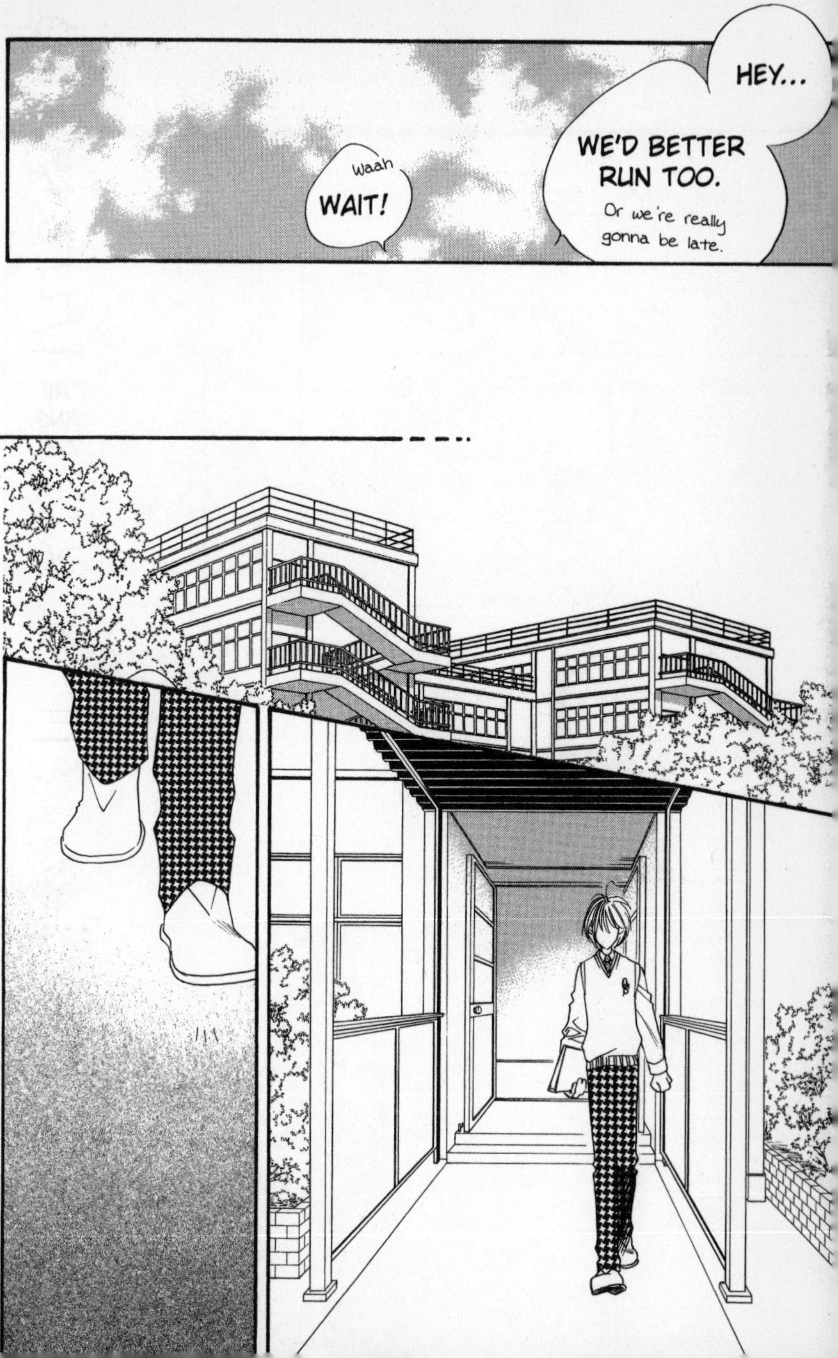
HEY...
WE'D BETTER RUN TOO.
Or we're really gonna be late.
Waah
WAIT!

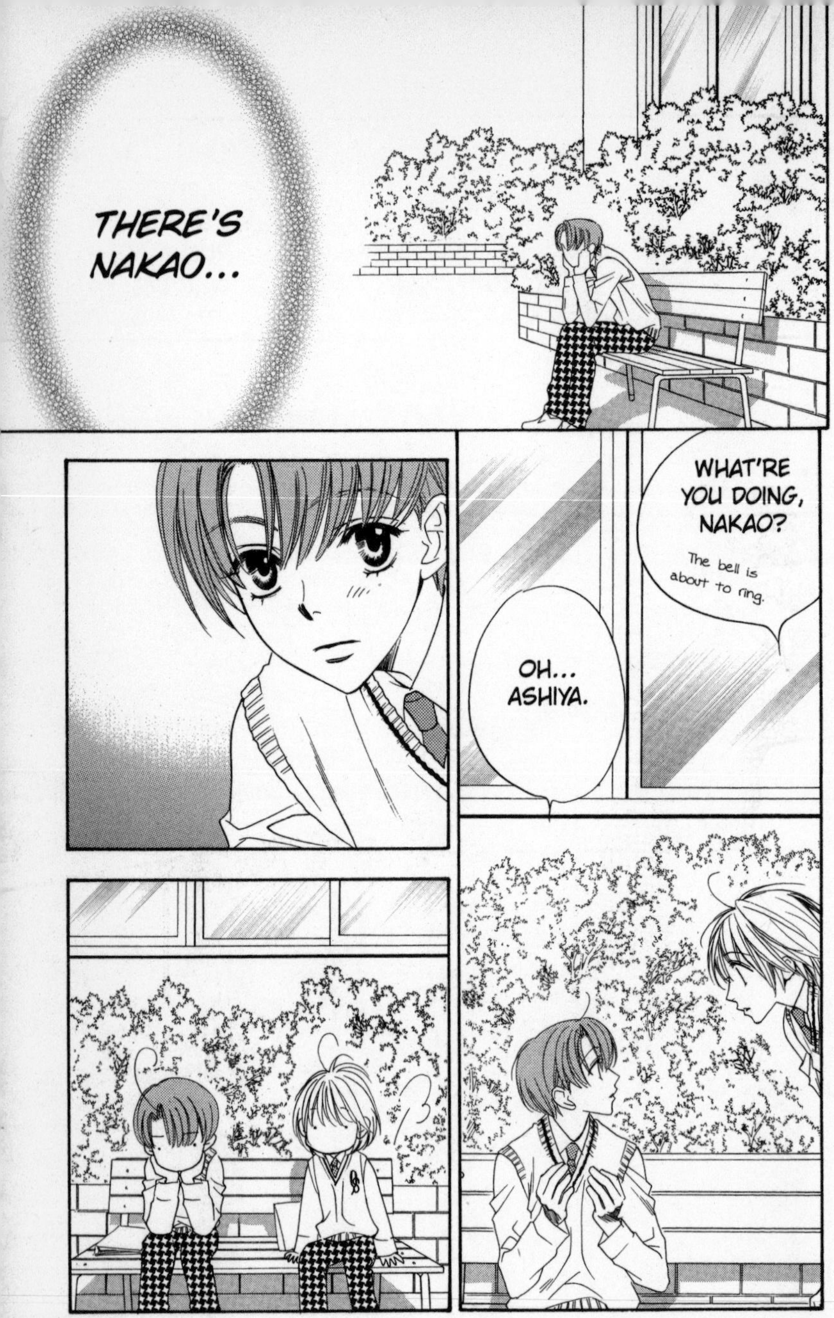
THERE'S NAKAO...
WHAT'RE YOU DOING, NAKAO? The bell is about to ring.
OH... ASHIYA.

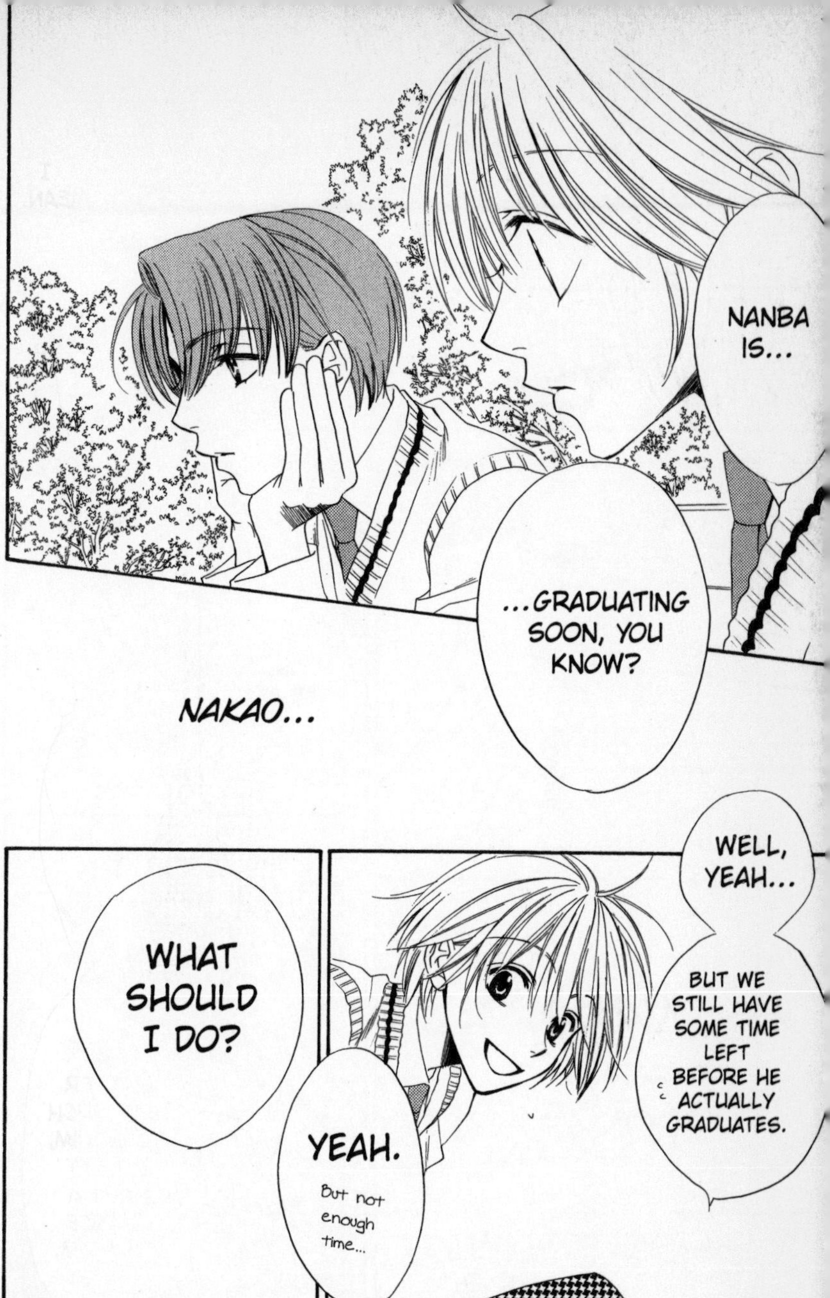
NANBA IS...
...GRADUATING SOON, YOU KNOW?
NAKAO...
WELL, YEAH...
BUT WE STILL HAVE SOME TIME LEFT BEFORE HE ACTUALLY GRADUATES.
YEAH.
But not enough time...
WHAT SHOULD I DO?

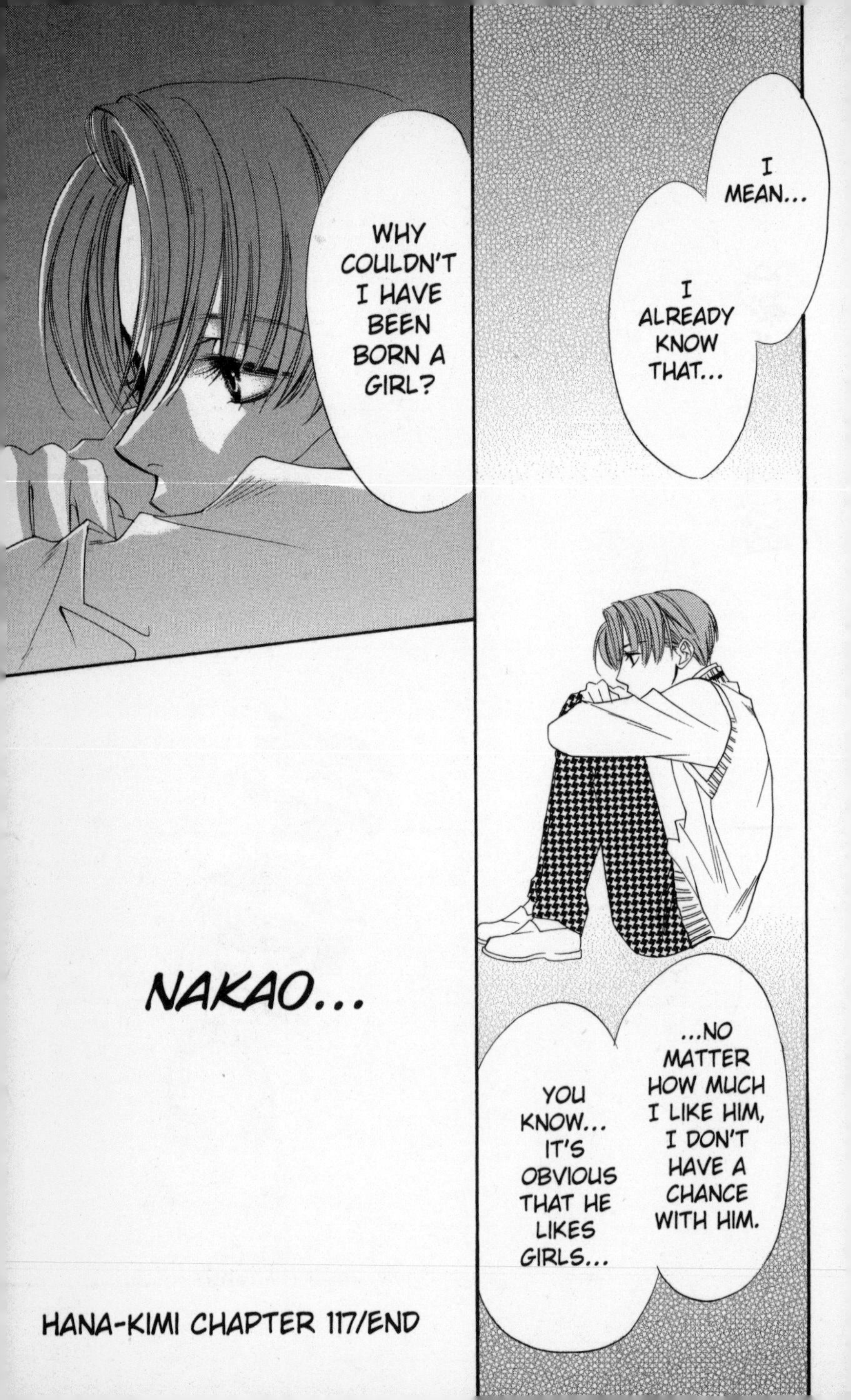
I MEAN...
I ALREADY KNOW THAT...
...NO MATTER HOW MUCH I LIKE HIM, I DON'T HAVE A CHANCE WITH HIM.
YOU KNOW... IT'S OBVIOUS THAT HE LIKES GIRLS...
WHY COULDN'T I HAVE BEEN BORN A GIRL?
NAKAO...
HANA-KIMI CHAPTER 117/END

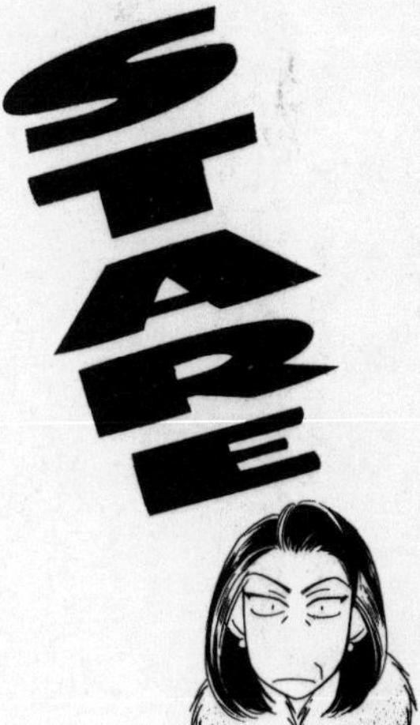
STARE

Hana-Kimi

For You in Full Blossom

CHAPTER 118

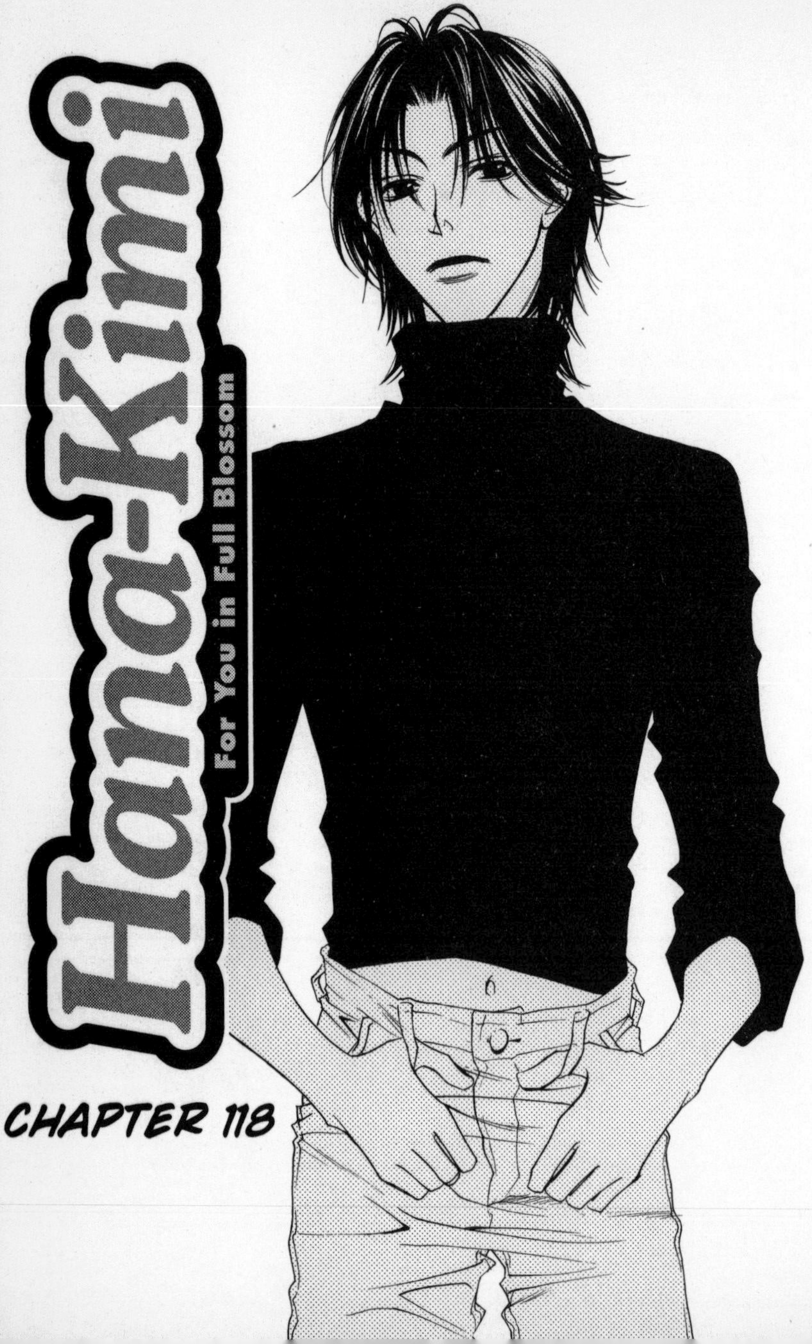

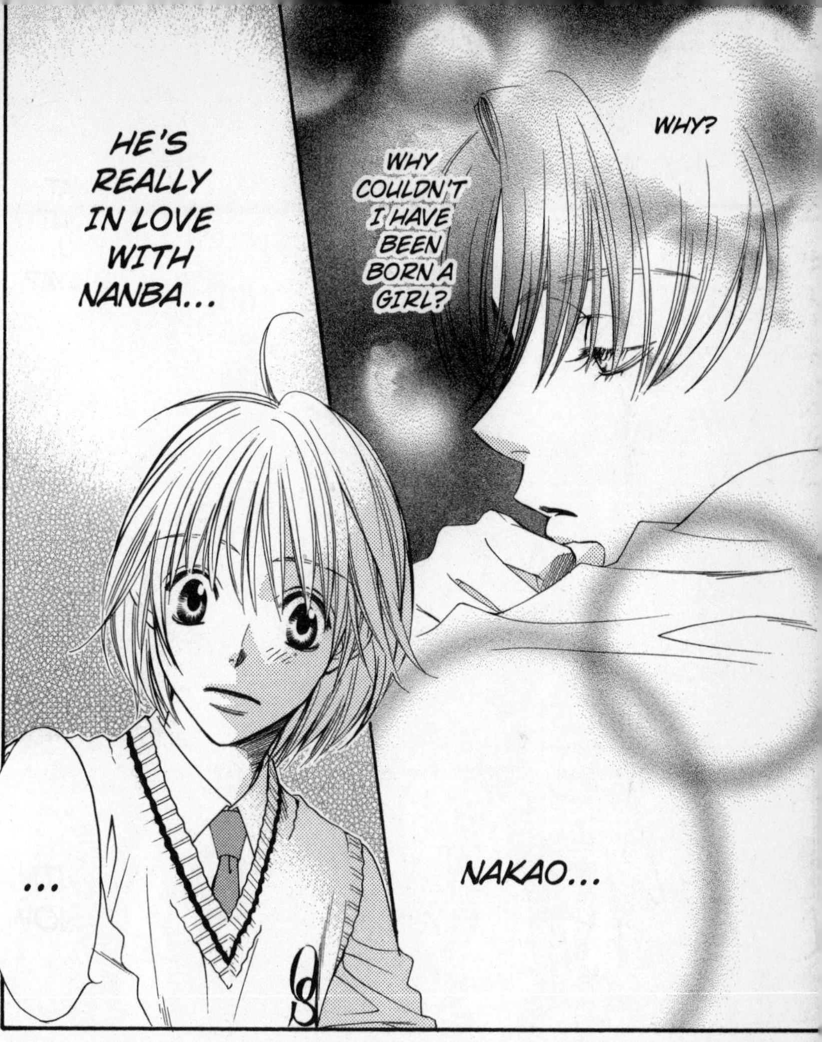
WHY?
WHY COULDN'T I HAVE BEEN BORN A GIRL?
HE'S REALLY IN LOVE WITH NANBA...
NAKAO...
...

WHAT I'M INTO THESE DAYS

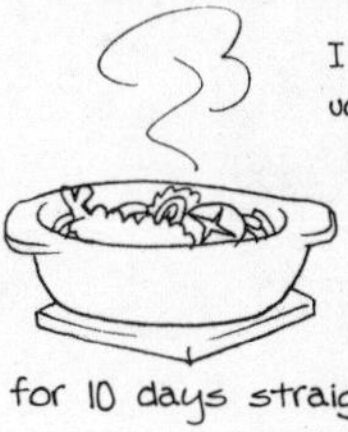

I ate Kitsune udon, Tempura udon, Miso udon and other types too.

I ate udon for 10 days straight.

↖ It was easy.

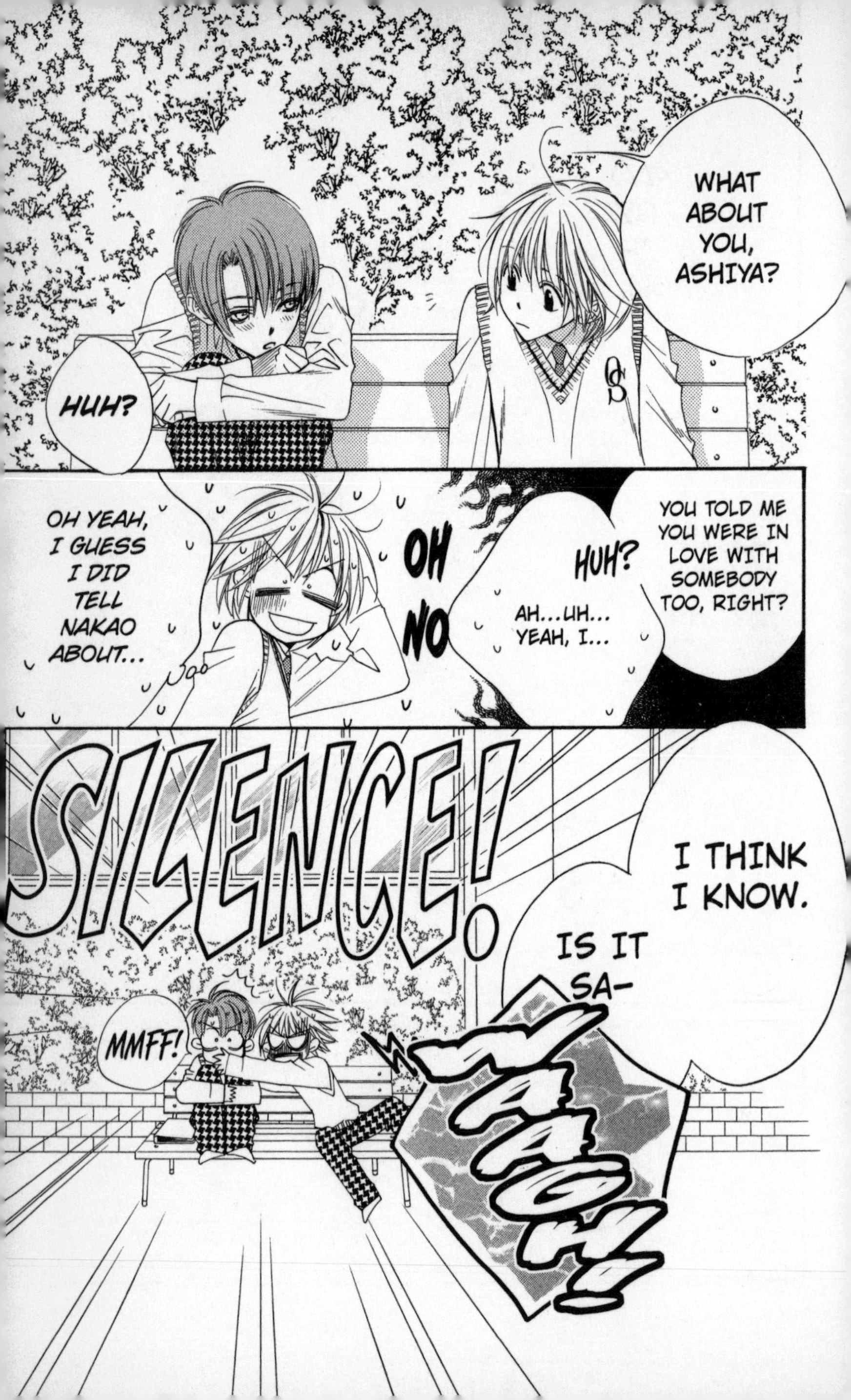
WHAT ABOUT YOU, ASHIYA?
HUH?
YOU TOLD ME YOU WERE IN LOVE WITH SOMEBODY TOO, RIGHT?
HUH?
AH...UH... YEAH, I...
OH NO
OH YEAH, I GUESS I DID TELL NAKAO ABOUT...
I THINK I KNOW.
IS IT SA-
SILENCE!
MMFF!

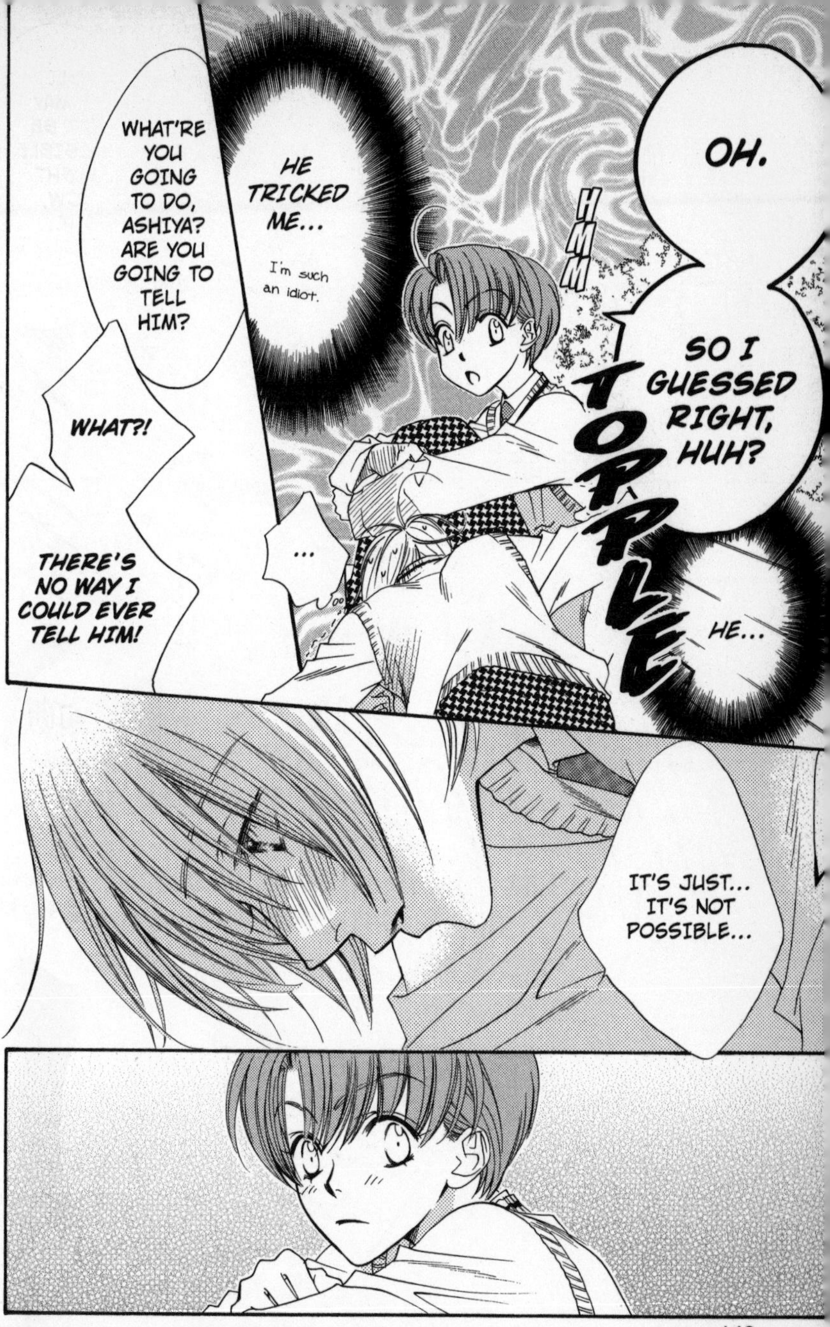
OH.
HMMM
SO I GUESSED RIGHT, HUH?
TOPPLE
HE TRICKED ME...
I'm such an idiot.
HE...
...
WHAT'RE YOU GOING TO DO, ASHIYA? ARE YOU GOING TO TELL HIM?
WHAT?!
THERE'S NO WAY I COULD EVER TELL HIM!
IT'S JUST... IT'S NOT POSSIBLE...

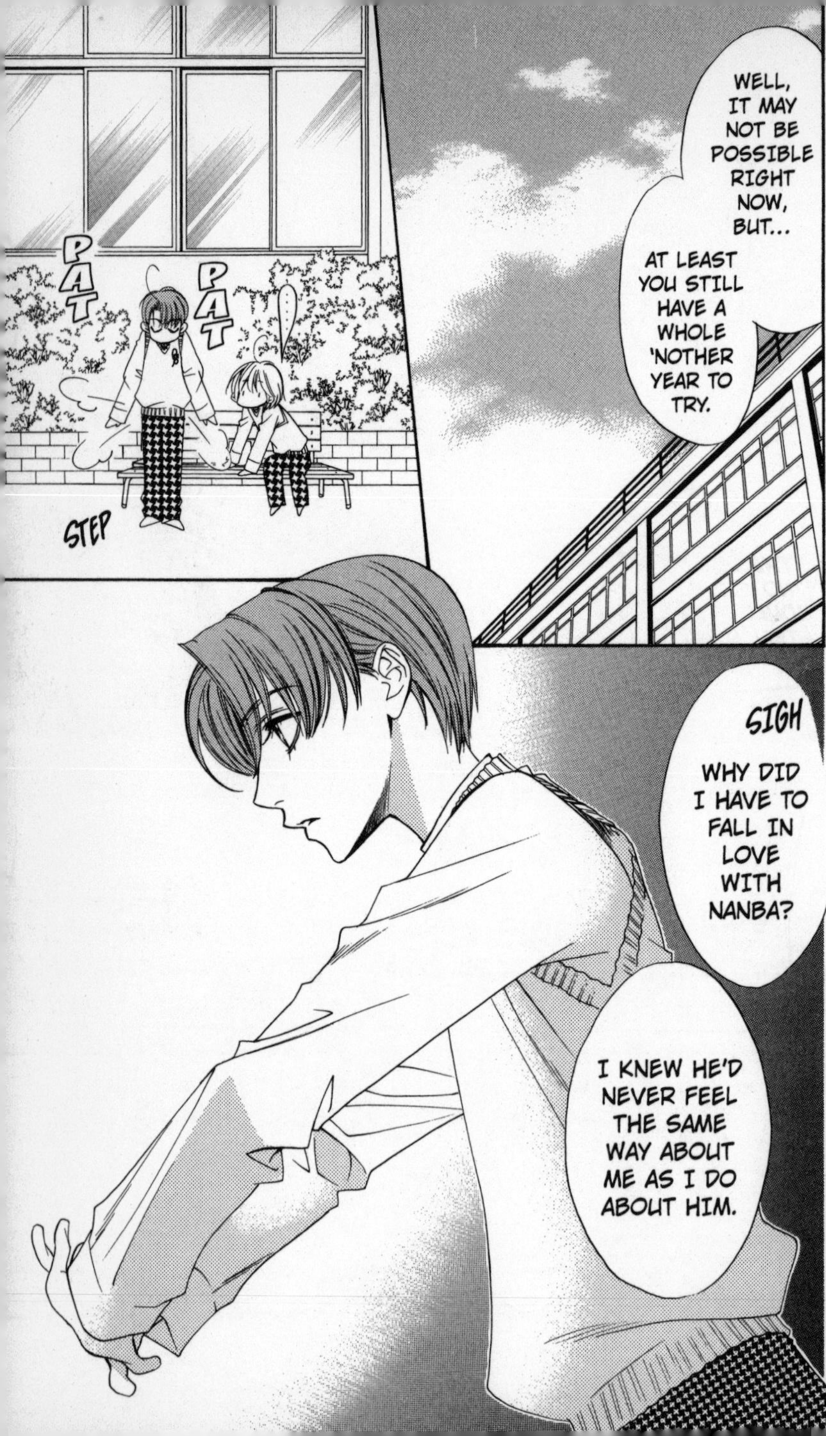
WELL, IT MAY NOT BE POSSIBLE RIGHT NOW, BUT...
AT LEAST YOU STILL HAVE A WHOLE 'NOTHER YEAR TO TRY.
PAT
PAT
!
STEP
SIGH
WHY DID I HAVE TO FALL IN LOVE WITH NANBA?
I KNEW HE'D NEVER FEEL THE SAME WAY ABOUT ME AS I DO ABOUT HIM.

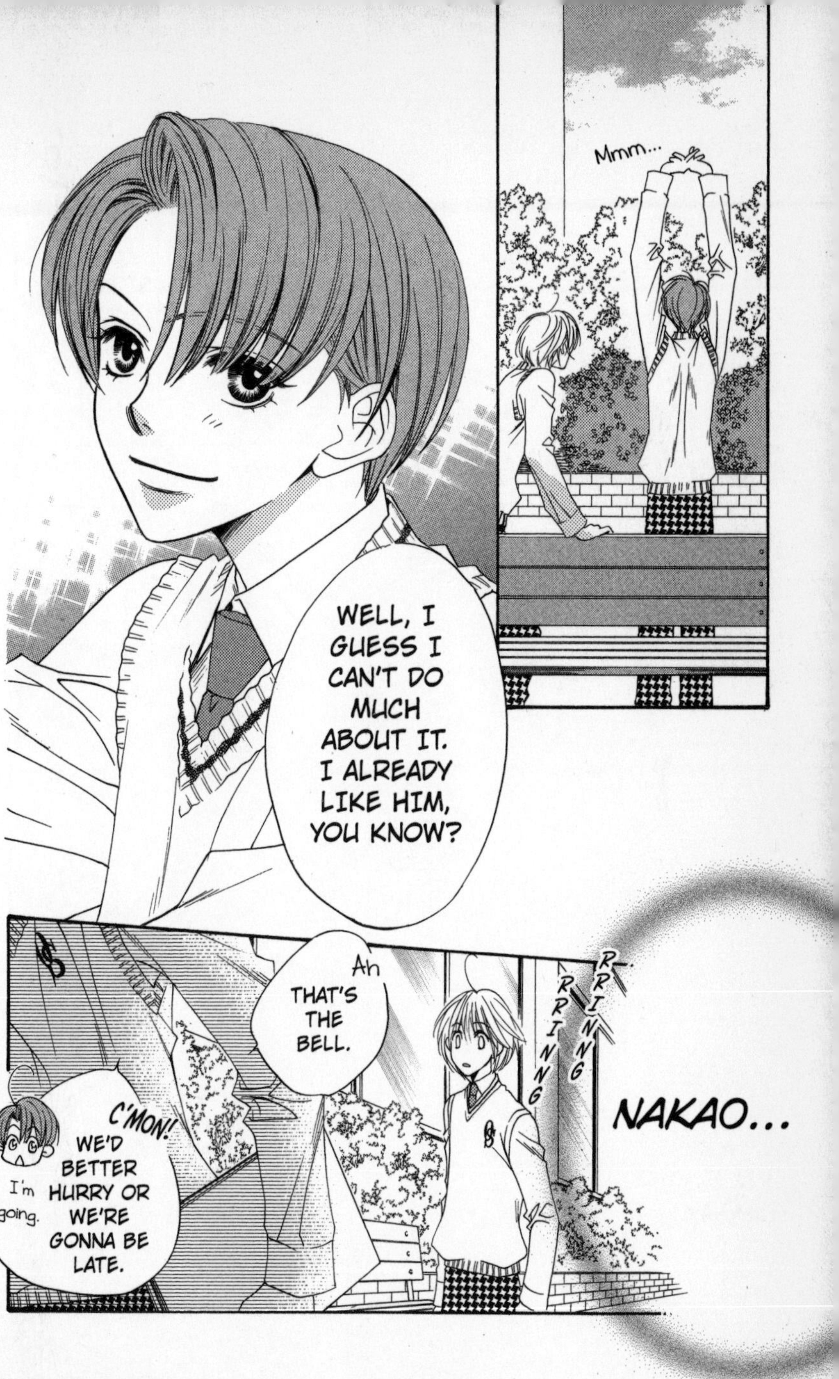
Mmm...
WELL, I GUESS I CAN'T DO MUCH ABOUT IT. I ALREADY LIKE HIM, YOU KNOW?
RRING
RRING
Ah THAT'S THE BELL.
NAKAO...
C'MON! WE'D BETTER HURRY OR WE'RE GONNA BE LATE.
I'm going.

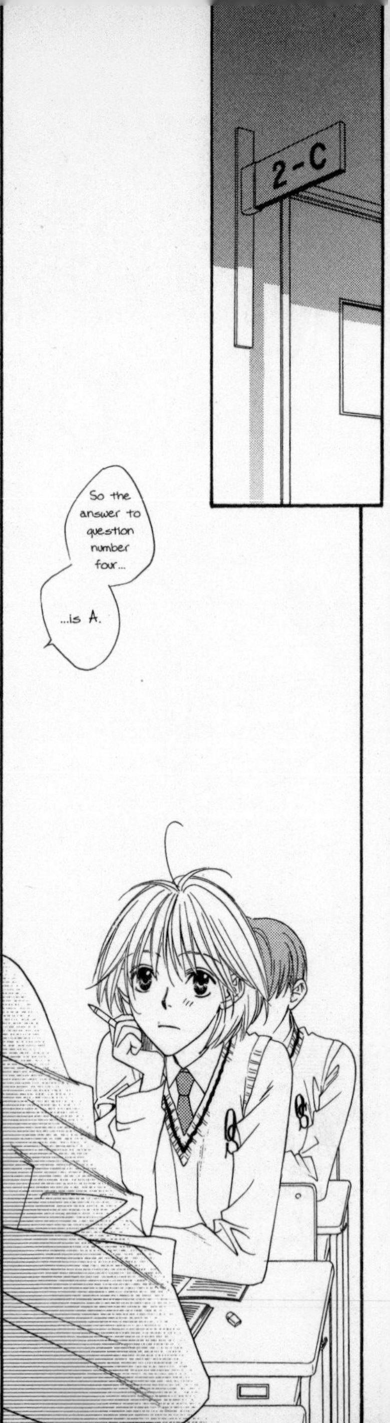
2-C
So the answer to question number four...
...is A.

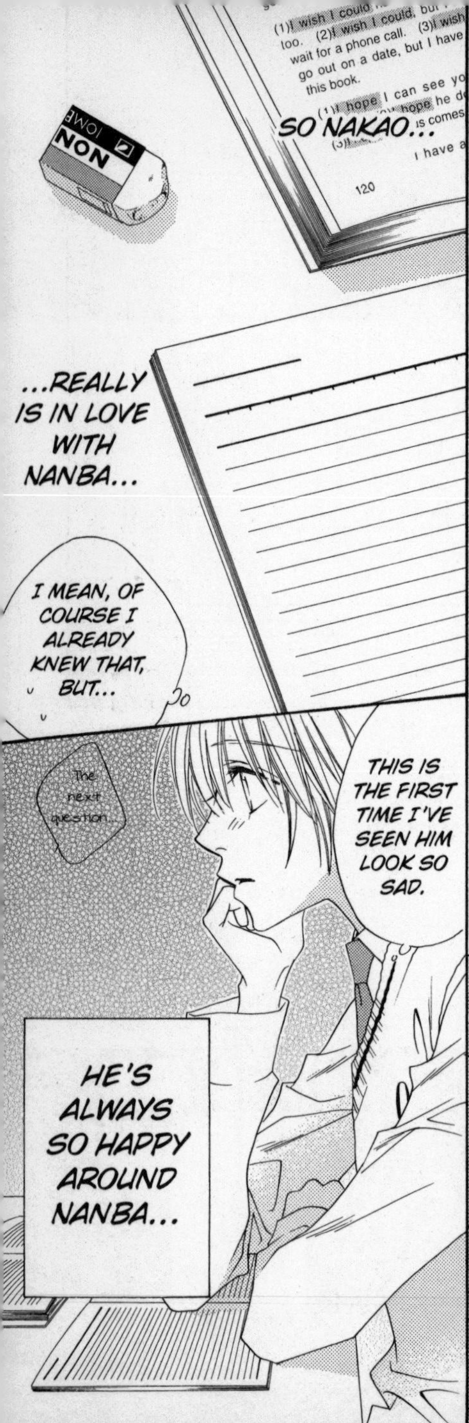
SO NAKAO...
120
...REALLY IS IN LOVE WITH NANBA...
I MEAN, OF COURSE I ALREADY KNEW THAT, BUT...
THIS IS THE FIRST TIME I'VE SEEN HIM LOOK SO SAD.
The next question...
HE'S ALWAYS SO HAPPY AROUND NANBA...

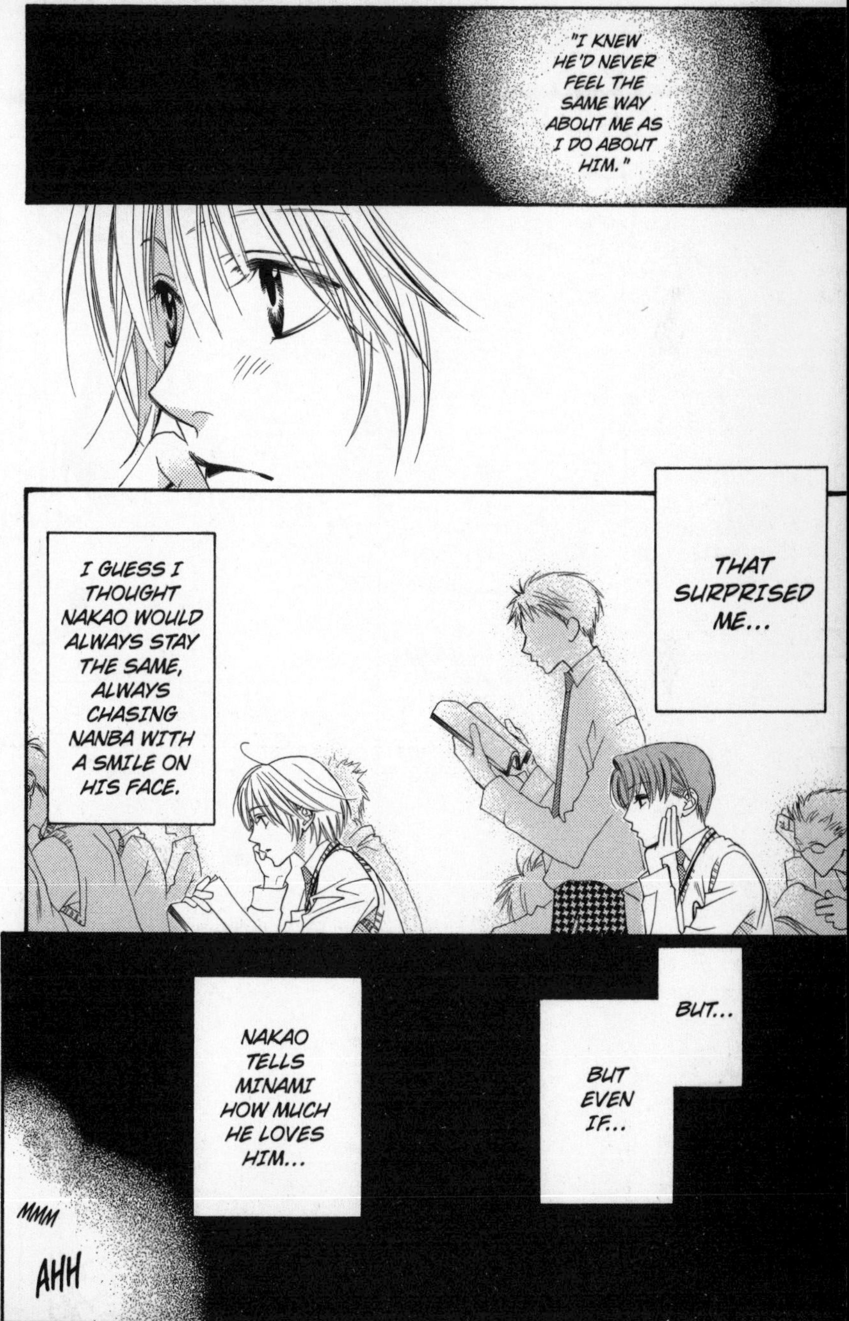
"I KNEW HE'D NEVER FEEL THE SAME WAY ABOUT ME AS I DO ABOUT HIM."
THAT SURPRISED ME...
I GUESS I THOUGHT NAKAO WOULD ALWAYS STAY THE SAME, ALWAYS CHASING NANBA WITH A SMILE ON HIS FACE.
BUT...
BUT EVEN IF...
NAKAO TELLS MINAMI HOW MUCH HE LOVES HIM...
MMM
AHH

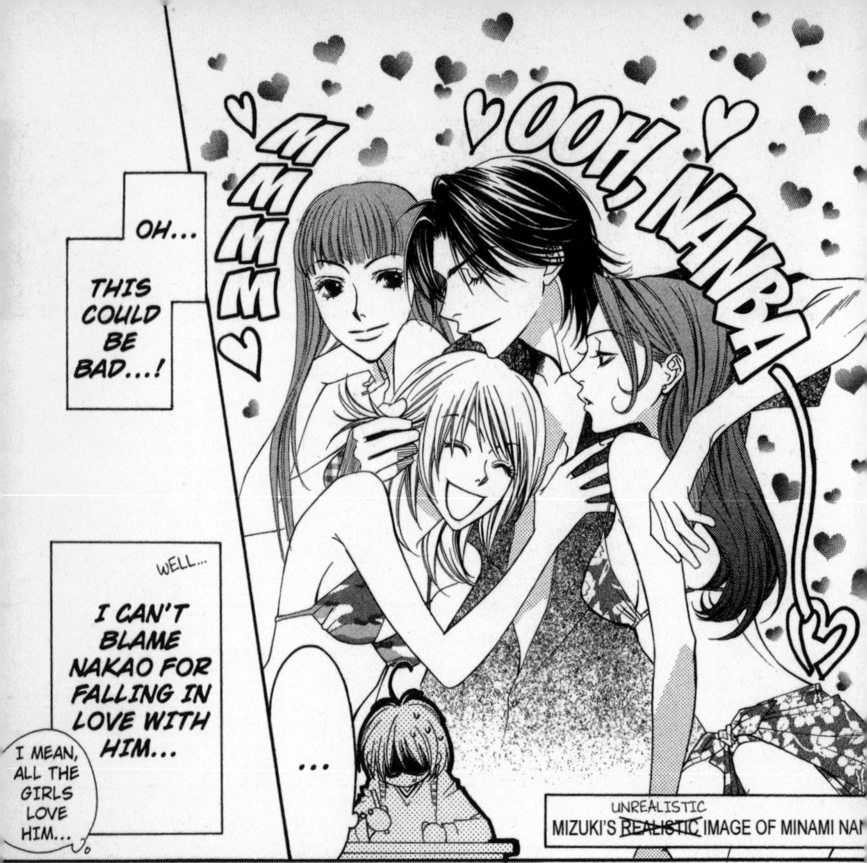
OOH, NANBA!
MMMM
OH... THIS COULD BE BAD...!
...
WELL... I CAN'T BLAME NAKAO FOR FALLING IN LOVE WITH HIM...
I MEAN, ALL THE GIRLS LOVE HIM...
MIZUKI'S UNREALISTIC ~~REALISTIC~~ IMAGE OF MINAMI NA

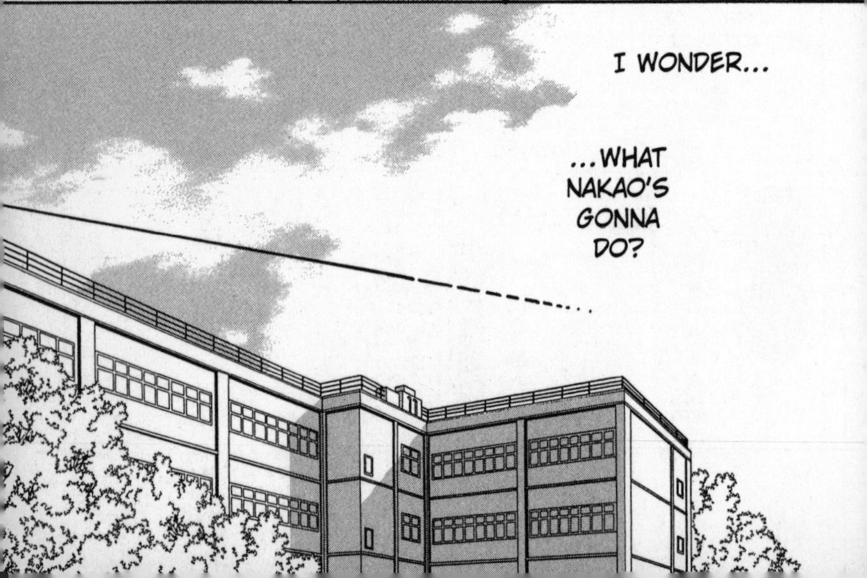
I WONDER...
...WHAT NAKAO'S GONNA DO?

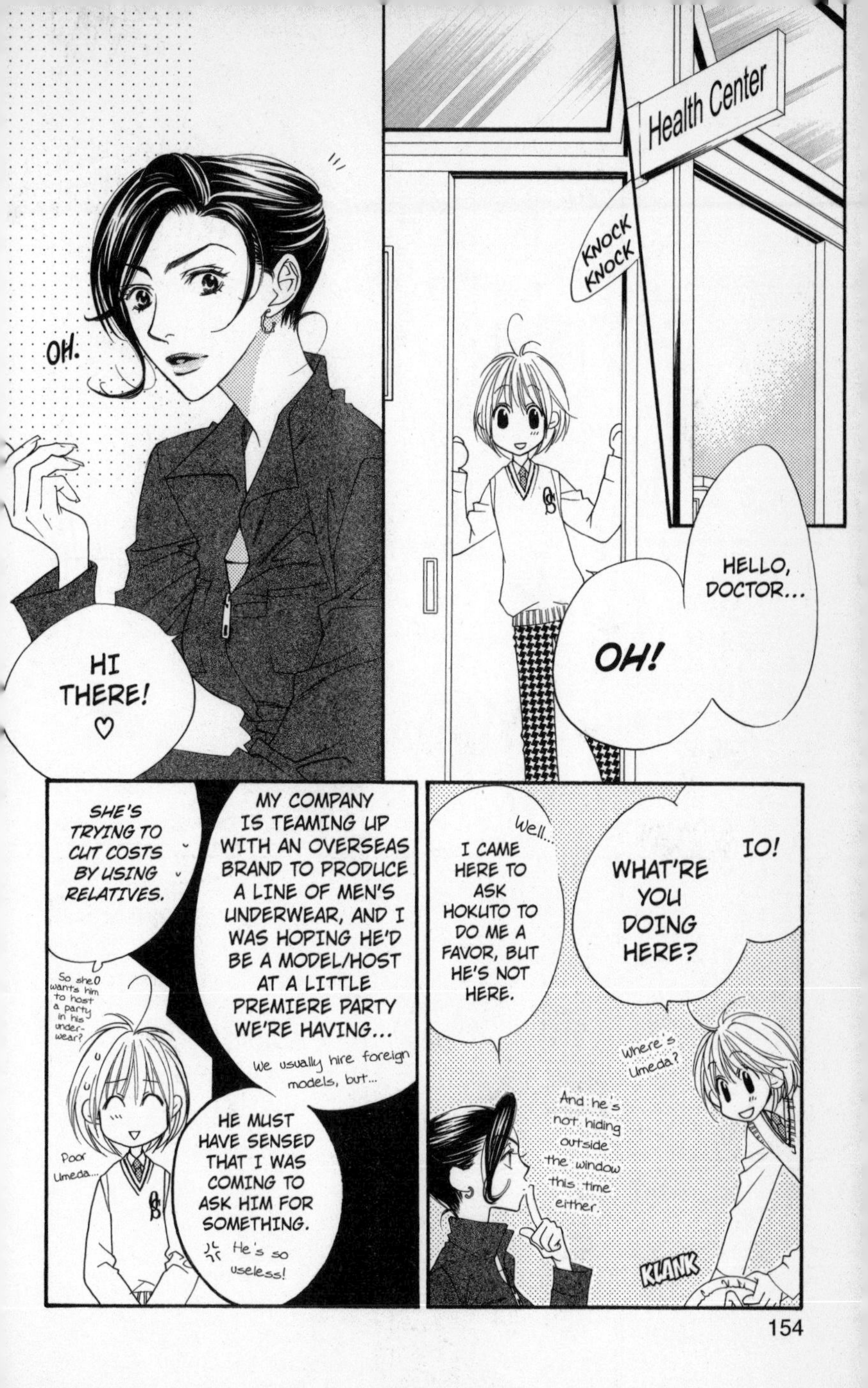
Health Center
KNOCK KNOCK
HELLO, DOCTOR...
OH!
OH.
HI THERE! ♡
IO!
WHAT'RE YOU DOING HERE?
Well...
I CAME HERE TO ASK HOKUTO TO DO ME A FAVOR, BUT HE'S NOT HERE.
Where's Umeda?
And he's not hiding outside the window this time either.
KLANK
MY COMPANY IS TEAMING UP WITH AN OVERSEAS BRAND TO PRODUCE A LINE OF MEN'S UNDERWEAR, AND I WAS HOPING HE'D BE A MODEL/HOST AT A LITTLE PREMIERE PARTY WE'RE HAVING...
SHE'S TRYING TO CUT COSTS BY USING RELATIVES.
We usually hire foreign models, but...
So she wants him to host a party in his underwear?
HE MUST HAVE SENSED THAT I WAS COMING TO ASK HIM FOR SOMETHING.
He's so useless!
Poor Umeda...

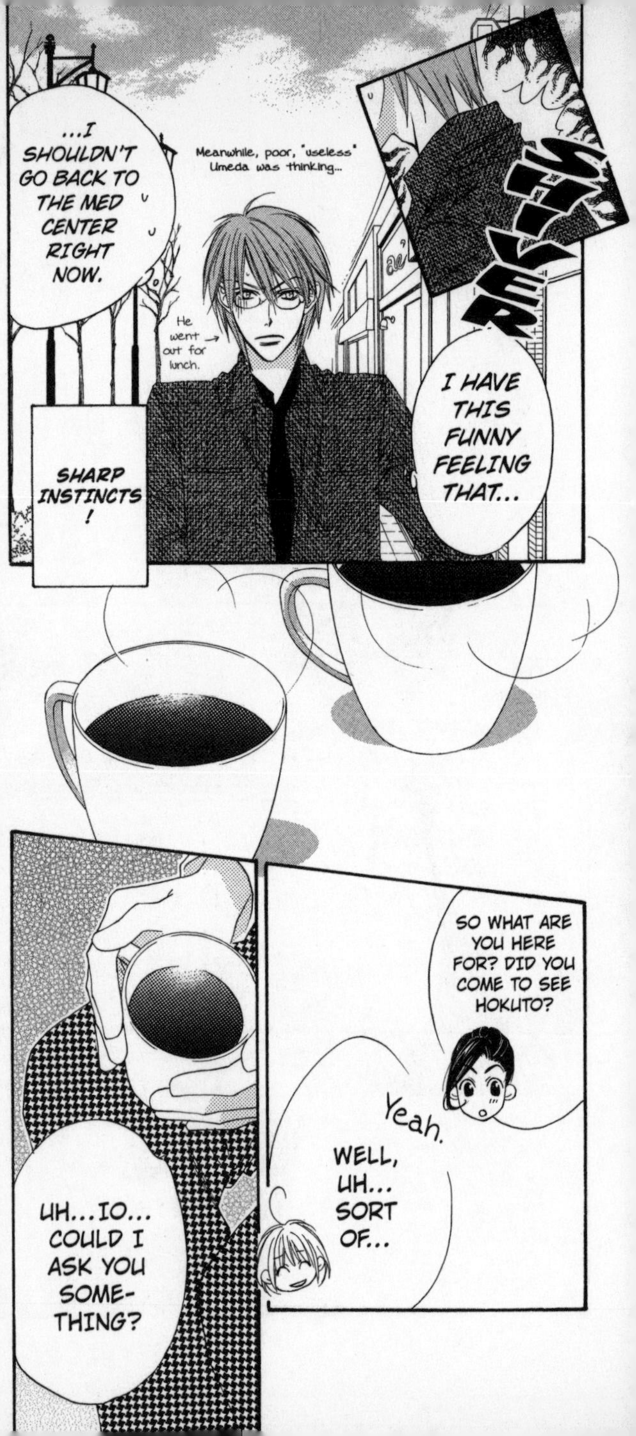
SHIVER
I HAVE THIS FUNNY FEELING THAT...
Meanwhile, poor, "useless" Umeda was thinking...
...I SHOULDN'T GO BACK TO THE MED CENTER RIGHT NOW.
He went out for lunch.
SHARP INSTINCTS!
SO WHAT ARE YOU HERE FOR? DID YOU COME TO SEE HOKUTO?
Yeah.
WELL, UH... SORT OF...
UH...IO... COULD I ASK YOU SOMETHING?

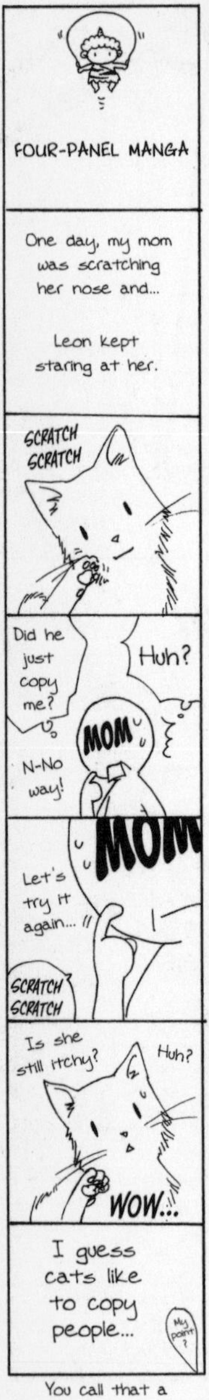
FOUR-PANEL MANGA
One day, my mom was scratching her nose and...
Leon kept staring at her.
SCRATCH SCRATCH
Did he just copy me?
Huh?
MOM
N-No way!
MOM
Let's try it again...
SCRATCH SCRATCH
Is she still itchy?
Huh?
WOW...
I guess cats like to copy people...
My point?

You call that a four-panel manga...?

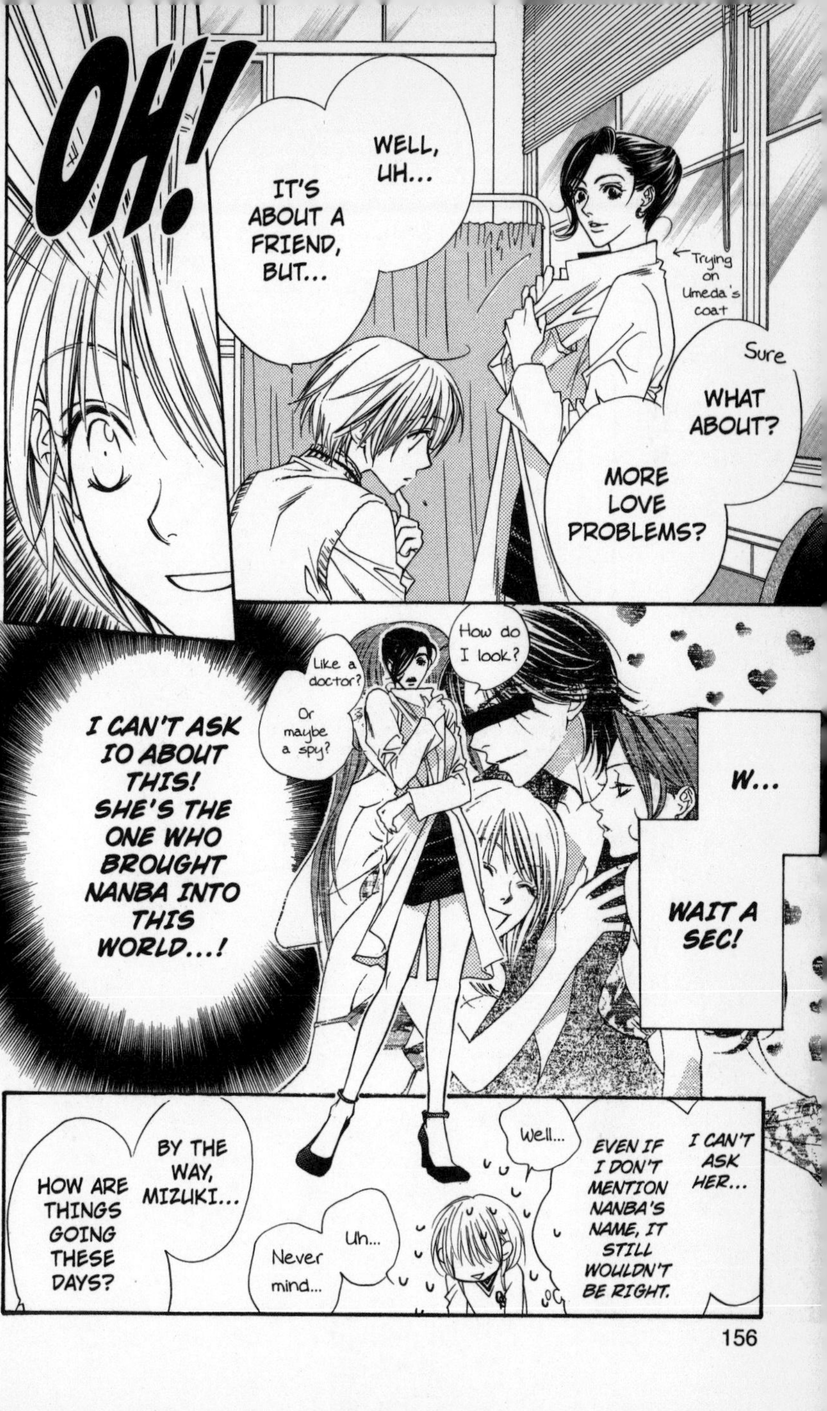

Trying on Umeda's coat
Sure
WHAT ABOUT?
MORE LOVE PROBLEMS?
WELL, UH...
IT'S ABOUT A FRIEND, BUT...
OH!
W...
WAIT A SEC!
How do I look?
Like a doctor?
Or maybe a spy?
I CAN'T ASK IO ABOUT THIS! SHE'S THE ONE WHO BROUGHT NANBA INTO THIS WORLD...!
I CAN'T ASK HER...
EVEN IF I DON'T MENTION NANBA'S NAME, IT STILL WOULDN'T BE RIGHT.
Well...
Uh...
Never mind...
BY THE WAY, MIZUKI...
HOW ARE THINGS GOING THESE DAYS?

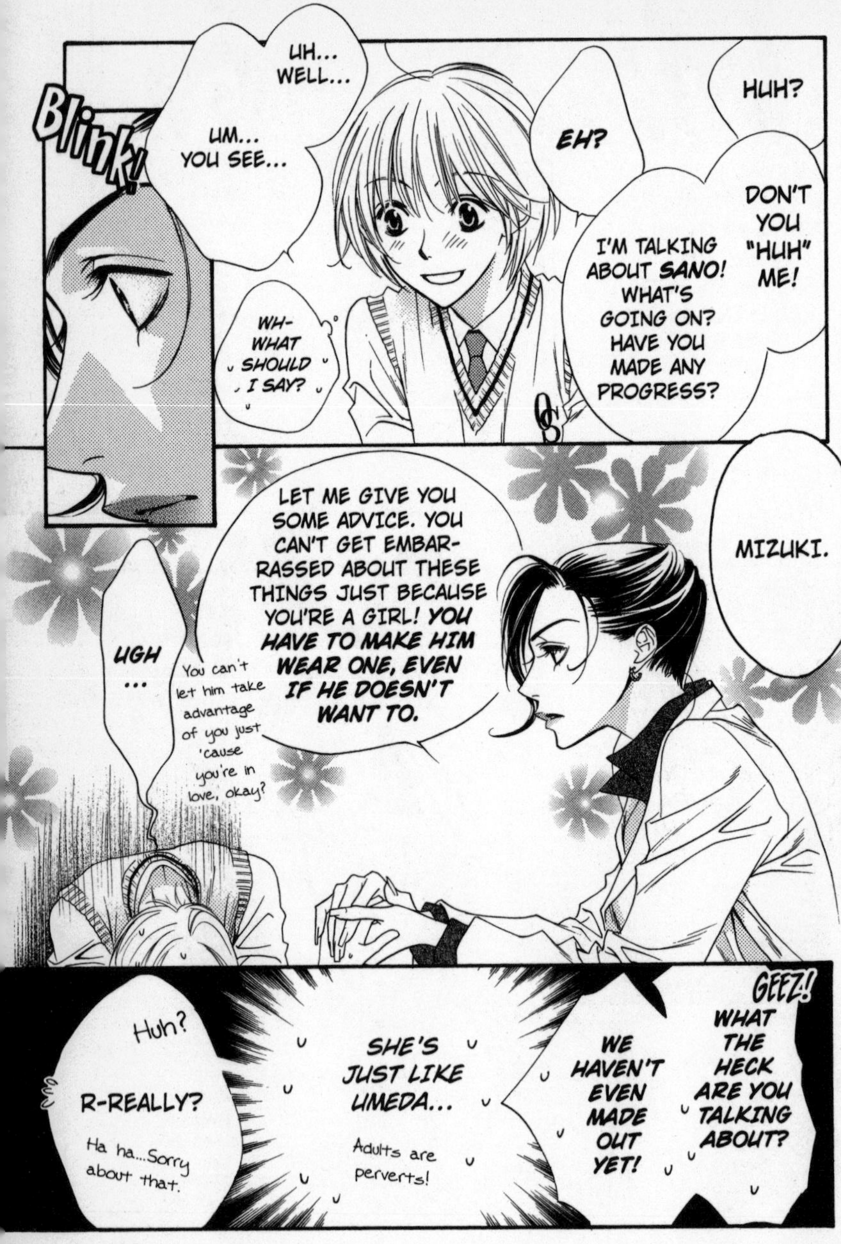
HUH?
DON'T YOU "HUH" ME!
I'M TALKING ABOUT SANO! WHAT'S GOING ON? HAVE YOU MADE ANY PROGRESS?
EH?
UH... WELL...
UM... YOU SEE...
WH-WHAT SHOULD I SAY?
Blink!
MIZUKI.
LET ME GIVE YOU SOME ADVICE. YOU CAN'T GET EMBARRASSED ABOUT THESE THINGS JUST BECAUSE YOU'RE A GIRL! YOU HAVE TO MAKE HIM WEAR ONE, EVEN IF HE DOESN'T WANT TO.
You can't let him take advantage of you just 'cause you're in love, okay?
UGH...
GEEZ!
WHAT THE HECK ARE YOU TALKING ABOUT?
WE HAVEN'T EVEN MADE OUT YET!
SHE'S JUST LIKE UMEDA...
Adults are perverts!
Huh?
R-REALLY?
Ha ha...Sorry about that.

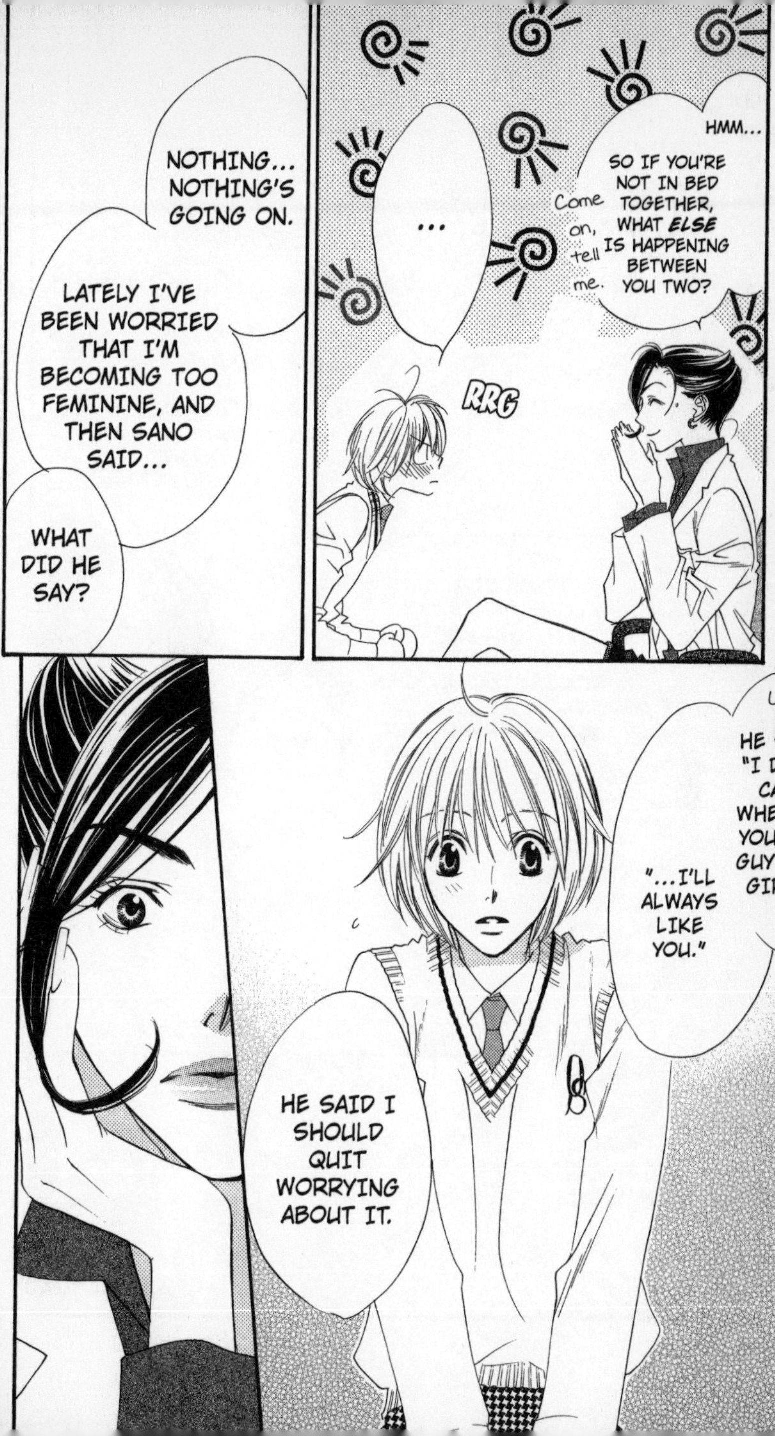
HMM...
SO IF YOU'RE NOT IN BED TOGETHER, WHAT *ELSE* IS HAPPENING BETWEEN YOU TWO?
Come on, tell me.
...
RRG
NOTHING... NOTHING'S GOING ON.
LATELY I'VE BEEN WORRIED THAT I'M BECOMING TOO FEMININE, AND THEN SANO SAID...
WHAT DID HE SAY?
Um...
HE SAID, "I DON'T CARE WHETHER YOU'RE A GUY OR A GIRL...
"...I'LL ALWAYS LIKE YOU."
HE SAID I SHOULD QUIT WORRYING ABOUT IT.

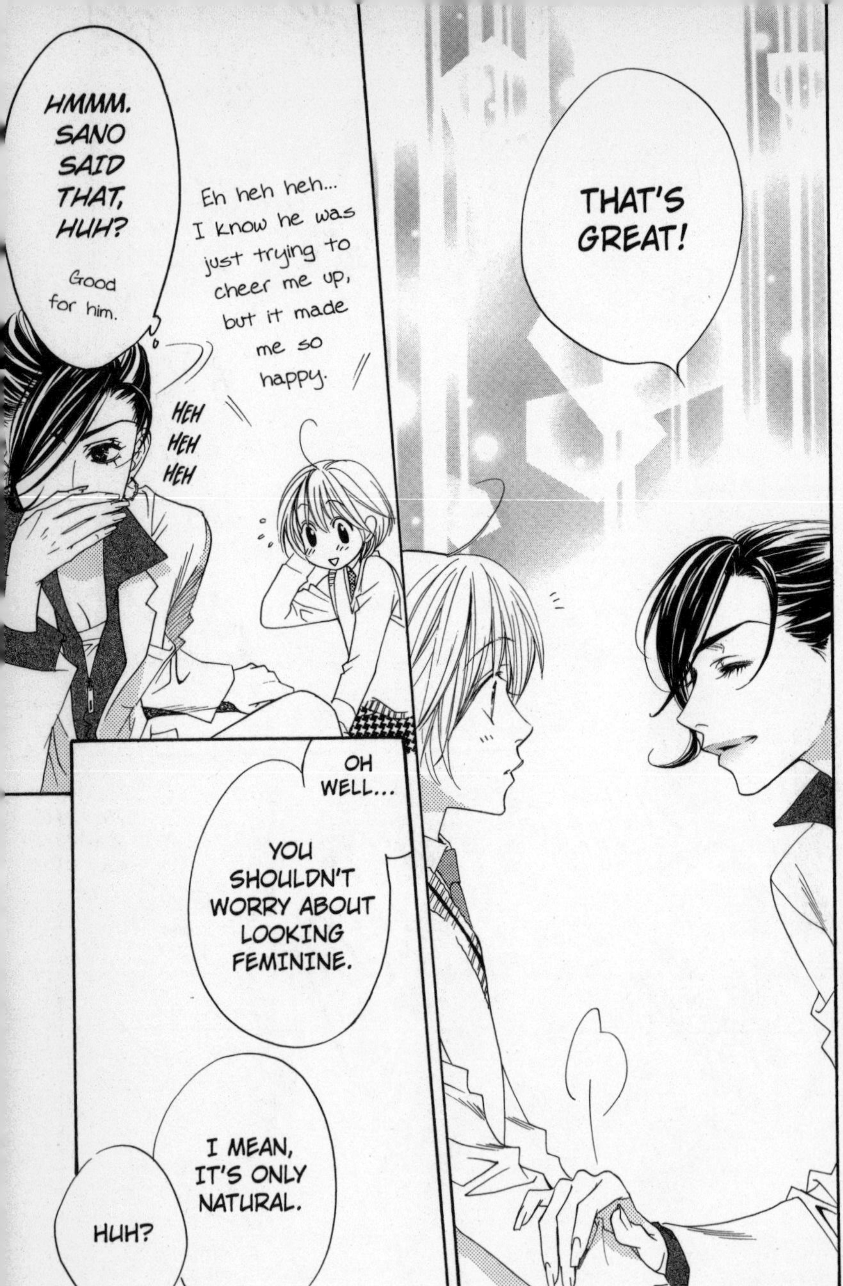
THAT'S GREAT!
HMMM. SANO SAID THAT, HUH?
Good for him.
Eh heh heh... I know he was just trying to cheer me up, but it made me so happy.
HEH HEH HEH
OH WELL...
YOU SHOULDN'T WORRY ABOUT LOOKING FEMININE.
I MEAN, IT'S ONLY NATURAL.
HUH?

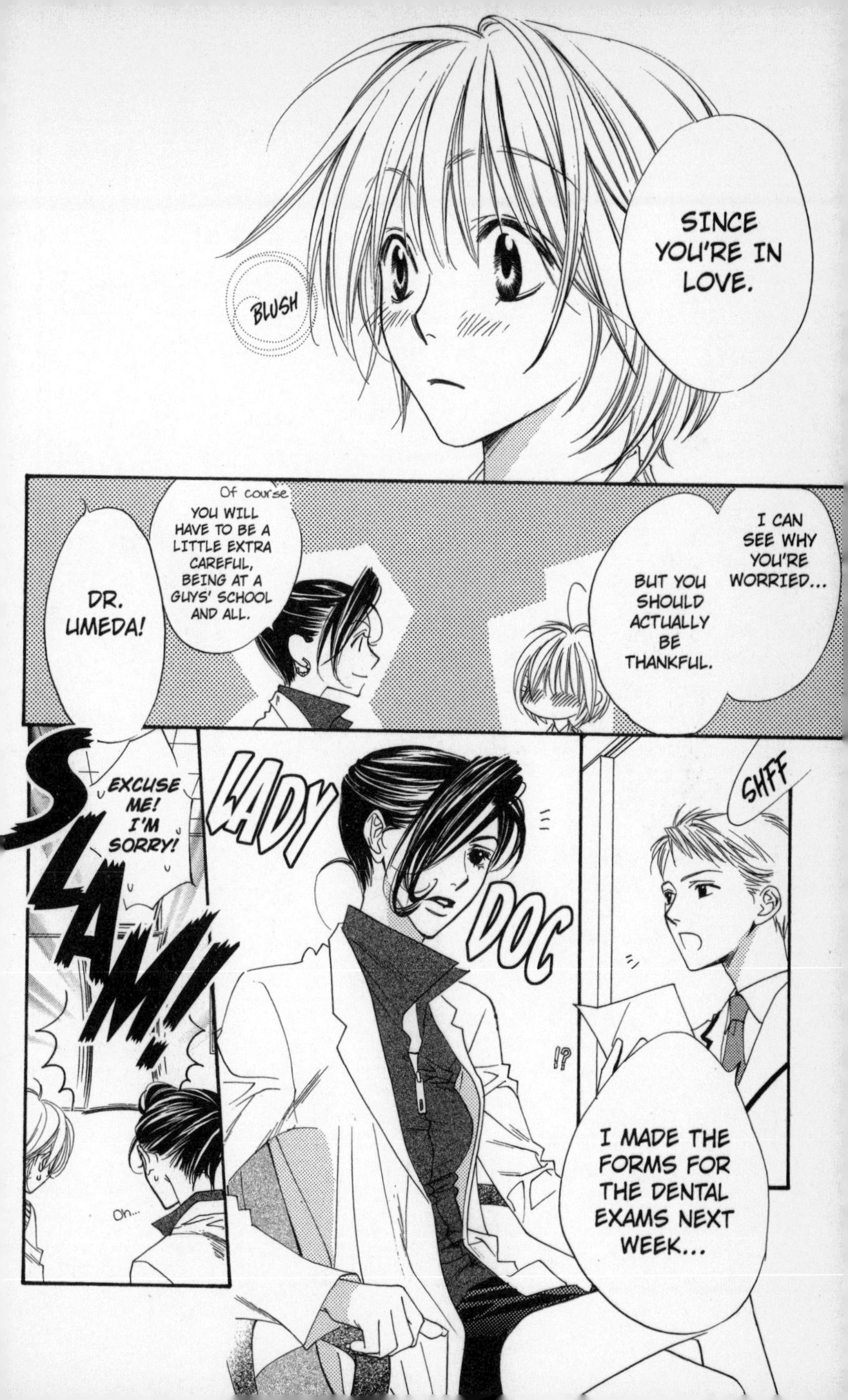
SINCE YOU'RE IN LOVE.
BLUSH
I CAN SEE WHY YOU'RE WORRIED...
BUT YOU SHOULD ACTUALLY BE THANKFUL.
Of course YOU WILL HAVE TO BE A LITTLE EXTRA CAREFUL, BEING AT A GUYS' SCHOOL AND ALL.
DR. UMEDA!
SHFF
I MADE THE FORMS FOR THE DENTAL EXAMS NEXT WEEK...
!?
LADY DOC
SLAM!
EXCUSE ME! I'M SORRY!
Oh...

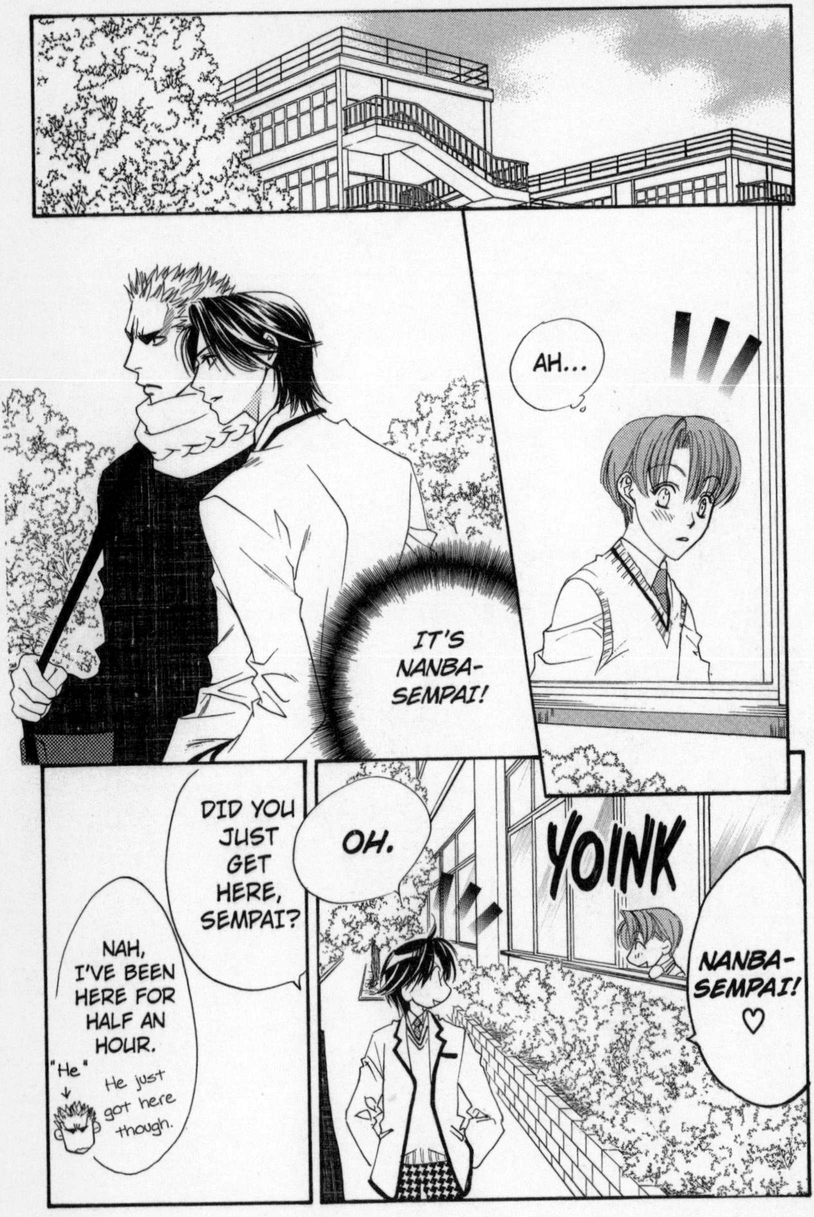
AH...
IT'S NANBA-SEMPAI!
YOINK
NANBA-SEMPAI! ♡
OH.
DID YOU JUST GET HERE, SEMPAI?
NAH, I'VE BEEN HERE FOR HALF AN HOUR.
"He"
He just got here though.

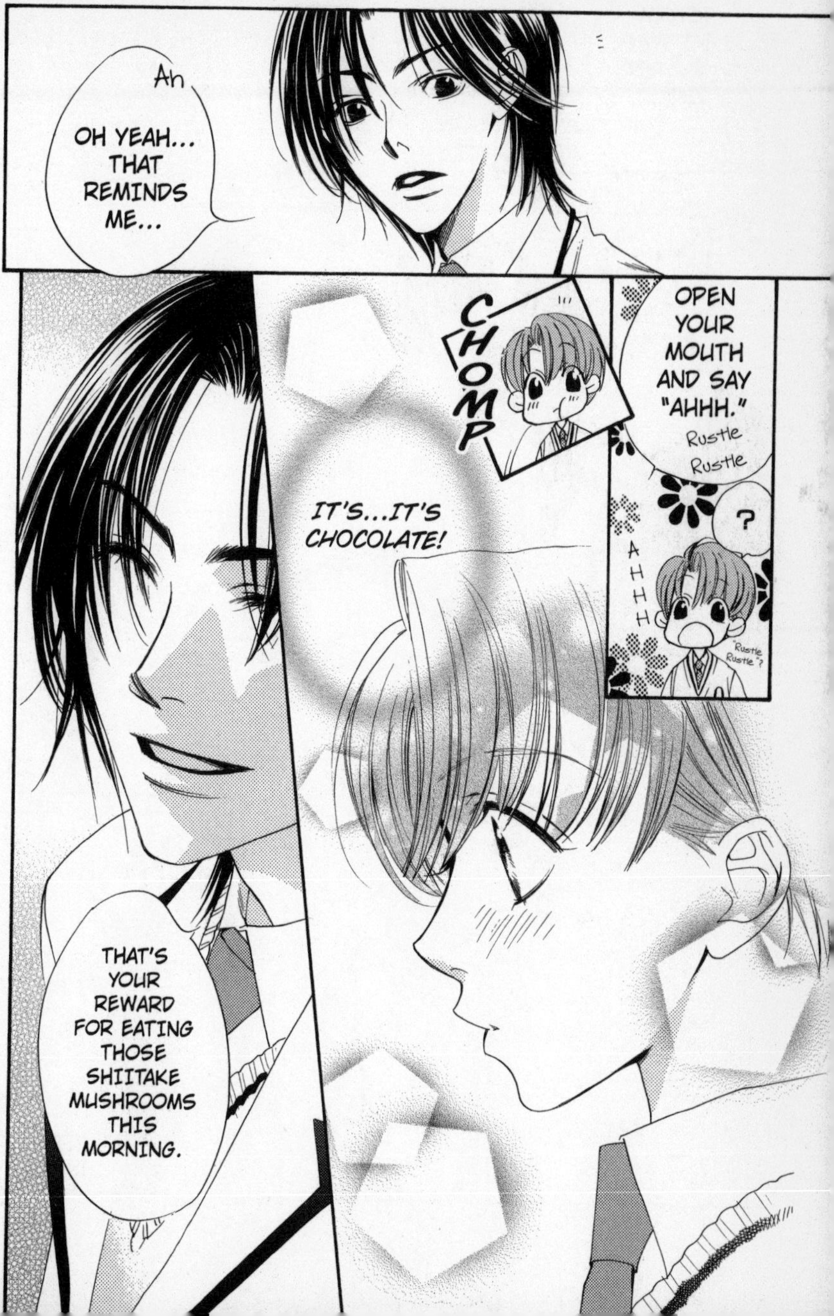
Ah
OH YEAH... THAT REMINDS ME...
OPEN YOUR MOUTH AND SAY "AHHH."
Rustle Rustle
?
AHHH
"Rustle Rustle"?
CHOMP
IT'S...IT'S CHOCOLATE!
THAT'S YOUR REWARD FOR EATING THOSE SHIITAKE MUSHROOMS THIS MORNING.

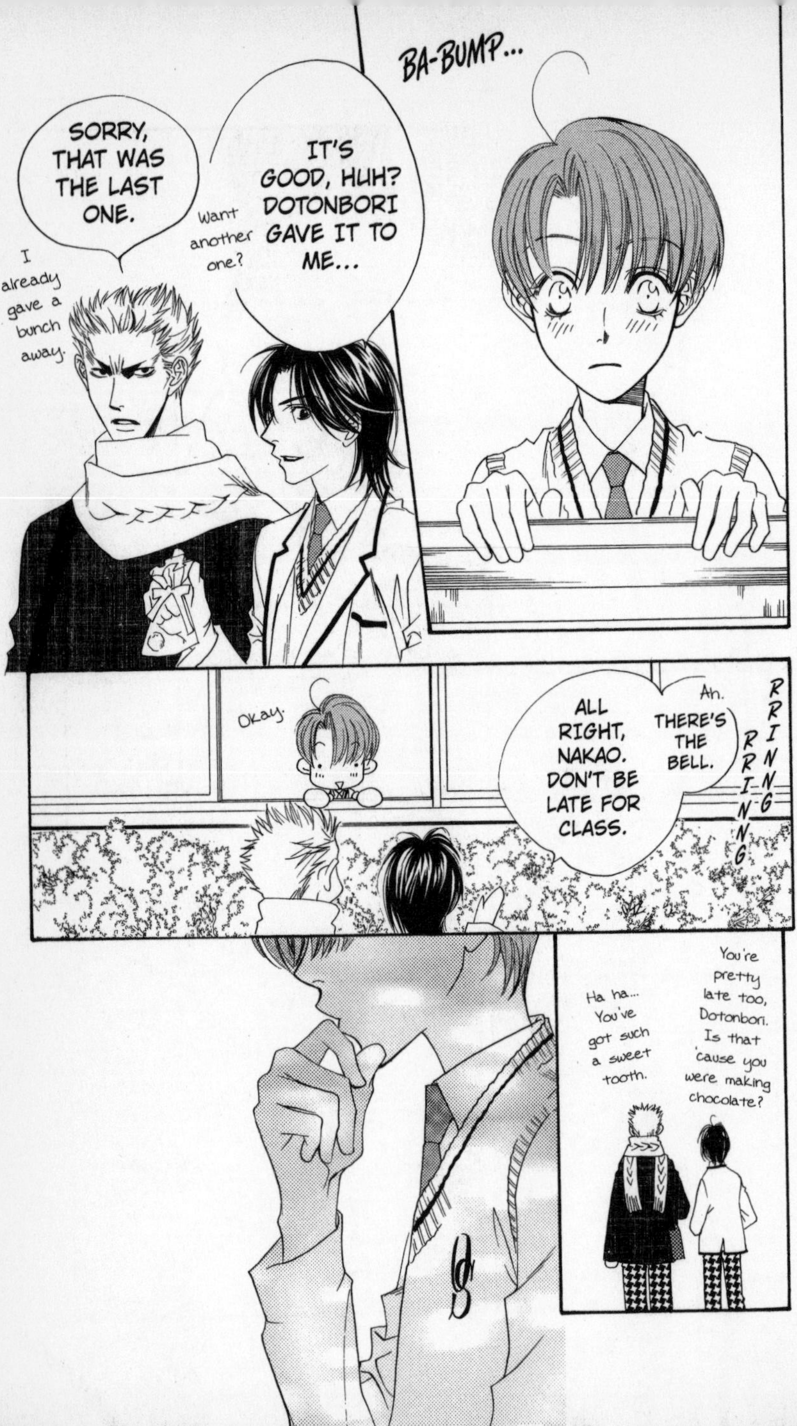
BA-BUMP...
IT'S GOOD, HUH? DOTONBORI GAVE IT TO ME...
Want another one?
SORRY, THAT WAS THE LAST ONE.
I already gave a bunch away.
RRING RRING
Ah. THERE'S THE BELL.
ALL RIGHT, NAKAO. DON'T BE LATE FOR CLASS.
Okay.
You're pretty late too, Dotonbori. Is that 'cause you were making chocolate?
Ha ha... You've got such a sweet tooth.

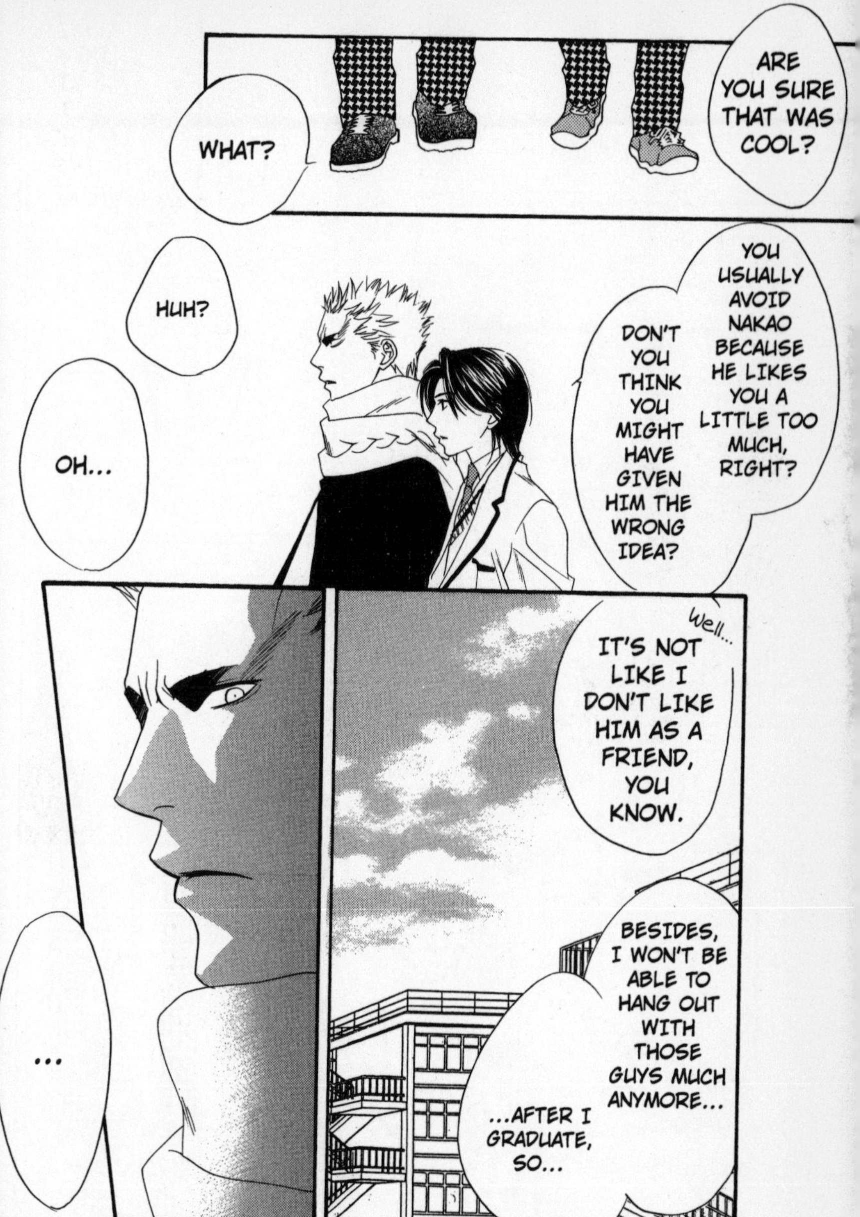
ARE YOU SURE THAT WAS COOL?
WHAT?
YOU USUALLY AVOID NAKAO BECAUSE HE LIKES YOU A LITTLE TOO MUCH, RIGHT?
DON'T YOU THINK YOU MIGHT HAVE GIVEN HIM THE WRONG IDEA?
HUH?
OH...
Well...
IT'S NOT LIKE I DON'T LIKE HIM AS A FRIEND, YOU KNOW.
BESIDES, I WON'T BE ABLE TO HANG OUT WITH THOSE GUYS MUCH ANYMORE...
...AFTER I GRADUATE, SO...
...

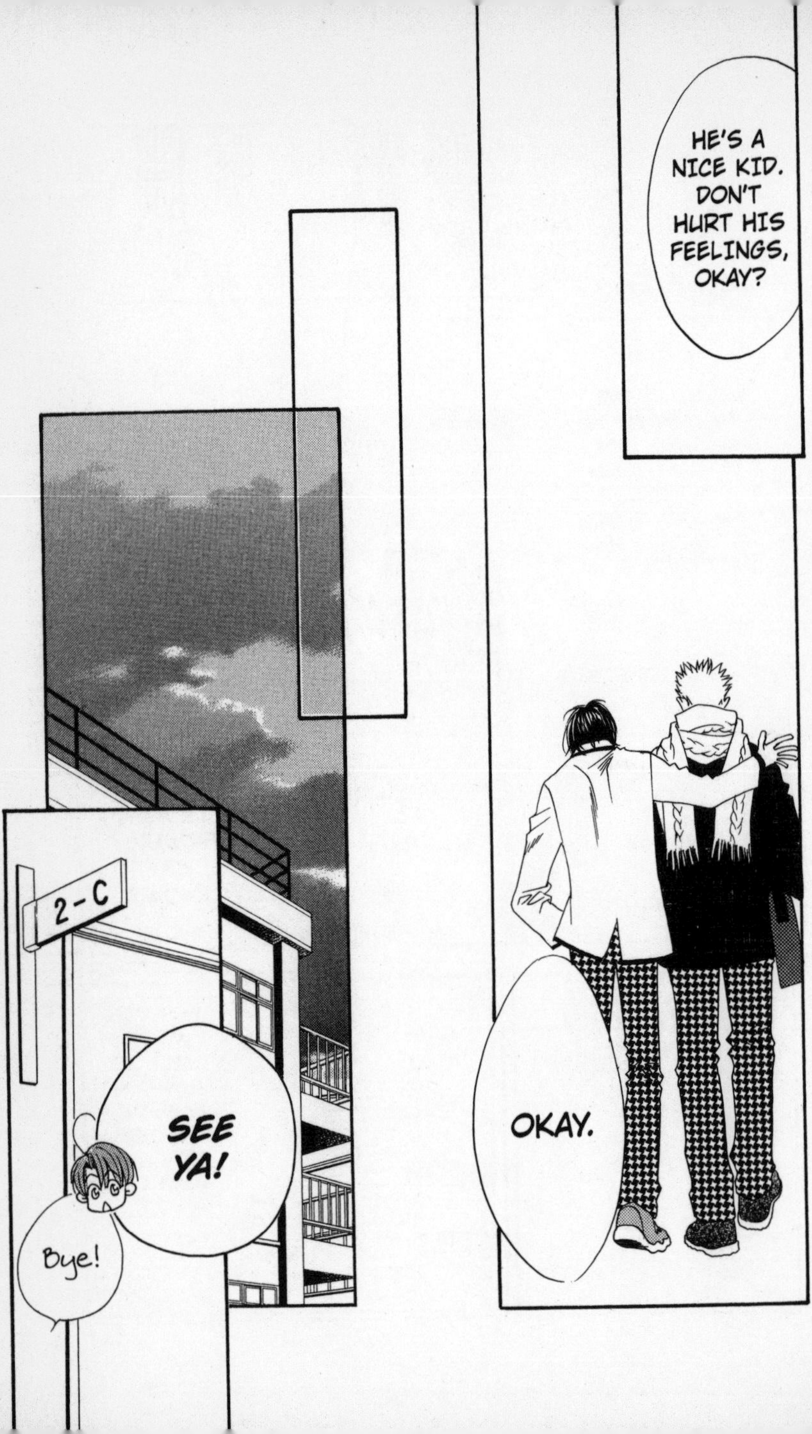
HE'S A NICE KID. DON'T HURT HIS FEELINGS, OKAY?
OKAY.
2-C
SEE YA!
Bye!

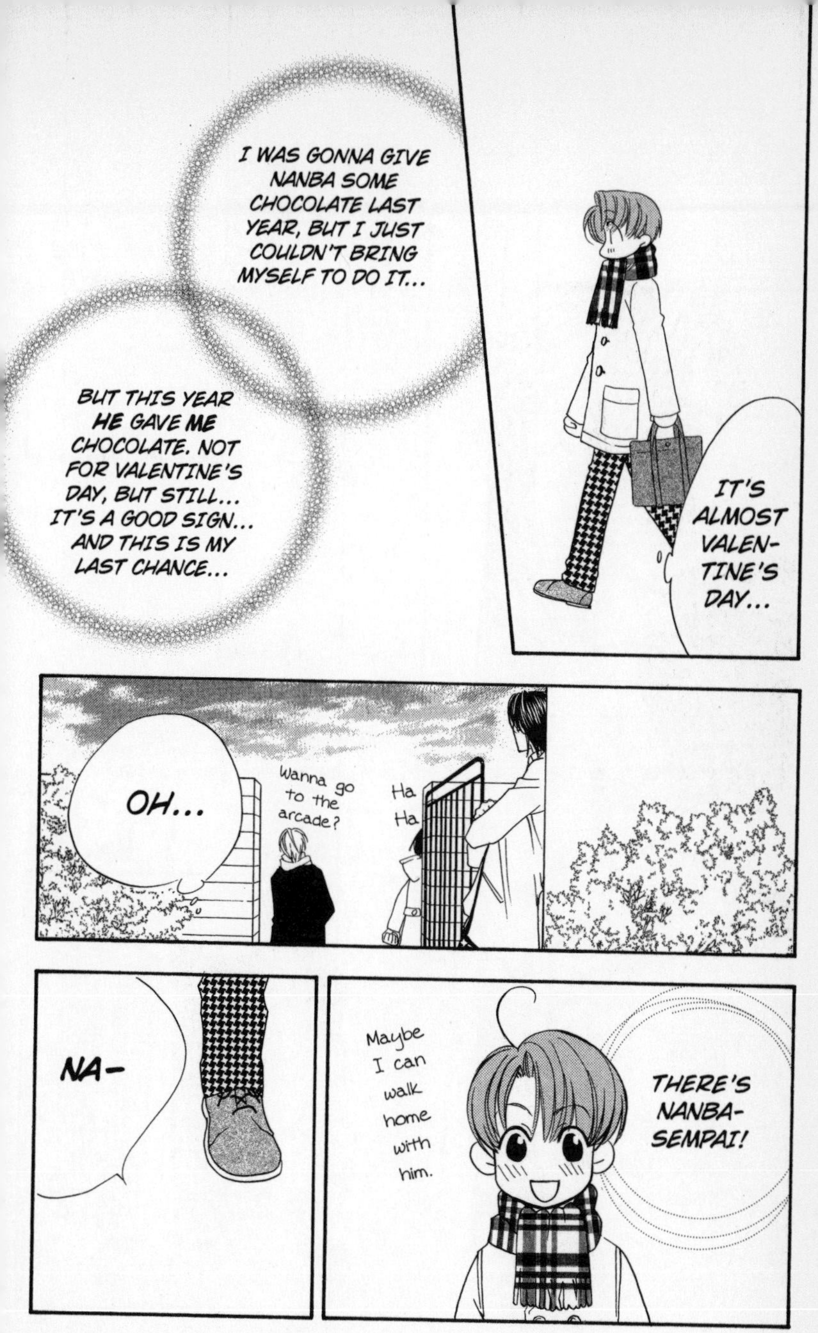
IT'S ALMOST VALENTINE'S DAY...
I WAS GONNA GIVE NANBA SOME CHOCOLATE LAST YEAR, BUT I JUST COULDN'T BRING MYSELF TO DO IT...
BUT THIS YEAR HE GAVE ME CHOCOLATE. NOT FOR VALENTINE'S DAY, BUT STILL... IT'S A GOOD SIGN... AND THIS IS MY LAST CHANCE...
Ha Ha
Wanna go to the arcade?
OH...
THERE'S NANBA-SEMPAI!
Maybe I can walk home with him.
NA-

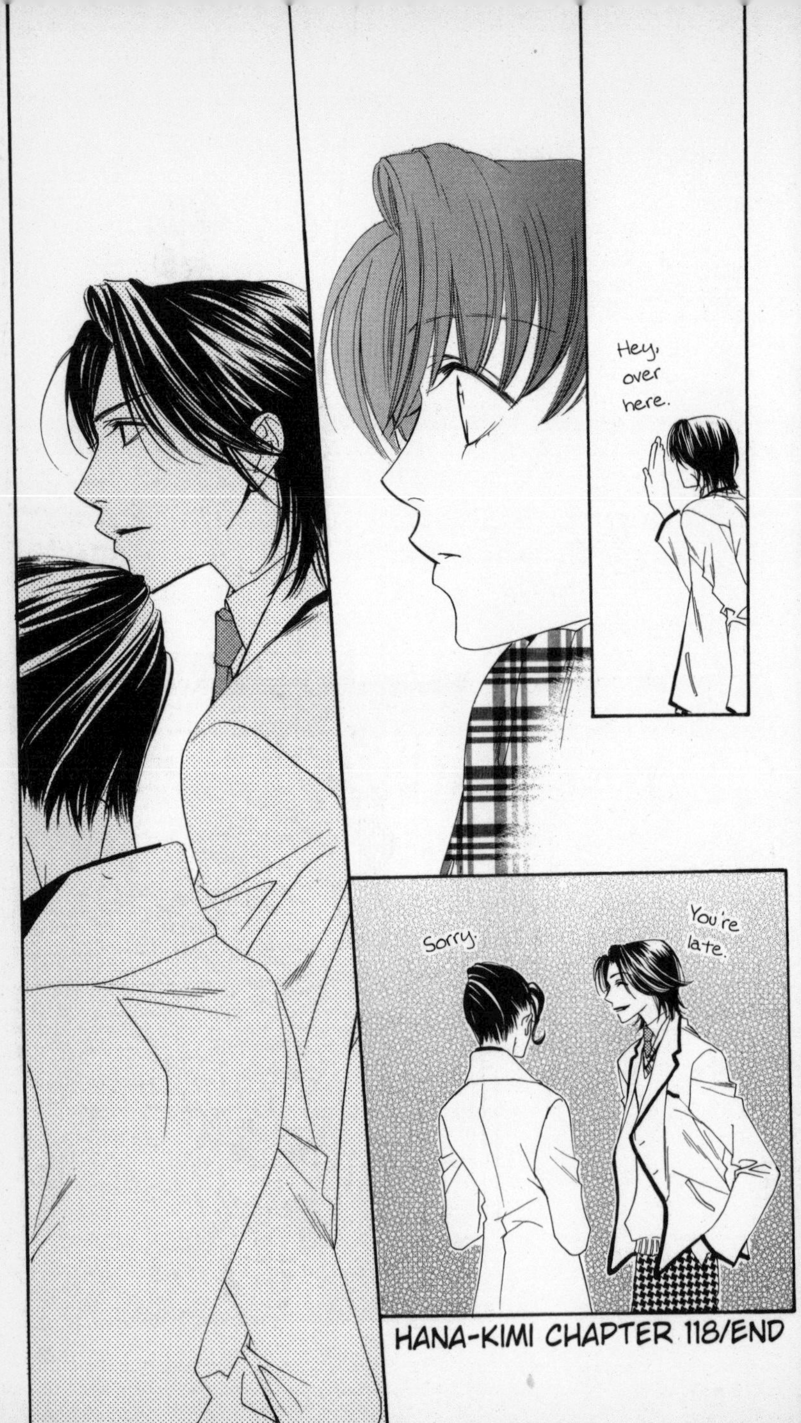
Hey, over here.
You're late.
Sorry.

HANA-KIMI CHAPTER 118/END

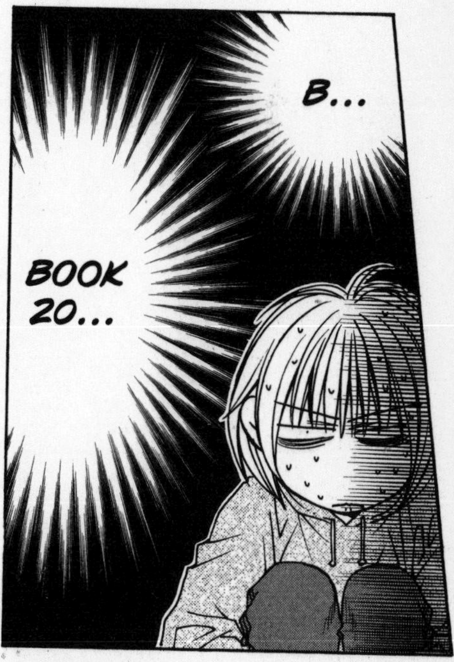
B...
BOOK 20...

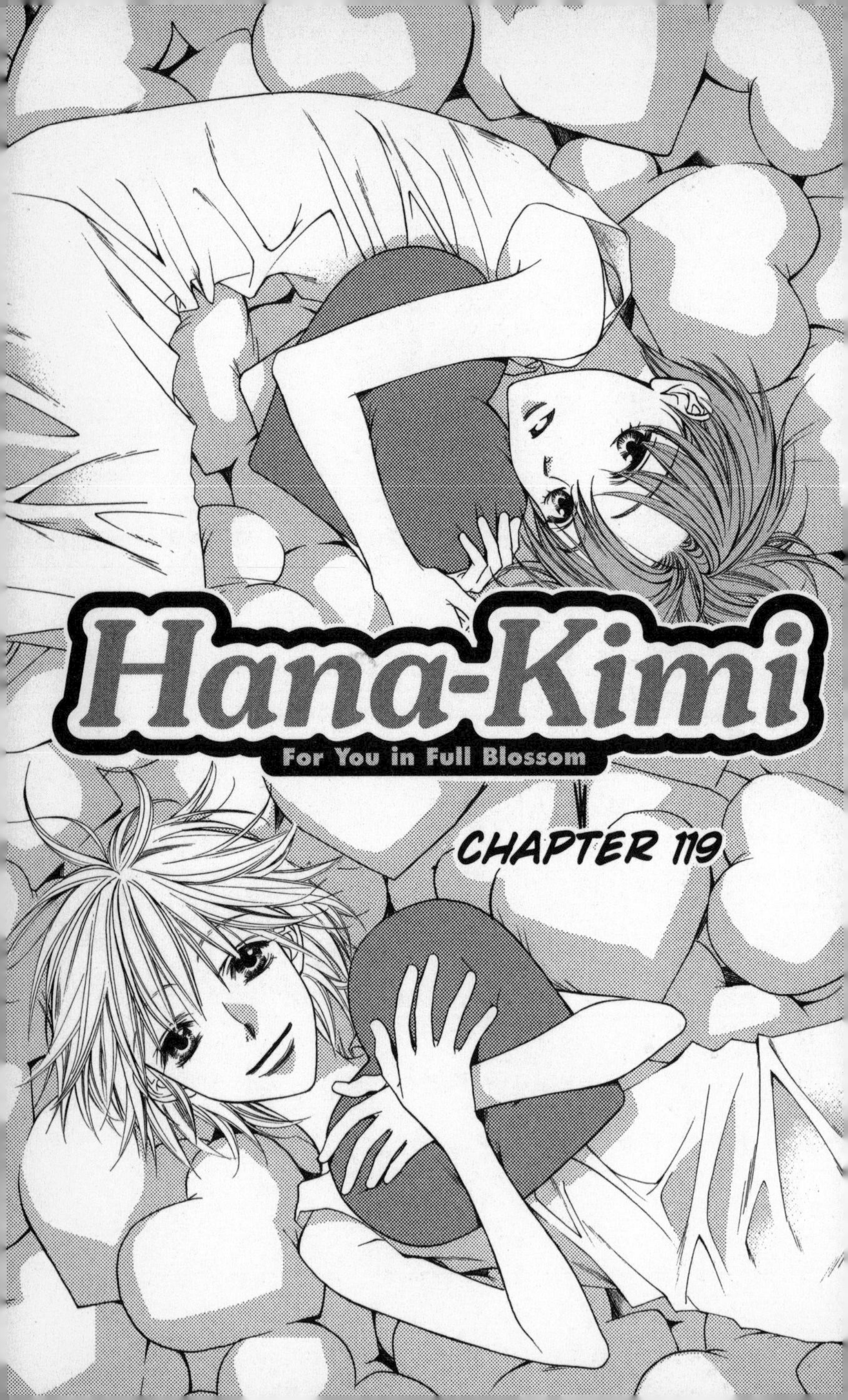
Hana-Kimi
For You in Full Blossom
CHAPTER 119

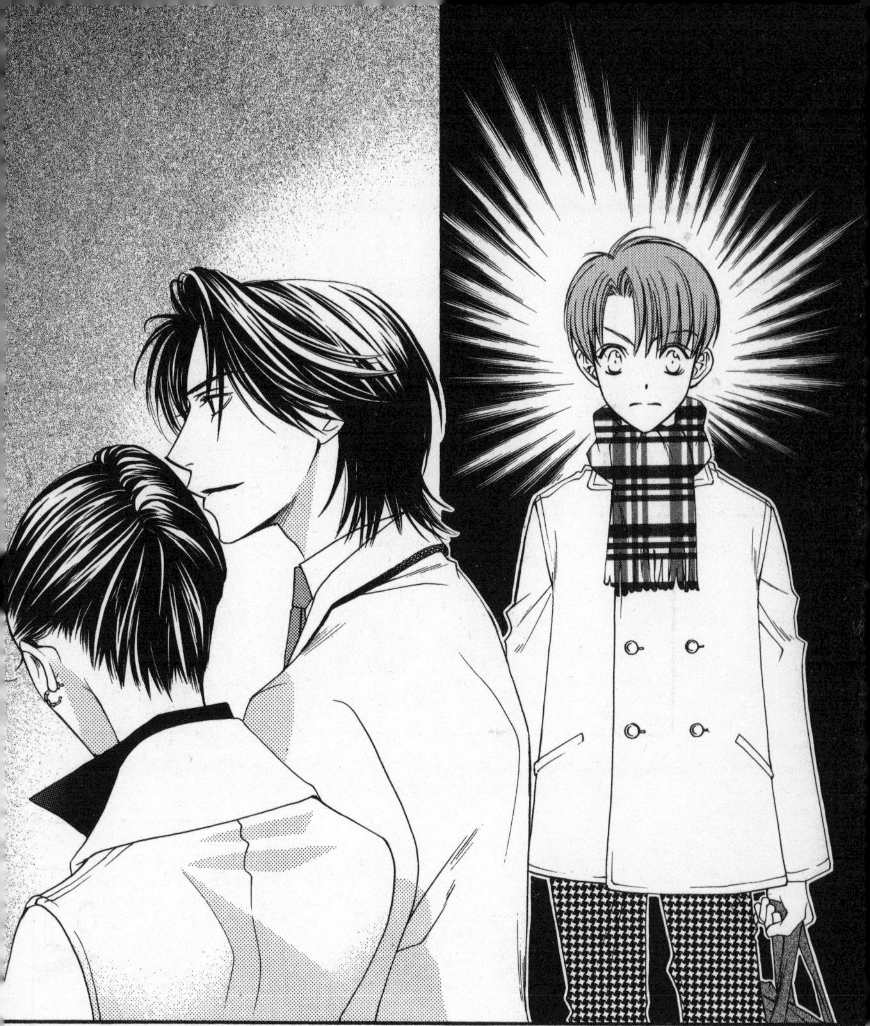

MY LATEST PROBLEM...

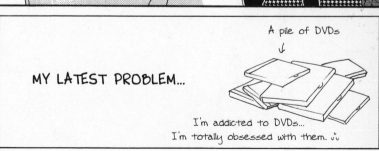

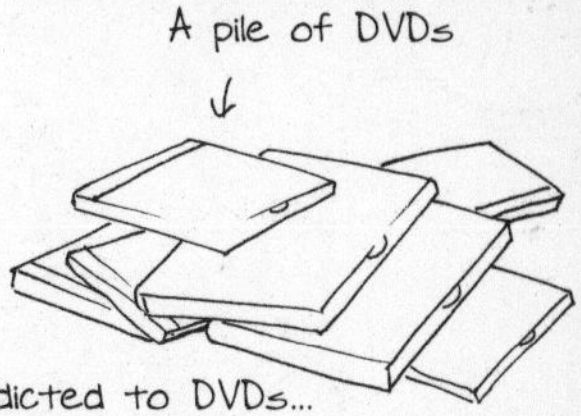
A pile of DVDs

I'm addicted to DVDs...
I'm totally obsessed with them.

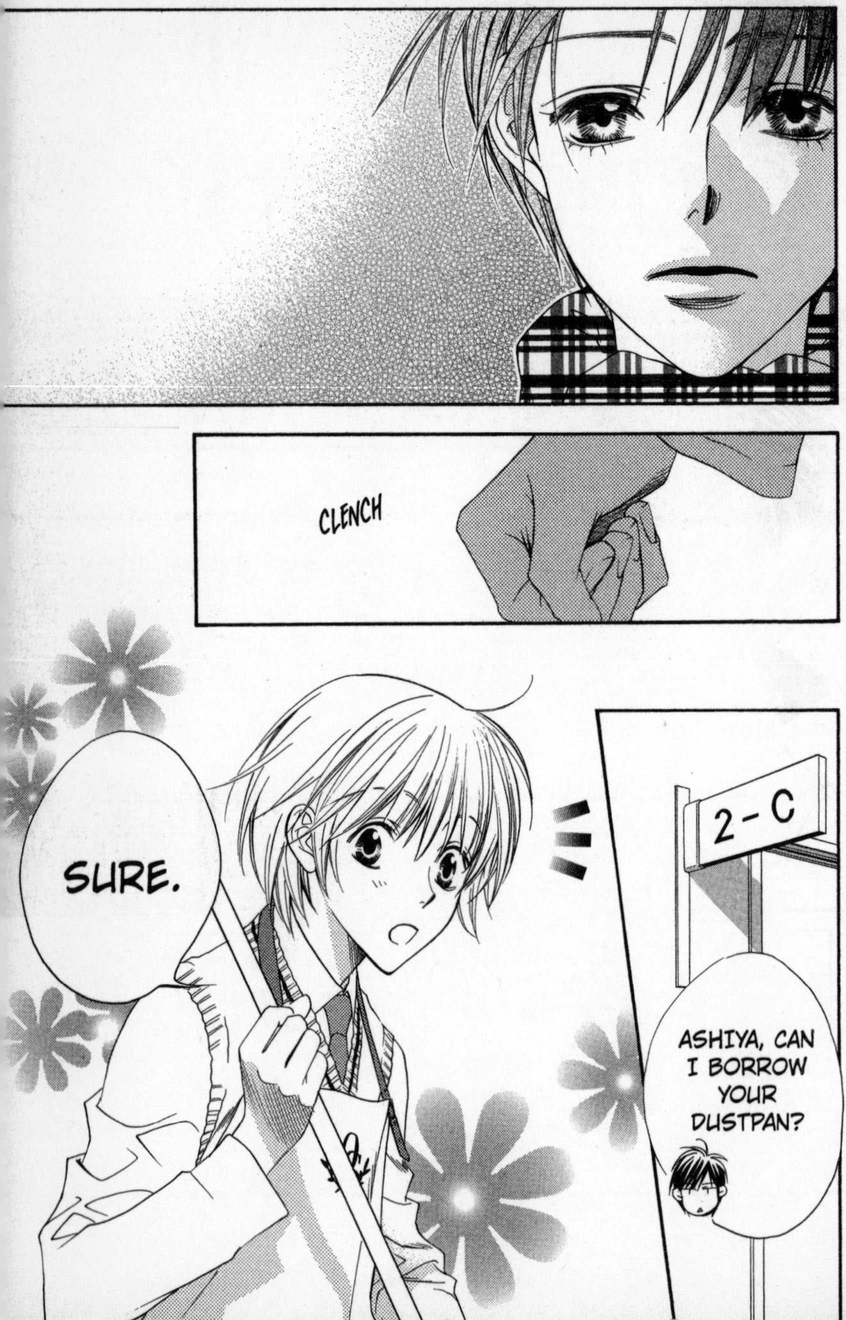
CLENCH
2-C
ASHIYA, CAN I BORROW YOUR DUSTPAN?
SURE.

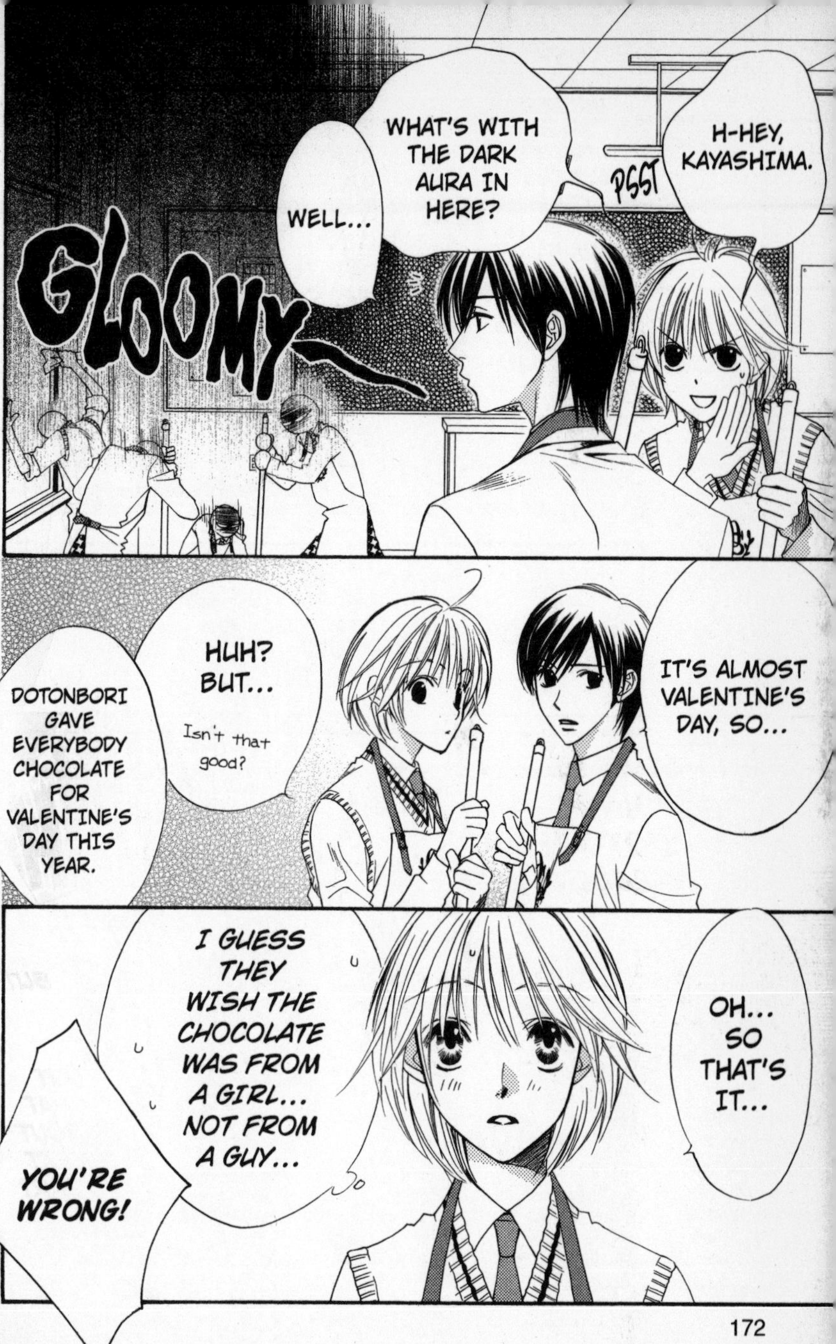
H-HEY, KAYASHIMA.
PSST
WHAT'S WITH THE DARK AURA IN HERE?
WELL...
GLOOMY
IT'S ALMOST VALENTINE'S DAY, SO...
HUH? BUT...
Isn't that good?
DOTONBORI GAVE EVERYBODY CHOCOLATE FOR VALENTINE'S DAY THIS YEAR.
OH... SO THAT'S IT...
I GUESS THEY WISH THE CHOCOLATE WAS FROM A GIRL... NOT FROM A GUY...
YOU'RE WRONG!

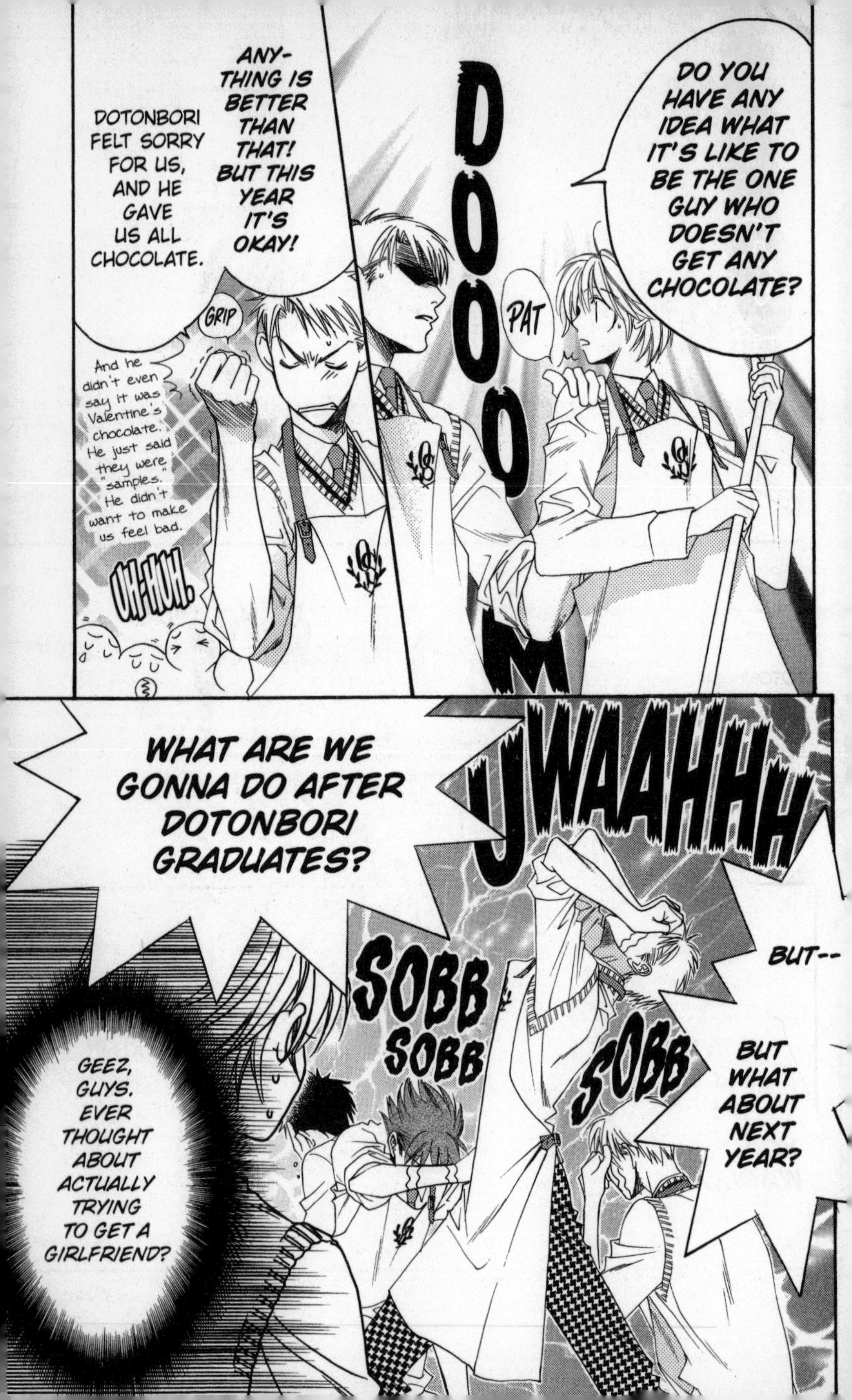
DO YOU HAVE ANY IDEA WHAT IT'S LIKE TO BE THE ONE GUY WHO DOESN'T GET ANY CHOCOLATE?
PAT
DOOOM
ANY-THING IS BETTER THAN THAT! BUT THIS YEAR IT'S OKAY!
DOTONBORI FELT SORRY FOR US, AND HE GAVE US ALL CHOCOLATE.
GRIP
And he didn't even say it was Valentine's chocolate. He just said they were "samples." He didn't want to make us feel bad.
UH-HUH.
BUT--
BUT WHAT ABOUT NEXT YEAR?
UWAAHHH
WHAT ARE WE GONNA DO AFTER DOTONBORI GRADUATES?
SOBB
SOBB SOBB
SOBB
GEEZ, GUYS. EVER THOUGHT ABOUT ACTUALLY TRYING TO GET A GIRLFRIEND?

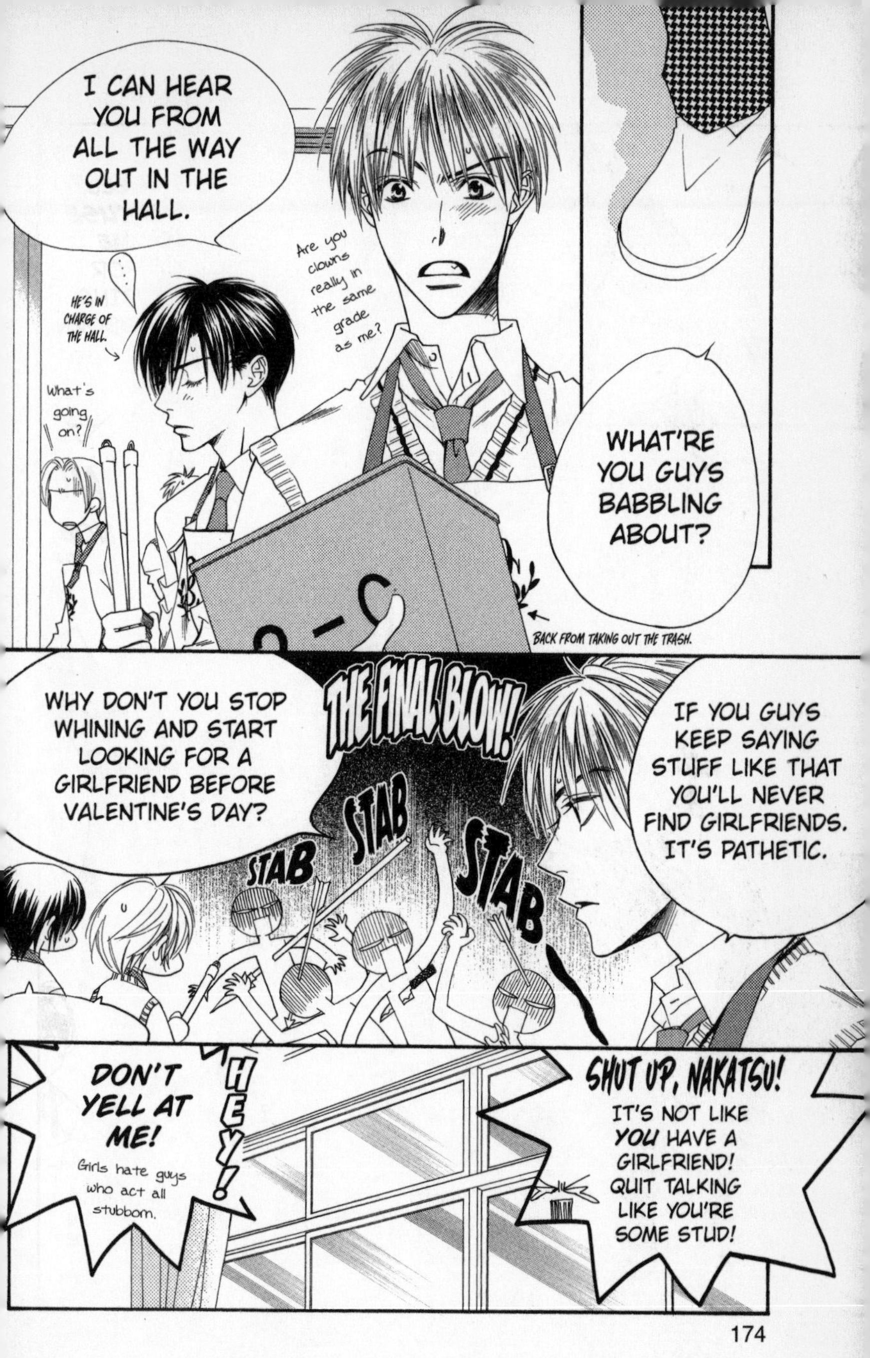
I CAN HEAR YOU FROM ALL THE WAY OUT IN THE HALL.
WHAT'RE YOU GUYS BABBLING ABOUT?
Are you clowns really in the same grade as me?
...
HE'S IN CHARGE OF THE HALL.
What's going on?
BACK FROM TAKING OUT THE TRASH.
IF YOU GUYS KEEP SAYING STUFF LIKE THAT YOU'LL NEVER FIND GIRLFRIENDS. IT'S PATHETIC.
THE FINAL BLOW!
WHY DON'T YOU STOP WHINING AND START LOOKING FOR A GIRLFRIEND BEFORE VALENTINE'S DAY?
STAB
STAB
STAB
SHUT UP, NAKATSU!
IT'S NOT LIKE *YOU* HAVE A GIRLFRIEND! QUIT TALKING LIKE YOU'RE SOME STUD!
HEY!
DON'T YELL AT ME!
Girls hate guys who act all stubborn.

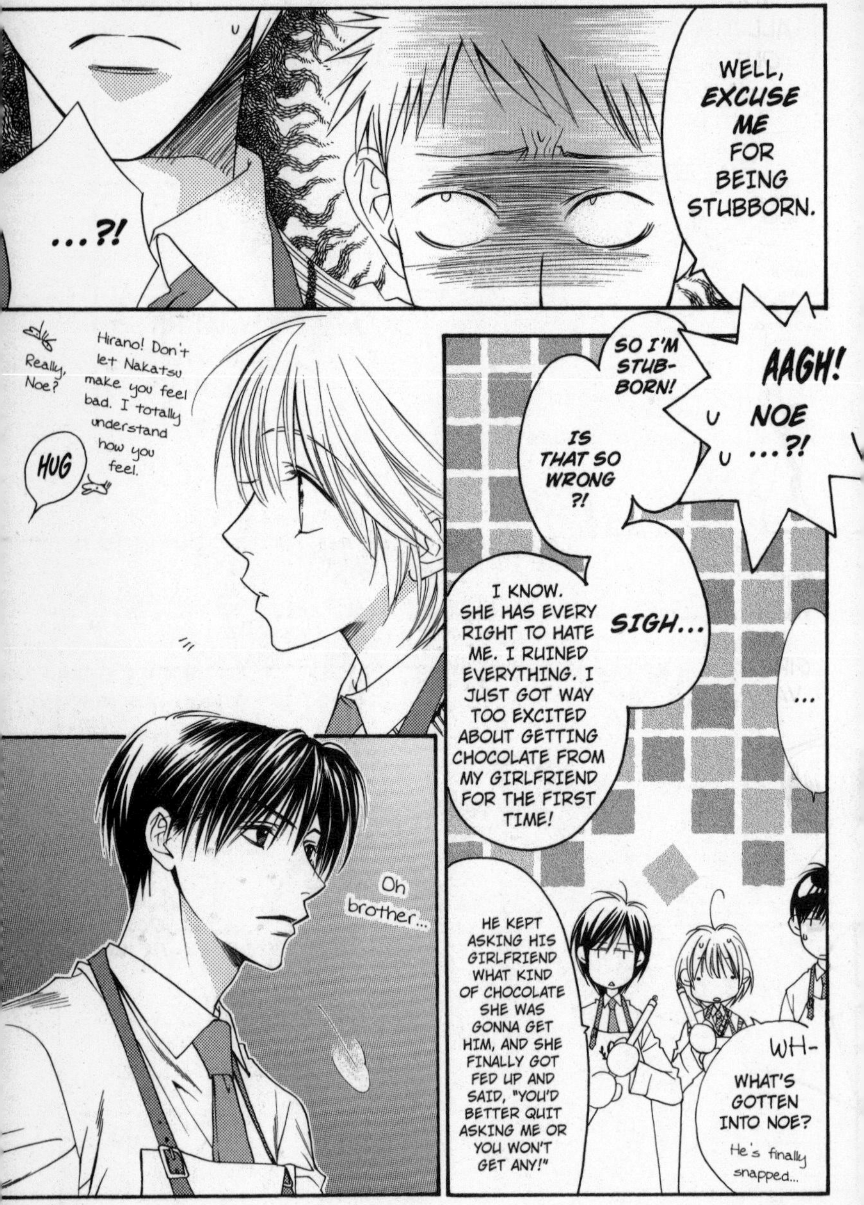
WELL, EXCUSE ME FOR BEING STUBBORN.
...?!
AAGH! NOE ...?!
SO I'M STUB-BORN!
IS THAT SO WRONG ?!
SIGH...
I KNOW. SHE HAS EVERY RIGHT TO HATE ME. I RUINED EVERYTHING. I JUST GOT WAY TOO EXCITED ABOUT GETTING CHOCOLATE FROM MY GIRLFRIEND FOR THE FIRST TIME!
...
WH- WHAT'S GOTTEN INTO NOE?
He's finally snapped...
HE KEPT ASKING HIS GIRLFRIEND WHAT KIND OF CHOCOLATE SHE WAS GONNA GET HIM, AND SHE FINALLY GOT FED UP AND SAID, "YOU'D BETTER QUIT ASKING ME OR YOU WON'T GET ANY!"
Hirano! Don't let Nakatsu make you feel bad. I totally understand how you feel.
HUG
Really, Noe?
Oh brother...

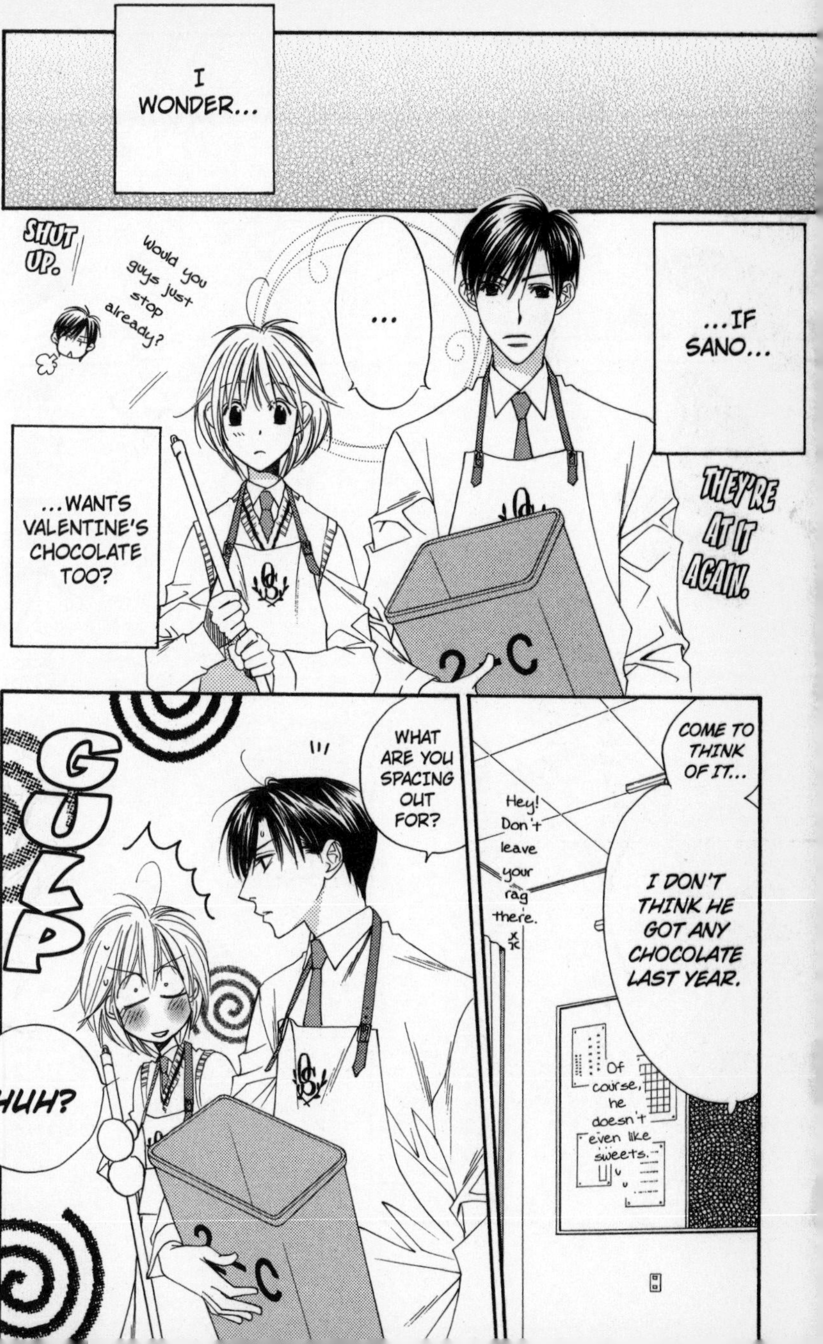
I WONDER...
...IF SANO...
THEY'RE AT IT AGAIN.
...
Would you guys just stop already?
SHUT UP.
...WANTS VALENTINE'S CHOCOLATE TOO?
COME TO THINK OF IT...
I DON'T THINK HE GOT ANY CHOCOLATE LAST YEAR.
Hey! Don't leave your rag there.
Of course, he doesn't even like sweets.
WHAT ARE YOU SPACING OUT FOR?
GULP
HUH?

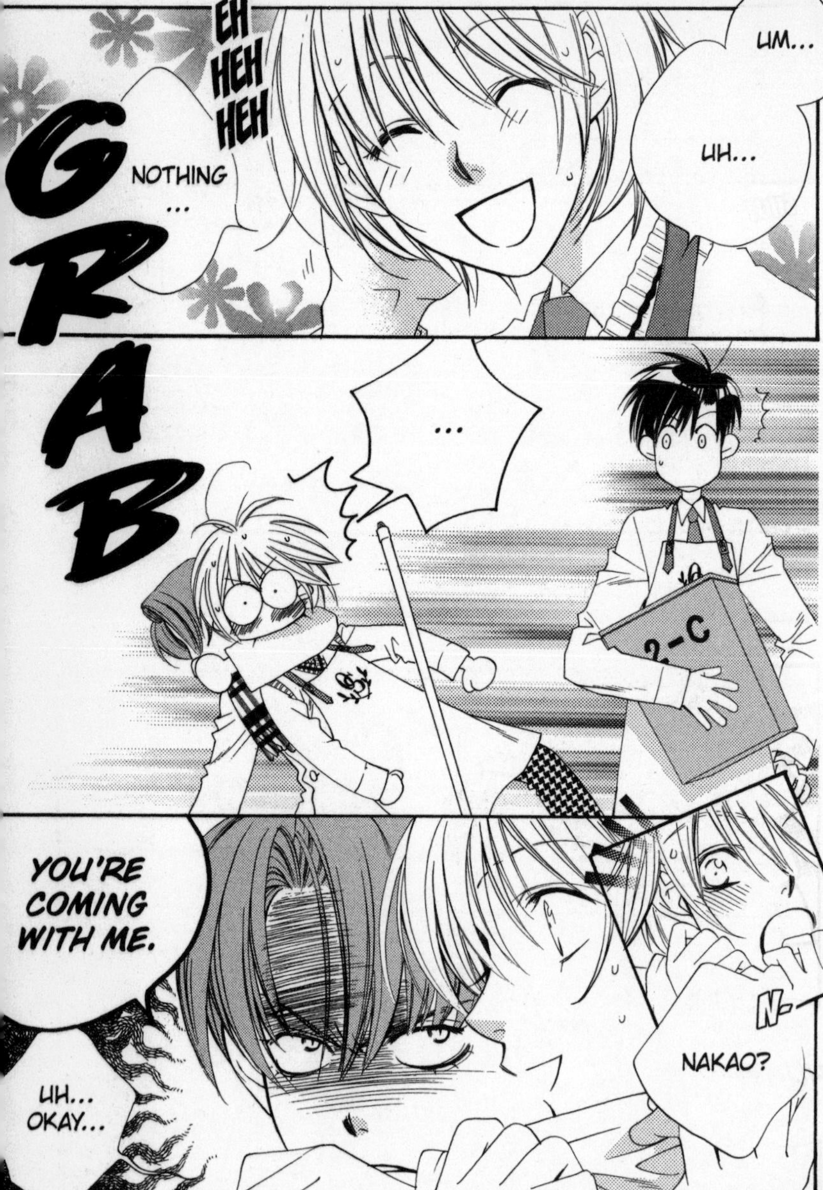
UM...
UH...
EH HEH HEH
NOTHING ...
GRAB
...
N-
NAKAO?
YOU'RE COMING WITH ME.
UH... OKAY...

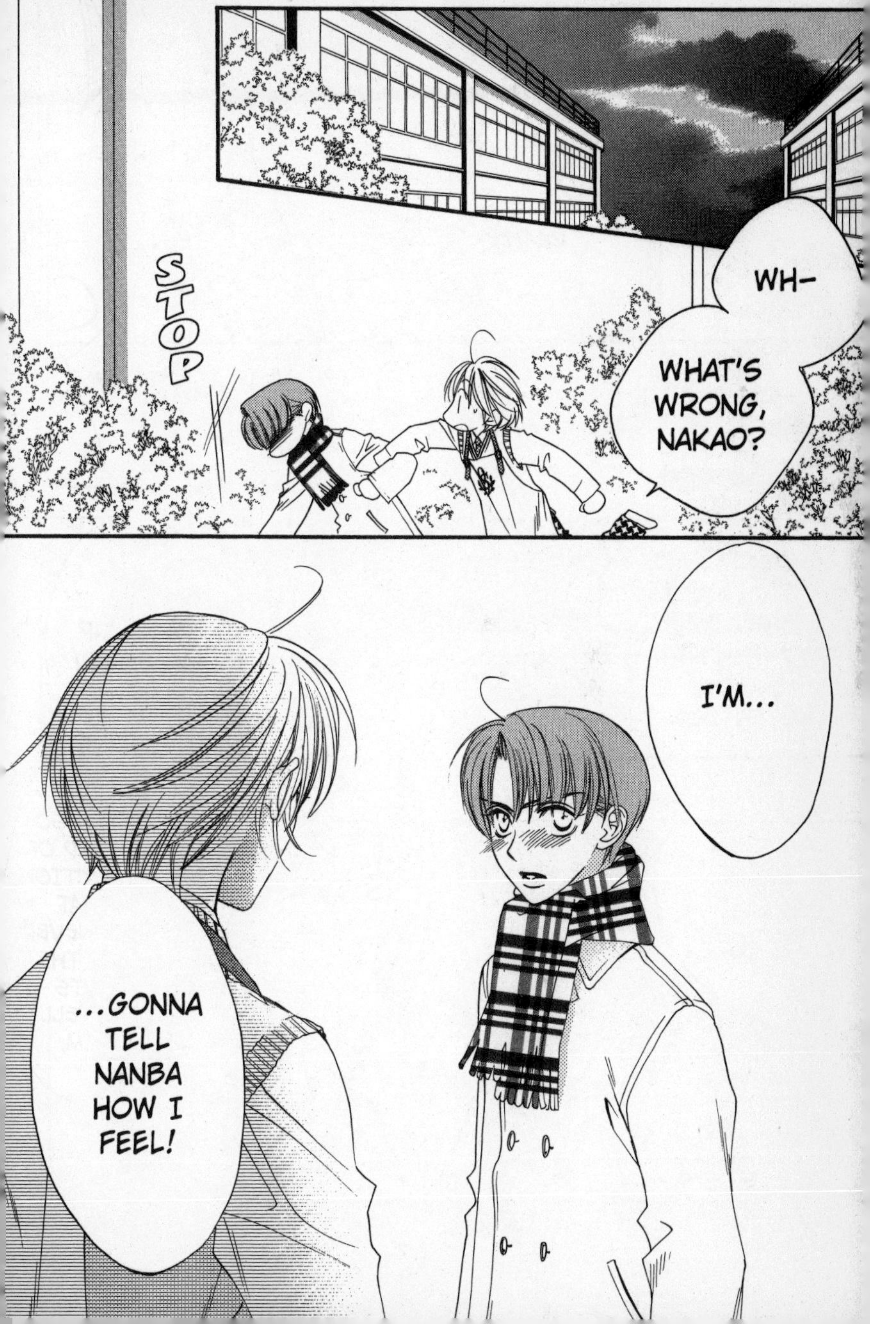
WH-
WHAT'S WRONG, NAKAO?
STOP
I'M...
...GONNA TELL NANBA HOW I FEEL!

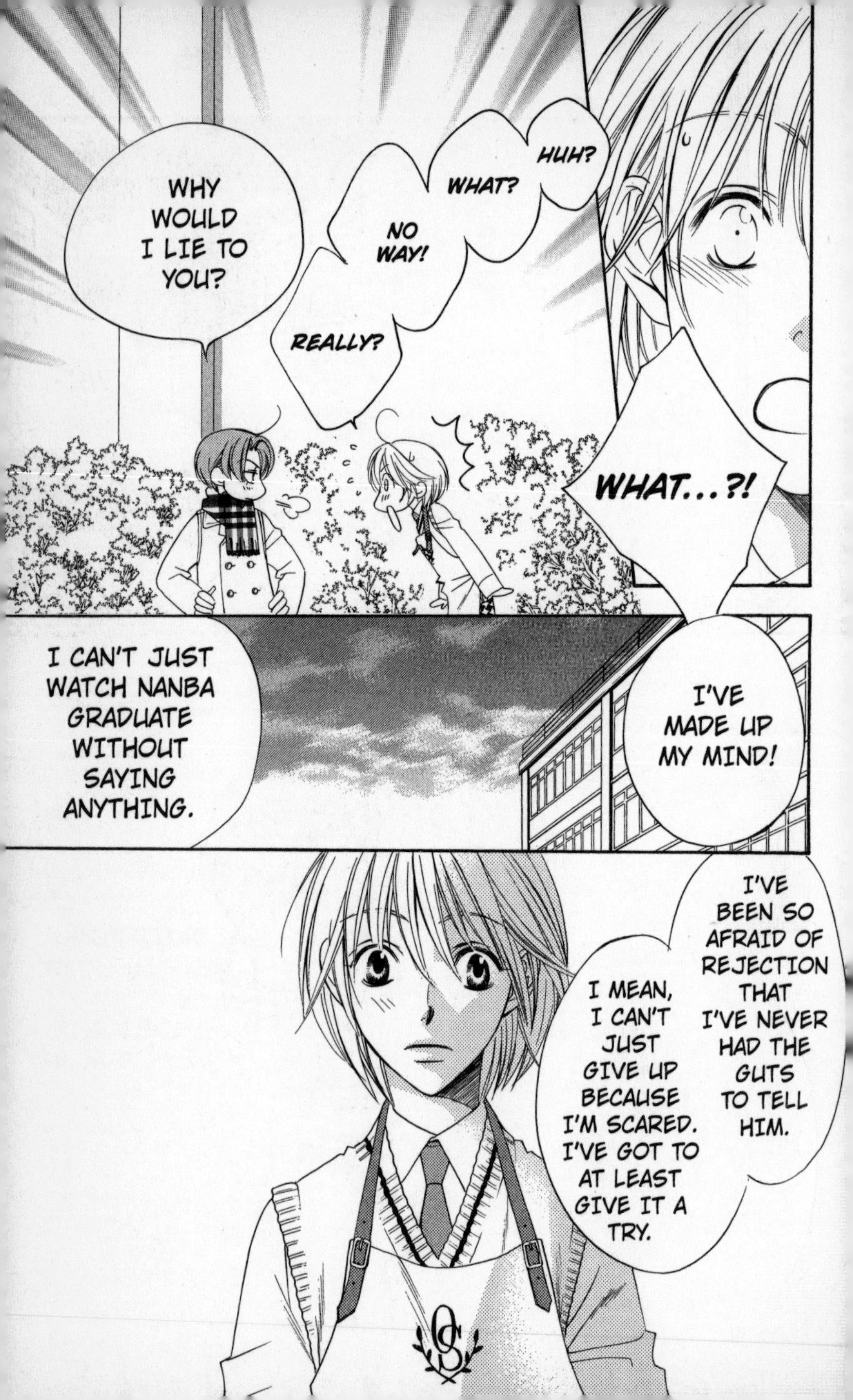
WHAT...?!
HUH? WHAT? NO WAY! REALLY?
WHY WOULD I LIE TO YOU?
I'VE MADE UP MY MIND!
I CAN'T JUST WATCH NANBA GRADUATE WITHOUT SAYING ANYTHING.
I'VE BEEN SO AFRAID OF REJECTION THAT I'VE NEVER HAD THE GUTS TO TELL HIM.
I MEAN, I CAN'T JUST GIVE UP BECAUSE I'M SCARED. I'VE GOT TO AT LEAST GIVE IT A TRY.

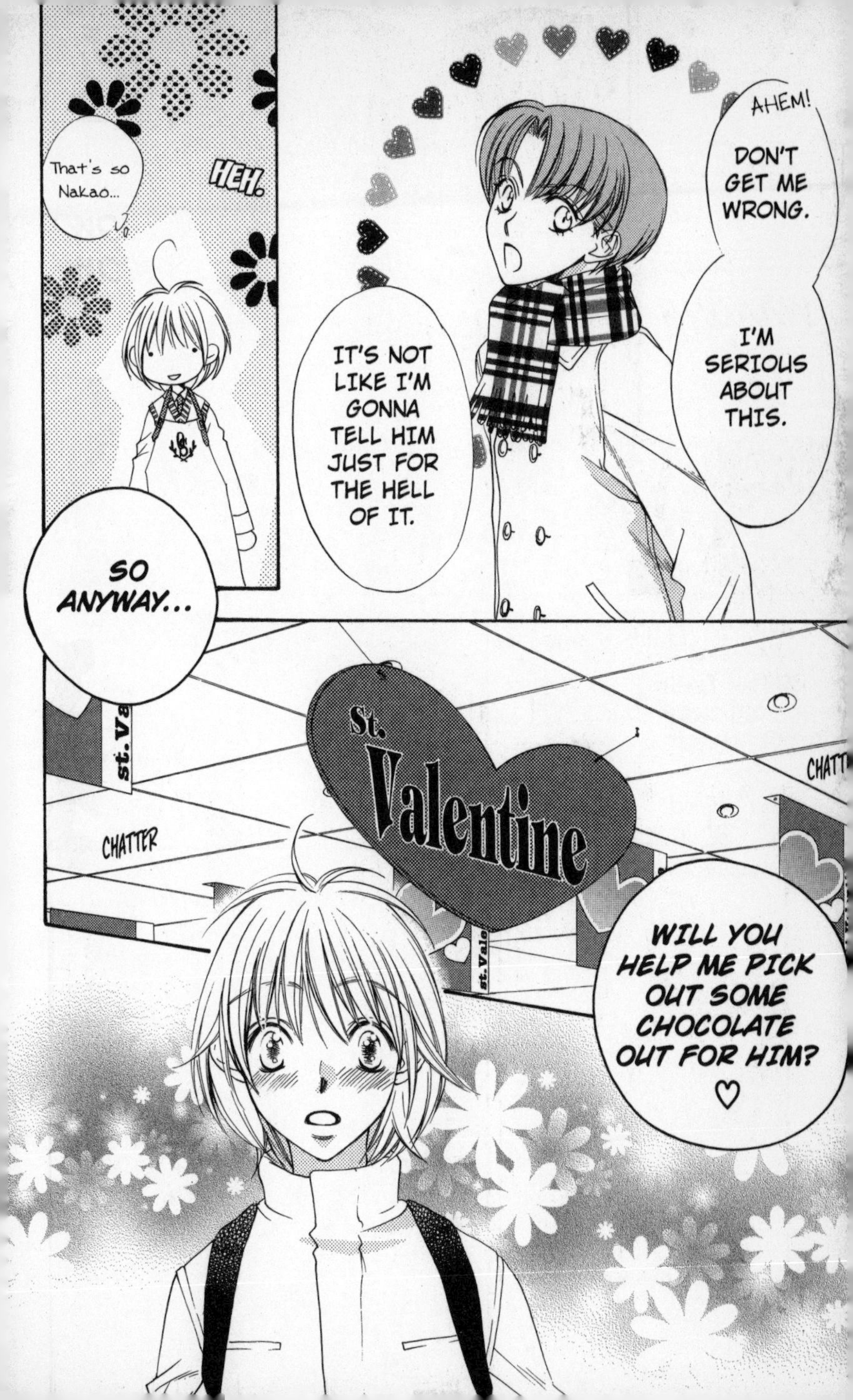
AHEM!
DON'T GET ME WRONG.
I'M SERIOUS ABOUT THIS.
IT'S NOT LIKE I'M GONNA TELL HIM JUST FOR THE HELL OF IT.
HEH.
That's so Nakao...
SO ANYWAY...
WILL YOU HELP ME PICK OUT SOME CHOCOLATE OUT FOR HIM? ♡
St. Valentine
CHATTER
CHATTER

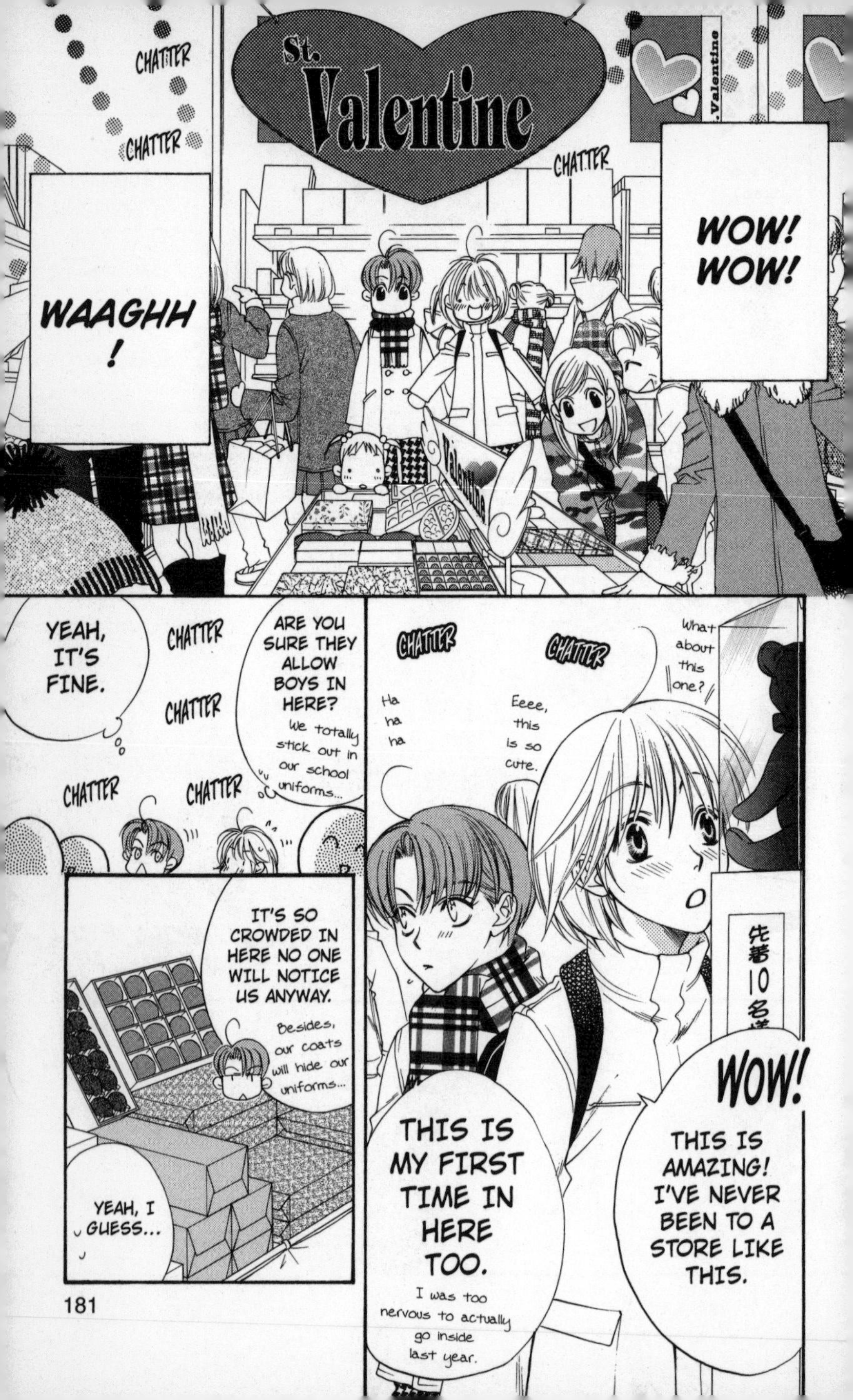
WOW! WOW!
CHATTER
St. Valentine
CHATTER
CHATTER
WAAGHH!
What about this one?
CHATTER
CHATTER
Eeee, this is so cute.
Ha ha ha
先着10名
WOW!
THIS IS AMAZING! I'VE NEVER BEEN TO A STORE LIKE THIS.
THIS IS MY FIRST TIME IN HERE TOO.
I was too nervous to actually go inside last year.
ARE YOU SURE THEY ALLOW BOYS IN HERE?
We totally stick out in our school uniforms...
CHATTER
CHATTER
YEAH, IT'S FINE.
CHATTER
CHATTER
IT'S SO CROWDED IN HERE NO ONE WILL NOTICE US ANYWAY.
Besides, our coats will hide our uniforms...
YEAH, I GUESS...

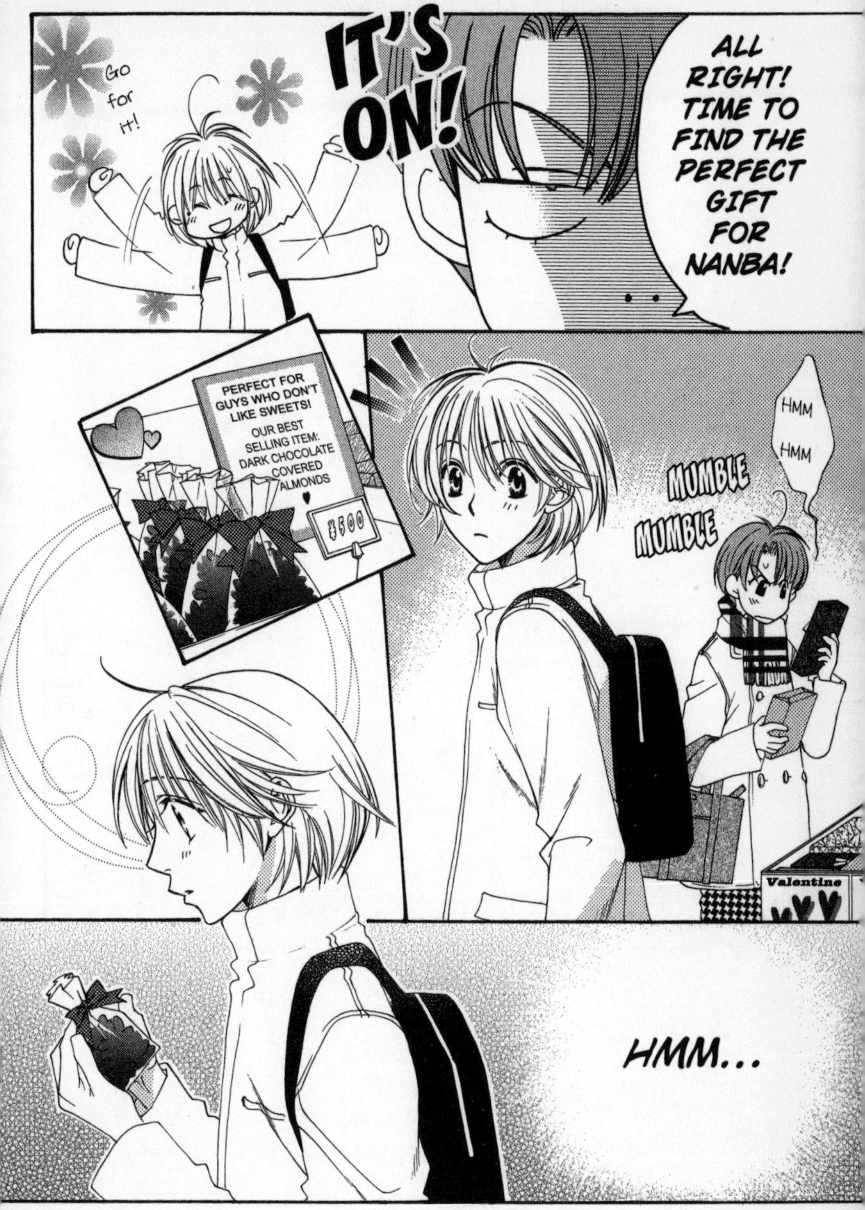
ALL RIGHT! TIME TO FIND THE PERFECT GIFT FOR NANBA!
IT'S ON!
Go for it!
HMM
HMM
MUMBLE
MUMBLE
Valentine
PERFECT FOR GUYS WHO DON'T LIKE SWEETS!
OUR BEST SELLING ITEM: DARK CHOCOLATE COVERED ALMONDS
¥500
HMM...

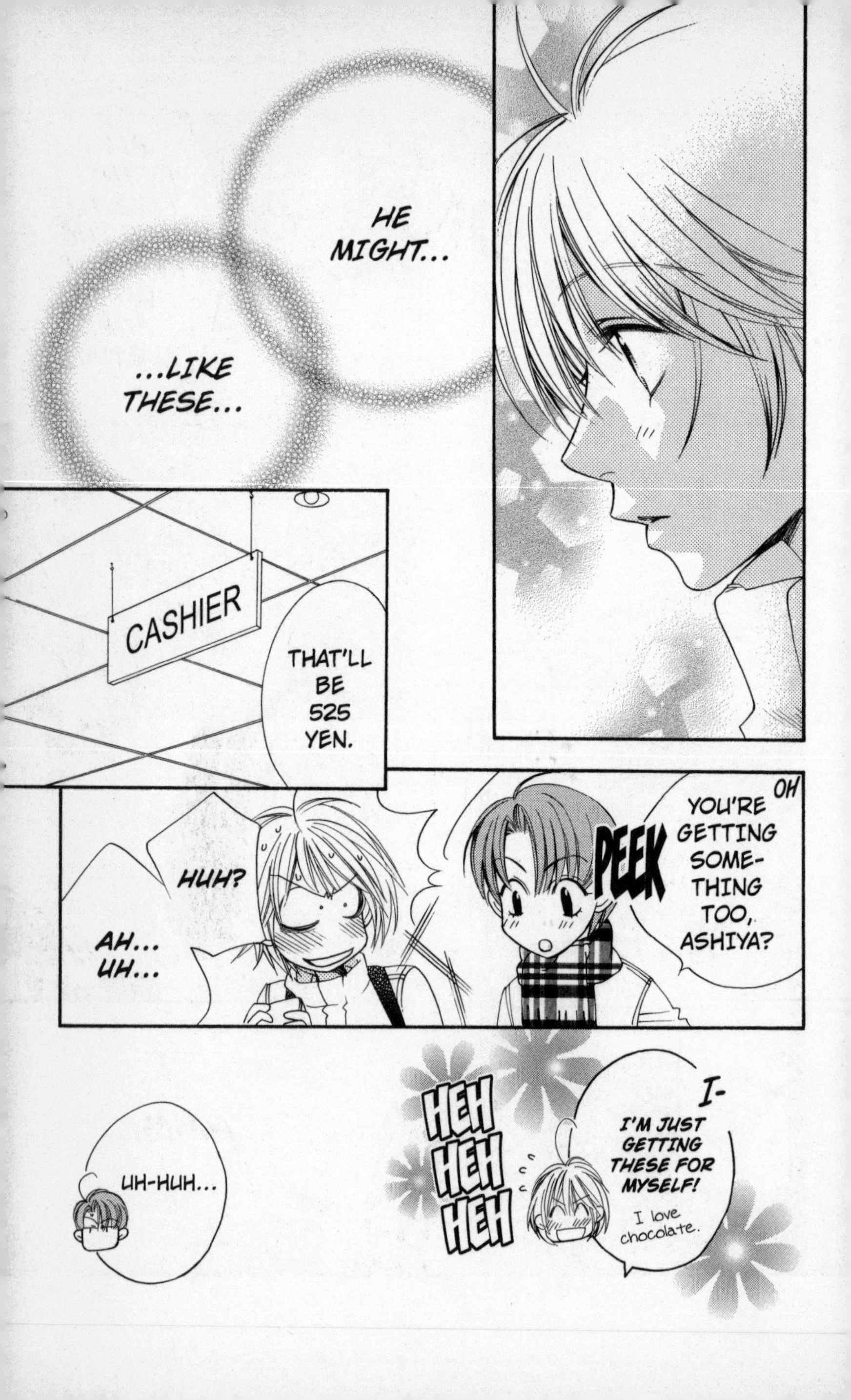
HE MIGHT...
...LIKE THESE...
CASHIER
THAT'LL BE 525 YEN.
OH
YOU'RE GETTING SOME-THING TOO, ASHIYA?
PEEK
HUH?
AH... UH...
I-
I'M JUST GETTING THESE FOR MYSELF!
I love chocolate.
HEH HEH HEH
UH-HUH...

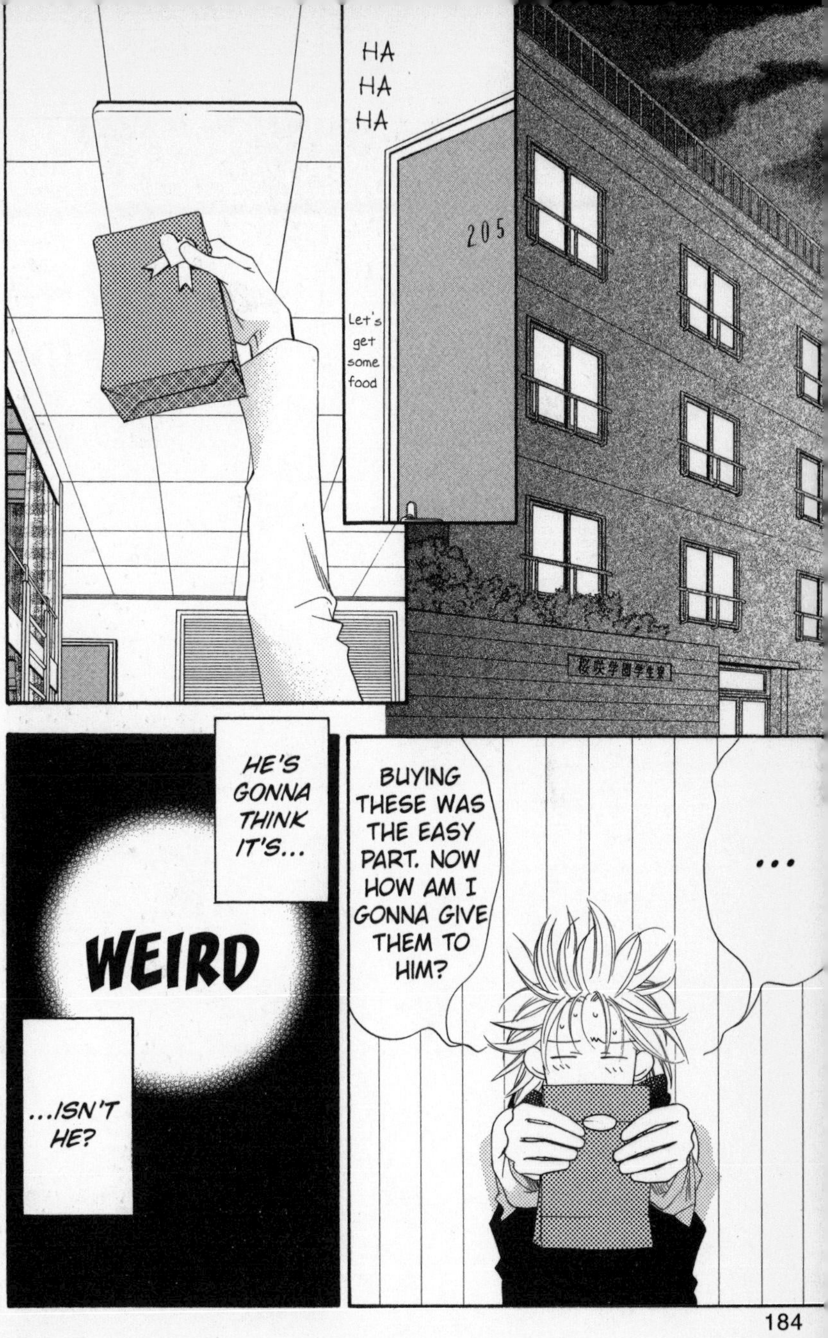
HA
HA
HA
205
Let's get some food
...
BUYING THESE WAS THE EASY PART. NOW HOW AM I GONNA GIVE THEM TO HIM?
HE'S GONNA THINK IT'S...
WEIRD
...ISN'T HE?

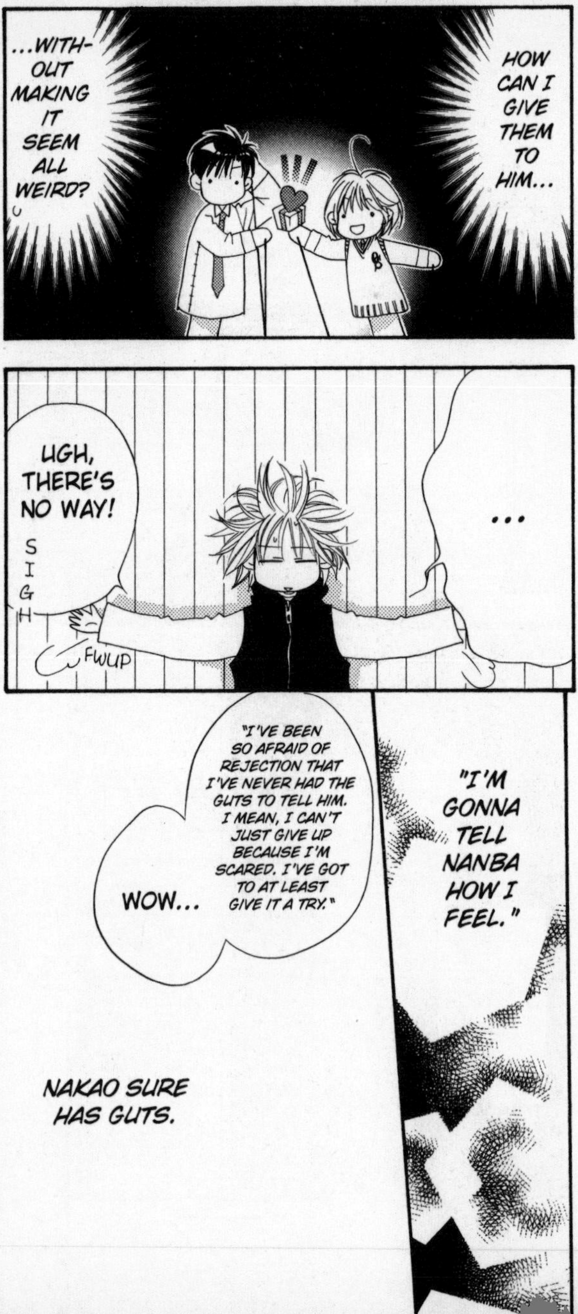
HOW CAN I GIVE THEM TO HIM...
...WITH-OUT MAKING IT SEEM ALL WEIRD?
...
UGH, THERE'S NO WAY!
SIGH
FWUP
"I'M GONNA TELL NANBA HOW I FEEL."
"I'VE BEEN SO AFRAID OF REJECTION THAT I'VE NEVER HAD THE GUTS TO TELL HIM. I MEAN, I CAN'T JUST GIVE UP BECAUSE I'M SCARED. I'VE GOT TO AT LEAST GIVE IT A TRY."
WOW...
NAKAO SURE HAS GUTS.

It's Hana-Kimi book 20. Yay!

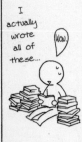

I actually wrote all of these...

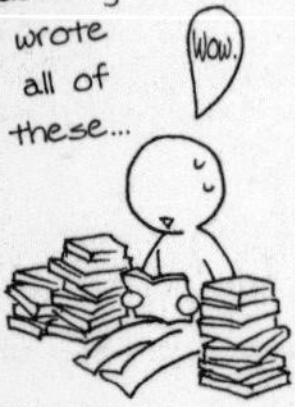
Wow.

New readers who are just picking up book one are gonna have to fork over quite a bit of dough to buy the whole series. I really appreciate your support... I feel kind of bad saying, "Please buy book 21 too!" (ha ha) but I do hope you'll stick around.

March 2003

I got a letter from a reader who complained, "I'm running out of money." (Sorry...)

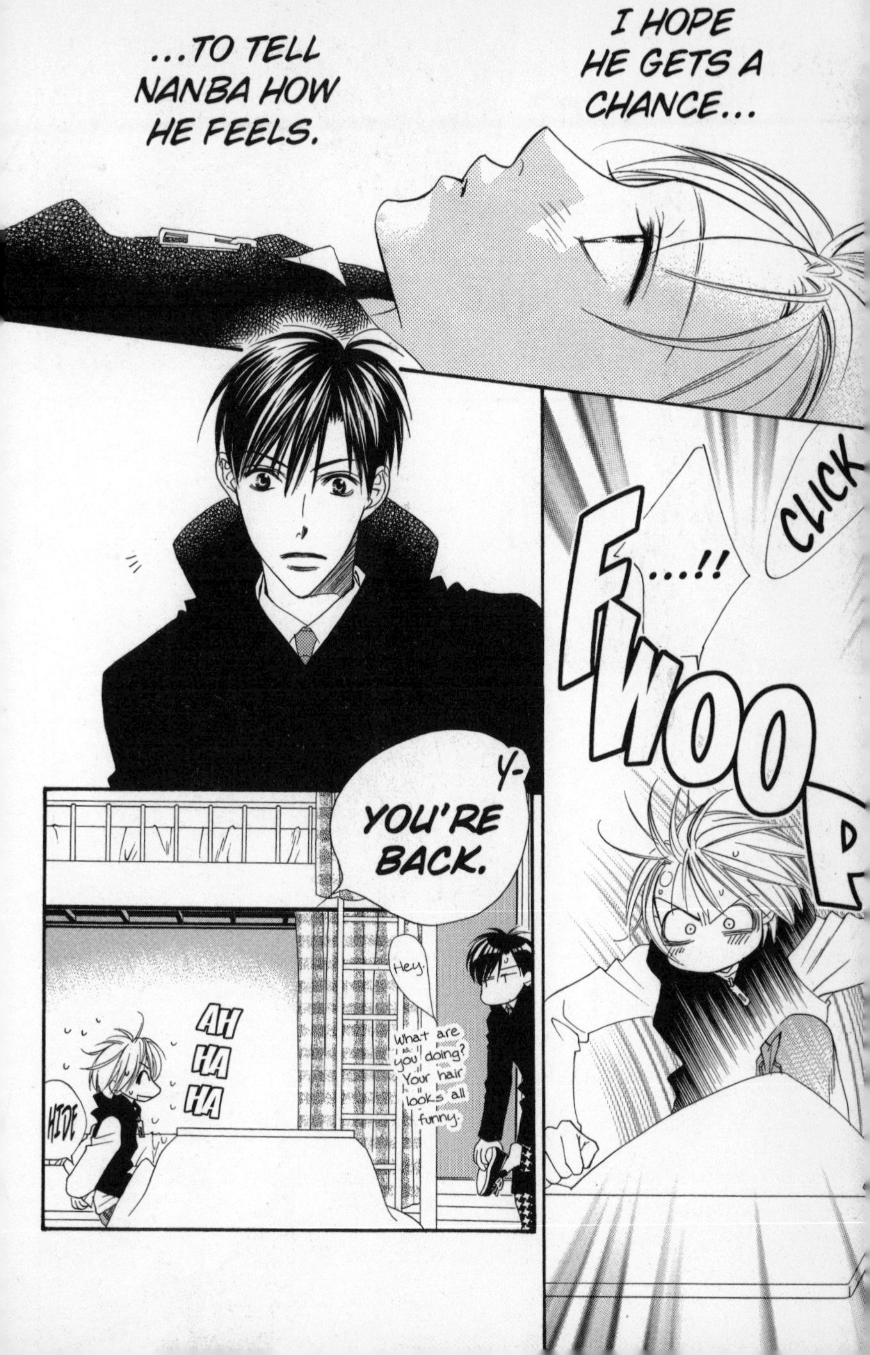
I HOPE HE GETS A CHANCE...
...TO TELL NANBA HOW HE FEELS.
CLICK
...!!
FWOOP
Y- YOU'RE BACK.
Hey.
What are you doing? Your hair looks all funny.
AH HA HA
HIDE

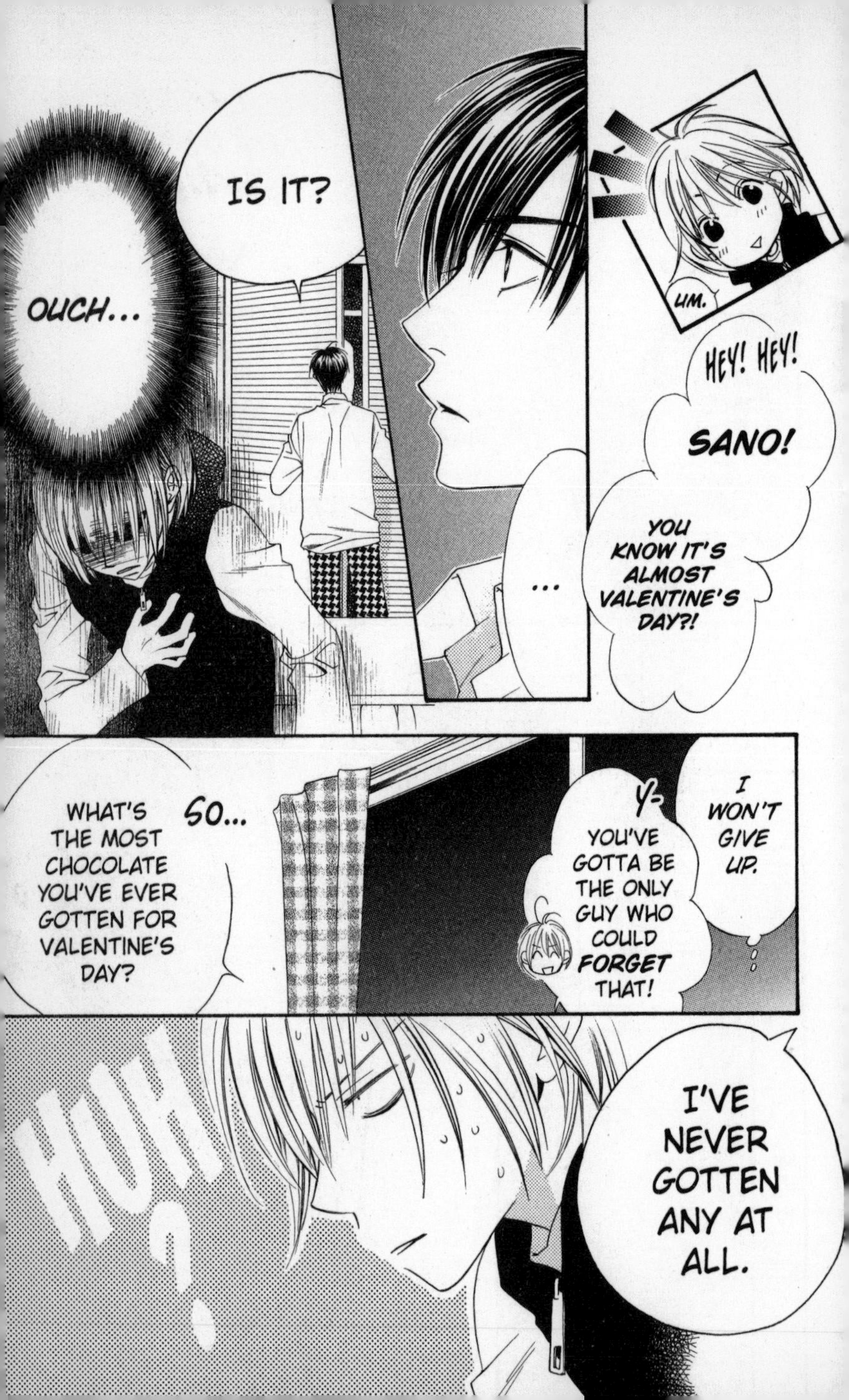
UM.
HEY! HEY!
SANO!
YOU KNOW IT'S ALMOST VALENTINE'S DAY?!
...
IS IT?
OUCH...
I WON'T GIVE UP.
Y-
YOU'VE GOTTA BE THE ONLY GUY WHO COULD FORGET THAT!
SO...
WHAT'S THE MOST CHOCOLATE YOU'VE EVER GOTTEN FOR VALENTINE'S DAY?
I'VE NEVER GOTTEN ANY AT ALL.
HUH?

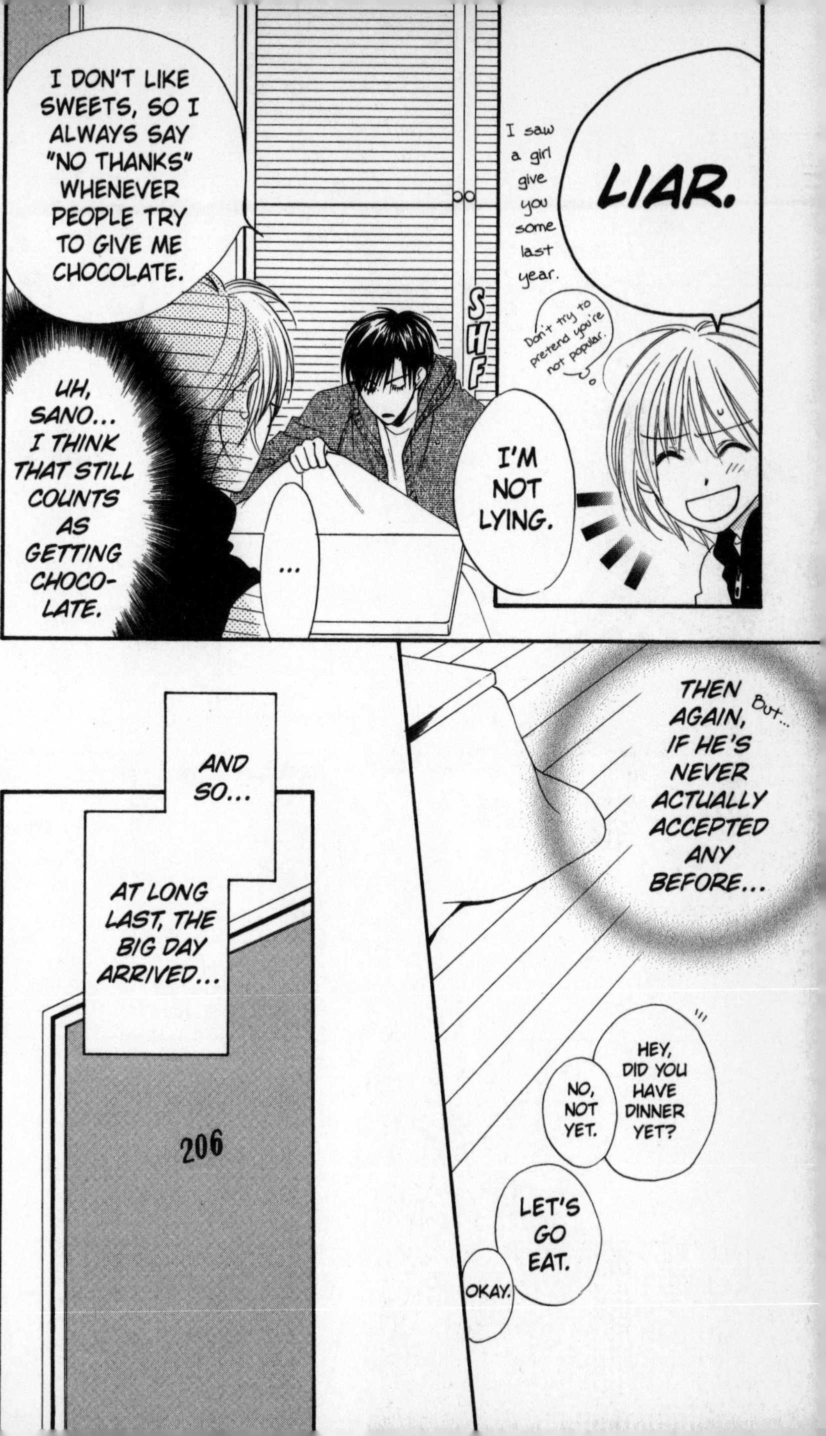
LIAR.
I saw a girl give you some last year.
Don't try to pretend you're not popular.
I'M NOT LYING.
I DON'T LIKE SWEETS, SO I ALWAYS SAY "NO THANKS" WHENEVER PEOPLE TRY TO GIVE ME CHOCOLATE.
SHF
...
UH, SANO... I THINK THAT STILL COUNTS AS GETTING CHOCO-LATE.
THEN AGAIN, IF HE'S NEVER ACTUALLY ACCEPTED ANY BEFORE...
But...
HEY, DID YOU HAVE DINNER YET?
NO, NOT YET.
LET'S GO EAT.
OKAY.
AND SO...
AT LONG LAST, THE BIG DAY ARRIVED...
206

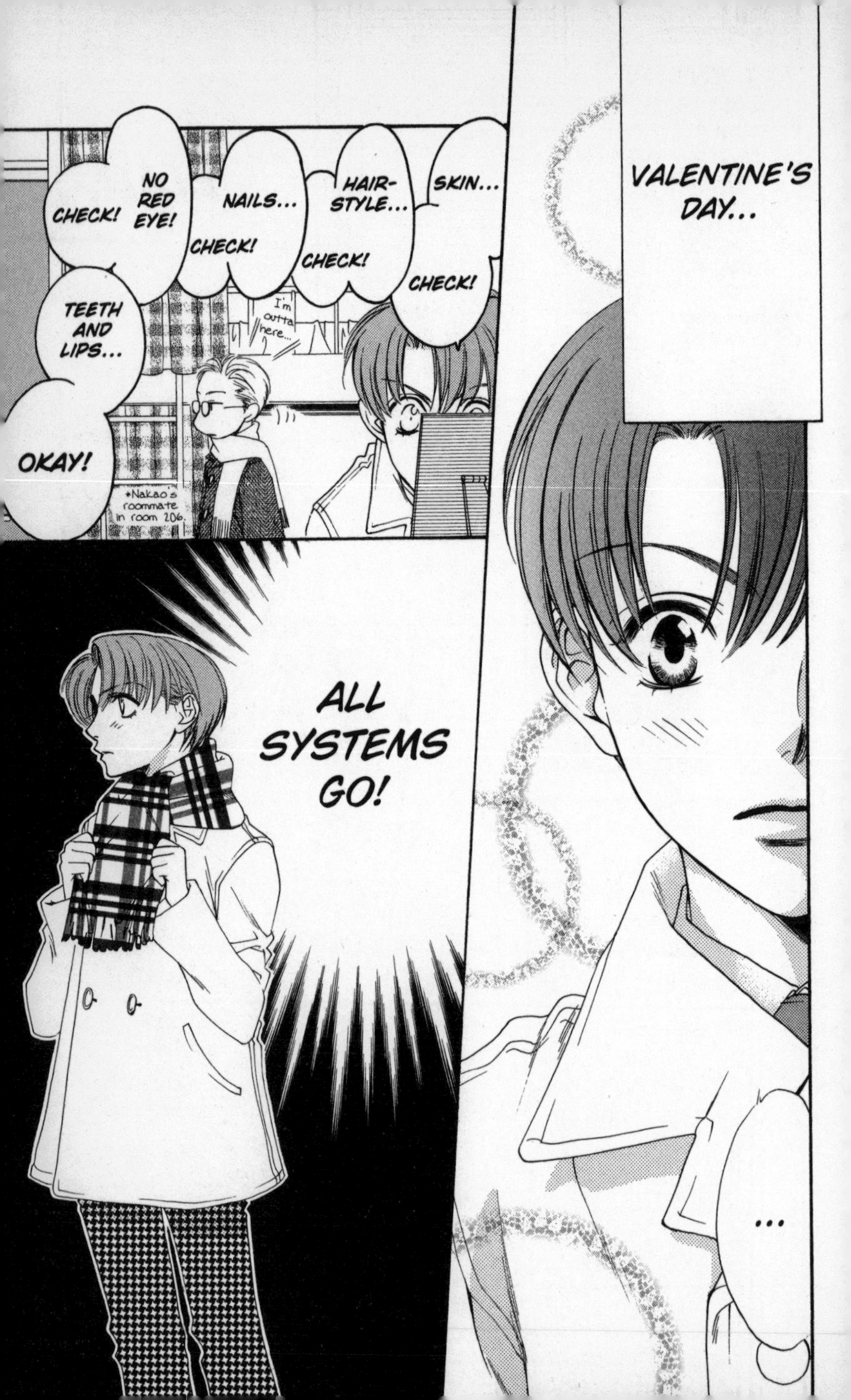
VALENTINE'S DAY...
...
SKIN...
CHECK!
HAIR-STYLE...
CHECK!
NAILS...
CHECK!
NO RED EYE!
CHECK!
TEETH AND LIPS...
OKAY!
I'm outta here...
*Nakao's roommate in room 206.
ALL SYSTEMS GO!

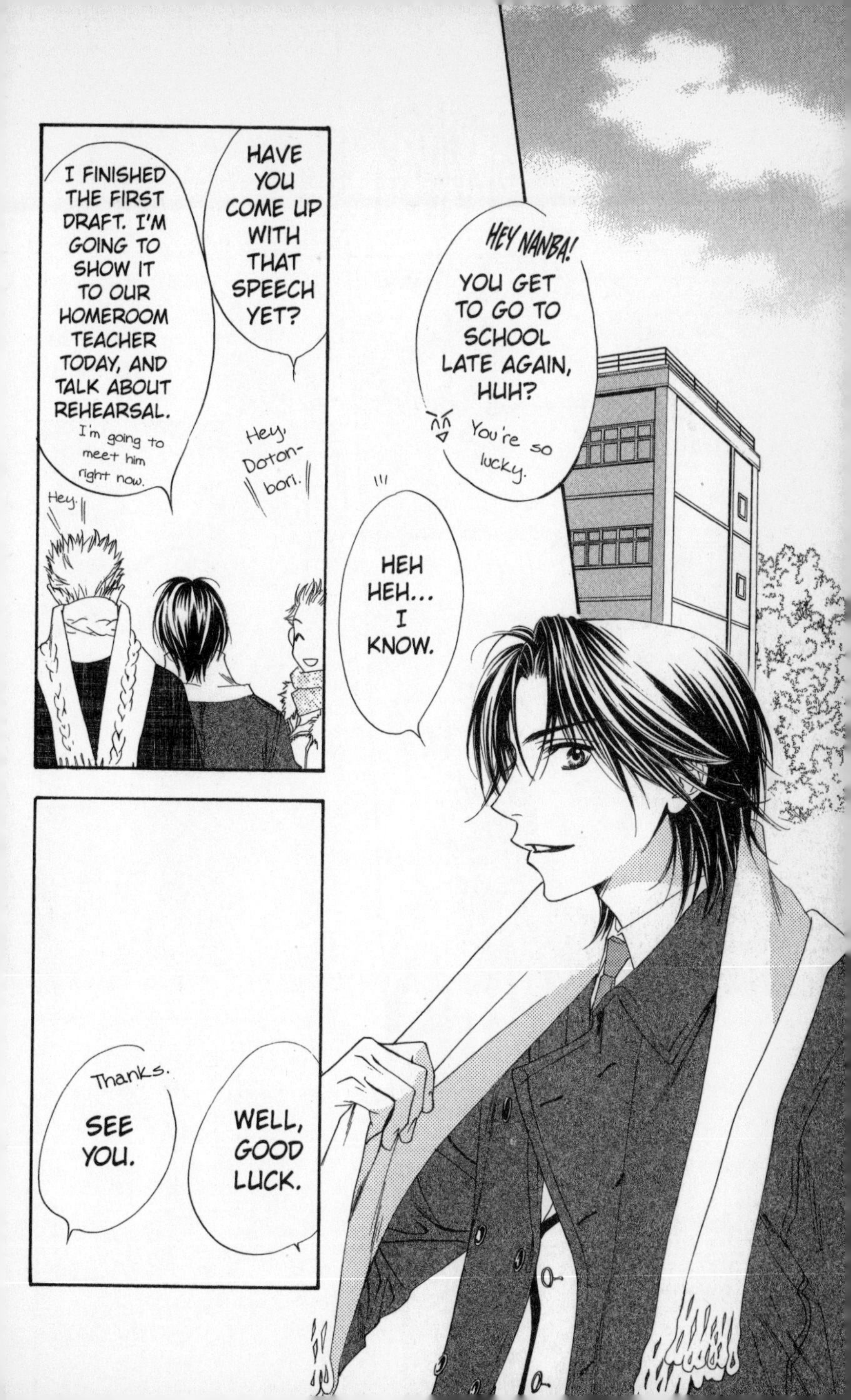
HEY NANBA!
YOU GET TO GO TO SCHOOL LATE AGAIN, HUH?
You're so lucky.
HEH HEH... I KNOW.
HAVE YOU COME UP WITH THAT SPEECH YET?
Hey, Doton-bori.
I FINISHED THE FIRST DRAFT. I'M GOING TO SHOW IT TO OUR HOMEROOM TEACHER TODAY, AND TALK ABOUT REHEARSAL.
I'm going to meet him right now.
Hey.
WELL, GOOD LUCK.
Thanks.
SEE YOU.

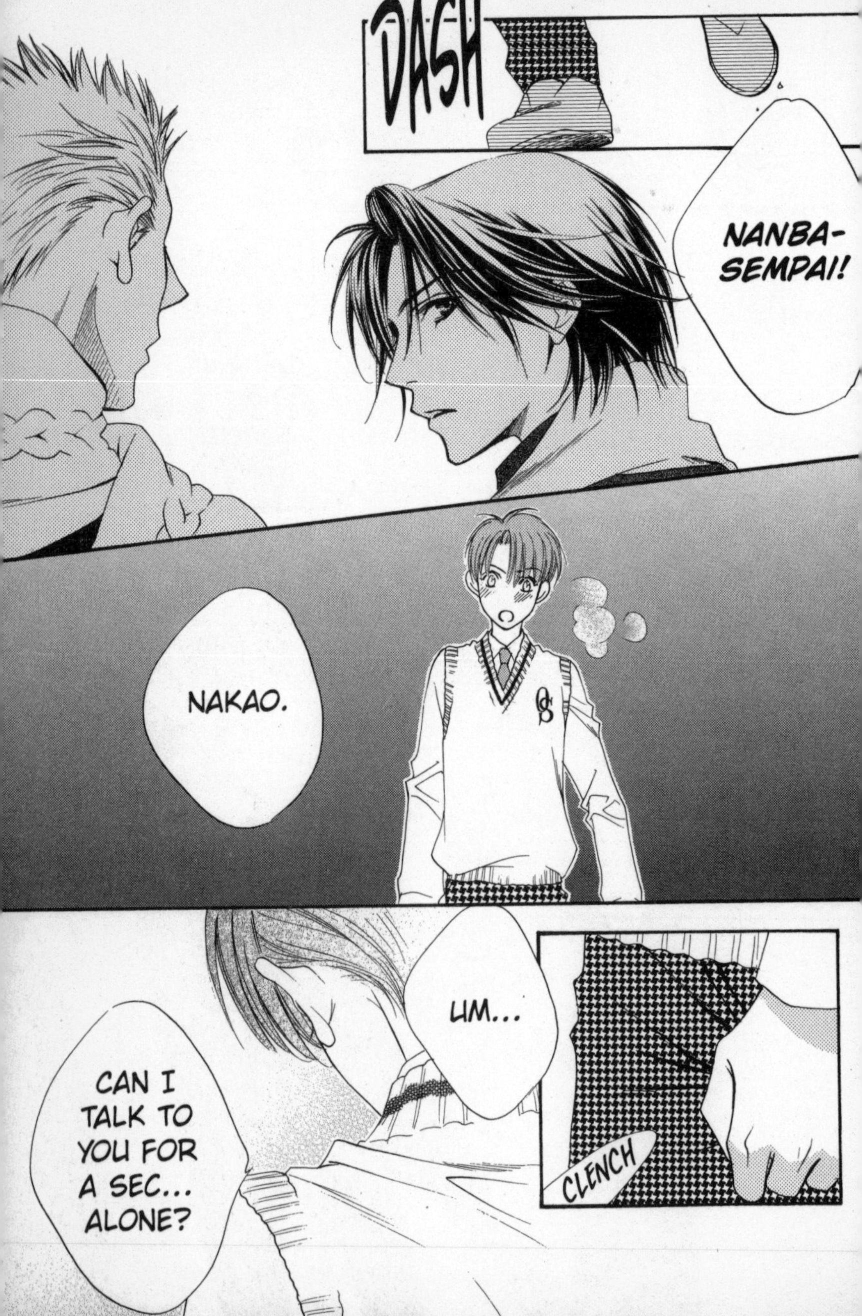
DASH
NANBA-SEMPAI!
NAKAO.
CLENCH
UM...
CAN I TALK TO YOU FOR A SEC... ALONE?

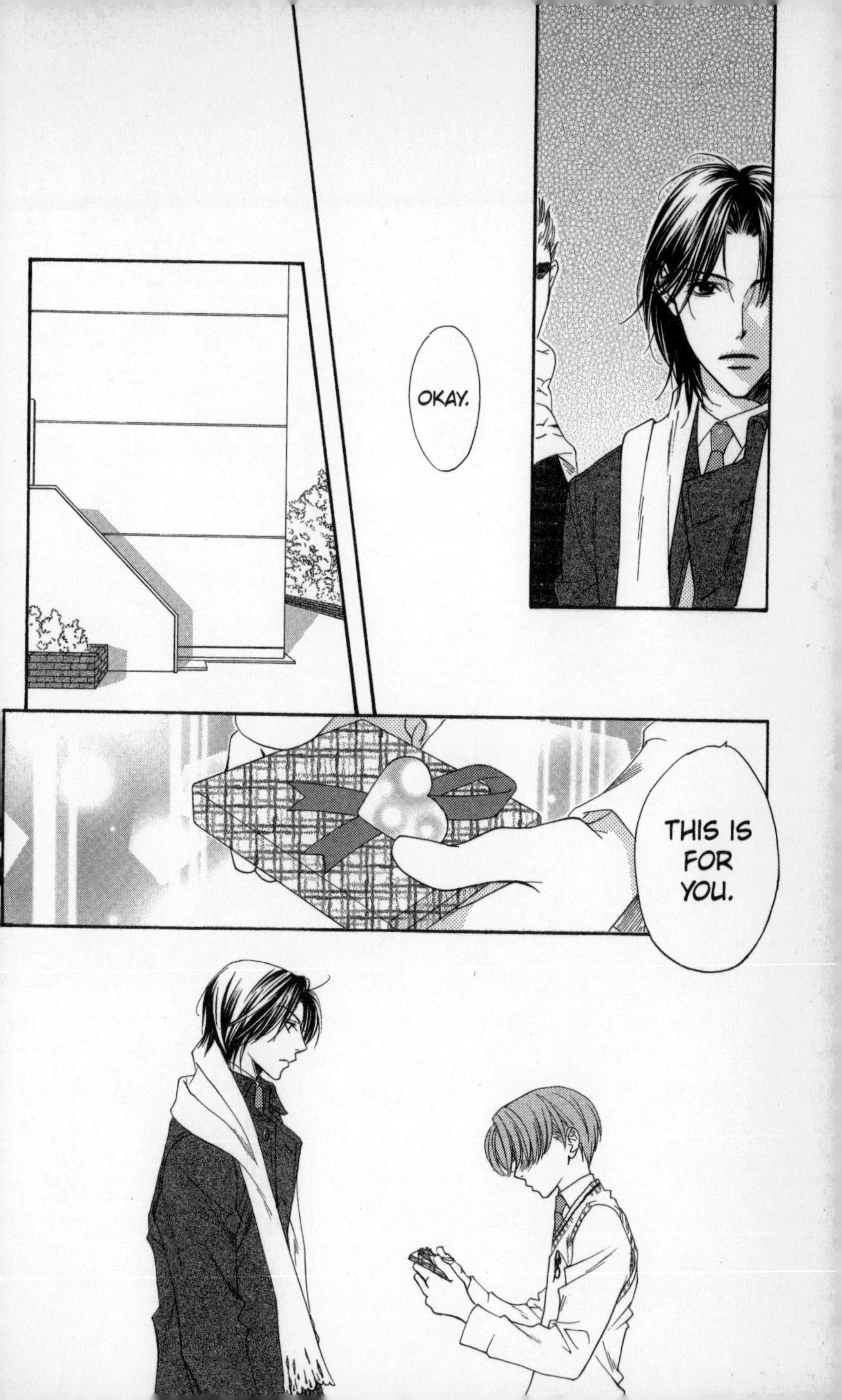
OKAY.
THIS IS FOR YOU.

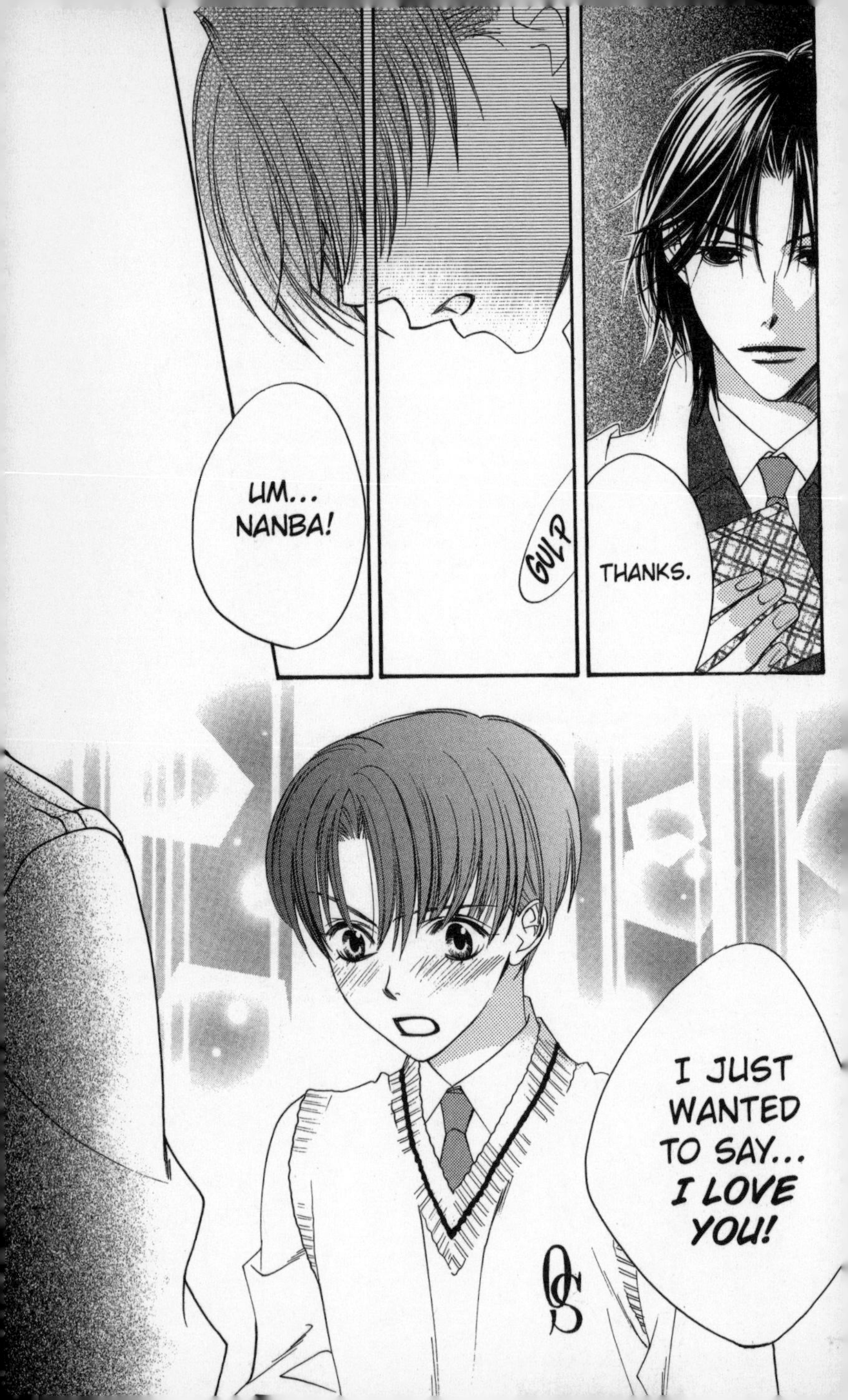
THANKS.
GULP
UM... NANBA!
I JUST WANTED TO SAY... *I LOVE YOU!*

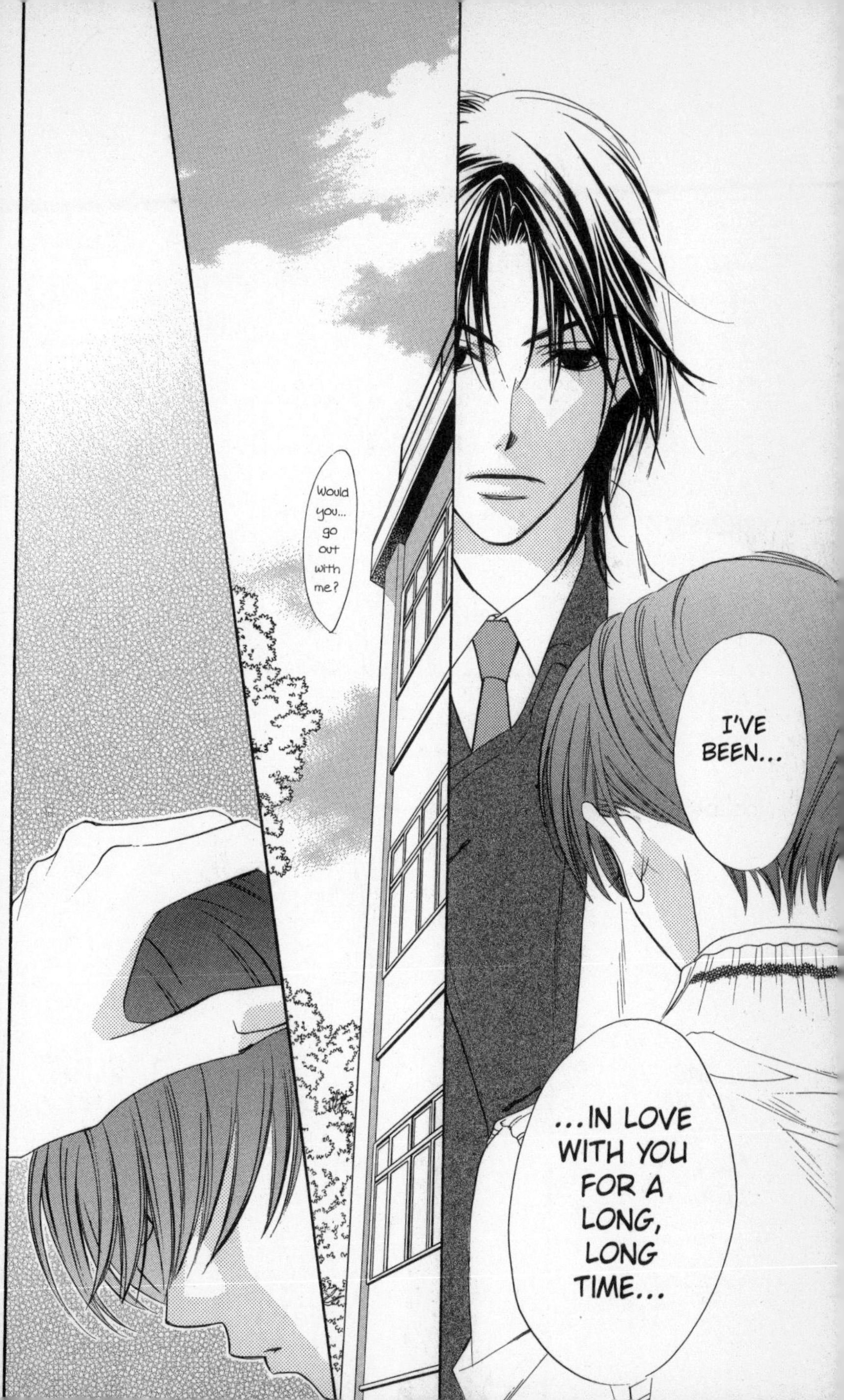
I'VE BEEN...
...IN LOVE WITH YOU FOR A LONG, LONG TIME...
Would you... go out with me?

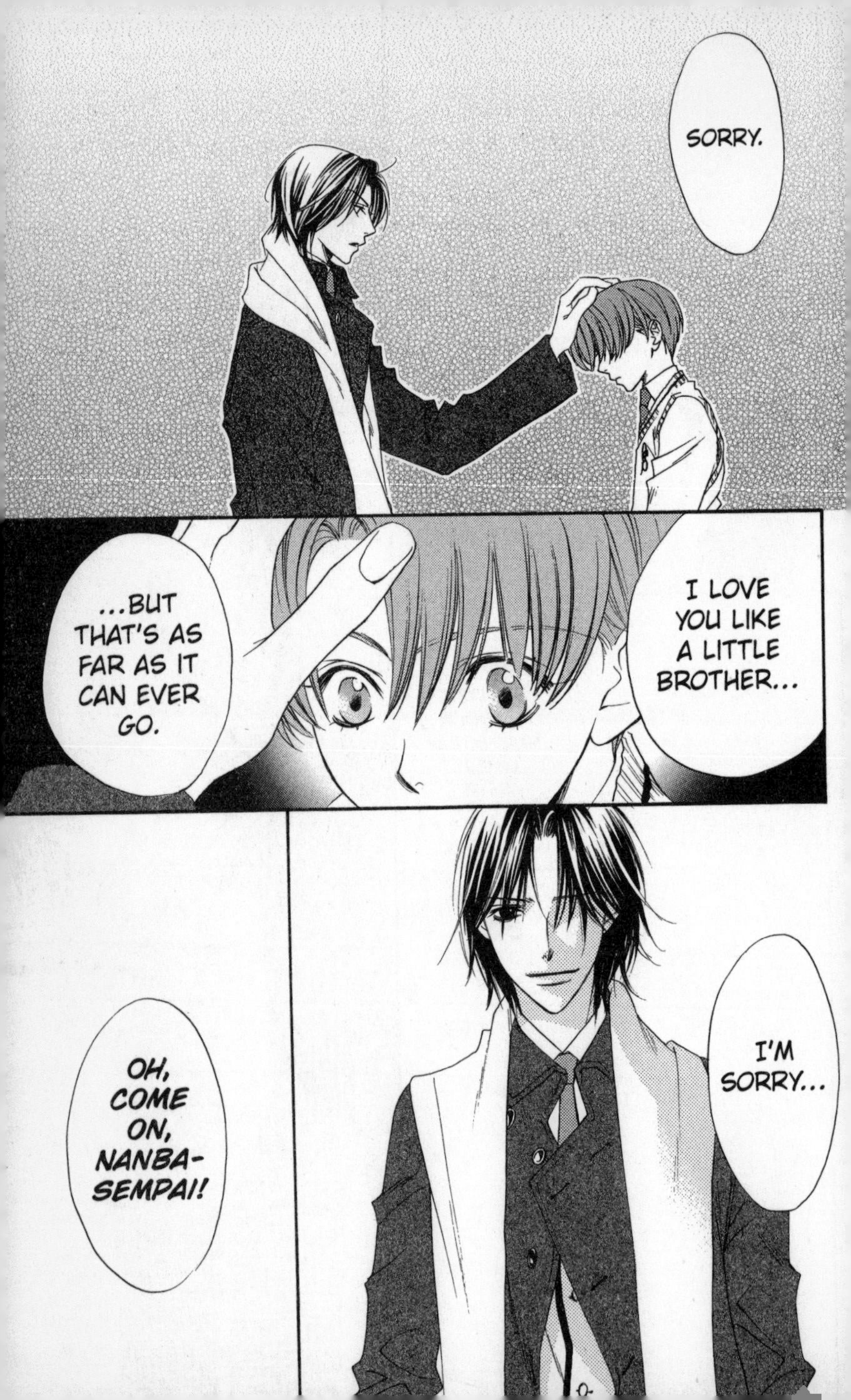
SORRY.
I LOVE YOU LIKE A LITTLE BROTHER...
...BUT THAT'S AS FAR AS IT CAN EVER GO.
I'M SORRY...
OH, COME ON, NANBA-SEMPAI!

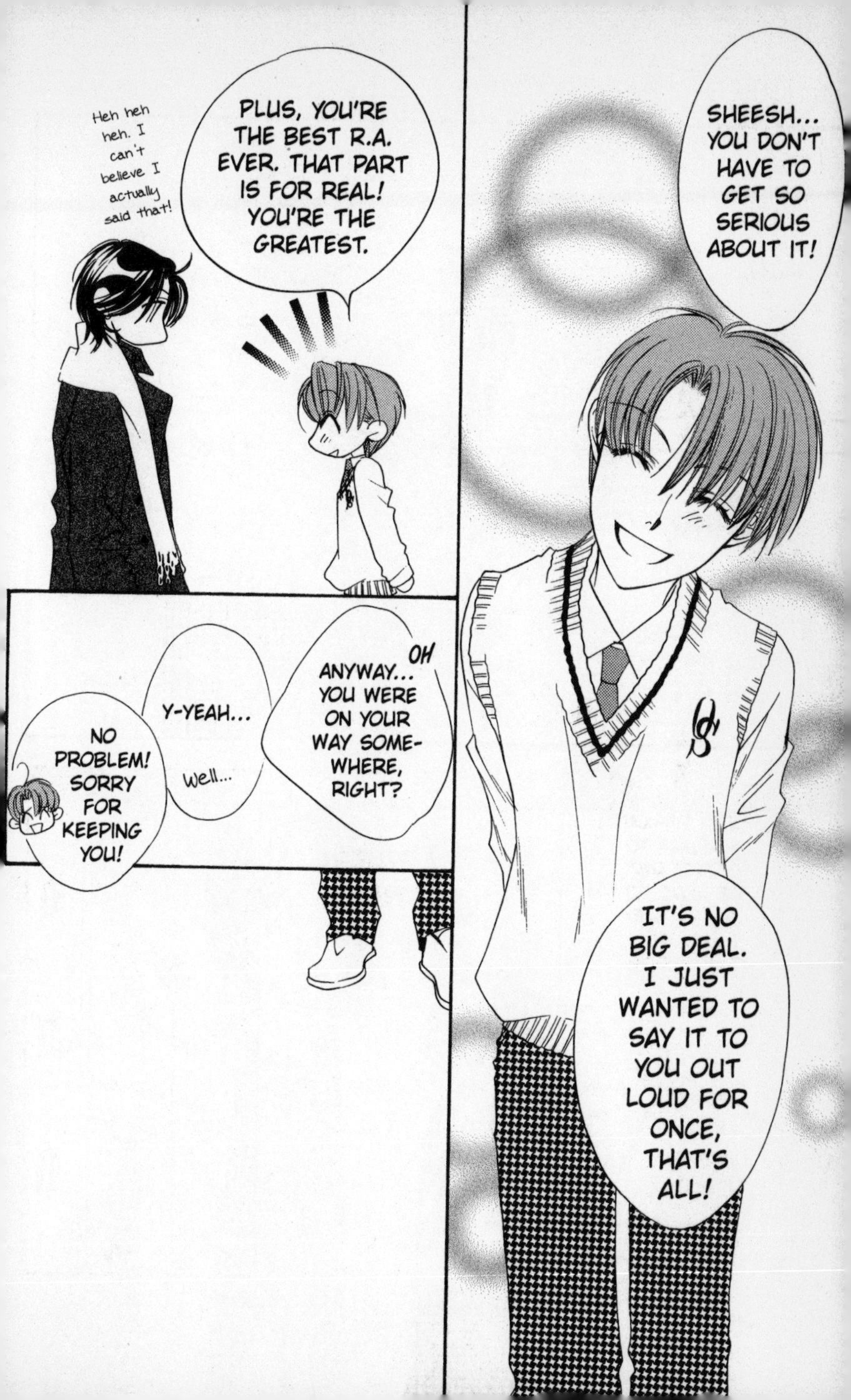
SHEESH... YOU DON'T HAVE TO GET SO SERIOUS ABOUT IT!
IT'S NO BIG DEAL. I JUST WANTED TO SAY IT TO YOU OUT LOUD FOR ONCE, THAT'S ALL!
PLUS, YOU'RE THE BEST R.A. EVER. THAT PART IS FOR REAL! YOU'RE THE GREATEST.
Heh heh heh. I can't believe I actually said that!
OH
ANYWAY... YOU WERE ON YOUR WAY SOME-WHERE, RIGHT?
Y-YEAH...
Well...
NO PROBLEM! SORRY FOR KEEPING YOU!

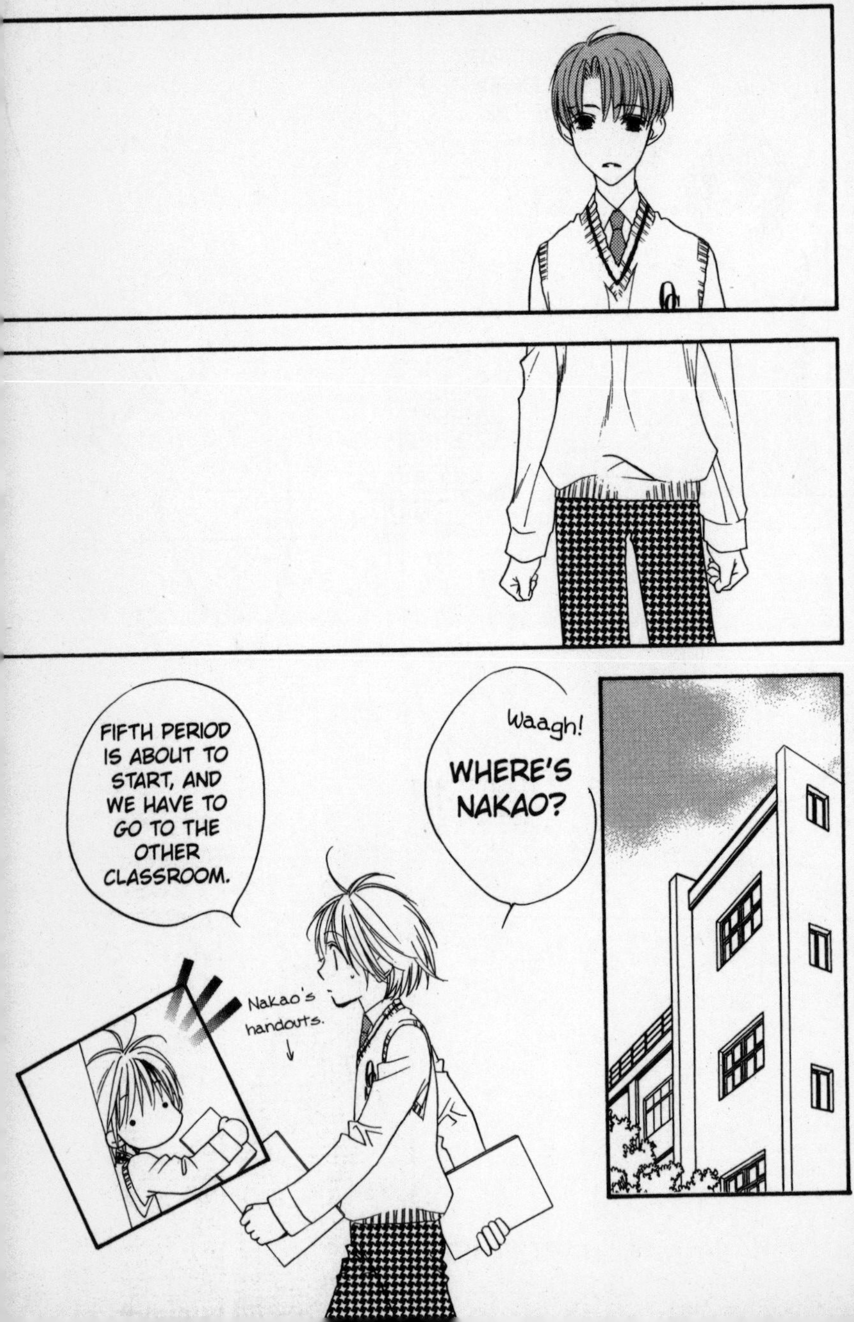
Waagh! WHERE'S NAKAO?
FIFTH PERIOD IS ABOUT TO START, AND WE HAVE TO GO TO THE OTHER CLASSROOM.
Nakao's handouts.

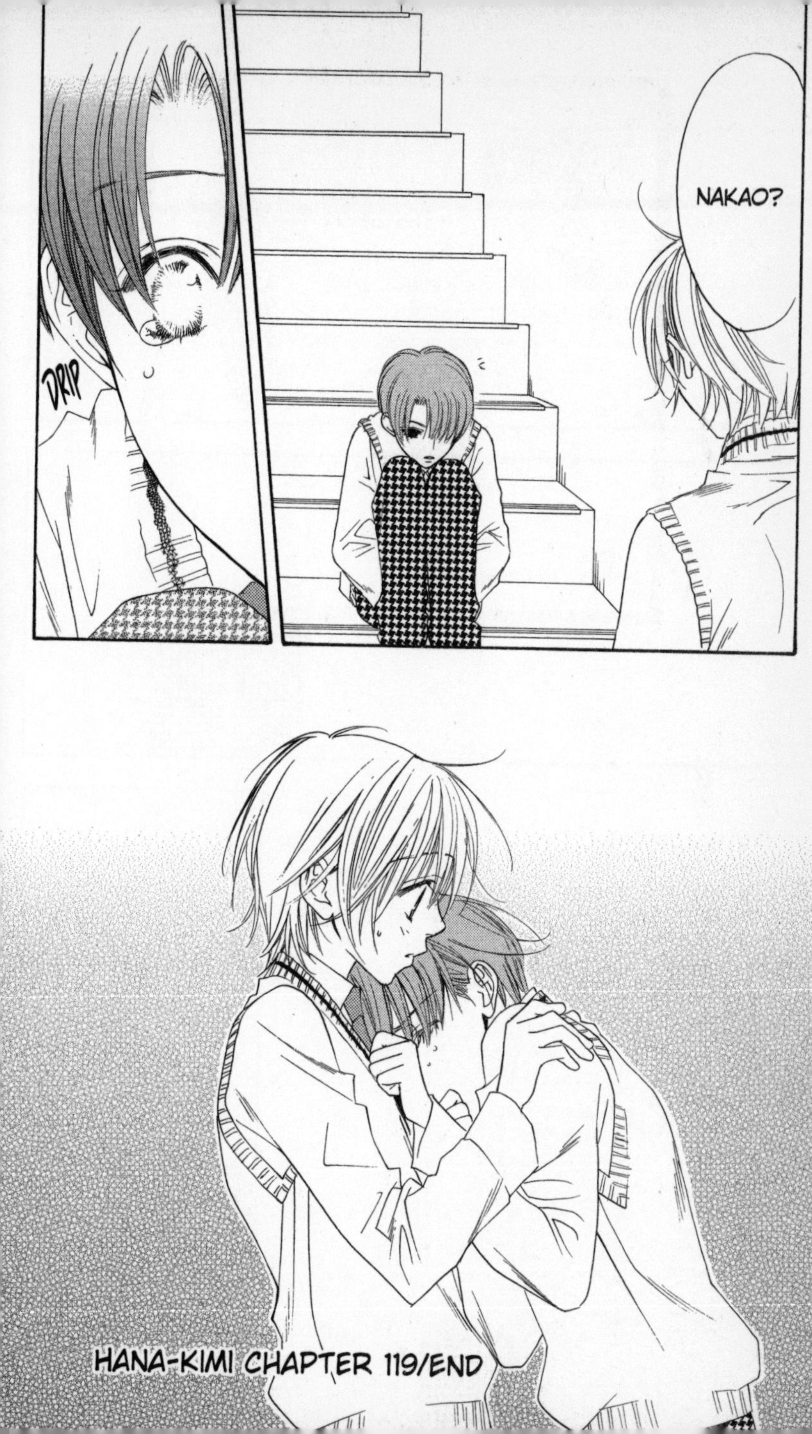
NAKAO?
DRIP
HANA-KIMI CHAPTER 119/END

ABOUT THE AUTHOR

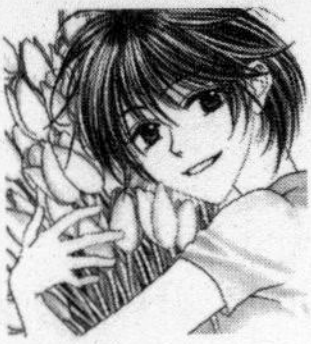

Hisaya Nakajo's manga series **Hanazakari no Kimitachi he** (For You in Full Blossom, casually known as **Hana-Kimi**) has been a hit since it first appeared in 1997 in the shôjo manga magazine **Hana to Yume** (Flowers and Dreams). In Japan, two **Hana-Kimi** art books and several "drama CDs" have been released. Her other manga series include **Missing Piece** (2 volumes), **Yumemiru Happa** (The Dreaming Leaf, 1 volume) and **Sugar Princess**.

Hisaya Nakajo's website:
www.wild-vanilla.com

IN THE NEXT VOLUME...

Love is in the air at Osaka High School—
bittersweet and true, as Nakao confesses his
feelings for Minami, and Noe receives a
Valentine's Day chocolate from a girl. While
the whole gang goes to the bowling alley,
Mizuki finds some time alone with Sano.
How much longer can she pretend to be a
boy? How much longer can she hide who
she is...and who she loves?

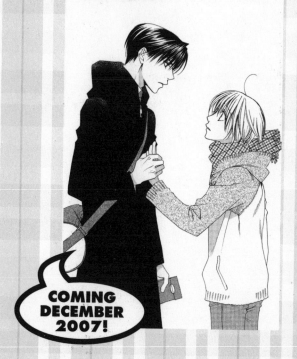

花ざかりの君たちへ

**COMING
DECEMBER
2007!**